The Archaeology of Urban Landscapes

Explorations in Slumland

This exciting collection on a new movement in urban archaeology investigates the history of urban slums. The stuff that is dug up – broken kitchen china, glass grog bottles, and innumerable tonnes of building debris, nails and plaster samples – will not quickly find its way into museum collections. But, properly interpreted, it yields evidence of lives that have left little in the way of written records. Including eleven case studies, five on cities in the United States and one each on London and Sheffield, and further chapters on Cape Town, Sydney, Melbourne and Quebec City, this collection maps out a new field, which will attract the attention of a range of students, including those outside archaeology such as historical sociologists and historians.

ALAN MAYNE is Associate Professor in the Department of History, University of Melbourne. His publications include *Fever, Squalor and Vice* (1982), *Representing the Slum* (1991), *The Imagined Slum* (1993) and *Reluctant Italians* (1997).

TIM MURRAY is Professor of Archaeology and Head of the School of Historical and European Studies at La Trobe University. He has written, with Judy Birmingham, *Historical Archaeology of Australia: A Handbook*, and edited *The Archaeology of Aboriginal Australia* (1998), *Time and Archaeology* (1999), *The Great Archaeologists*, 2 vols. (1999), (with Atholl Anderson) *Australian Archaeologist* (2000) and *History and Discoveries*, 3 vols. (2001).

NEW DIRECTIONS IN ARCHAEOLOGY

NEW DIRECTIONS IN ARCHAEOLOGY

The Archaeology of Urban Landscapes

Explorations in Slumland

Edited by

ALAN MAYNE
University of Melbourne

and

TIM MURRAY
La Trobe University

PUBLISHED BY THE PRESS SYNDICATE OF THE UNIVERSITY OF CAMBRIDGE
The Pitt Building, Trumpington Street, Cambridge, United Kingdom

CAMBRIDGE UNIVERSITY PRESS
The Edinburgh Building, Cambridge, CB2 2RU, UK
40 West 20th Street, New York, NY 10011-4211, USA
477 Williamstown Road, Port Melbourne, VIC 3207, Australia
Ruiz de Alarcón 13, 28014 Madrid, Spain
Dock House, The Waterfront, Cape Town 8001, South Africa

http://www.cambridge.org

First published 2001

Printed in the United Kingdom at the University Press, Cambridge

Typeface Monotype Times NR 9/11 pt.   *System* QuarkXPress™   [SE]

A catalogue record for this book is available from the British Library

ISBN 0 521 77022 X hardback
ISBN 0 521 77975 8 paperback

Contents

Figures

Contributors

Réginald Auger
CELAT and Department of History
Université Laval
Quebec, Canada G1K 7P4

Mary C. Beaudry
Department of Archaeology
Boston University
Boston, MA 02215 USA

Paul Belford
Ironbridge Archaeology
The Archaeology Unit of the Ironbridge Gorge
    Museum Trust
The Wharfage, Ironbridge
Telford, Shropshire TF8 7AW

Grace Karskens
School of History
University of New South Wales
Sydney, NSW, 2052 Australia

Nancy J. Kassner
Department of Consumer and Regulatory Affairs
Historic Preservation Division
614 H. St, NW
Room 305
Washington, DC 20001 USA

Dr Barbara J. Little
National Register of Historic Places, Ste. 400
National Park Service
1849 C St, NW
Washington, DC 2024 USA

John P. McCarthy
Project Director
Applied Archaeology and History Associates, Inc.
615 Fairglen Lane
Annapolis, MD 21401 USA

Antonia Malan
Historical Archaeology Research Group
Department of Archaeology
University of Cape Town
7701 Rondebosch, South Africa

Alan Mayne
Department of History
University of Melbourne
Parkville, Victoria, 3052 Australia

William Moss
Design et Patrimoine
Hotel de Ville
C.P. 700, Haute-Ville
Quebec (Quebec) Canada G1R 4S9

Stephen A. Mrozowski
Department of Anthropology
University of Massachusetts at Boston
Boston, MA 02125 USA

Professor Tim Murray
Department of Archaeology
La Trobe University
Bundoora, Victoria, 3083 Australia

Ellen Ross
School of Social Science and Human Services
Ramapo College of New Jersey
505 Ramapo Valley Road
Mahwah, New Jersey 07430–1680 USA

Elaine-Maryse Solari
Anthropological Studies Center
Sonoma State University Academic Foundation, Inc.
Sonoma State University
Rohnert Park, CA 94928-3609 USA

Elizabeth van Heyningen
Department of History
University of Cape Town
Private Bag
Rondebosch 7700, South Africa

Rebecca Yamin
John Milner Associates, Inc.
1216 Arch Street
Philadelphia, PA 19107 USA

1
The archaeology of urban landscapes: explorations in slumland

ALAN MAYNE AND TIM MURRAY

In a handful of modern city places, archaeologists and historians together are probing within the all-but-forgotten local horizons of vanished inner-city neighbourhoods. In every case, the past textures of these places have been obscured by distorting 'slum' stereotypes. The researchers' focus in time is the urbanisation spurt which, beginning in Britain late in the eighteenth century, transformed both the parent society and its settler-colonies during the following two centuries. This book brings together their findings. It unravels conventional historical understandings in order to trace the actualities of working-class lives in neighbourhoods that have been marginalised and demonised as notorious slums where poverty, deviance and criminality intersected. Case studies are presented from both the hubs and the outlying regions of the English-speaking urban world system: from London and Sheffield; from Cape Town, Sydney and Melbourne; from the cities of New York and Quebec; from Lowell, Minneapolis and West Oakland. In so doing, *The Archaeology of Urban Landscapes* introduces the methods that underpin these new research agendas, and clarifies the concepts and conclusions that link and sustain them.

Urban digs fascinate the general community. The excavations seem to bridge present and past, as the archaeologists' trowels uncover evidence of earlier occupations. The integration of history and archaeology has frequently been urged in order comprehensively to reveal the hidden layers of the urban past, and explain their forms to the present. In practice, however, the material traces of past places have all too often been erased, denied and trivialised. Neighbourhoods have been bulldozed, rebuilt or selectively commemorated according to inappropriate taxonomies of historical significance. Memories of place have been lost or fragmented. Hopes for the effective integration of urban history and archaeology have largely been disappointed. City dwellers today, thereby denied an informed and abiding sense of their urban past, are sometimes said to live in a wilderness of both time and place.[1]

These paradoxes are highlighted by the misunderstandings that cloud public knowledge about historic central-city neighbourhoods that endured as centres of working-class work and residence well into the middle of the twentieth century. The complexities of these places – their variety of social worlds, and their complex patterns of continuity and change through time – are obscured by the homogenising, universalising and changeless qualities of slum myths. Slum stereotypes underpinned clearance programmes and redevelopment schemes which, between the late nineteenth and the mid-twentieth centuries, largely destroyed these neighbourhoods. The archaeological sites upon which this book is based attest to the magnitude of these changes: these sites are today betwixt-and-between places, with weed plots and parking lots where communities once lived. Freeways and high-rise towers have transformed the local skylines.

Slums are constructions of the imagination: a stereotype that was fashioned in the early nineteenth century by bourgeois entertainers and social reformers, and that obscured and distorted the varied spatial forms and social conditions to which it was applied.[2] Historians have perpetuated this slum myth. Mesmerised by the dramatic intensity of the caricatures that remain embedded in the documentary record, they have insisted that 'the essence of slums was their "environmental reality"'.[3] They have confused and thereby inadequately conflated the imagined reality of slums with the actualities of working-class neighbourhoods that were labelled in this way. Historians tend to regard material evidence from such neighbourhoods as providing, at best, illustrations of what they have already framed as the major themes of historical inquiry. Often they disregard material things altogether. Rarely has their tunnel vision been effectively challenged by a consideration of the archaeological record.[4] Some historical archaeologists concede that artefacts do serve merely to 'confirm and illustrate the historical record'. Others, with an insularity similar to that of some historians, refuse to engage in cross-disciplinary debate and claim to find documentary evidence helpful simply as corroboration of the archaeology.[5]

Resolving these debates about the relationships between history and historical archaeology requires archaeologists to engage their sceptics. By tapping the rich local idioms of vanished places, it is possible to demonstrate unequivocally the advantages of interpretations that draw upon a broad appreciation of what constitutes the historical record. Finding these new facts is only the first step in developing such interpretations.[6] By interweaving documentary, oral and material evidence, both archaeologists and historians are compelled to develop concepts and arguments with which to interrogate these diverse sources, to highlight their significance and to pursue the questions that arise when juxtaposing and melding these data sets. As Carmel Schrire remarks, the test of historical significance has less to do with 'what new facts were revealed but rather what new emphases were [thereby] stressed'.[7] It must be conceded, however, that to date historical archaeology has hesitated to proceed from the first to the second of these steps. It has produced discrete data inventories rather than synthesising interpretations of urban sites. Schrire's proposition has yet to be demonstrated. The archaeology of modern cities has lacked compelling intellectual frameworks and questions to drive inquiry forward.[8] Urban historical archaeologists – in the main consultants and cultural resources managers – have tended to respond to the work briefs offered to them, and the scope of their work is often further constrained by limited time and money. Purely academic research on the archaeology of modern cities is comparatively rare.

A kick-start is needed. We think it is to be found by pursuing the contexts of the data we study. The archaeological record of itself is stuff retrieved from the dirt. The historical record of itself is flotsam thrown up upon an alien shore. Independently, both are indeterminate: relics from a world that has gone, anchorless, preserved in plastic bags and archival cartons. Their meanings today are ambiguous. Yet the archaeological and historical evidence of vanished working-class communities is idiomatic to the particular contexts of their past production and use. They were anchored in specific times and places. It follows that interpreting these data in order to piece together those contexts can provide a key to cultural worlds in the past which have hitherto been obscured by the universalising effects of elite-driven stereotypes.

The first step in such analysis is relatively easy: to critique these stereotypes.[9] However neither historians nor archaeologists have proceeded far beyond this threshold. They deconstruct slum myths and compile descriptive artefact inventories, but they do not go on to explore the enveloping social and cultural milieux of vanished inner-city communities. In order to do so, a synthesising analytical model is required that recognises the historical significance of individual lives and particular locales in the past, without surrendering thereby to directionless parochialism or antiquarianism: a model that simultaneously interweaves these local stories into broader historical arguments, without privileging present-day constructions of historical significance over the local actualities of past lives and places.

Archaeologists and historians are outsiders to the past. We can only pretend to speak as insiders. Its idioms are not our own. The immediacies of social experience then and now are not the same. The local stuff from past places perplexes us with its humdrum profusion and uncertain provenance. The local knowledge of those who once occupied these places eludes us. Our efforts to fashion historical significance for these local things by constructing possible social contexts for them produce ambiguous results, and afford no clear pathways for developing broader historical arguments. Judy Birmingham and Tim Murray conceded over a decade ago that

> A great deal of material data emerges during the excavation of most historic sites and by far the greater proportion of them are remarkably undistinguished. Broken kitchen china, glass grog bottles, and innumerable tonnes of building debris, nails and plaster samples are sources of social and economic information rather than cultural and aesthetic values. One challenge on such sites is to translate this assemblage of refuse and discarded material into a valid database for social and cultural interpretation.[10]

Our attempts at translation, however, have fashioned not windows upon the past, but 'mirrors, infinitely reflecting back to us our own worn visages'.[11]

The Archaeology of Urban Landscapes meets these challenges by starting where things are seemingly most opaque: with the particular – but vanished – places to which these undistinguished artefact assemblages are tied, and which lie behind the assumed realities of public knowledge and general histories. The book necessarily begins by acknowledging the enduring influence of the slum genre, which 'crated' real neighbourhoods as grotesque underworlds in public imagination. Thus Ellen Ross, in her chapter about the middle-class women who visited and chronicled disadvantaged communities in London between 1860 and 1940, unravels the potent narrative tropes of exploration which visualised these places in the imaginations of outside readers. The book proceeds, however, beyond these old narrative conventions. It attempts to present the local horizons of particular places in narrative vignettes that are as compelling to readers today as the slum genre was in the past. Compelling, and more credible. It constructs ethnographies of place.[12] Upon these deep-driven foundations are built broader arguments about the past social landscapes of modern cities, without ever losing sight of the particular lives and places where interpretation begins. This is a transparent epistemology of the urban past.

In the following chapters, assemblages are related to the social landscapes of particular places in the urban past, and to a matrix of life stories about identifiable households and even individuals. Rebecca Yamin, whose chapter concludes this book, remarks that artefacts recovered from the Five Points neighbourhood in New York City 'are evidence of daily life in a place that until now has been portrayed as a living hell'.[13] But in the light of archaeological and historical evidence from this and central-city sites elsewhere, how should daily life in such neighbourhoods now be described? Not as constituting an homogeneous underclass. Nor as drip-down imitations of bourgeois prosperity and propriety. The material culture from such sites, researchers agree, is 'mundane'. By and large, one finds cheap and mass-produced homewares and domestic knick-knacks. They are intrinsic to the everyday lives of the inhabitants of these vanished communities. As James Deetz argues, 'in the seemingly little and insignificant things that accumulate to create a lifetime, the essence of our existence is captured'.[14] These objects – a decorated plate, for example, or a moulded clay pipe – are simultaneously functional and symbolic. They express personal and local identity. They exude a pride in self and place that is at variance with outside constructions by elite observers and later historians. Far from denying inequality, *The Archaeology of Urban Landscapes* focuses upon the ignored material residues of inequality on the edges of mainstream history making.

To call life in these places 'hell' makes impossibly remote the social contexts that shaped the data we study. It drains them of human agency. It saps the data of the immediacy that connected them to past lives. It denies the individual and collective strategies by which neighbours and communities maximised circumscribed life chances, and pursued goals other than those legitimised by hegemonic cultural determinants. Life in these communities *was* hard, but it was not uniformly so, nor was it inescapably so. Lives that to outsiders seemed to be played out upon the edge, and boxed in by unmitigated ugliness, were inevitably known very differently by neighbours. Imagine a local streetscape, as slum narratives so often did. But read against the grain of one's expectations. What might a neighbour have seen? One open door perhaps reveals hard-won comfort, vulnerable, though often consolidated by the next generation. A neighbouring door might reveal scenes unambiguously unpleasant: in which a treasured heirloom, and a modicum of slowly accumulated possessions, could not altogether compensate for cramped living

space, preventable ill health, and an inequitable and intermittent wage. These locales knew frustration, hurt and anger. Yet there was still laughter in the poorest of households, and achievements, and dignity displayed there in forms that diverged from the codes of respectability that were enshrined by manuals of bourgeois etiquette. Working-class radicalism and resistance were nurtured in these places. But we also find military buckles (kept with pride, perhaps, or misplaced and easily forgotten?) in these house sites, and patriotic figurines. There are buttons, too, and tablewares that imitated the trends of well-to-do fashion. There are toys, and cleaning brushes. Everywhere in these places are to be found the prosaic residues of lives that were centred around family and neighbourhood.

We miss this humdrum immediacy – and with it, the plurality of experiences, opinions, strategies, and the open-endedness of neighbourhood outcomes – if we stress the marginality of such places. Any locale is necessarily immediate to its occupants. Individually and collectively, we fashion overarching imaginary templates which give coherence to our material surroundings, making them intelligible and knowable, and which guide our efforts to modify those surroundings. Thus it is, says Simon Schama, 'our shaping perception that makes the difference between raw matter and landscape'. Herein lies the distinction between what sociologist Herbert Gans called 'potential' and 'effective' environments: the intervention of human artifice whereby – in Michel de Certeau's words – space is fashioned into 'a *practiced place*'.[15] These mental and emotional constructs form the roots of community life, providing the matrix for neighbourhood identity and interaction.

It requires historical imagination to strip away the overlays and access those roots. As David Lowenthal aptly remarks, 'we can no more slip back to the past than leap forward to the future. Save in imaginative reconstruction, yesterday is forever barred to us.'[16] How far can this imagination extend, as we experimentally fashion social contexts from archaeological and historical data? Clifford Geertz cautions that:

> We cannot live other people's lives . . . it is with expressions, representations, objectifications, discourses, performances . . . that we traffic . . . Whatever sense we have of how things stand with someone else's inner life, we gain it through their expressions, not through some magical intrusion into their consciousness.[17]

Schrire concludes that past landscapes and their embedded meanings must necessarily be imagined in their reinterpretation today. 'Palpable though the documents and artifacts may be', she writes, 'in the end their deeper messages can only be read through acts of imagination.' Anne Yentsch pushes the limits of historical imagination still further. Her goal, influenced by Geertz, is 'to see the people through the things they left behind'. Yentsch challenges us to 'reach beyond data' in order to make 'the imaginative effort to feel' as people in the past once felt.[18]

Yentsch's goal to 'feel' at one with people and places in the past is as dangerous as it is potent. Historical imagination, as the contributors to this book attest, must be grounded in hermeneutics rather than in the pretence of empathy. This style of analysis demands intimate collaboration between archaeologist and historian, as site-specific historical research is driven by the excavation data, and is painstakingly reinterpreted through engagement with the material culture. Herein lies the pathway for achieving a 'from the inside out' rather than a contrived 'bottom up' perspective upon the past.[19] As Geertz explains,

> The truth of the doctrine of cultural relativism is that we can never apprehend another people's or another period's imagination neatly, as though it were our own. The falsity of it is that we can never therefore genuinely apprehend it at all. We can apprehend it quite well enough, at least as well as we apprehend anything else not properly ours, but we do so not by looking *behind* the interfering glosses that connect us to it but *through* them.[20]

Yamin describes this hermeneutic circle as 'a manner of reasoning . . . that moves back and forth between past and present, between different categories of data – archaeological evidence, oral history, written sources, ethnographic data, anthropological theory, human experience – until the part and the whole begin to make sense'.[21] In so doing, one strives constantly to anchor the embedded artifice of document or artefact in the context of its past production and use. Eschewing the siren lure that one can 'see things from the native's point of view . . . [through] some unique form of psychological closeness . . . with our subjects', hermeneutics takes as axiomatic that the 'only way to discover who people actually are is through their expressions, through their symbolic systems'.[22]

This process of unleashing our imaginations, and the historical narratives we can construct as a result, are supported in turn by a revitalised ethnography that draws upon well-established anthropological principles and recent history making.[23] These ethnographic models entail three methodological principles. First, by reading through – instead of imposing upon – the available evidence, ethnographic interpretation 'begins with the most difficult thing of all to see: the experience of past actors as they experienced it, and not that experience as we in hindsight experience it for them'. It follows that such interpretations must acknowledge the actions of past people in creating meaning – and thereby the multivocal, contested and dynamic nature of the past – if we are 'to enter into the experience of those actors in the past who, like us, experience a present as if all the possibilities are still there'.[24] Second, ethnographies of the past are structured in spiral sequences of particular case studies, rich in local texture, together with broader synthesising arguments that connect and are continually tested by the local studies that sustain them. Thick description and enveloping historical arguments are thus seamlessly combined. Third, ethnographic narratives are not only tools of rigorous description and argument in the hands of a research team; they must communicate findings to, and engage the attention of, broader audiences. Wide-ranging historical arguments, enriched by local texture, produce compelling stories which should be both entertaining and reflective.

The Archaeology of Urban Landscapes comprises twelve chapters, which are grouped in two sections. Contributors to Part I pursue themes of setting, scope and approach. Contributors in Part II range further into applications and conclusions. The first and last chapters of both sections act as 'book-ends', in order to consolidate arguments begun in this introductory chapter, and to stress the book's unifying concepts of exploration, imagination and narrative.

Part I contains five chapters. It begins with Ellen Ross's 'Slum journeys: ladies and London poverty 1860–1940'. Ross, a distinguished social historian, argues that narratives of slumland exploration decisively shaped public knowledge about urban poverty in London. She examines the nineteenth- and early-twentieth-century narrative conventions that fashioned slums in public imagination, and focuses upon the aural confrontations between women of different classes that are contained in this narrative genre. In chapter 3 ('The making of an archaeological site and the unmaking of a community in West Oakland, California'), Elaine-Maryse Solari describes how slum myths fed into public policies which, in the name of urban renewal, unravelled an inner-city community. In all the studies contained in this book, archaeologists and historians have had to explore vanished communities: neighbourhoods which were torn apart by the redevelopment pressures that flowed from slum myths. The complexities of doing so are highlighted in chapters 4 and 5. In the first of these, 'Twice removed: Horstley Street in Cape Town's District Six, 1865–1982', archaeologist Antonia Malan and historian Elizabeth van Heyningen set about describing a neighbourhood that was bulldozed by South Africa's apartheid regime, and recreated imaginatively in opposition to that regime through music, story telling, and the tapping of memories. In the next chapter, 'Archaeology in the alleys of Washington, DC', Barbara J. Little and Nancy J. Kassner review the development of historical archaeology in the US capital. Part I concludes with 'Small things, big pictures: new perspectives from the archaeology of Sydney's Rocks neighbourhood', in which historian Grace Karskens reflects upon the approaches used at the trail-blazing Cumberland and Gloucester Streets archaeological investigation since 1994. Karskens highlights the uneasy interface between slum stereotypes and the actualities of working-class life in 'the Rocks'.

Part II consists of six detailed case studies of the material culture of urban disadvantage in the modern city. It begins with 'Imaginary landscapes: reading Melbourne's "Little Lon"', where Tim Murray and Alan Mayne mesh archaeological and historical evidence from households in the Little Lonsdale Street precinct of Melbourne. In so doing they underline arguments used already by Ross and Karskens, setting aside nineteenth- and twentieth-century slumland depictions, and later historical interpretations, in order to tell an 'inside-out' story about a complex and long-enduring working-class locale. In chapter 8 ('Work, space and power in an English industrial slum: 'the Crofts', Sheffield, 1750–1850'), Paul Belford separates the early development of 'the Crofts' district in Sheffield from the later slum stereotypes which grew up around it. Mary C. Beaudry and Stephen A. Mrozowski continue this theme in chapter 9 ('Cultural space and worker identity in the company city: nineteenth-century Lowell, Massachusetts') and, building upon Belford, pay particular attention to archaeological readings of worker resistance. In Chapter 10 (The archaeology of physical and social transformation in Québec City's waterfront: 'high times, low times and tourist floods') Réginald Auger and William Moss apply archaeological perspectives to the cycle of abandonment and revitalisation which has characterised Quebec City's waterfront district. John P. McCarthy narrows the focus in chapter 11, ('Values and identity in the "working-class" worlds of late-nineteenth-century Minneapolis') to an examination of the particularities of neighbouring households within late-nineteenth-century Minneapolis, exploring the material record for variations by social class and ethnicity. This fine-textured perspective upon the local horizons of household and neighbourhood is maintained in the final chapter, Rebecca Yamin's 'Alternative narratives: respectability at New York's Five Points'.

Yamin juxtaposes the exploration tropes of narrative conventions in the past that constructed slums, and present-day ethnographies that deconstruct them. Yamin's 'narrative vignettes' about life within New York's notorious Five Points district underlines how new directions in historical archaeology can explore beyond slum myths, in order to address the complexities of working-class life in an urbanising world.

Although there is a unity of purpose in each of the contributions to *The Archaeology of Urban Landscapes*, there is a diversity of solutions to the pertinent question of how we achieve our goal. Given the present state of our explorations of the archaeology of the modern city, and the clear need to foster an environment where traditional divisions between disciplines and approaches are broken down, this diversity is both warranted and welcome. Understanding life in the city, especially in those parts which have been demolished in urban renewal programmes or demonised as exemplars of all that is reprehensible about living in cities, must first and foremost be built around an understanding of the contexts of neighbourhood, work, gender, class, ethnicity, childhood and old age, poverty, oppression and prejudice, but above all of possibility. In the nineteenth-century city, people from rural areas as well as immigrants from all over the world found work, found community, indeed found patterns of interaction which came to be increasingly the hallmark of life in the modern world. In the nineteenth century (as well as the twentieth) the city was celebrated as being the great engine of social and cultural differentiation, whether it was in the Parisian slums so memorably portrayed by Emile Zola in *L'Assomoir*, or by Charles Dickens' depictions of London slums in *Oliver Twist*. Notwithstanding these great literary feats, it is true to say that the nature of life in the poorest sections of the great cities of the western world was of a richer texture than that captured by either writer, and our job as historical archaeologists is to imagine the existence of other lives on the basis of the empirical information we have before us.

The agenda of this book, that our understanding of such places is not fixed by the writings of social reformers, novelists and evangelists, nor by historical convention, is an encouragement to explore those urban contexts and to integrate such diverse sources of information as documentary history, oral history and archaeology as a basis upon which to imagine different social worlds.

Notes

1 S. B. Warner Jr., *The Urban Wilderness: A History of the American City* (New York: Harper & Row, 1972),

p. 4. See also M. Christine Boyer, *The City of Collective Memory: Its Historical Imagery and Architectural Entertainments* (Cambridge, MA: MIT Press, 1996); Dolores Hayden, *The Power of Place: Urban Landscapes as Public History* (Cambridge, MA: MIT Press, 1995).

2 Alan Mayne, *The Imagined Slum: Newspaper Representation in Three Cities 1870–1914* (Leicester: Leicester University Press, 1993), p. 1.

3 S. Martin Gaskell, *Slums* (Leicester: Leicester University Press, 1990), p. 1. See also Alan Mayne, 'On the edge of history', *Journal of Urban History* 26:2 (2000), 249–58.

4 Two exceptions are Randall H. McGuire and Robert Paynter (eds.), *The Archaeology of Inequality: Material Culture, Domination and Resistance* (Oxford: Blackwell, 1991) and LuAnn Wurst and Robert K. Fitts (eds.), *Confronting Class* special issue, *Historical Archaeology* 33:1 (1999).

5 Helen Proudfoot, Anne Bickford, Brian Egloff and Robyn Stocks, *Australia's First Government House* (Sydney: Allen & Unwin and the New South Wales Department of Planning, 1991), p. 159. These issues are discussed by Beaudry in Mary C. Beaudry (ed.), *Documentary Archaeology in the New World* (Cambridge: Cambridge University Press, 1988), pp. 1–2, 43.

6 See Clifford Geertz, *After the Fact: Two Countries, Four Decades, One Anthropologist* (Cambridge, MA: Harvard University Press, 1995).

7 Carmel Schrire, *Digging through Darkness: Chronicles of an Archaeologist* (Charlottesville: University Press of Virginia, 1995), p. 111. See Little's introductory comments in Barbara J. Little (ed.), *Text-Aided Archaeology* (Boca Raton, FL: CRC Press, 1992), p. 4.

8 Little has changed during the twenty years since Roy Dickens expressed a similar concern in Roy S. Dickens Jr. (ed.), *Archaeology of Urban America: The Search for Pattern and Process* (New York: Academic Press, 1982), p. 1.

9 Alan Mayne, 'A barefoot childhood: so what? Imagining slums and reading neighbourhoods', *Urban History* 22:3 (1995), 380–9.

10 Judy Birmingham and Tim Murray, *Historical Archaeology in Australia: A Handbook* (Sydney: Australian Society for Historical Archaeology, 1987), p. 91.

11 Henry Glassie, *Passing the Time in Ballymenone: Culture and History of an Ulster Community* (Bloomington: Indiana University Press, 1995), p. 11. Glassie expands this argument in the chapter 'History', in Henry Glassie, *Material Culture* (Bloomington and Indianapolis: Indiana University Press, 1999), pp. 5–39. See also Geertz, 'Found in translation: on the social history of the moral imagination', in Clifford Geertz, *Local Knowledge: Further Essays in Interpretive Anthropology* (New York: Basic Books, 1983), pp. 36–54.

12 Alan Mayne and Susan Lawrence, 'Ethnographies of place: a new urban research agenda', *Urban History* 26:3 (1999), 325–48.

13 Rebecca Yamin, 'New York's mythic slum: digging Lower Manhattan's infamous Five Points', *Archaeology* 50:2 (1997), 47. See also Grace Karskens, 'Making the "slums", making the Rocks', in Karskens, 'Main report', Godden Mackay Heritage Consultants, *The Cumberland/Gloucester Streets Site, the Rocks: Archaeological Investigation Report* (Sydney: Godden Mackay Logan, 1999), vol. 2, pp. 187–94.

14 James Deetz, *In Small Things Forgotten: The Archaeology of Early American Life* (New York: Doubleday, 1977), p. 161. See also Deetz's foreword in Anne E. Yentsch, *A Chesapeake Family and Their Slaves: A Study in Historical Archaeology* (Cambridge: Cambridge University Press, 1994), p. xix.

15 Simon Schama, *Landscape and Memory* (London: Fontana Press, 1995), p. 10. Herbert J. Gans, *People and Plans: Essays on Urban Problems and Solutions* (New York: Basic Books, 1968), pp. 4–11. Michel de Certeau (trans. Steven F. Rendall), *The Practice of Everyday Life* (Berkeley: University of California Press, 1984), p. 130.

16 David Lowenthal, *The Past Is a Foreign Country* (Cambridge: Cambridge University Press, 1985), p. 4.

17 Clifford Geertz, 'Making experiences, authoring selves', in Victor Turner and Edward M. Bruner (eds.), *The Anthropology of Experience* (Urbana: University of Illinois Press, 1986), p. 373.

18 Schrire, *Digging through Darkness*, p. 5. Yentsch, *A Chesapeake Family*, pp. xxii, 294, 330. Note also the recent enthusiasm for 'storytelling' in historical archaeology, as expressed in Adrian Praetzellis (ed.), *Archaeologists as Storytellers*, special issue, *Historical Archaeology* 32:1 (1998), and continued in a multipart 'Forum' in *ibid.* 34:2 (2000), 1–24.

19 See Glassie, *Passing the Time*, p. 86.

20 Geertz, *Local Knowledge*, p. 44.

21 Rebecca Yamin and Karen Bescherer Metheny, *Landscape Archaeology: Reading and Interpreting the American Historical Landscape* (Knoxville: University of Tennessee Press, 1996), p. xiv.

22 Clifford Geertz, '"From the native's point of view": on the nature of anthropological understanding', in Geertz, *Local Knowledge*, p. 56. Greg Dening, *The Death of William Gooch: A History's Anthropology* (Melbourne: Melbourne University Press, 1995), p. 157.

23 We note, especially, the influence of Victor Turner – see, for example, Victor Turner, *On the Edge of the Bush: Anthropology as Experience* (Tuscon: University of Arizona Press, 1985) – and of the 'Melbourne School' of ethnographic history, many of the contributors to which are included in Donna Merwick (ed.), *Dangerous Liaisons: Essays in Honour of Greg Dening* (University of Melbourne History Department, 1994).

24 Dening, *The Death of William Gooch*, p. 157. Greg Dening, *Performances* (Melbourne: Melbourne University Press, 1996), p. xvi. See also Mary C. Beaudry, 'Public aesthetics versus personal experience: worker health and well-being in 19th-century Lowell, Massachusetts', *Historical Archaeology* 27: 2 (1993), 91; and Mary E. D'Agostino, Elizabeth Prine, Eleanor Casella and Margot Winer (eds.), *The Written and the Wrought: Complementary Sources in Historical Anthropology*, Kroeber Anthropological Society Papers 79 (Berkeley: Department of Anthropology, University of California at Berkeley, 1995).

PART I

Setting, scope and
approaches

2
Slum journeys: ladies and London poverty 1860–1940

ELLEN ROSS

In South London's miles of impoverished streets, wrote Alexander Paterson in *Across the Bridges* (1911), 'where it is not possible to find a good tailor or a big hotel', one might none the less catch a glimpse of 'a woman of another world, with the exotic appearance of a suburb or the West [End]', a lady who 'gives advice, and drops a leaflet on "Pure Milk"'.[1] The middle-class women who journeyed to poor London districts ranged from clergymen's wives to suffrage organisers; from Marie Hilton, a Quaker who established a day nursery in waterside Ratcliff in the 1870s; to Eleanor Marx, daughter of Karl; from part-time visitors like Lady Constance Battersea whose weekly destination was Whitechapel; and those, like educator Clara Grant, who devoted their remaining adult lives to their slum work. Their numbers, in London, can only be guessed: several thousand in any year before 1930. A single settlement, Blackfriars Women's University Settlement, for example, in 1901 had about a hundred part-time volunteers and twenty-five residents.[2] In the Stepney parish of St Dunstan's at about the same time, with a population of 22,000, the Church of England alone had 7 paid lady workers and 150 mostly female part-time volunteers. The Methodist East End Mission in 1897 employed, in addition to its ministers and 'evangelists', twenty ladies who did 'house-to-house visiting of the poor and sick'. Forty settlements in London alone are listed in *The Woman's Year Book* for 1923–4.[3]

The female visitors, however much they differed, had a great deal in common in this period of philanthropic activism. Nearly all had wealth and education superior to their clients; they shared assumptions – evangelical, 'humanitarian' in Thomas Laqueur's sense,[4] or, eventually, socialist – about the value of serving the poor. And

what they saw and heard in 'the slums', women and men charity-givers alike, was structured, as Alan Mayne points out in his book on slum journalists in this period, by common reading in a literature on London poverty that included Dickens, Mayhew, both Booths, George Sims and other popular journalists.[5]

My chapter, based on London from 1860 to 1940, is, for one thing, a reminder to all students of neighbourhood life that volunteer or official providers of services and advice, many of them non-resident, were active participants in the survival systems of poor neighbourhoods even in the interwar years. Secondly, I build on Mayne's *Imagined Slum*,[6] suggesting that the slums created through the discourses of philanthropic women and men diverged, in part because they were commentaries on different sensory confrontations with poverty: *aural* versus *visual*. Urban poverty, when 'heard', appears less exotic and dangerous than when it is 'seen'; more human, familiar and pathetic. Finally, in this chapter I explore an element of the slum encounter neglected by historians: conversation between women of different classes as represented in women's writings about poverty and the city, evangelistic publications and works of social reformers in particular.[7]

A discussion of talk among these long-dead Londoners might be seen as an improbable beginning to a collective project in urban archaeology. What our approaches share, however, is a way into the lives of 'slum' people that circumvents the standardised discourses of prestigious contemporary observers, views that continue to cramp our understanding of the history of urban poverty.

Gender and 'the erotics of talk'

Female 'slum travel' works from the 1860s through to the 1920s are remarkably conscious of the speech of poor subjects. Perhaps because the ladies were themselves throwing aside the Victorian injunction to silence, they include, on the whole, more dialogue than male writers do, whether quoted directly or indirectly, or fictionalised. Lady visitors, usually without formal position, in fact had to establish their authority mainly through talk in many forms: declaiming, questioning, listening, praying. Probably rare was real 'conversation' between women as imagined by feminists today, and which is defined by Carla Kaplan in *The Erotics of Talk* as talking between social peers that brings about 'recognition, reciprocity, and understanding'.[8] None the less I scrutinise power differences and the conventions of talk and of its print reproduction for these moments.

Male and female slum writings emerge from different locations within the worlds of slum philanthropy and exploration, a point well illustrated by the two separate worlds of East London's Toynbee Hall. On the one hand there was the all-male institution whose residents conducted boys' clubs and a wide range of classes for working men; on the other, the women's world centred on the dynamic and appealing Henrietta Barnett: mothers' meetings, 'lady' rent collecting, parish visiting, and programmes for female servants and schoolchildren.[9] Congregationalist-affiliated Mansfield House and its sister Canning Town Women's Settlement displayed a slightly different sexual division of labour into the 1930s: clubs, teams, classes and lectures for boys and men at the men's settlement; an emphasis on social services for women and children (which even included a small hospital and a very active dispensary) at the women's settlement.[10]

Scholars have cited a great many other gender differences among 'slummers', many of which imply disparities in access to, or interest in opportunities to talk intimately with inhabitants of poor districts. Jane Lewis notes that men were interested in policy-making committees of organisations, while women were more active as visitors in workers' homes; and F. K. Prochaska has demonstrated women's special effectiveness as charity fundraisers. Anne Summers has pointed out that the 'domestic service paradigm' played a major role in shaping the behaviour and expectations of well-off women active in voluntary work. In contrast, many male social explorers were actually on their way to positions in government service.[11] Ross McKibbin contrasts the 'subjective' approach of most women investigators with the efforts of Booth, Bowley and Rowntree, among other prominent men, to formulate 'objective' (usually statistical) standards for measuring poverty. Seth Koven has explored the erotic valence that attracted so many well-connected men to settlement and child-rescue work; for Martha Vicinus, on the other hand, passion also pulled women into the slums, but it was the irrepressible appetite for work rather than for love.[12] Clearly, urban poverty offered different vistas for male and female explorers.

Street scenes

Experiencing and reading the slum as spectacle was an established gentlemanly enterprise. The privileging of the visual, an axiom of modern science since Galileo, intensified in the nineteenth century.[13] Many men slum visitors use *visual* metaphors of tint such as light/dark, clear/foggy, sunshine/shade; they 'draw' lines around bad districts; or, using cartographical references, refer to slums as continents, distant lands or separate nations.[14]

Indeed urban journeys are often illustrated, from the Dore–Jerrold collaboration (1869–72), to John Thompson and Adolphe Smith's photographic *Street Life in London* (1877), to George Sims' four-volume edited compendium of newspaper articles, *Living London* (1902), lavishly accompanied by photographs.

Raymond Williams equates the modern written representation of the modern city with 'a man walking, as if alone, in its streets' – the Baudelairian *flâneur* – and Deborah Nord adds to this equation the man's 'penetrating gaze'.[15] Not surprisingly, the male gaze more often dwelt on the cityscape, what could be seen outdoors in the boulevards and lanes. At least some women were aware of their different 'place' in the city. As Helen Dendy (later Bosanquet), a Charity Organisation Society (COS) caseworker in Shoreditch for five years, wrote rather scornfully in the 1890s, such often stereotyped views of poverty were 'the impression of the outsider who confines his investigations to the main thoroughfares, or makes official visits during the business hours'. Marie Hilton criticised slum journalists as too ready to judge from a glance, which produced depictions obviously 'written by people who do not look below the surface'.[16]

Streetscapes almost by definition minimise the human by directing the eye (or the mind's eye) to a built environment which is endowed with personality. To take one example: Thomas Archer's walk through what was, in the 1860s, getting to be the notorious Old Nichol in Bethnal Green places readers squarely in the street, moving their glance across the depressing landscape, both human and built.

> Even though here and there a falling tenement is propped up by a shoring-beam, to prevent a wall from bulging over into the street, there are still the remains of poor respectability in some places; and ragged, dirty children, and gaunt women, from whose faces almost all traces of womanliness have faded, alternate with the clean-looking and even well-dressed families of some of the shopkeepers.[17]

The description of the bulging wall is actually more vivid and less hackneyed than that of the 'dirty children' or 'gaunt women'.

George Sims' dozens of *Living London* contributors also highlight what can be seen outdoors. In many of the articles, as in 'London sweethearts' by Sims himself, the author/*flâneur* is at the boundary of propriety ('Discreetly, modestly, and with the tenderest consideration for the feelings of the inhabitants, let us take a stroll this quiet summer evening through Love-land in London'), and the reader follows unaware young couples who are 'seen' from behind.[18] To be sure, Victorian photographers like John Thompson, John Galt or Paul Martin pictured far more than street scenes, rendering many revealing close-ups. But photographic images may render their subjects formal or distant, in much the same way as the development of statistical approaches to poverty such as Chadwick's attempted to reify the fluidity and activity of slum life. Contemporaries debated the meaning of photography in particular and recognised its potential as a tool of surveillance.[19]

A *flâneuse* was almost a logical impossibility in the nineteenth century. A well-dressed unaccompanied female walking the streets risked street harassment by men of all kinds and could even be arrested as a prostitute. The female shoppers who began to circulate in the West End in the 1870s were obliged to make new claims for ladies' movements in public spaces. Freedom to 'walk the streets' was, until the early twentieth century, accorded only to women in uniform, a privilege warmly appreciated by Salvation Army 'lasses' and district nurses.[20]

Women's slum vantage point was thus often the inside of a dwelling. Women had business in homes as parish visitors, district nurses, Bible-sellers, as collectors of funds for country holidays. A characteristically British style of offering both charitable aid and missionary work, as well as such paid services as clothing purchases and insurance premium payments, and even vaccination after 1898, visiting the poor was an old social form.[21] It had been adapted to urban missionary activities in the 1820s by the innovative all-male London City Mission, followed in 1857 by Ellen Ranyard's all-female London Bible and Domestic Mission. Women's visiting expertise was acknowledged in the appointment of a large female minority among London's first School Board visitors (truant officers), a number that declined as the profession came to be associated with neighbourhood hostility and even violence.[22]

'Sketch of life in Buildings', by 'A Lady Resident' in Booth's First Series,[23] reads like an experiment in aural investigation within domestic spaces, with the author as an eavesdropper (the aural equivalent of a 'voyeur') reporting on what she hears through her flat's thin walls. The average day in 'T Buildings' is described entirely in terms of what a woman, home a good part of the day herself, would hear from her own flat. The man upstairs wakes up very early for work; the baby cries; the wife asks the husband to give the baby something to eat ('a sip of tea and crust'); the wife, who has been heard sewing until 1 a.m. the previous night, stays in bed until 10 o'clock. Morning gossip on the common balcony outside the Lady Resident's door is heard; children are called in to lunch; afternoon topics included the illness of a neighbour, an unwanted visit from a clergyman, and the bad temper of one of the buildings' children. As dinner is being cooked in the buildings, someone finally crosses the author's threshold and is 'seen' by readers. This arrival also places the writer inside the elaborate social networks of the buildings for the first time: Mrs A from upstairs has sent her 'most careful child' in with sprats, the author's favourite food.[24]

The male–female difference I am pointing to in this section is, of course, one of degree rather than of dichotomy. Giving victims voice had long been a characteristic of humanistic narratives exemplified by the working people included among witnesses at Parliamentary hearings. Men in such 'talking' professions as police court magistrates, court missionaries and National Society for the Prevention of Cruelty to Children inspectors told personal stories and quoted subjects in their writings. Henry Mayhew's ability to engage in conversations yielded some of the best interviews in journalism history; Charles Booth's massive study of London is also based on hundreds of interviews. Also, the characteristic feminine method of recording in print conversations or narratives also arrests the flow of speech, and many quoted passages in both female and male writings are little more than affectionate jokes on the slum dweller's cockney accent and quaint ideas. Again, women mass-market journalists' articles – like those of Elizabeth Banks or Olive Christian Malvery – can closely resemble those of their male co-workers. Judith Walkowitz, in her study of Malvery's photojournalistic series, 'The heart of things', in *Pearson's Magazine* (1905) indeed contrasts Malvery's stilted and stereotype-filled text with its playful and vivid photographs.[25]

The art of talk

Most of the women active in slum work in the nineteenth century were there as volunteers lacking official position and power. They had to 'talk' their clients into accepting their authority. Sparked by her first meeting with the energetic Octavia Hill disciple Emma Cons in August of 1885, Beatrice Potter (later Beatrice Webb) drew up a sketch of the 'governing and guiding women' who were appearing in slum settings in the 1880s. They spoke with 'the dignity of habitual authority'. Emma Cons, in particular, conversed with tenants 'with that peculiar combination of sympathy and authority which characterises the modern type of governing woman'.[26]

The talking associated with female philanthropy did not have a particularly good reputation. Emilia Dilke, Women's Trade Union League organiser, classed it with an outmoded form of social action which dispensed 'charity' rather than justice. As Dilke put it, the solution to the problems of modern industry required study and analysis; it would come 'not by mere talking, not by mere gifts of money, but by taking trouble'.[27] Working-class clients or potential clients warily expected 'talk' as well. 'I don't want any of your talk!', said a young street walker in her first encounter with a rescue worker who approached her late one night in May 1896, as she came out of St James's Restaurant, Piccadilly. 'At the beginning of each case the woman seemed to steel herself to sit patiently and bear it while the expected questions or teaching of something should follow', wrote Maud Pember Reeves of the Lambeth mothers who were the subjects of a Fabian Women's Group research project early in the twentieth century.[28]

None the less, the spoken word was valorised in guides and commentaries for slum workers. In their 1932 text-book for social investigators, Beatrice and Sidney Webb pointed to the value of being a 'good listener' who genuinely wants 'to hear what others have to say'. Helen Bosanquet eventually renamed this talent 'communications' in her own social work textbooks, but earlier guides stressed 'tact', meaning special skill in talking about unpleasant subjects with strangers. 'Tact' implied educated upper-class women, as in this 1908 formulation by a LCC health official on the inspection of foster homes:

> English people do not like official inspection, especially in matters concerning their private domestic lives. Where capable, tactful and educated women Inspectors are employed to visit the homes, this objection would easily be overcome, and the nurse-mothers would welcome these visits. [29]

When a district nursing superintendent in 1886 described what made a probationer nurse unacceptable, she wrote that she had 'no love for the poor, and no knowledge or tact how best to deal with them'.[30] Alice Hodson, a young settler at Lady Margaret Hall settlement, Lambeth, in the 1900s, admitted that house-to-house expeditions exhausted her verbal abilities. Though a lady and well educated, perhaps she was still too young to have cultivated 'tact'. She doubted she could ask to view the pawn tickets of a 'lady who was trying to look superior' or to persuade a 'hard-hearted' daughter to support her elderly mother. 'A very clever, tactful visitor can sometimes make a good impression under such circumstances, but the ordinary nervous amateur is apt to make the people abusive . . . I have sometimes been spoken to most severely.'[31]

Some organisations ingeniously structured opportunities for easier, more informal talk, such as day-long country outings or advertised visiting hours. Some Sisters of the People, an uncloistered religious 'order' sponsored by the (Methodist) West London Mission, resorted to a time-honoured way of making contact with the families who shared their crowded court in Somers Town: in the hot summer nights of 1894 they went outside and sat on their doorstep. In the darkness people escaping from the heat and bugs came over to talk with them.[32] At Beatrice House in Rotherhithe near the Surrey Docks, part of the women's branch of the Bermondsey Settlement (also Methodist), Monday afternoon and Tuesday evening 'Socials' drew about fifty wives of water-side workers to hear suffrage speakers, learn about factory legislation, or talk with the celebrity friends of the settlement workers such as Evelyn Sharp, Emmeline Pethick Lawrence and Elizabeth Robins. Settler Laura Robinson apparently enjoyed herself at these events, and brought her West End friends. She found the waterside women (said her friend Mary Simmons in an obituary article for Robinson in 1906) 'far more interesting to know than most of the West End or well-to-do middle class ladies she had ever met'.[33]

Mothers' Meetings were potential centres of talk, places where local women came to meet parish-based charity-givers, which could 'blend and unite classes that have been and still are too far separate', according to Elizabeth Twining, an early proponent. In Twining's view, the benefits of these meetings of the classes would not be one-sided; they would 'uplift' the poor, but also humble the 'pride' of the rich participants.[34] Mary Bayly, Kensington missionary during the 1850s and 1860s, began a 'Mothers' Society' in 1853, an institution quickly copied by many other church-affiliated volunteers so that by the late Victorian era hundreds of thousands of women in England were attending these meetings. Bayly provided the women with patterns, sewing equipment, and bargain cloth on which to work while they were being lectured. She found that it was domestic subjects that stimulated conversation among the mothers and between them and the missionaries. Among the successful topics were efficient preparation of Sunday dinners and encouraging children's creative play. Earnest private conversations with the missionary could take place before and after the meetings.[35]

'Ideal speech situations'?

However eagerly middle-class women welcomed the chance to experience the 'joy', as one church worker put it, 'of being allowed to enter the inner side of many a life',[36] they brought to these conversations their privileges, their ignorance, and, of course, their accents. The philan-thropic encounter obviously did not represent Habermas' 'ideal speech situation' of mutuality in which participants are free of 'external pressures and internal distortions'.[37] The working-class words lovingly reproduced in middle-class texts were often obtained with great awkwardness.

One barrier to real 'conversation' was the ubiquity of the mistress–servant relation. Anne Summers has argued that managing servants was so deeply 'imprinted' in the identities and practices of middle-class women that it structured many of the public projects in which they engaged.[38] Though London girls were less likely to become domestic servants than those of many other areas, they signified servants to many philanthropists. When settlement worker Alice Hodson grew especially fond of a talented local member of a Girls' Friendly Society she thought of her as 'just the sort of person I should like for my own private attendant, secretary, and housekeeper'. Edith Simcox, a passionate advocate for female shirtmakers, urged in 1879 that ladies should come forward as 'civilised managers' of co-operative garment workshops so as to rescue working women from the greed of the 'lowest class of speculators'.[39] Helpful ladies often found domestic service placements for local girls, and the Metropolitan Association for Befriending Young Servants which institutionalised this practice was a favourite cause of such progressive women as Henrietta Barnett of Toynbee Hall and Anna Martin of the Bermondsey Settlement. The beleaguered nurse-narrator of *Five Months in a London Hospital* (1911), a lady trainee loaded down with menial chores, dreams of a hospital where the nurses are all ladies, and the chores are done by charwomen, cooks and maids.[40]

The mechanics of speech – voice and accent – consti-tuted another obvious barrier to slum conversations. Writing in the 1930s as a post-Victorian, Virginia Woolf gives her character Eleanor Pargiter in her novel *The Years* considerable self-consciousness about her class-based speech as she confronts, in the 1891 part of the book, the lower-middle-class contractor who has botched her slum building job: '"If you can't make a good job of it", she said curtly, "I shall employ somebody else". She adopted the tone of the Colonel's daughter; the upper middle-class tone that she detested. She saw him turn sullen before her eyes.'[41] Margaret Bondfield comments on charity activist (later LCC member and MP) Susan Lawrence's 'posh' high and quavering voice in a speech at a factory gate in East London. 'But Susan's voice had not been trained for speaking to an East End audience, who treated her as a comic turn and roared with laughter.' The girls 'had never before heard that kind of voice'. Lawrence

could not run for political office in working-class districts without transforming her voice, so she set to work.[42]

Many practitioners and investigators, in any case, were less interested in conversational exchanges than in extracting specific kinds of information or carrying out their tasks. They did their best to restrict and order the talking, yet their appearance of leisure and focused atten-tion probably stimulated talk in those being questioned. Nursing journals' humour columns are filled with garru-lous patients side-stepping the nurse's or doctor's single-minded effort to get a case history. Clementina Black and her wealthy colleague Adele Meyer, in their 1908 investi-gation of women home workers, found that even women who were paid by the piece might want to stop and talk:

> It is . . . necessary to let them tell their story in their own way. One has to hear far more than merely the industrial facts that one sets out to learn. The addi-tional information is often very interesting – as a glimpse into any human life can hardly fail to be – but listening to it is apt to take a long time. Few persons who have not tried would guess how small is the number of 'cases' that a competent investigator can collect in a day.[43]

With a ghoulish wit generated by her scepticism, Virginia Woolf portrays her housing-reformer heroine Eleanor Pargiter's attempts to discover the source of a leak in a deaf old woman's ceiling while the woman presses on with her own talk of pain and loneliness:

> 'And the pain –' Mrs. Potter stretched out her hands; they were knotted and grooved like the gnarled roots of a tree.
> 'Yes, yes,' said Eleanor. 'But there is a leak; it's not only the dead leaves,' she said to Duffus [the contrac-tor].[44]

Women, talking and the pathetic

When visited at home by figures with relatively open agendas, clients did more of the talking. In practice, it may have been parish visitors or missionaries rather than female investigators or social reformers who communi-cated most with poor and working-class women. The con-versations that resulted were often reported in the pathetic vein, meant to elicit sympathy, or even tears. These meet-ings might not always foster 'understanding' or 'recogni-tion', elements of real conversation in Kaplan's sense, but they could demonstrate some form of reciprocity.

London, like other large cities, contained its share of lonely and neglected people. As a minimum, these people could exchange their stories and attention with a middle-class visitor for whom the visit had a special meaning as a part of her own vocation. Socially sophisticated Maude Stanley defended conventional parish visiting in the late 1870s as 'the best method of really reaching the homes and hearts of working people' despite seeming even then 'old-fashioned', 'sectarian', even 'inquisitorial'.[45] A South London Baptist 'sister' who kept notes on four months of parish visits in the late 1890s backs up Stanley's position. She became intimate with dozens of women, spending a lot of her time with 'shut-ins'. One parishioner 'had been hoping someone would call to read and pray with her sick sister'. Another woman had been housebound for twenty-seven years. Still another old and disabled woman 'sits in a back room day after day', so the visitor 'read and talked to her and prayed, spending some time trying to make it clear and plain'. This visitor, who paid 941 visits during the 5 months she kept track of her activities, provided a number of services, not least of which was talking and listening, services also rendered to her.[46]

In her 1878 book on visiting in Soho, Stanley refers to the 'pathetic beauty to be found in the lives of the poor', and recounts dozens of quite detailed histories of people she encountered or aided in the Five Dials district as *pathos*, 'a queer ghoulish emotion', in Northrop Frye's terms, involving isolation or loss, and in imaginative literature usually generated by a child or a woman.[47] Missionary Mary Bayly's accounts also rely heavily on the pathetic. A focus on Christ-like suffering was a natural approach for evangelical writers, but one found in many kinds of slum writings, including those of male journalists and, occasionally, of later female social reformers.

Pathos became a science, and part of a well-thought-out fundraising programme, in the publications of the Ranyard Female Bible Mission.[48] Ellen Ranyard's Bible-women, from 1857, and her district nurses (founded in 1868) combined a belief in the value of 'declaring of God's message by women to women',[49] with house-to-house visiting, attendance on the sick and dying, and vivid interest in deathbed conversions, the varieties of human sin, and the possibility of redemption for all. However it was Ranyard's use of paid local working-class women, many of them people with troubled pasts, as her missionaries that best explains the freedom of conversation so characteristic of the Ranyard system. The combination generated hours of talk, and thousands of pages of recorded conversation in the mission's monthly magazine and in the books Ranyard herself wrote using the cases: all mesmerising reading because of their closeness to the daily texture of poverty. Mary Poovey refers to this discourse as a 'feminized epistemology of sympathy', the

antithesis of the attempt by statistician or camera to capture pattern rather than feeling in slum life.[50]

The Ranyard quarterly magazines offer deathbed accounts, but also, equally pathetic, stories of courage and generosity among the very poorest: a sickly eleven-year-old girl, 'Father's Darling', hoping for her chance to get a job and help her mother; a thirteen-year-old trying to manage the household and praying three or four times a day to Jesus 'to let mother stay a little longer, and don't take her for a few days, please'. Or a bedridden paralysed widow depending on an Odd Fellows pension which stopped coming:

> It has been a sore trial to helpless Mrs. P—, who told me how she lies and thinks till her head aches, how and where she can save a penny. She has had another great trouble lately in the very serious illness of the youngest child, Maggie. For five weeks she lingered between life and death, only soothed by the unwearying attention of the Nurse . . . It was a terrible time for them in the one room, with the one bed and the lessened income, but no murmur ever escaped the poor mother.[51]

The repeated 'trials' (obviously instances of the clients' grinding poverty), the recognition of emotional and physical pain, and the subjects' stoicism, all place these accounts in the realm of pathos rather than tragedy or melodrama.

In the oddly disembodied setting of a maternity hospital, the pseudonymous author of *Five Months in a Maternity Hospital* (1911), 'Katherine Roberts', recounts intimate conversations between the narrator (the generic 'Sister') and her patients, all addressed as 'Mother' in hospital parlance. Stories of poverty, violence and loss are recounted, and the author advertised the book as 'a personal narrative of intense interest in which pathos and humour combine to throw a lurid light on hospital methods'.[52] Ostensibly written as an indictment of this and other hospitals' nurse training programmes, *Five Months* is a lady's account of her midwifery training in an unnamed central London lying-in hospital, probably Queen Charlotte's, in 1903.[53] The patients themselves, and their stories, are the book's second agenda. In what she says is her first encounter with 'a class of people whom one had never even vaguely realised the existence of', the narrator chats with them by the hour. They talk about pregnancy, abortion, children and husbands, though the nurse reveals very little of herself in the process. The narrator is presented as a curious and sympathetic listener, who admires the generosity and fortitude particularly of the married women in her wards. One woman's account 'interested me much', she says, and the nurse encouraged her to talk freely. This mother went on to tell of her own childhood of neglect and abuse and her plans to work as a charwoman to support her six children; her uncomplaining determination made the comfortably off nurse feel 'ashamed' of her own dissatisfaction with her far easier life.[54]

Five Months in a London Hospital is, in all likelihood, the work of wealthy and well-connected suffragist Mildred Ella Mansel, who eventually became a high-ranking member of the Pankhursts' suffrage organisation, the Women's Social and Political Union.[55] Mansel's feminism is expressed more in the narrator's defiance of officious and unfeeling doctors than in the highlighting of the sufferings of her working-class patients to make a statement about the consequences of women's disenfranchisement. Mansel's suffrage conversion came in 1909, and it is tempting to think that feminism gave Mansel a new interest in the lives of previously invisible working-class women. The pathos of their monologues is relieved by Mansel's admiring comments on the women's pluck, good humour and coping skills, and recognition that they are 'sister women'.[56]

A social worker connected with a popular Euston Road infant health clinic, the Mothers and Babies Welcome (founded in 1907) in the 1900s, represented a different kind of intimate talk among women. She pioneered the newly professionalising language of domestic management which was connecting rich and poor women all over Europe in the early twentieth century. 'The Pudding Lady' was the affectionate nickname given by Somers Town children to Florence Petty, who called herself a 'lecturer and demonstrator in health foods'.[57] Her mandate was limited to showing in six lessons how to cook cheaper, tastier and more nutritious food than they had been doing. She was able to ask very naturally about the family's diet and income and to demonstrate her own 'understanding' and 'recognition' of the families' trials, offering no moral judgement. Her case notes on the 'O. Family' (parents, a baby and a sixteen-year-old), like the others, are distillations of a great deal of conversation. Petty's focus on the improvement in diet which the new recipes promised, and her technical interest in her subjects, operates to limit both the pathetic and the sensationalist revelations of poverty conditions. Suffering is translated into practical problems amenable to solution by voluntary agencies or local government.

Remarks. – The mother is very grateful for lessons, and anxious to learn to make cheap dishes that will do for baby presently. The husband worked on the tube railways for three years, and was put on to drive a train,

but lost his nerve, and nearly caused a bad accident, therefore was dismissed, and has worked in mineral water factories since. This, however, means only about 15s. per week, and dismissal for about three to four months of each year.[58]

The father appears in this case to have grabbed the social worker's attention to recount his dramatic story of losing his nerve in the tube. But the mother's anxiety about feeding a baby who would soon be weaned was what probably brought Petty into the home for a conversation about foods for infants.

A politics of voice

The generations of women 'slum' travellers after the 1890s drew on the visiting tradition and that of the capturing of sorrow and pathos on paper. Their writing, however, makes the individual sufferer less a soul deserving of care and sympathy, more an emblem of the needs of all women or of those of the working populations. Indeed, many who had begun their careers as missionaries or settlers intent on conversion or charity in God's name agonised as they shifted from one reading of their conversations among the poor to another. These included Emmeline Pethick, who left the Sisters of the People and eventually became a major suffrage leader, along with several relatives and her friend Mary Neal. Bermondsey settler Ada Brown and her fiancé Alfred Salter made a similar transition to the Independent Labour Party.[59]

Socialist, feminist and sociological women writers championed poor women in national political debates, incorporating into a wider politics the conversations which had provided them with detailed knowledge of working-class life. They supported 'working women' against charges that they were wrong to take paid jobs, to buy food in small quantities, to keep elder children home from school as helpers, or to refuse to serve oatmeal and other nutritious but unpopular foods. They inserted a new female counter-narration into such national political conversations as the freedom to divorce, the payment of maternity benefits and women's claims for full citizenship.[60] Women slum investigators recognised their responsibility to help working-class women find a 'voice'. In the late 1890s Emmeline Pethick formulated a set of political obligations based on her direct contact with women in poverty: 'By an actual knowledge and experience gained in direct contact with the people, we are fitted to become their voice, and to give utterance to their claim upon society, for a life that is worth the living.'[61] In their Introduction to *Makers of Our Clothes*, Black and Meyer plead for a better life for the long-silenced seamstresses: 'They are such good human material and for the most part so wasted. In a world of clamour the silent and long-suffering are exceedingly apt to be overlooked, although their patience forms an additional claim.'[62] Representing working-class women's words themselves became a solemn obligation for these activist women: Maud Pember Reeves, the Women's Cooperative Guild, Anna Martin, Clementina Black – all shared their pages with the women for whom they were advocates.

The voices of 'slum' women of the generations before the Second World War are not plentiful and the published and unpublished middle-class records of their conversations are an important way in which this social group has become audible to us. The daily struggles and successes of poor women could not be recognised by the 'eyewitness' journalists, social reformers and officials who glanced their way but did not stay to converse. Historical archaeology too, as Karskens puts it in her chapter for this collection, 'speaks' of people living daily lives and sharing a 'common language of things' (ch. 6) with which we might enter in conversation. The spoken evidence that we can salvage may be read alongside the testimony of material culture now being unearthed to furnish new zest and excitement to the study of urban history.

Acknowledgements

The author would like to thank Caitlin Adams, of the University of Michigan, for her help with this project's research; and, for their valuable thoughts on this work, Martha Vicinus, Judith Walkowitz and George Behlmer. Graduate students at York and Carleton Universities, at Queen's University, and at the University of Washington have also enriched this study with their ideas. My thanks also to Ramapo College's Research and Sabbatical Funds for financial support.

Notes

1 Alexander Paterson, *Across the Bridges, or Life by the South London River-Side* (London: Edward Arnold, 1911), pp. 1, 59.
2 Martha Vicinus, *Independent Women: Work and Community for Single Women 1850–1920* (Chicago: University of Chicago Press, 1985), p. 231. I have written more about London charity in 'Hungry children: housewives and London charity, 1870–1918', in Peter Mandler (ed.), *The Uses of Charity: The Poor on Relief in the Nineteenth-Century Metropolis*

(Philadelphia: University of Pennsylvania Press, 1990); and 'Good and bad mothers: lady philanthropists and London housewives before World War I', in Dorothy O. Helly and Susan M. Reverby (eds.), *Gendered Domains: Rethinking Public and Private in Women's History* (Ithaca, NY: Cornell University Press, 1992).
3 Charles Booth, *Life and Labour of the People in London, Third Series: Religious Influences* (London: Macmillan, 1902), vol. 1, p. 3; 'East End Mission Anniversary', *Methodist Times*, 14 October 1897, p. 705; G. Evelyn Gates (ed.), *The Woman's Year Book 1923–24* (London: Women Publishers, 1924), pp. 646–7.
4 Thomas Laqueur, 'Bodies, details, and the humanitarian narrative', in Lynn Hunt (ed.), *The New Cultural History* (Berkeley: University of California Press, 1989).
5 Alan Mayne, *The Imagined Slum: Newspaper Representation in Three Cities 1870–1914* (Leicester: Leicester University Press, 1993), pp. 129–47.
6 *Ibid.*, pp. 1, 4. See also, for a parallel account, Peter Fritzsche, *Reading Berlin 1900* (Cambridge, MA: Harvard University Press, 1996).
7 Melanie Tebbutts' wonderful study, *Women's Talk: A Social History of 'Gossip' in Working-Class Neighbourhoods, 1880–1960* (Aldershot, Hants: Scolar Press, 1995), is about women of the same or similar classes, though Tebbutts shows how gossip, especially in the period after 1930, established class demarcations.
8 Carla Kaplan, *The Erotics of Talk: Women's Writing and Feminist Paradigms* (New York: Oxford University Press, 1996).
9 Seth Koven, 'Henrietta Barnett 1851–1936: the (auto)biography of a late Victorian marriage', in Susan Pedersen and Peter Mandler (eds.), *After the Victorians: Private Conscience and Public Duty in Modern Britain* (London: Routledge, 1994), p. 44.
10 Based on a reading of Mansfield House and Canning Town Women's Settlement *Annual Reports* and Canning Town Settlement Minute Books, materials at the Newham Local Studies Centre and the London Metropolitan Archives. See also Seth Koven, 'Culture and poverty: the London Settlement House Movement 1870 to 1914', PhD thesis, Harvard University (1987), pp. 528–50.
11 Jane Lewis, *Women and Social Action in Victorian and Edwardian England* (Stanford: Stanford University Press, 1991), p. 10; Frank K. Prochaska, *Women and Philanthropy in Nineteenth Century England* (Oxford:

The Clarendon Press, 1980); Anne Summers, 'Public functions, private premises: female professional identity and the domestic-service paradigm in Britain, c. 1850–1930', in Billie Melman (ed.), *Borderlines: Genders and Identities in War and Peace, 1870–1930* (New York: Routledge, 1998).

12 Ross McKibbin, 'Class and poverty in Edwardian England', in *Ideologies of Class: Social Relations in Britain 1880–1950* (Oxford: Clarendon Press, 1990), pp. 167–9; Seth Koven, 'From rough lads to hooligans: boy life, national culture and social reform', in Andrew Parker, Mary Russo, Doris Sommer and Patricia Yaeger (eds.), *Nationalisms and Sexualities* (New York: Routledge, 1992); Seth Koven, 'Dr. Barnardo's "artistic fictions": photography, sexuality, and the ragged child in Victorian London', *Radical History Review* 69 (Fall 1997), 39; Vicinus, *Independent Women*.

13 See Deborah E. Nord, *Walking the Victorian Streets: Women, Representation, and the City* (Ithaca, NY: Cornell University Press, 1995); Jonathan Crary, *Techniques of the Observer: On Vision and Modernity in the Nineteenth Century* (Cambridge, MA: MIT Press, 1990); Mary Poovey, *Making a Social Body: British Cultural Formation, 1830–1864* (Chicago: University of Chicago Press, 1995), ch. 4.

14 Mayne, *Imagined Slum*, pp. 12, 157–60.

15 Raymond Williams, *The Country and the City* (New York: Oxford University Press, 1973), p. 233; Nord, *Walking the Victorian Streets*, p. 1. Baudelaire often situated the artist as a *flâneur*, a man of privilege who has the free run of the city's tantalising streets. The character of the *flâneur* has been explicated in more detail by Walter Benjamin in *Baudelaire: A Lyric Poet in the Era of High Capitalism*, trans. Harry Zohn (London: New Left Books, 1973); and by Susan Buck-Morss, who deals more with Benjamin than with Baudelaire, in 'The flâneur, the sandwichman, and the whore: the politics of loitering', *New German Critique* 39 (Fall 1986), 99–140. See also Nord's 'Introduction: rambling in the nineteenth century', in *Walking the Victorian Streets*.

16 Bosanquet, 'Children of working London', in *Aspects of the Social Problem* (London: Macmillan, 1895), p. 29; quoted in John Deane Hilton, *Marie Hilton: Her Life and Work 1821–1896* (London: Isbister and Company, 1897), pp. 90, 95.

17 Thomas Archer, *The Pauper, the Thief and the Convict: Sketches of Some of Their Homes, Haunts and Habits* (London: Groombridge and Sons, 1865), p. 10.

18 George Sims (ed.), *Living London*, 3 vols. (London: Cassell, 1902), vol. 2, pp. 118–25.

19 Koven, 'Dr. Barnardo's "artistic fictions"', pp. 32, 37; Judith Walkowitz, 'The Indian woman, the flower girl, and the Jew: photojournalism in Edwardian London', *Victorian Studies* 42:1 (1998–9), 3–46; John Tagg, *The Burden of Representation: Essays on Photographs and Histories* (Minneapolis: University of Minnesota Press, 1983); Poovey, *Making a Social Body*, ch. 5.

20 Nord, *Walking the Streets*, pp. 10–12; Erika D. Rappaport, *Shopping for Pleasure: Women and the Making of London's West End* (Princeton: Princeton University Press, 1999); Judith Walkowitz, 'Going public: shopping, street harassment, and streetwalking in late Victorian London', *Representations* 62 (Spring 1998), 1–30.

21 Beth Fowkes Tobin, *Superintending the Poor: Charitable Ladies and Paternal Landlords in British Fiction, 1770–1860* (New Haven: Yale University Press, 1993; M. Jeanne Peterson, *Family, Love and Work in the Lives of Victorian Gentlewomen* (Bloomington: Indiana University Press, 1989), p. 34. On home vaccination see George Behlmer, *Friends of the Family: The English Home and Its Guardians, 1850–1940* (Stanford: Stanford University Press, 1998), p. 91.

22 *Ibid.*, pp. 33–46; also see Donald M. Lewis, *Lighten Their Darkness: The Evangelical Mission to Working-Class London, 1828–1860* (New York: Greenwood Press, 1986); Kathleen Heasman, *Evangelicals in Action: An Appraisal of Their Social Work in the Victorian Era* (London: Geoffrey Bles, 1962), pp. 36–7. On vaccination: Behlmer, *Friends*, p. 96.

23 A Lady Resident, 'Sketch of life in Buildings', in Charles Booth, *Life and Labour of the People in London, First Series: Poverty* (London: Macmillan, 1902), vol. 3, pp. 37–41. This series was first published in 1889 and 1891. This is not the block of buildings which Beatrice Potter mentioned in her *Pall Mall Gazette* article of 18 February 1886, 'A lady's view on the unemployed in the East' (p. 11), and I have been unable to go beyond the pseudonym. Some candidates, all of whom lived for at least a time in such buildings are: Margaret Nevinson (though her quarters were larger), Margaret Harkness, Constance Black (Clementina's sister), Ella Pycroft.

24 'Life in Buildings', pp. 39, 41.

25 Walkowitz, 'The Indian woman', pp. 3–46.

26 Norman and Jeanne MacKenzie (eds.), *The Diary of Beatrice Webb*, vol. 1: 1873–1892 (Cambridge, MA: Harvard University Press, 1982), entry for 12 August

1885, pp. 136–7. Potter underestimated Cons. Cons had already bought the notorious Old Vic music hall and converted it into a successful temperance entertainment centre. When she was coopted by the London County Council (LCC) for a seat as London Alderman in 1889, Cons proved a dogged and efficient public servant. She fought to hold on to this position in the face of subsequent court rulings against females holding LCC offices. See Janet E. Courtney, *The Women of My Time* (London: Lovat Dickson [1934]), pp. 103–8; and Patricia Hollis, *Ladies Elect: Women in English Local Government 1865–1914* (Oxford: Clarendon Press, 1987), pp. 310–17.

27 Kali Israel, *Names and Stories: Emilia Dilke and Victorian Culture* (New York: Oxford University Press, 1999), p. 191.

28 'The Sisters' hour', *Methodist Times*, 14 May 1896, p. 323; Maud Pember Reeves, *Round About a Pound a Week* (1913) (reprinted London: Virago Books, 1979), p. 16.

29 Sidney and Beatrice Webb, *Methods of Social Study* (London: Longmans, 1932), p. 33. Chapter 6, 'The spoken word', written by Beatrice, actually deals with extracting information from male union officers. Bosanquet's textbooks are mentioned by Ross McKibbin, in *Ideologies of Class*, p. 178. The quotation is from Susan Pennybacker's *A Vision for London 1889–1914: Labour, Everyday Life and the LCC Experiment* (London: Routledge, 1995), p. 167.

30 Hon. Inspector's Report, Metropolitan and National Nursing Association for Providing Trained Nurses for the Sick Poor, Florence Lees (Mrs Dacre Craven), Guildhall Manuscript Library (14,626/2 [1886]).

31 A. L. Hodson, *Letters from a Settlement* (London: Edward Arnold, 1909), p. 28.

32 Mrs George Unwin and John Telford, *Mark Guy Pearse: Preacher, Author, Artist* (London: Epworth, 1930), pp. 164–5. The activities of the Sisters of the People may be followed through *The Methodist Times* and the West London Mission's monthly newsletter, *Advance!*

33 *Bermondsey Settlement Magazine*, February 1907, pp. 17–19. The number attending, fifty, dates from 1919, according to Martin's letter to Elizabeth Robins (Elizabeth Robins Papers, Series 2, Subseries B, Box 18, Fales Library, New York University). My thanks to Angela John for making me a copy of this correspondence.

34 Quoted from Elizabeth Twining, *Readings for Mothers' Meetings* (1861) in Behlmer, *Friends*, p. 62. See Frank K. Prochaska, 'A mother's country:

mothers' meetings and family welfare in Britain, 1850–1950', *History* 74 (October 1989), 336–48, and Behlmer, *Friends*, pp. 62–73. The Mothers' Union, founded in 1876, modelled on mothers' meetings, had over 400,000 members into the 1980s (Frank K. Prochaska, *The Voluntary Impulse: Philanthropy in Modern Britain* (London: Faber and Faber, 1988), pp. 12, 57).

35 The estimate is Behlmer's, *Friends*, p. 62; [Mary] Bayly, *Ragged Homes and How to Mend Them* (Philadelphia: American Sunday School Union, 1864), pp. 138, 150–3; Heasman, *Evangelicals in Action*, pp. 26, 32, 261.

36 'An appeal', *Methodist Times*, 7 April 1892, p. 335.

37 Kaplan, *Erotics of Talk*, pp. 9, 15.

38 Summers, 'Public functions'.

39 Hodson, *Letters from a Settlement*, pp. 108–9; Edith Simcox entry by Christine Devonshire, in Janet Todd (ed.), *British Women Writers: A Critical Reference Guide* (New York: Continuum Books, 1989), p. 615. This position was presented in an article in *Fraser's Magazine*, November 1878.

40 Katherine Roberts, *Five Months in a London Hospital* (Letchworth: Garden City Press, 1911), p. 106.

41 Virginia Woolf, *The Years* (1937) (New York: Harcourt Brace Jovanovich, 1965), p. 100.

42 See Hollis, *Ladies Elect*, p. 415. It is quoted by Anne Summers in 'Public functions', p. 369.

43 Mrs Carl [Adele] Meyer and Clementina Black, *Makers of Our Clothes* (London: Duckworth, 1909), p. 10.

44 Woolf, *The Years*, pp. 98–9.

45 [Maude Stanley], *Work about the Five Dials* (London: Macmillan, 1878), p. 3.

46 Booth, *Life and Labour, Third Series*, vol. 4, *Inner South London*, pp. 193–6.

47 *Five Dials*, p. 67; Northrop Frye, *Anatomy of Criticism* (Princeton: Princeton University Press, 1957), pp. 38–9.

48 Ellen Ranyard entry in *Dictionary of National Biography*, vol. 16 (Oxford: Oxford University Press, 1977); Frank K. Prochaska, 'Body and soul: Bible nurses and the poor in Victorian London', *Historical Research* 143 (October 1987), 336–48; Poovey, *Making a Social Body*, pp. 43–52.

49 Ellen Ranyard, *Nurses for the Needy* (London: James Nesbet, 1875), p. 169.

50 Poovey, *Social Body*, p. 43.

51 *The Missing Link Magazine*, June 1883, p. 170; April 1883, p. 111; February 1878, p. 47.

52 The advertisement ran in *The Suffragette* (newspaper

of the WSPU) 6 June 1913, p. 558. The author, who by that time was working full-time in the WSPU office, probably composed the ad herself.

53 Which is how it was reviewed in the *British Journal of Nursing*, 11 October 1911, pp. 363–4.

54 Roberts, *Five Months*, pp. 60–3, 131–3.

55 References to events in the suffrage struggle in the two other books 'Roberts' wrote made it possible to trace her through newspaper lists and police records of women arrested. The pseudonym may have been because she was a close relative, a cousin, of a fairly prominent Liberal politician. I have had no luck finding proof that she ever trained as a midwife, so it is possible that she based her hospital account on the diaries or stories of a friend or relative.

56 Roberts, *Five Months*, pp. 106–7. The conversion is portrayed in *Pages from the Diary of a Militant Suffragette* (Letchworth: Garden City Press, 1910). The WSPU's *Votes for Women* published short biographies of the approximately one hundred women arrested on 29 June 1909; Mansel states that she 'has now decided to devote her services exclusively to the W.S.P.U. till the vote is gained' (2 July 1909, p. 878).

57 According to her entry in *Who Was Who among English and European Authors 1931–1949*. Miss Bibby, Miss Colles, Miss Petty and Dr Sykes, *The Pudding Lady: A New Departure in Social Work* (London: The St Pancras School for Mothers [1910]). On the new 'domestic' language of this period, see Bonnie Smith, *On Writing Women's Work* (pamphlet, European University Institute Working Papers in History, Florence, 1991).

58 *Pudding Lady*, pp. 66–7.

59 Emmeline Pethick Lawrence, *My Part in a Changing World* (London: Gollancz, 1938) describes this shift. On the Salters, see Fenner Brockway, *Bermondsey Story: The Life of Alfred Salter* (reprinted London: Stephen Humphrey, 1995), ch. 2.

60 Smith, *On Writing Women's Work*, p. 5.

61 Emmeline Pethick, 'Working girls' clubs', in Will Reason (ed.), *University and Social Settlements* (London: Methuen, 1898), p. 114.

62 Meyer and Black, *Makers of Our Clothes*, pp. 17–18.

3

The making of an archaeological site and the unmaking of a community in West Oakland, California

ELAINE-MARYSE SOLARI

Fig. 3.1 'Wrecker uses Sherman tank to blitz old homes.' The contractor, hired in 1960 to clear an area for a huge postal facility, levelled nineteenth-century houses in ninety minutes instead of the two days that it would have taken if he had used more conventional equipment. (Reproduced by permission of the Oakland Enquirer.*)*

West Oakland embattled

On 15 August 1960, a former racing-car driver using a World War II Sherman tank, a 73,000-pound dreadnought, levelled six Victorian-era houses in West Oakland, California (Fig. 3.1).[1] City officials were impressed. They hired him to clear a 20-acre site, which required the relocation of more than 300 lower-income families, in order to build a huge postal facility. The site remained vacant for more than five years, even though the City of Oakland suffered an acute shortage of housing affordable to lower-income citizens.[2]

This image of war aptly illustrates the recent history of West Oakland (Fig. 3.2). Since the 1930s, West Oakland, one of the oldest communities in the City of Oakland, has been embattled: the war against poverty waged by a city confronted with innumerable social problems; the struggle by residents to keep their homes; the fear of a race war in the turbulent 1960s; and a continuing political and class battle for power and environmental justice. Four decades of 'urban renewal' have blighted the landscape of West Oakland all because government officials considered the area a slum (Fig. 3.3).[3]

Although much of the urban fabric of West Oakland has been devastated by 'renewal', the community has survived with a sense of identity. After the 1989 Loma Prieta Earthquake destroyed a major freeway that had bisected West Oakland and had isolated the Prescott District from the rest of the city, West Oakland residents successfully fought to have the freeway rerouted around their community. This rerouting of the freeway and requisite compliance with federal and state environmental laws led to one of the largest urban archaeological excavations in the

United States. The Anthropological Studies Center at Sonoma State University, under contract with the California Department of Transportation, excavated 22 city blocks, evaluated 765 features (pits, privies and wells), and analysed more than a quarter of a million artefacts.[4] This archaeological project – which garnered much local interest – provided scholarly and popular reports, a video, and travelling exhibits that describe the development of a vital and important community in stark contrast to the popularly held view of West Oakland today.[5]

This chapter assesses the cumulative effect of urban renewal and other government projects on West Oakland, probing the relationship between land condemnation and the creation of public housing, and between urban renewal and the politicisation of the African American community.

From hub to 'slum'

West Oakland, located in the 'flatlands',[6] was mostly marshland and oak groves when the town of Oakland was incorporated in 1852. Its strategic importance for transportation was quickly realised, and a wharf at Oakland Point near the foot of Seventh Street was constructed in 1863 to provide a ferry service to San Francisco, located across the bay. Daily local railroad services along Seventh

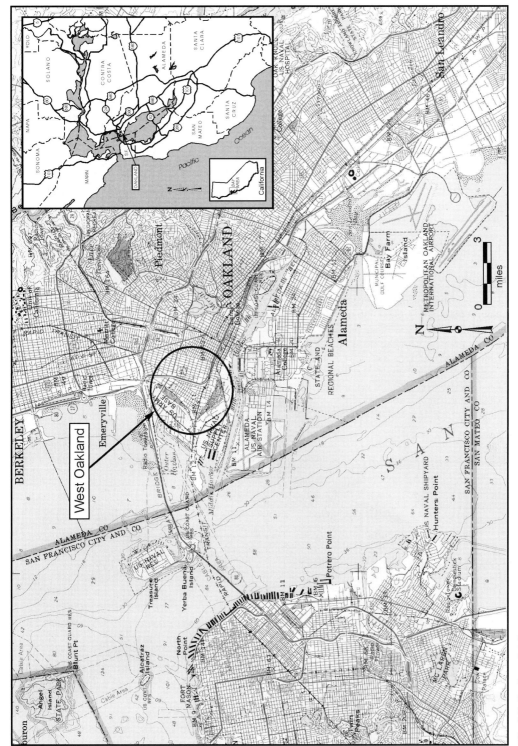

Fig. 3.2 Project vicinity.

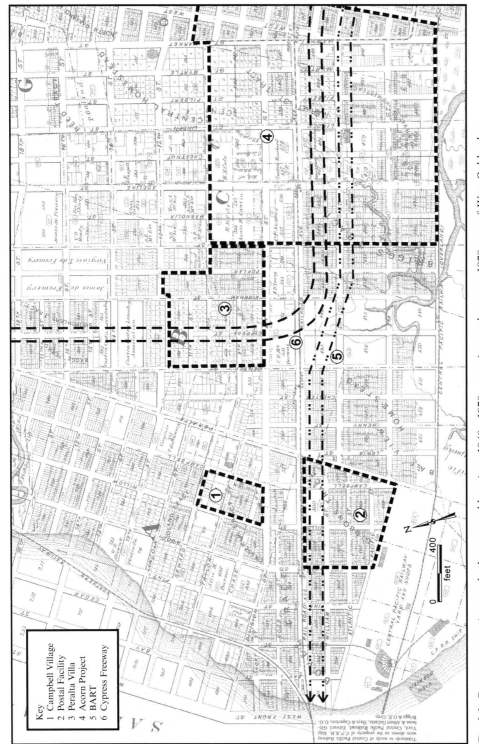

Fig. 3.3 *Government projects and urban renewal locations, 1940s–1970s, superimposed upon an 1878 map of West Oakland.*

Street soon connected downtown Oakland to the new ferry terminal, and Seventh Street became the commercial centre of West Oakland. In 1869 Oakland Point became the western terminus for the transcontinental railroad, elevating Oakland to a transportation node of national importance. Because of its excellent access by rail and sea, large industries grew up in the area and Oakland developed into a major city.[7]

Most residents in West Oakland, including many Irish, Italian and Portuguese immigrants, worked for the railroad and related industries, businesses and professions. African Americans, also early residents of the neighbourhood, founded the first African Methodist Episcopal Church in 1858, along with a variety of black charitable and self-improvement societies. West Oakland in the nineteenth century was an ethnically as well as economically mixed neighbourhood, with middle-class African Americans living next door to working-class European Americans, and elaborate Victorian houses situated next to small workers' cottages.[8]

By the turn of the century, although the neighbourhood was still ethnically mixed, West Oakland was attracting more and more African American residents because of its proximity to the railroad yards (a major source of employment), the affordability of the area, and racial discrimination, which excluded blacks from many other neighbourhoods. A local African American business and professional community developed, mainly along Seventh Street, and West Oakland became the social and cultural centre for Oakland's African Americans for the next five decades. Its nightclubs, such as Slim Jenkins' Place and the Creole Club, became nationally known centres for jazz.[9] In 1916 the first major industrial plant was built away from the main railroad line and began a mix of residential and industrial use that later, to its detriment, became characteristic of West Oakland. In the mid-1930s, much of West Oakland was officially zoned for heavy industry. Although few houses were actually replaced by industry, the maintenance, morale and property values of the area declined because of this designation.[10]

West Oakland's economy, much of it tied to the transportation industry, declined when transportation technology changed. When the San Francisco–Oakland Bay Bridge opened to automobile traffic in 1936, West Oakland lost the auto ferries that had made Seventh Street the link between San Francisco and the entire East Bay.[11] The increasing use of automobiles instead of trains by the middle classes compounded the problem. As a result, businesses along Seventh Street declined.[12]

West Oakland, because of its port and rail facilities, became a major centre for defence-related industry during the two world wars. This industry recruited thousand of labourers, many of them unskilled. During World War II thousands of labourers, including many African Americans from the South, came to work in the shipyards, warehouses and factories engaged in war industries. Oakland's African American population more than quadrupled from 1940 to 1945. At the height of the war effort, there were 500,000 jobs in the San Francisco Bay metropolitan area, many of which were temporary in nature. Wartime housing facilities were hastily set up in the East Bay to house the flood of workers. A survey for the Oakland Housing Authority (OHA) in 1942 indicated a shortage of at least 7,000 family-housing units based on the number of families living in the city.[13]

After the war more than 30,000 war housing units were demolished or abandoned in the East Bay. The African Americans who had resided in government housing found themselves limited in the main to housing choices in West Oakland because of higher prices and racial prejudice elsewhere. An acute housing shortage caused three to four families to reside in units originally constructed to house a single family. Many defence workers could not find new employment after the war's end, and high unemployment rates became chronic in West Oakland. As a result, both the houses and the neighbourhood amenities declined.[14]

By 1950, 85 per cent of the 47,562 African Americans living in Oakland resided in West Oakland. The conversion of trains from steam to diesel in the 1950s eliminated numerous jobs, because less extensive maintenance facilities were required. In the early 1950s, forty trains per day departed from West Oakland; by the late 1960s that number had dropped to three. Between 1959 and 1963, Oakland's unemployment rate had been at least 70 per cent higher than that of the San Francisco Bay metropolitan area and at least 50 per cent higher than the state and national rates. Up to 30 per cent of the employed minority population was thought to be underemployed.[15]

West Oakland was designated 'blighted' in 1949. The industrial zoning, predominance of pre-1900 housing, and the lowered socio-economic status of its residents made the area a prime target for urban renewal and other government projects. The inhabitants, mainly lower-income minorities, had little political clout, and decisions that drastically affected their lives were made without their input. Under the auspices of 'renewal', hundreds of nineteenth-century single-family homes were demolished, and the poorest tenants relocated into large public housing projects. With the urban renewal projects in full swing by the mid-1950s, middle-income white residents fled to the suburbs, and the inner city lost much of its tax base and economic stability. West Oakland, once a vibrant multi-ethnic working- and middle-class community with its own commercial district, became a 'blighted' area interspersed with large housing projects and isolated pockets of single-family housing.[16]

In the early 1960s, one-fifth of Oakland's total household population of 365,500 persons lived in poverty. The poorest section of the city, West Oakland, had a 46 per cent poverty rate. Most of these poor residents were African American. In the Prescott District, a major neighbourhood in West Oakland, the population plummeted from 22,000 in 1950, to 11,000 in 1970, and to fewer than 6,000 in 1980. Most of the residents who remained were poor black tenants, many in public housing projects.[17]

West Oakland 'renewed'

Every city in this country faces the actual or potential danger of becoming a ghost town. The cost in terms of human and economic values is enormous. THE TIME FOR ACTION IS NOW – OR NEVER. We CAN face the situation squarely, we CAN stop the spread of slums – we CAN create a new face for America.[18]

In the 1930s a war against slums swept the nation. Much of the housing stock was ageing and lacked modern amenities. Almost all houses built before 1900 were considered substandard, although when originally constructed many were of a desirable type. In 1931 President Hoover convened the 'President's Conference on Home Building and Home Ownership' to study America's housing problems. In the federal government's view, there was a close connection between housing and health, safety, morals, and family and general welfare. Policy makers believed that the housing problem had become a national emergency that only the federal government, with co-operation from state and local housing authorities, could solve. Advocates of slum clearance and urban renewal cited grim statistics: 'Slum' & 'Blighted' ('semi-slum') districts, which comprised only about 20 per cent of city residential areas, drained 45 per cent of the total city service costs while contributing only about 6 per cent of the real estate revenue. Reportedly a third of the population resided in slum or blighted areas, where 45 per cent of the major crimes occurred as well as 50 per cent or more of juvenile delinquency, arrests, disease and tuberculosis victims. If this trend continued, it was feared that American cities would face bankruptcy.[19]

The language used in describing slum problems was dramatic and fear inspiring: slums were equated with cancer or a contagious disease that could spread to surrounding areas if left to rot and fester. Slums were dangerous and threatened the destruction of entire urban communities. By the beginning of the 1940s, the United States Housing Authority (USHA) had 890 projects under contract nationwide. The Housing Act of 1949 provided federal aid to local governments to assist in slum-clearance projects and the construction of low-rent public housing projects. By the mid-1950s, 191 American cities had adopted redevelopment programmes using federal assistance; 8 of these cities were in California, including Oakland.[20]

The City of Oakland was caught in the urban renewal frenzy. Almost all the houses in residential West Oakland had been built between 1870 and 1900. These houses were growing old at the same time, and the Victorian style was in disfavour with middle-class tastes of the 1930s. During the Depression, many West Oaklanders could not afford to maintain their homes and by the late 1930s many houses needed painting and some repair.[21]

The *Oakland Observer*, a weekly progressive paper, strongly advocated urban renewal and chronicled its progress from the 1940s through the 1960s. The tone of the articles reflects the national mood of the time. After touring some of Oakland's neighbourhoods, an editor posed the question: 'Is it any wonder that you have juvenile troubles, race friction, drunken women cluttering up your dimly lighted taverns, and rats galore?' By 1948 the editor called for the clearance of thousands of substandard dwellings that occupied valuable land. In florid terms, the *Observer* described the slum tours that its reporters had taken with government officials, interested citizens and other press members. They visited the 'more seamy residences, with five children to the bed and three beds to the room', and 'rat-infested, filthy hovels'. The residents were described as being on welfare and having large numbers of illegitimate children. In other editorials, the *Observer* reiterated government statistics comparing the cost of services provided in relation to tax monies received; praised the goal of eliminating 'multi-unit insanitary, illegal, re-conversions that reap high profits to absentee landlords who do little or nothing to keep their properties habitable at the expense of the poor tenants'; and decried any delays in the renewal process. The editor dismissed those who protested against the urban renewal programme as 'West Oakland residents who did not understand the scope of Urban Renewal, and selfish interests who preferred slums, illegal conversions and a tidy profit on their holdings in the depressed area'.[22]

West Oakland's 'projects' begin

In the late 1930s, West Oakland was chosen for two USHA housing projects, Peralta Villa and Campbell

Fig. 3.4 Looking north-east from Cypress and Eighth Streets, 1940–41. These homes were demolished, despite strong resistance by homeowners, as part of the largest 'slum clearance' project in the East Bay. The houses were replaced by the Peralta Villa housing estate. (Courtesy Oakland Public Library, Oakland History Room.)

Village. These projects were intended to prevent further deterioration and preserve a normal, healthy community life before continuing decay resulted in serious social problems. Combined, Peralta Villa and Campbell Village were to provide 550 units on 24.6 acres of West Oakland land. When the housing authorities chose a densely built area with more than 300 'slum units' for the Peralta Villa and Campbell Village housing projects, the African American community suspected that the authorities had unjustly targeted their community for removal. The area chosen was located in one of the oldest neighbourhoods in Oakland, it did not have the worst housing, and, even before the mass migration during World War II, it had a large percentage of African Americans.[23]

Peralta Villa, completed in 1942, was the largest slum clearance project in the East Bay. Thirty-five two-storey residential buildings and one administration building, in a stripped-down International Style, represented the radical new social ideas and planning concepts of the New Deal as advocated by the USHA. These projects were intended to change entire neighbourhoods. One

hundred and fifty nineteenth-century detached wood-frame structures located on traditional neighbourhood streets were replaced by complexes on 'superblocks' (Figs. 3.4 and 3.5). The new structures could be arranged according to a master plan expressing the community structure the New Deal planners envisioned. This new type of planned community – initiated and controlled from outside the neighbourhood – established a pattern of development that negatively influenced West Oakland for decades. The poorest residents were concentrated in housing projects surrounded by 'blight', that forever altered the structure and character of West Oakland. Ironically, Peralta Villa, originally intended to provide better housing for those whom it displaced, only housed defence workers, many of whom were not original residents of the area, when it was eventually completed.[24]

'Renewal' on a larger scale

By the end of the 1940s, the Oakland Redevelopment Agency (the Agency) considered much of West Oakland

Fig. 3.5 Peralta Villa Housing Project, an example of 1930s social planners' attempt to reshape the lives and social habits of working-class West Oaklanders by imposing social order through new housing forms and building arrangement. (Courtesy Oakland Public Library, Oakland History Room.)

a 'blighted area', even though substantial numbers of blocks and individual properties had been well maintained and were either in good shape or could economically be brought into minimum compliance with housing codes (Fig. 3.6). The Agency determined that the area was in need of urban renewal – a combination of conservation, rehabilitation, clearance and redevelopment – in order to restore the whole neighbourhood. A combination of criteria were examined: crowding of the land by buildings, intermixture of business and industrial uses with residences, proximity to major streets and railroad, adequacy of public utilities, and the availability of essential community services. In 1958 the Agency estimated that as much as 55 per cent of the area might need to be cleared because the location of housing in industrial areas and the physical deterioration of the housing stock created generally unhealthy conditions. According to the Agency, residences should be separate from industry, each taking about half of the area. Accordingly it proposed that 'all of the residentially blighted land south of 7th and north-west of 14th and Cypress should be cleared and reused for industrial purposes'.[25]

As a result of its 'blighted' designation and the lack of

Fig. 3.6 Snapshot of young African American girl with doll standing in front of home. This photograph was filed in evidence by a landowner in the land condemnation case for the postal facility, c. 1960. (Courtesy National Archives, San Bruno.)

political clout among the residents – mainly poor African Americans – most of the government projects that benefited the public generally, at the expense of local residents, were located in West Oakland. In 1958 the double-deck portion of the Nimitz Freeway located on Cypress Street was built, bisecting West Oakland and isolating the Prescott neighbourhood from the rest of Oakland rather than going around it. Homes were destroyed, families relocated, and the character of the area was changed by both a physical and visual barrier.[26]

As of 1960 about a quarter of the population in Oakland earned less than $4,000 yearly and were eligible for public housing or federal rent subsidies. The Agency estimated that 90 per cent of these families would be affected by freeway and Bay Area Rapid Transit (BART) construction, code enforcement, urban renewal and other public action. That same year, the Postmaster General declared, 'We're doing this area a favor' when the postal service chose a location in the Prescott District of West Oakland for a huge new postal facility (Fig. 3.7). Local residents disagreed. Hundreds of families lost their homes, some landowners had to litigate for several years to get justly compensated, the project was long delayed, and, when finally completed, did not employ as many local people as the neighbourhood might have hoped or expected. Most of the 4,000 employees working at the new facility, when it was finally completed 9 years after the land had been cleared, were transferees from other postal facilities.[27]

During the same period that residents were being relocated to make room for the postal facility, the Oakland Citizens' Committee for Urban Renewal endorsed and the city approved, without representation from West Oakland, the 200-acre Acorn Renewal Project, which required the demolition of more than 300 buildings and the relocation of 9,000 residents in West Oakland. The residents to be displaced contended, to no avail, that 41 per cent of the demolished buildings could have been repaired.[28]

The Agency recognised early on that the families ordered to vacate the urban redevelopment areas would have difficulty finding new housing, because the units in new construction were largely one-bedroom apartments, the rent range was too high, and few units were available to families with children. It optimistically believed, however, that the present relocation programme was 'sufficient'.[29] As thousands of relocated families were to discover, the Agency had been over-optimistic.

Government officials did not have a relocation plan for residents to be evacuated when they condemned the twelve-block area for the postal facility. A survey established that about half of the families did not have sufficient income to rent or purchase homes in other sections of the city and would probably require public housing. Many of the families were on welfare or had incomes too low to permit payment of anything more than token rent.[30] Less than two months before the first families were required to move, a survey of the 'evacuation plans and procedures' of West Oakland residents being ousted for the postal facility indicated that most were seriously unprepared. Almost a third were not convinced the government would take over by 1 August; a third were undecided where they would go. Reportedly, the largest families were the least prepared and some were hoping 'something would happen to prevent the calamity'. Residents displaced by the postal facility had difficulty finding decent housing, because they were competing for housing with residents displaced by the Acorn Renewal Project, which had its own relocation problems.[31] All the residents were low-income and less than 12 per cent were believed to be able to reapply for new housing when constructed. Oakland clearly had difficulties in relocating thousands of lower-income residents, when there was already an acute shortage of affordable housing. The Federal Housing Authority and Home Finance Agency rejected a housing redevelopment project in West Oakland during the same time period, in part because the Agency needed to provide more evidence that 'the city can successfully relocate families to be displaced by slum clearance'.[32]

Turning a 'slum' into a slum?

Between 1960 and 1965, 8,000 housing units (of which 6,000 were located in the flatlands and occupied by low-income people) were demolished in Oakland. Although 13,000 new units were built during the same period, most were in the hills and lake area, affordable only to moderate- and high-income people. In 1966 public housing reportedly amounted to less than 1 per cent of the city's 146,000 housing units, and the OHA had a waiting list of over 500 eligible families. Throughout the 1960s and 1970s, residents were forced to relocate as older homes continued to be destroyed owing to code enforcement, and the construction of BART and the Grove-Shafter Freeway, yet another highway project that passed through West Oakland.[33]

Not just residences were targeted. Much of the black commercial district on Seventh Street was torn down for BART. This greatly reduced the services available to West Oaklanders: they had to go elsewhere (generally downtown) to shop and no longer patronised the businesses that remained. Commercial activity changed. There were not enough grocery stores and too many liquor stores.[34]

Fig. 3.7 On 18 July 1960 the Postmaster General and his entourage tour the 20-acre
site chosen for the location of a huge new postal facility. Although demolition of
numerous nineteenth-century homes would soon begin, the postal facility was not
completed for almost a decade. (Reproduced by permission of the San Francisco
Chronicle.)

This destruction of much of the African American commercial district has been criticised as racist:

> For some strange reason [the BART train tracks] had to go through Oakland's predominantly Black commercial business district above ground, while the tracks coursed through the predominantly white commercial business districts of Berkeley and San Francisco below ground.[35]

In the name of urban renewal, the community also lost schools, churches and social organisations. For example, when a school was condemned to make room for the huge postal facility, the students who had attended it had to be absorbed into neighbouring schools, causing overcrowding and a reduction in services. The New Century Club, 'one of Oakland's oldest philanthropic and social service organisations and considered one of the most revered landmarks in West Oakland', was also demolished to make room for the postal facility. That community centre and recreation area was greatly needed and sorely missed.[36]

The massive 'slum clearance' and relocation of residents had a negative impact on the entire West Oakland community in what one local newspaper, *The Flatlands*, called 'shifting slums'. A year after residents were relocated from the Acorn Renewal Project area, the paper observed 'greedy landlords subdivided old Victorian homes to create conditions as bad as those Acorn planners were supposed to replace'. Once neat, lower-middle-class single-family dwellings turned into overcrowded poverty traps. Houses on the private market were generally overpriced, unsafe, insanitary, and located in the 'ghetto'.[37]

Losing their homes through compulsory purchase turned many homeowners into renters. Although the federal constitution requires the government to pay 'just compensation' for the property it takes, the process can be unfair, particularly to the poor. The government can take the property and evict the owner before paying the landowner, and if the price offered in the declaration of taking is not accepted – it takes years to litigate or settle the matter. The government generally pays 'the fair market value' of the property, which in 'slum' areas is usually much less than is needed to buy another home elsewhere. Low-income homeowners do not have the resources to find new homes, pay litigation costs, and wait several years to be compensated. Thus, many are forced by circumstance to agree to the government's initial offer even if it is less than they paid or would not be sufficient to buy a comparable home elsewhere.[38]

Robert Valva, a real estate broker in West Oakland who liaised between the state agencies and the residents to be relocated for both the postal facility and the Nimitz (Cypress) Freeway, described it in these terms:

> [W]hen they got $7000 for their house that they paid $1800 for, that was a lot of money. But, the cheapest house that they could go find, better up, was ten or fifteen [thousand dollars]. And a four or five thousand dollar difference was a lot of money to them. How did they make those payments? I mean, they were $25, $50 a month, which was a lot of money for them . . . We had problems there because even though they got a profit, they couldn't get a house that price anywhere else. Because they were in a lower category, when you look where the Nimitz Freeway went through, and where the Post Office is, those were the cheapest houses in the whole Bay Area. Even though they got a top price, the house they were going to buy was more money. And there were a lot of older people, you know, they were settled.[39]

The elderly were the hardest hit because they were too old to get loans and could not afford to make house payments with their limited incomes. An 85-year-old homeowner of twenty years, before being forced to relocate in 1966 because of BART construction, was a typical example: 'They offered me $7,000 but for something comfortable like now it will cost $14,000 or up. With $7,000 if I'm not replaced, I'll have to rent.'[40]

Displaced renters were also put at a disadvantage because they, too, had to look elsewhere for housing when the housing supply for the poor was sharply decreased. Those evicted were frequently worse off than before, since with their limited income they could afford only to live in an area just as dilapidated. As a result of the condemnations, many of the poor went from being landowners or tenants in single-family dwellings, albeit frequently substandard, to living in housing projects.

Because of the various construction projects and code enforcement, some families in the area faced having their home demolished more than once. According to one family, living in a dilapidated house owned by Southern Pacific, the 'house we lived in ten years ago – that's been tore out. The other one also tore out. There's no house I lived in since I been here that's still up except this one. I guess we paid enough rent to have bought a home.'[41] As the decade passed, even the editorial staff of the *Observer* expressed disillusion:

> [When the urban renewal] first started [it] had the laudatory intent of providing low rent housing in the depressed areas (translate slums). However, since urban renewal projects have not been able to provide

Fig. 3.8 *Life in a housing project – an insider's view.*
*(Courtesy Oakland Public Library, Oakland History
Room.)*

even one-room apartments for less than $94 a month
rental which is too high for these self-same residents
whose homes have been bulldozed out. They are now
listed as 'displaced persons'.[42]

The Acorn Renewal Project lay vacant for almost ten years
between when the government started land acquisition and
clearance and when it started construction. Meanwhile
about 1,600 families, many of whom had owned their own
houses, were moved off their land. The African American
community bitterly resented the city's tendency to clear
housing and let the land remain vacant for years, even
though affordable housing was in acute shortage.[43]

The cumulative effect of four decades of government
projects, frequently for the benefit of the general public at
the expense of the local community, contributed greatly
to the social and economic decline of West Oakland. In
the name of urban renewal, the government destroyed
entire neighbourhoods, including their churches and businesses. At the same time, the poorest residents were concentrated in public housing projects that were frequently
'dehumanizing, dangerous, and eventually drug super-
markets' surrounded by 'blight'. An artistic and imaginative tenant considered living in Peralta Villa the same as
living in a concentration camp (Fig. 3.8). One African
American resident commented, when showing a federal
official the large area bulldozed by the Sherman Tank for

the postal facility then left vacant for years, 'They say out
here, Urban Renewal is just Negro Removal.'[44]

Politicisation of a community

The construction of Peralta Villa and Campbell Village
in the 1930s may have been the beginning of the end for
old West Oakland, but it also marked the start of many
years of community resistance that culminated in the
social unrest of the 1960s. It established a pattern of
urban redevelopment – initiated and controlled from
outside the neighbourhood – which influenced public
policy for years. While city officials considered West
Oakland blighted and in need of massive slum clearance,
local residents disagreed and viewed the government's
decisions with suspicion. 'West Oakland didn't have the
slums they said we had. It was pure racism.'[45] The
African American community questioned, from the first
urban renewal project onward, the government's motives
and choice of locations.

Resistance began with the proposed housing projects of
the 1930s. Local residents who protested that they had a
healthy neighbourhood with sound, owner-occupied
houses, bitterly resisted the destruction of their homes. As
C. I. Dellums, a black civil rights activist, noted:

> [T]here were quite a number [of homeowners who]
> couldn't understand why [the government] wanted to
> take over their home for that price while all the places
> over there on Pine Street and Wood Street and Cedar
> Street were in much worse condition than theirs. The
> people had kept their homes up . . . They were always
> presentable.[46]

The bitter resistance and allegations of racism were probably due in part to the knowledge that much of the property on Pine, Wood and Cedar belonged to the Southern
Pacific Railroad Company, which, according to one chief
housing inspector, owned 'collectively the worst housing
in all Oakland', because of the railroad's refusal to repair
their rental property on the grounds of unprofitableness.[47]

At one city council meeting, the riot police had to be
called in when a group of 350 protestors, mostly from West
Oakland, descended on the meeting to protest against the
housing projects. Believing that they were not being
offered a fair price for their homes, homeowners refused to
sell to the housing authorities. This required the government to condemn the property through compulsory purchase and contributed to the projects' long delay.[48]

Although local residents could not prevent entirely the
imposition of government projects, community resistance
enabled some families to save their homes. According to

Arthur Patterson, the reason that his family's property, from the corner of Lewis and Fifth extending up to Peralta Street, was not cleared for the postal facility was due to his mother's strenuous fight to prevent the property from being included in the demolition:

> Mama wouldn't move! And all these neighbors around here wouldn't move, that's why it stopped where it is. They would have taken this whole thing. Mama wouldn't move! . . . She was a strong, energetic woman and she was in on the town meeting, that was going on, Mama was there . . . [Three women on the same street who opposed the relocation would go with her] down there and tie up the whole meetin' . . . And when they got to Peralta they had to deal with my Mama and three or five of these other women up and down the street here . . . So there are three families that are still here that were there when all of this was in dispute. So they stopped . . . the line right here. And everything on that side of Peralta was demolished, and everything on this side of Peralta they left.[49]

By the 1960s, the devastation of West Oakland, with its ever-increasing poverty, led to social unrest and political activism. Tenants in public housing began to organise, demand certain rights, and take action. In June 1965, pursuant to a mandate from Washington to 'beautify' the area, the OHA began, without giving advance notice, to tear down backyard fences that the tenants themselves had paid for at the Peralta Villa housing project. Outraged, tenants formed the Peralta Improvement League (PIL) within three days to protest at the destruction of their fences. Joined by tenants from other OHA housing projects and the Students for a Democratic Society (SDS), the PIL stopped youth work gangs from removing the remaining fences by picketing and staging 'sit-ins'. As a result of these protests, the OHA abandoned its attempts to remove the remaining fences. The PIL, continuing as a permanent tenants' union at Peralta Villa, worked closely with two other public housing tenant groups in Oakland to protest against other OHA actions, including an attempt to ban illegitimate children from Oakland's public housing. They also worked on community improvement projects.[50]

Facing hostility from both the OHA and the housing project management, PIL officers claimed that the management had tried to evict them in retaliation for their activities. One OHA commissioner's attitude was 'public housing is inadequate in Oakland so they should be grateful they are in there at all'.[51]

In 1965 and 1966 political activity flourished. *The Flatlands*, a newspaper whose motto was 'Tell it like it is

and do what is needed', challenged the poor flatlanders to 'get up off their butts' and take action: 'We've got one good thing going. The weak points in the structure – they're our strong points. They're the issues flatlands people are beginning to get hot about. They're the points we can band together on. We've got to take them one by one. We've got to push each one through.'[52]

The SDS began 'The West Oakland Community Project' in an effort 'to build a movement of ordinary people to change Oakland'. In a door-to-door campaign, they discussed the pressing social problems of the day, one of which was the destruction of housing for public projects that were not constructed for years.[53] The Council of Social Planning, with members from various tenants' rights leagues, organised seventy-five people to form the Citizen's Committee on Housing. Although the Committee was successful in its bid for voter approval for 2,500 more public housing units, it failed to successfully reform the OHA.[54] Activists, however, were successful in motivating community members to take action. Various organisations banded together to protect tenants. For example, when one welfare mother and her four children faced eviction by a landlord, who literally tore up part of her apartment to make repairs, several community groups, the press and neighbours went to the house to help the family. The landlord had to stop (at least temporarily) until the case could be heard in court.[55]

The Flatlands, unabashedly one-sided from the poor's point of view, vividly set forth the mood of the times:

> Welcome to Oakland, the all-American city; welcome to Oakland, the 'city of Pain' . . . Seems like Watts made the federal government jumpy. People from Washington, they come all the way down here. They ask us what's going on in the flatland. They want to know how long we can wait. Some of these national magazines and newspapers write about us too. They say the flatlands is an area in which we have a so-called 'potential explosion'.[56]

The mayor, who took the potential for a race riot very seriously, warned that Oakland would become 'another Watts' unless city officials acted immediately to improve communications with minority groups and the poor. The mayor had good reason to worry. In the mid-1960s, waves of riots had engulfed other African American ghettos across the country. The *Wall Street Journal* and other news sources expressed fear that Oakland was ripe for a 'Watts' Riot, and Oakland 'became a symbol of this dangerous urban confrontation'. There were many rumours in West Oakland suggesting a possible riot: Molotov cocktails being manufactured in empty garages; arms caches being discovered; and the discussion of new riot tactics (burning City Hall, the business district, and the homes of the whites in the hills, rather than burning the ghetto).[57]

The federal government sent both advisors and massive sums of monetary aid to stabilise the situation. As a pilot project, the Economic Development Agency (EDA) used large amounts of money to create jobs and relieve the racial tensions. The EDA's plans, however, did not go smoothly. Oakland was deadlocked in a struggle between 'the power structure' (the mayor and city administration, businessmen, and labour unions) and the community activists from West Oakland on how anti-poverty funds were to be used. Their economic policies were diametrically opposed. City officials and their supporters primarily emphasised economic expansion: that Oakland's economic future depended upon the city's ability to attract and retain private capital investors. Economic growth would expand the city's tax base, creating resources that could be reinvested in the city's advancement, and would create employment opportunities, so that the citizens could be productive rather than public liabilities. In essence, they expected the economic benefits, from the federal aid, to trickle down to West Oakland residents. The West Oakland leaders desired policies that would genuinely redistribute wealth. They demanded that the government activity specifically improve the economic status of West Oakland residents, rather than generate policies that sought to adjust West Oakland residents to the existing distribution of advantages and disadvantages.[58]

In 1967 Oakland was one of sixty-three cities given funds under the Model Cities Program, a federal plan for 'changing the quality of urban life' in run-down areas. Oakland received $201,000 for planning and expected to receive millions of dollars for implementation.[59] The same year, the newly formed West Oakland Planning Council, a delegate assembly of more than 150 West Oakland organisations (a representative from every major organisation in the district), joined forces with Percy Moore, the executive director of the Oakland Economic Development Council (OEDC), in an attempt to control the federal funds. The OEDC had dropped its official affiliation with the city government because of major political differences. Moore contended:

> [T]he new model cities program should be controlled by black people for the benefit of black people [because] what motivates Congress to appropriate the money is the rising militancy of black people . . . Burn his buildings down and Congress responds. Congress

is part of the racist system. Money comes to Oakland because of black people . . . We are here to see to it that Oakland does not solve its problems by getting rid of black people . . . West Oakland citizens could veto the model cities program if they do not get what they want because the federal law requires citizen participation. The city wanted the model cities program because it has certain problems including the threat of racial disorders.[60]

West Oakland leaders, through sophisticated political manoeuvring, succeeded in extracting concessions from the city and eventually gained control of the agencies responsible for urban-renewal projects. Their push for community-based economic diversity failed, however, owing to concerted federal, state and local opposition. The federal funds were cut off and West Oakland's infrastructure continued to decline. The massive amounts of federal funds poured into Oakland did successfully prevent a major riot in the mid-1960s, however, and, unlike some other African American ghettos, it did not go up in flames.[61]

Political activity in West Oakland reached its zenith in 1966 with the organisation of the Black Panthers, whose politics were 'based in the misery of Oakland's black ghetto'.[62] David Hillard, the former National Chief of Staff of the Black Panthers, described West Oakland during this period: 'From the piers up to Lake Merritt you're in West Oakland, a tract of largely treeless streets filled with broken glass, boarded up houses, and decrepit schools – a ghetto whose squalor seems even worse to me than Mobile's, larger, grayer, more inescapable.'[63]

According to Hillard, you couldn't understand the Panthers without having a sense of Oakland's history, a 'unique blend of southern black, militant trade union, and western American cultures'.[64] Huey Newton, the co-founder of the Black Panthers, was born, raised and murdered in West Oakland. He and Bobby Seale, the other co-founder of the party, held the party's first meeting in a clubhouse on Peralta Street. In 1970 the Panthers' National Headquarters and Ministry of Information was also located on Peralta Street.[65]

Although the Panthers first began as an armed group who monitored the police and advised black citizens being arrested of their rights, they quickly evolved into a national organisation, advocating militant resistance to discrimination and exploitation.[66] Adequate housing for African Americans was a critical issue in their broad social policy.[67]

Although the Panthers are more apt to be remembered by some for their calls for Black Power, their violent rhetoric, their murder trials and their armed march to the State Capitol in 1967, the party set up and ran a variety of social programmes, including schools, medical clinics and food programmes both in Oakland and nationwide. Although their national influence declined in the 1970s, the Black Panthers enjoyed wide support among African Americans in West Oakland and their still considerable local influence strongly contributed to Lionel Wilson's election as Oakland's first black mayor in 1977.[68]

West Oakland deconstructed

The ultimate irony of urban renewal in West Oakland is that it created the blight that it sought to ameliorate. The situation in West Oakland was by no means unique. Old neighbourhoods were being ripped apart and communities destroyed throughout the United States during the 1930s–1960s, as cities struggled with deteriorating city cores. Housing projects built to replace the ageing housing stock soon became major problems as income ghettos, centres for juvenile gangs and areas where social disintegration became institutionalised. Urban renewal also engendered the problem of 'shifting slums' and mass evictions, and still it could not provide enough affordable units for those who had been driven away. The result was the creation of 'new slums' and intensified pressure within the old centres of disadvantage, particularly for minority groups.[69]

Many of the organisations begun in the 1960s in opposition to the displacement caused by urban renewal continue to thrive and play an important role in the ongoing revitalisation of West Oakland's neighbourhoods. After the Loma Prieta Earthquake, Caltrans proposed that the Cypress Freeway be rebuilt in the existing right of way. The local community, spearheaded by the Citizens Emergency Relief Team (CERT), strongly opposed that course of action. In response the Oakland City Council passed two resolutions opposing any construction in the existing corridor. After evaluating several alternate routes, Caltrans chose one that went around the residential neighbourhood in West Oakland. Community groups, social activists and politicians used the freeway issue to focus attention on social, economic and environmental problems in West Oakland.[70]

Historical archaeology for the Cypress Freeway relocation is helping to dispel some of the modern images of blight and slumland that cling to West Oakland by reviving the truths of this once-vital area through historical research, oral history and archaeology. Studies have shown that, far from being a downtrodden mono-cultural ghetto, West Oakland in the nineteenth century was a centre of commerce and was inhabited by people of diverse ethnic, cultural and economic backgrounds. On one city block, a wealthy white capitalist lived two doors away from an African American widow in the early 1880s. The capitalist and his family occupied an elaborate, Victorian-style home on a corner lot with bay widows and set their table in high fashion with matching sets of gilt porcelain and pressed glassware. Their neighbour, the widow, took in boarders and lived in a plain one-storey cottage that she furnished as well as she could. Working with limited means, she set her table with odds and ends of old-fashioned china that, from a distance, could have appeared to be a matched set. These two families illustrate the diversity that was West Oakland, where rich and poor lived side by side, and most strove to accommodate the Victorian ideals of public display that informed American middle-class society at that time.[71]

West Oakland is again faced with huge plans for redevelopment. One proposed redevelopment plan would raise more than $1 billion in funds over a fifty-year period. Some local businesses and residents, perhaps on the basis of historical experience, fear that it would displace long-time businesses and residents: 'Redevelopment is supposed to be making a better world, and what we're ending up with is a complete catastrophe.'[72] Only time will tell whether the city has learned from its previous forays into 'renewal'. Perhaps with planning and an eye to the past, the City of Oakland can build on the community that is already there, instead of unmaking it all over again.

Acknowledgements

The author would like to thank the following people for their comments and suggestions on earlier drafts of this chapter: Grace H. Ziesing, Mary Praetzellis and Jack McIlroy. I am particularly indebted to Ms. Ziesing for her editorial assistance with the final draft of this chapter and her encouragement throughout the project. I appreciate the skilled assistance with the graphics by Maria Ribeiro and Nelson ('Scotty') Thompson. William Sturm, at the Oakland History Room of the Oakland Public Library, and Betty Marvin, at the Oakland Cultural Heritage Survey Office, have graciously shared their extensive knowledge of Oakland history and provided patient guidance to their archives. I also wish to extend a special thanks to Mary Praetzellis and Adrian Praetzellis for their encouragement and understanding, which made this chapter possible.

Notes

1 West Oakland refers to the area west of Market Street extending to the bay. The Prescott District is bounded by West Grand Avenue, Cypress Street, Third Street,

and the Southern Pacific Classification Yards. California Department of Transportation, *Final Environmental Impact Statement/Report,* vol. 1, *I-880/ Cypress Replacement, Alameda County, California* (1991), pp. 5–17.

2 *Oakland Tribune,* 16 August 1960, E-13; *Tribune,* 15 July 1963, 1, 4.

3 War references are frequently used by the American press when reporting governmental action on social issues; e.g. the 'War on Poverty', the 'Battle with the Slum', and more recently the 'War on Drugs'. See Alan Mayne, 'A just war: the language of slum representation in twentieth-century Australia', *Journal of Urban History* 22 (1995), 75–107. For a discussion of the slum as myth see Alan Mayne, *The Imagined Slum: Newspaper Representation in Three Cities 1870–1914* (Leicester: Leicester University Press, 1993).

4 Jack McIlroy, 'The Cypress Archaeology Project', paper presented at the California Preservation Federation Conference, Berkeley, California, 8 May 1998, p. 6.

5 Mary Praetzellis (ed.), *West Oakland – A Place to Start From: Research Design and Treatment Plan Cypress I-880 Replacement Project,* vol. 1, *Historical Archaeology* (Rohnert Park, CA: Sonoma State University, Anthropological Studies Center, 1994); Suzanne Stewart and Mary Praetzellis (eds.), *Sights and Sounds: Essays in Celebration of West Oakland* (Rohnert Park, CA: Sonoma State University, Anthropological Studies Center, 1997); California Department of Transportation, *Privy to the Past* (co-produced with Alpha Spectrum Educational Films, Oakland; and the Anthropological Studies Center, Sonoma State University, Rohnert Park, CA, 1999).

6 The flat areas of Oakland were generally occupied by lower-income residents; whereas the suburban neighbourhoods, predominately white, were located in the nearby hills.

7 Beth Bagwell, *Oakland: The Story of a City* (Novato, CA: Presidio Press, 1982), pp. 33, 47, 53.

8 Nancy and Roger W. Olmsted, 'History of West Oakland', in Praetzellis (ed.), *West Oakland,* p. 98; Oakland Citizens Committee for Urban Renewal (OCCUR), *Neighborhood Profiles: West Oakland* (1988), pp. 5–6 (on file at Environmental Design Library (EDL), University of California, Berkeley).

9 Donald Hausler, 'Blacks in Oakland, 1852–1987' (MS on file at the Oakland Public Library, Oakland History Room (OHR), 1987), pp. 35–6, 123; Willie R. Collins, 'Jazzing up Seventh Street: musicians, venues,

and their social implications', in Stewart and Praetzellis (eds.), *Sights and Sounds,* pp. 295–324.

10 Oakland Cultural Heritage Survey (OCHS), *Historic Property Survey Report,* 4 vols. (Oakland City Planning Department, 1990), vol. 1, pp. 11–12.

11 The counties surrounding San Francisco Bay are referred to as the Bay Area; the East Bay refers to the communities on the east side of the bay, most notably Oakland and Berkeley.

12 Olmsted, 'History of West Oakland', pp. 170–1.

13 *Tribune,* 16 August 1942, B11:5; Redevelopment Area Organization, *Provisional Economic Development Program for the City of Oakland* (Oakland, 1964, on file EDL).

14 William L. Nicholls II, *Poverty and Poverty Programs in Oakland* (Survey Research Center, University of California, Berkeley, 1966), pp. 136–8; Redevelopment Area Organization, *Provisional Economic Development,* pp. 3–11.

15 City Manager of Oakland California, 'Application for planning grant, model cities program, City of Oakland' (City of Oakland, 1966); Redevelopment Area Organization, *Provisional Economic Development,* pp. 7–8. Olmsted, 'History of West Oakland', pp. 172–3.

16 OCHS, *Survey,* vol. 3, A-10, A-228:14.

17 Nicholls, *Poverty Programs in Oakland,* p. 137; Lawrence P. Crouchett, Lonnie G. Bunch III and Martha Kendall Winnacker, *Visions toward Tomorrow: The History of the East Bay Afro-American Community 1852–1977* (Oakland: Northern California Center for Afro-American History and Life, 1989), p. 45. Hausler, *Blacks in Oakland,* p. 22. According to the 1980 census, the district was almost 90 per cent black, almost 40 per cent had household incomes under $5,000, and fewer than 22 per cent of the housing units were owner occupied. The district had 16 OHA projects for a total of 737 housing units. OCCUR, *Neighborhood Profile,* pp. 5–6.

18 National Association of Home Builders, *A New Face for America: A Program of Action Planned to Stop Slums and Rebuild Our Cities* (Washington, DC: Department of Housing Rehabilitation, 1953), p. 1.

19 Edith Elmer Wood, *Slums and Blighted Areas in the United States* (Federal Emergency Administration of Public Works, Housing Division Bulletin 1, 1935); A. R. Desai and S. Devadas Pillai (eds.), *Slums and Urbanization* (Prakashan: Bombay Popular, 1970), pp. 37–8.

20 William Grigsby, 'Slum clearance: elusive goals', in *ibid.,* pp. 255–60, 256 (reprinted from the *Annals of the*

American Academy of Political and Social Science 352, March 1964). *Observer*, 19 February 1955, 4:2–5:1.

21 Olmsted, 'History of West Oakland', p. 169.

22 *Observer*, 16 September 1944, 2:1; 8 May 1948, 1:2; 26 February 1955, 1:1–2; 22 September 1956, 1:1–2; 29 September 1956, 4:1; 13 October 1956, 1:2; 8 December 1956, 1:1–2; 11 November 1967, 2:1–2.

23 Housing Authority of the City of Oakland, *Fourth Annual Report* (Oakland, 1942–3, on file at OHR), pp. 5–6; OCHS, *Survey*, vol. 3, A-228:9.

24 OCHS, *Survey*, vol. 3, A-228:10–12; *Post Enquirer*, 14 July 1939, 1:8; *Tribune*, 16 August 1942, B11:5.

25 Redevelopment Agency of the City of Oakland, *GNRP Progress Report to City Council* (Oakland, 1958), pp. 4–10.

26 Hausler, *Blacks in Oakland*, p. 125; OCHS, *Survey*, vol. 1, p. 6.

27 *San Francisco Chronicle*, 19 July 1960 7:1–4; 20 July 1969, B-10.

28 Crouchett *et al.*, *Visions toward Tomorrow*, pp. 45, 56.

29 Department of Urban Renewal, *Workable Program* (Oakland, 1959), pp. 11–12.

30 *Tribune*, 28 August 1959, 1, 3.

31 *California Voice*, 22 January 1960, 1:6–7; 19 February 1960, 1:7; 4 March 1960, 1:1; 11 March 1960, 1:3; 10 July 10, 1959, 1:7; *Flatlands*, 26 March 1966, 1:1–5; *Oakland Tribune*, 28 August 1959, 1, 3; Crouchett *et al.*, *Visions toward Tomorrow*, p. 56.

32 *California Voice*, 25 December 1959, 1:4; 29 April 1960, 1:4, 8.

33 *Flatlands*, 26 March 1966, 1:1–5; 9 April 1966, 1–3:1–5; Ruth Goodman, 'The housing problem in Oakland' (photocopy of typescript, dated 10 March 1966, in vertical file 'Oakland Housing (1960–1969)/Peralta Villa Housing I' at OHR).

34 OCCUR, *Neighborhood Profiles*, p. 4.

35 Hugh Pearson, *The Shadow of the Panther: Huey Newton and the Price of Black Power in America* (Menlo Park, CA: Addison-Wesley, 1994), p. 238.

36 United States District Court, Northern District of California, Southern Division, *United States of America v. Certain Lands in the City of Oakland* (Civil Case #38477, filed 26 August 1959, amended pre-trial agenda for tracts 103, 104 and 105, on file at the National Archives, San Bruno), p. 5; *Tribune*, 28 August 1959, 3:5.

37 *Flatlands*, 26 March 1966, 1:1–5, 3:2; Council of Social Planning, 'Statement on low income housing in Oakland' (typescript, 27 April 1966, in vertical file 'Oakland Housing (1960–1969)/Peralta Villa Housing I' at OHR).

38 Those who litigated or 'held out' for a year or more

before settling generally received 10–20 per cent more than the government's initial offer. The small increase in value probably did not offset the cost of litigation or justify the wait for compensation for some of the landowners owning the less valuable tracts. United States District Court, *USA v. Certain Lands*.

39 Robert Valva, interviewed by Karana Hattersley-Drayton on 2 and 17 March 1995 as part of the Cypress Freeway Replacement Oral History Project (transcript on file at Anthropological Studies Center, Sonoma State University, Rohnert Park, CA), pp. 6–7.

40 Betty Stenyard interviewed in *Flatlands*, 18 November–2 December 1966 1:5, 3:1–5.

41 *Flatlands*, 5–18 June 1966, 3:2.

42 *Observer*, 17 September 1965, 4:1–2.

43 *Flatlands*, 9 April 1966, 1:1; *Observer*, 11 November 1967, 4:1.

44 Pearson, *The Shadow of the Panther*, p. 314; Armory Bradford, *Oakland's Not for Burning* (New York: David McKay Company, 1968), p. 6.

45 A comment by an African American resident in West Oakland in Donald Hausler, 'The Cypress structure and the West Oakland black community', *From the Archives*, Northern California Center for Afro-American History and Life, 1 (1990), 2.

46 C. L. Dellums, 'International president of the brotherhood of sleeping car porters and civil rights leader', typescript (Berkeley: Regional Oral History Office, Bancroft Library, 1973), p. 71.

47 Reginald Major, *A Panther is a Black Cat* (New York: William Morrow & Company, 1971), pp. 10–11.

48 *Post Enquirer*, 14 July 1939, 1:8.

49 Arthur Patterson, interviewed by Marta Gutman on 8 June 1995, in Oral History Project, pp. 50–1.

50 *Tribune*, 4 and 13 July 1965 A2:7–8, E5:4–5; *Montclarion*, 4 August 1965 (clipping from PIL vertical file); Peralta Improvement League (PIL), letter, 12 August 1966 in PIL vertical file at Oakland Public Library, Oakland History Room.

51 *Montclarion*, 4 August 1965 (clipping from PIL vertical file).

52 *Flatlands*, 19 March 1966, 1.

53 Students for a Democratic Society, 'Informational flyer' (*c.* 1965 in PIL vertical file); *Flatlands*, 14 September–8 October 1966, 2–3:1–3.

54 *Flatlands*, 11–24 March 1967, 1:1–3; 2:1–5; 7:4–5. Although social activists recognised the problems with public housing, they strongly advocated more public housing because of the acute housing shortage and the private sector's failure to provide decent low-cost housing. PIL Newsletter 15, January 1967 (in

vertical file 'Oakland Districts, West Oakland' at OHR).

55 *Flatlands*, 14 September–8 October 1966, 2–3:1–3.

56 *Flatlands*, 19 March 1966, 1. *The Flatlands*, a ghetto paper financed by small contributions, was mainly the work of two young women, Alexandra Close, who wrote most of the articles and Lynn Phipps, who took the photographs. The paper lasted from 1966 until 1968, when the publishers ran out of money. Bradford, *Not for Burning*, p. 87.

57 *Tribune*, 21 April 1966 1:3, 2:2–3; Roger Biles, 'Thinking the unthinkable about our cities thirty years later', *Journal of Urban History* 25 (1998), 57–64; Bradford, *Not for Burning*, pp. 188–9.

58 Bradford, *Not for Burning*, pp. 202–3; Judith V. May, *Two Model Cities: Negotiations in Oakland* (Department of Political Science, University of California, Davis, 1970); Shirley F. Barshay, *One Meaning of 'Citizen Participation': A Report on the First Year of Model Cities in Oakland California* (prepared under a grant from the Office of Economic Opportunity, Western Region, 1968; on file EDL).

59 *Tribune*, 10 December 1967 1:7, A:5–7; Barshay, *One Meaning*, pp. 4–5.

60 *Tribune*, 30 November 1967 1:3, 4:4.

61 Crouchett *et al.*, *Visions toward Tomorrow*, p. 59.

62 Major, *A Panther is a Black Cat*, p. 20.

63 David Hillard and Lewis Cole, *This Side of Glory: The Autobiography of David Hillard and the Story of the Black Panther Party* (Boston: Little, Brown, 1993), p. 68.

64 *Ibid.*, p. 67.

65 G. Louis Heath, *The Black Panther Leaders Speak: Huey P. Newton, Bobby Seale, Eldridge Cleaver and Company Speak Out through the Black Panther Party's Official Newspaper* (Metuchen, NJ: Scarecrow Press, 1976), p. 4; Hillard and Cole, *This Side of Glory*, pp. 1, 7; Pearson, *The Shadow of the Panther*, p. 8; Bobby Seale, *Seize the Time: The Story of the Black Panther Party and Huey P. Newton* (New York: Random House, 1970), p. 13.

66 Crouchett *et al.*, *Visions toward Tomorrow*, p. 59; Pearson, *Shadow of the Panther*, p. 3.

67 Policy 4 of the Black Panther Party's 10 Point Platform and Program, dated October 1966: 'WE WANT DECENT HOUSING FOR THE SHELTER OF HUMAN BEINGS. We believe that if the white landlords will not give decent housing to our black community, then the housing and the land should be made into co-operatives so that our community, with government aid, can build and make decent housing for its people.' Seale, *Seize the Time*, p. 67.

68 *Ibid.*, pp. 412–15; Crouchett *et al.*, *Visions toward Tomorrow*, p. 59; Pearson, *Shadow of the Panther*, p. 314.

69 Michael Harrington, 'Old slums, new slums', in Desai and Pillai (eds.), *Slums and Urbanization*, pp. 82–90 (reprinted from Michael Harrington, *The Other America* (New York: Macmillan, 1962)); Grisgsby, 'Elusive goals', in *ibid.*, pp. 255–60.

70 California Department of Transportation, *EIR* 5–18; *Tribune*, 28 August 1991 A3:4–5; Elihu M. Ellis, Memo from Oakland's Mayor regarding the I-880 Freeway Reconstruction Project (reprinted in *West Oakland Commerce Association Journal*, Redevelopment Section, July 1991).

71 California Department of Transportation, *Privy to the Past*.

72 *Montclarion*, 9 July 1991 1:1–6, 6:1–6.

4

Twice removed: Horstley Street in Cape Town's District Six, 1865–1982

ANTONIA MALAN AND
ELIZABETH VAN HEYNINGEN

Cape Town's most striking memorial to *apartheid* is several hectares of open, rubble-strewn land close to the Central Business District. This was District Six, once a vibrant but impoverished inner-city working-class area. (Fig. 4.1).[1] Although it was declared a white group area on 11 February 1966, removals only occurred on a large scale in the mid-1970s. The destruction of District Six became one of the central myths of the struggle against *apartheid*, shaped and reshaped in verse, novels, reminiscences, videos and even a musical.[2] Memory is a form of mourning, and 'Welcome to Fairyland' became the slogan that expressed the loss of a community destroyed not only by racial segregation but also by the forces of modernism in an industrialising society.

The very potency of Capetonian memories of District Six serves to obscure the daily reality and life in the District as it had evolved since the eighteenth century. Even before the *apartheid* years, nostalgia was integral to Capetonians' perception of themselves. From the comfortable white middle classes to the African resistance leader Phyllis Ntantala, all shared the view of the young communist Pauline Podbrey that 'On my heart you will find "Cape Town".' This did not mean that there was a common understanding of the city. On the contrary, experiences of life in Cape Town diverged widely. For outsiders District Six was a no-go area, a slumland, crime-infested, gang-ridden, to be avoided at all costs. On the other hand, ex-District Six residents remember their old home as a warm community in which conflict was rare. Since the mid-1980s the musicals of Taliep Petersen and David Kramer, including *District Six: The Musical*, *Welcome to Fairyland* and, most recently, *The Cat and the Kings*, now playing on Broadway, used the distinctive music of the

District to evoke a lost world. However, the stereotypical characters – the Jewish landlord, the gang member, the respectable Muslim, the good-hearted prostitute, the coarse bureaucrat enforcing Group Areas – illustrate the problem of mythologising.

Horstley Street was a street of about 100 single-storey terrace houses which ran down the steep mountain slope, meeting Hanover Street, District Six's main street, at right-angles. The origins of the name 'Horstley' are not known, but by 1900 the street had become a byword for its insanitary squalor. At that time a *Cape Argus* journalist, in the familiar language of slummer journalism, remarked of its houses that 'Filth is the only word which can be used to describe these dens.'[3] The street survived until the early 1980s, when a video, *Last Supper at Horstley Street*, captured the grief and alienation of a family torn from its roots and moved to Belhar on the Cape Flats. In these disparate images Horstley Street epitomised the best and the worst of this inner-city community.

Although much has been written about District Six, there is little detailed, critical research by historians. In spite of the fact that much of the area has not been built over since the removals and is consequently a unique opportunity for urban archaeologists, little has so far been excavated. It has resulted from grasping small opportunities rather than emerging from a properly strategised, community-based and focused research project on the material culture of District Six.[4] Though acknowledging the significance of District Six, researchers have often failed to collaborate formally. Indeed, this text is woven together from parallel researches that only partly coincide in time and place. This chapter is an attempt, within the context of related work in other cities, to recover the social and material context of life in the District through the collaboration of historical archaeologists and historians. The detailed, site-specific approach of the historical archaeologist has melded surprisingly well with the historian's records, productively raising many new questions from each researcher for future work.

Building Horstley Street

District Six developed as a suburb on the farm Zonnebloem, first granted as Freehold land to Claas Hendrik Dieperman in 1707, then passing through a number of hands in the eighteenth century.[5] During these years the farmstead was owned and occupied by elite military officers and their families. It was conveniently situated near the Castle, headquarters of the Cape garrison. The nineteenth century saw increased urbanisation and

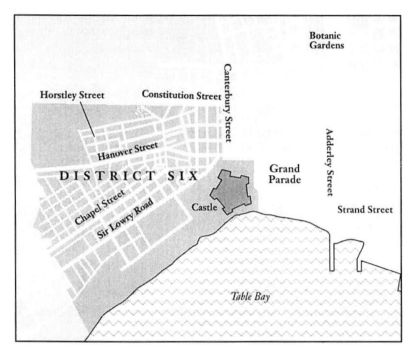

Fig. 4.1 Cape Town's District Six close to the Central Business District (Adderley and Strand Streets) and harbour.

the gradual collapse of prosperous market gardens on the slopes of Table Mountain. Farms were subdivided and the farmsteads adapted as 'gentlemen's residences' or commercial ventures.[6] By the 1860s District Six had been in existence for over a generation, owing its origins partly to the emancipation of slaves in 1834–8. This event created a substantial market for working-class housing while slave compensation money gave slave owners liquid capital which was frequently invested in property. However, the Horstley Street part of the Zonnebloem estate remained undeveloped until the 1860s.

Early-nineteenth-century developments in the District followed old farm boundaries and watercourses, unlike the gridded block form of eighteenth-century central Cape Town grants. For instance, archival research into the Tennant Street site documented a variety of semi-detached 'cottages' and row-houses being erected from the 1840s, arranged piecemeal around the outside of an irregular-shaped property before the central area was filled with short access alleys and buildings.[7] Unlike the Tennant Street block, Horstley Street developed linearly, with short, regular rows of dwellings extending up from Hanover Street. The first trace of Horstley Street appeared in the *Cape Almanac* in 1865, when three resi-

dents were recorded. By the end of the century Horstley Street had expanded by stretching up the mountain, past Ashley and Frere Streets. A row of dwellings was built opposite Roos Street by Robert Falconer on *erf* (lot) 7702 in 1897. The plot above these remained open, however, as did the land beside a watercourse behind the buildings (Fig. 4.2).

The new structures were surveyed by J. G. Hallack in 1897. He drew a simple outline plan of the footprint of nine dwellings, the uppermost of which was slightly larger.[8] According to evidence from the 1901 Municipal Valuation, describing a similar row lower down Horstley Street, the larger house (or 'home') was intended for the owner or a supervisor.[9] Situated at the top of the row, the occupant of the 'home' would have a dominant view and controlling position over the attached dwellings. Access to the original houses was a single external door leading straight onto the street. Two photographs, one taken in the 1960s and the other in 1973 on the eve of demolition of the remaining buildings on the street, show flat-fronted, flat-roofed, single-storey buildings with low parapets along the façades, stepped to allow for the steep slope of the street. This style, described by the *Cape Times* Special Commissioner in 1901 as 'offensively modern',

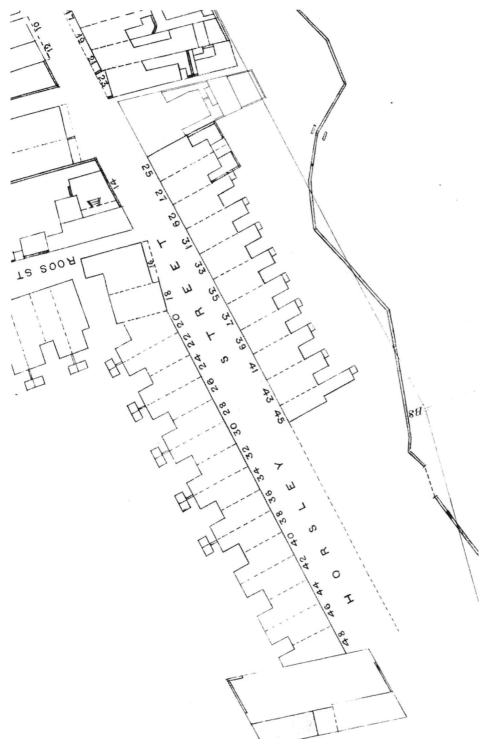

Fig. 4.2 Walter Thom's Survey of c. 1900 shows the footprints of the houses built for Robert Falconer on erf 7702 in 1897, originally numbers 29 to 45 Hors[t]ley Street.

Fig. 4.3 View up Horstley Street, towards Table Mountain. Erf 7702 is on the left, at the top, opposite the white car.

was reminiscent of the style of housing found in the first part of the nineteenth century (Figs. 4.3 and 4.4).[10]

Excavating Horstley Street

Despite the extent of open ground left by the bulldozing of District Six, there are few areas that are suited for archaeological excavation. In some places the ground has been completely scoured, removing all traces of foundations, while in other areas several metres of rubble cover the original land surface, making excavation impractical. In addition, landscaping for Cape Technikon buildings and car parks has obliterated all traces of the earlier urban fabric over a substantial area. The top segment of Horstley Street was initially chosen for fieldwork in 1992 because the foundations of several houses were still visible on aerial photographs and the cobbles and pavement had been left undisturbed. This offered a chance of relating excavated house plans to archival plans and nineteenth-century maps (Figs. 4.5 and 4.6).

Archaeological excavations at nos. 73 and 75 Horstley Street revealed an original core of two rooms, one behind

the other, with a passage connecting them along one side (Fig. 4.7). Later concrete slabs obscure the original provisions for sanitation or ablution, if any, though Thom's plan of *c.* 1900 showed small rear extensions. Foundations were constructed from blocks of Table Mountain Sandstone and walls were brick and mud mortar, plastered originally with mud and painted at various times with colours including light blue and ochre brown. In No. 75, traces of floorboards could still be seen. In No. 73, in the back room, a semi-circular brick feature on the stone foundation could have been the remains of a fireplace. There were no sheltering *stoeps* or decorative verandahs as in some of the dwellings built further down the street.[11] Neither were there provisions for workshops or garden allotments: domestic or household production was effectively curtailed by these structures.[12]

Lack of research on the interiors of Cape Town working-class housing makes it difficult to establish how typical these units were. The British experience is an unsatisfactory model for comparison since conditions were very different at the Cape. Though ideas of model housing, sanitation and administrative control may have

Fig. 4.4 View down Horstley Street, towards the harbour. Erf 7702 is on the right. Some of the dwellings were painted pale blue when this photograph was taken in 1970.

emanated from Britain, especially after the 1870s, their application in Cape Town was mediated by local physical, political and social structures.[13] A municipality was only established for the Table Valley area in 1840 and it was not until the late nineteenth century, after responsible government was granted in 1872, that Acts regulated buildings plans or public health. A range of 'cottages' as well as small houses, sometimes in rows or terraces, were built for a working class which was racially, ethnically and occupationally heterogeneous.[14] The fact that the poorest housing stock was destroyed, largely unrecorded, makes our research task still more difficult. Very little remains, either, of the poorest working people who, unable to afford even the rent of purpose-built lower-class housing, occupied dilapidated older houses, in miserable conditions.[15]

In general, development in Cape Town was low rise, and a lack of water meant that houses were often built without sanitation.[16] The self-interest of private enterprise, rather than philanthropy, motivated building stan-

dards. In the absence of town planning, *ad hoc* development by private individuals exacerbated poor street and service management. Although modifications occurred in Horstley Street, including the installation of sewerage and the provision of piped water, in the 1980s the basic structures still remained.

It is tempting to over-interpret the sparse evidence we have of the material world of the community in Horstley Street, District Six. While some meaning can be derived from the spatial context of Horstley Street, the excavated artefacts are most remarkable for their mundane nature and an archaeological context that defies interpretation.[17] Most of the assemblage was excavated from unstratified deposit beneath the floorboards of No. 75. The artefacts represent things that were broken or lost in the house, rather than general household refuse, and were small enough to have fallen through gaps in the floor.

There have been initiatives to combine the debris of the past with the political present. For instance, an exhibit of artefacts excavated from Stuckeris Street formed part of

Fig. 4.5 Aerial photograph taken in 1968, looking north towards the harbour, showing an intact Horstley Street and neighbourhood.

Fig. 4.6 Aerial photograph taken in 1992, looking north towards the harbour, showing open ground with some cobbled streets still visible. The Cape Technikon campus encroaches from top left and new thoroughfares cut across the old streetscape.

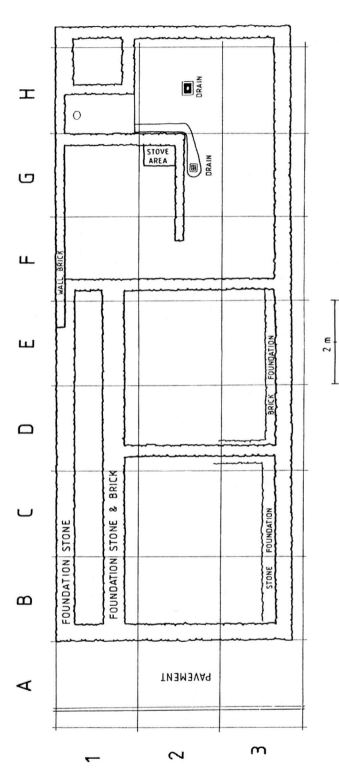

Fig. 4.7 Foundations, internal room layout and floor-level features revealed by archaeologists at No. 75 Horstley Street in 1994.

the District Six Museum public display, alongside salvaged street signs and personal photographs. The intention was to demonstrate both the importance of archaeological context for even the recent past and the symbolic value as well as tangible power of apparently useless rubbish. Reactions to an exhibition by artist Sue Williamson, comprising 'found objects' set in clear resin, such as plastic toys, broken ceramics and bits of string, exposed many controversies around District Six as 'myth'. Children and their history teachers from schools in Greater Cape Town participated in a salvage excavation at the Tennant Street site.[18]

Patterns of migrancy

Cape Town's street directories provide an uncertain guide to patterns of occupancy in Horstley Street, but they do, to some extent, reflect changes in the local economy. The 1890s were a period of prosperity in Cape Town, when the profits from Rand gold flowed into the city, attracting white working-class immigration from Britain, Europe and Australia. The growth in shipping increased the demand for dock labour, providing an alternative to the mines for migrant labourers from the Transkei. District Six did not grow as rapidly as nearby Woodstock but between 1891 and 1904 there was plenty of opportunity for the speculator.

Two new groups of immigrants entered the District from the late nineteenth century: 'poor white' Afrikaners and East European Jews. Both found accommodation in Horstley Street but it was the Jews who left their mark. The brothers Nathan and Moses Bloch both invested in property in Horstley Street, as did the Russian-born Bailen family. Even after they moved out of the District, the Bailens continued to own property there which provided them with 'a very good living'.[19] *Erf* 7702 was purchased for £400 by Louis Bailen from Frederick R. Henry Pocock in 1913.[20] On 27 May 1920 Annie Bailen (born Boner, married to Simon Bailen) took transfer with a mortgage worth £795.[21]

While the Jewish landlord became one of District Six's stereotypical 'characters', the Afrikaner residents of the street left little legacy but their names, not easily distinguishable from those of the coloured inhabitants. The policies that were introduced as a result of their presence in the District, however, ironically contributed to the creation of a black ghetto. One of the major reasons for the 1934 Slum Act and the 'poor white' upliftment programmes of the 1920s and 1930s was the fear of Afrikaner degeneration arising from miscegenation in this cosmopolitan community, in which many blacks

shared the language and church of the Afrikaner working class. Cape Town's first substantial sub-economic housing schemes, introduced between the two world wars, provided largely for whites who moved out of the District. The Jewish drive for social improvement, combined with 'poor white' upliftment programmes, meant that, even before the Second World War, District Six was becoming more exclusively black. Post-war *apartheid* speeded a shift of property ownership from whites to locally resident coloured people, especially Muslims.

Landlords and tenants

By 1890, patterns of ownership and tenancy had been established which would exist well into the twentieth century. The first listed residents of Horstley Street were Richard Trace, E. O. Fredrikse and F. W. Woodward. These were probably white artisans, for their occupations were given respectively as storeman, shipping clerk and moulder. Fredrikse and Woodward soon disappeared from the directories, but Trace, transformed into Richard Tracey, overseer, retained his links with the street for many years, from 1865 to 1891. Carl August Luck and members of his family owned property in the street for forty years between 1891 and 1931, living amongst their tenants. They owned a group of six cottages on the left side of the street, with a few other properties nearby. Carl August himself variously occupied Nos. 9, 23, 25, 29 and 45 at different times. The Lucks were careful landlords, urging the municipality to improve the road and sidewalks. Mrs Sophia Luck, sister-in-law of Carl August, who owned Nos. 25 to 29, wanted the side path outside her properties completed, explaining that her tenants were complaining:

> I luckily have good tenants which are hard to find at present, I should not like to lose them, & as it is already very difficult to manage to scrape together the rates, besides losing your tenant which would very likely mean a vacant property for about six months or more before one can secure a good tenant again.[22]

These tenants, William Jansen, John Collop and Isaac Schoonraad, were relatively stable residents. Schoonraad lived at No. 29 and then at No. 23 for almost twenty years, from 1908 to 1927.

This stability was a reflection, not only of the acceptability of the street despite its poor image, but of racial discrimination which made upward mobility more difficult for coloured people than for whites. Such immobility was probably even more typical of the mid-twentieth century, although it is difficult to establish since South Africa's racism extended to the directories which increasingly

Fig. 4.8 Typical corner store, in this case at the corner of Stuckeris and Aspeling Streets.

recorded blacks in District Six simply as 'coloured' or 'Malay'.[23] The occupants of the corner stores, however, hardly altered for years. No. 66, at the corner of Roos and Horstley Streets, was occupied between 1911 and 1946 by S. M. Mohamed and, from 1949 to 1971, by O. M. Parker, who owned both the shop and the adjoining house, while No. 36, on the corner of Frere Street also remained a corner store for years (Fig. 4.8).

A second category of landlord was the non-resident owner. Prosperous white Capetonians held Horstley Street properties from the 1890s to the Second World War. After Falconer acquired *erf* 7702 in 1896 and built the first houses, the properties were transferred to William Pocock and in 1913 to Louis Bailen.[24] Falconer was a considerable speculator in property, over time holding no fewer than forty-nine mortgages. William Frederick Henry Pocock was the only person connected with Horstley Street who was sufficiently notable to have an entry in the *Dictionary of South African Biography*. The nephew of J. T. Pocock, who established the family pharmaceutical business in Cape Town, William Pocock followed his father and uncle in the family firm, ultimately inheriting his uncle's share. He became a prominent spokesman for Cape pharmacists, a mayor of Rondebosch (a Cape Town suburban town), and later of Kalk Bay and Muizenberg, both villages on the False Bay coast.[25] His outstanding photographs are one of his most valuable legacies to Cape Town. He appears to have been an enlightened man, a supporter of women's education, sending his daughters to school at the prestigious Cheltenham Ladies College. One became South Africa's first colonial-born woman doctor. But this eminent man was also one of Horstley Street's slum landlords, a point noted in a *Cape Argus* article.[26]

Pocock's properties included houses in Roos and Stone Streets as well as numbers 71 to 87 in Horstley Street. His surviving financial records show a careful management of his investment. The Horstley Street tenants all paid a rental of 15 shillings a week in 1903 and 1904, although they were not always regular in their payment, particularly in 1904 as depression bit. The collection of rentals was contracted out, first to W. B. Jeffreys and, by Jeffreys, to A. Stoffers who received a commission of 12s 6d a week for his work which included the repair of the properties. Rents on the District Six houses brought Pocock about £61 a month in 1903. In the year ending June 1904 rentals and interest gave him an income of £2,257 13s 5d: a significant figure in a colony which did not yet have income tax.[27]

Pocock was well aware of the economic implications of property ownership, noting that the investment of profit from the sale of his fifteen District Six houses would yield about half the amount that he received in rentals.[28] He was a prudent landlord, commenting to Jeffreys, 'I am sorry that these [houses] require such constant attention, and therefore expense, but the only way to keep them in thorough habitable condition is by carefully watching them and doing what is required at once.' The need for diligence is hardly surprising since, as the archaeologists discovered, badly baked bricks and mud mortar had been used for construction of house walls on *erf* 7702. Although Pocock did repair his houses, Horstley Street residents complained to the municipality about their condition, which they considered the most disgraceful in Cape Town.[29]

In the early twentieth century East European immigrants first found their economic footing in the District. Like the Lucks, they lived locally, keeping a sharp eye on their tenants while they established and expanded other business interests. As the Jews became more prosperous they moved out to more affluent suburbs, such as Vredehoek and the Gardens, or beyond into the southern suburbs or Sea Point on the Atlantic coast. The extended Bailen clan demonstrated this pattern. Annie, Simon Bailen's wife, owned *erf* 7702 between 1913 and 1920, while his brother, Hyman, opened a draper's shop in Hanover Street, near the Horstley Street intersection. With his wife, Esther, Hyman went on to open two of the earliest cinemas in the District, one of which, the Union Bioscope, backed onto the Hanover Street end of Horstley Street. The Bailens continued to acquire properties in the District even after they moved into the wealthier, white Gardens neighbourhood.

Mrs Esther Bailen, who ran the business after Hyman died in 1927, was cautious about the tenants she acquired, demanding references from employers. Most of the Bailen tenants were coloured, although some were white, but the

Eaton Place property, as well as some others, had illegal African tenants on occasion. The Bailen children often had the job of rent collection, dealing on occasion with recalcitrant occupants. In Eaton Place the African tenants

> used to have like a shebeen, running a shebeen there, they used to sell Kaffir beer and they used to go a little berserk, and then you couldn't go there – my mother used to send my brother and I to go down and collect the rent and we'd go out. When we got there, they'd be so under the weather that you couldn't ask them for anything, so the weeks used to go by – about two or three weeks – before we'd got any payment of rent. So eventually we had to go to an attorney and have him pitched out.[30]

By the middle of the twentieth century this pattern of ownership had changed. White ownership gave way to ownership by black District Six residents. The social mobility of the Bailens was less available to the coloured residents of District Six. Although Cape Town was not formally segregated before the 1950s, the newer suburbs generally restricted property ownership to whites, while sub-economic housing schemes were invariably racially segregated. With such limited options District Six people, often Muslim businessmen, many of them corner store traders, increasingly invested some of their profits in property in District Six. *Erf* 7702 passed out of Bailen hands in 1930 when the Indian-born Muslim Ameer Camroodeen paid £1,950 for it.[31] The next transfer occurred in 1931 in favour of Osman Shaboodien.[32] While such landlords did not necessarily live in Horstley Street itself, they were often resident nearby, part of the local community. Camroodeen, for instance, was a general dealer at nearby No. 70 William Street. It was these people who were directly dispossessed by *apartheid* legislation, with inadequate compensation.

The first removals

By 1900 District Six was severely overcrowded. Refugees from the Transvaal goldfields waited out the years of the South African War (1899–1902) in District Six, while their small savings dwindled. They were joined by British immigrants who hoped to take advantage of a Rand under British control, and by African dockworkers from the Transkei, who preferred the freedom of the District to the docks barracks. Wages, at 4s 6d a day, were relatively good during these years but, as migrant labourers, the Africans wanted cheap accommodation. Some Horstley Street landlords willingly catered for this demand.

When plague broke out in Cape Town in February 1901, 'slum' living conditions became a matter of public concern.[33] The Horstley Street Africans, already identified as the source of infection, were the subjects of several newspaper articles. The *Cape Times* 'Special Commissioner' visited the area:

> At the time of my second visit a howling south-easter was blowing, and the natives were all within doors. This gave me an excellent opportunity of seeing to what extent the buildings were occupied. In Frere-street, near Horstley-street, the natives not only swarmed within the house, but lay sleeping along the verandahs – or stoeps – packed like so many herrings . . . In Horstley-street itself the houses were innocent of stoeps . . . So the herring-packing process was confined to the inside of the premises, and there scientifically carried out. Not an inch of space went abegging. Lights – very primitive indeed; coarse wick and oil, whose smoke thickened the already dense atmosphere – burned dimly in some of the rooms, and the natives huddled together in their filth and squalor, perfect pictures of misery.[34]

Archaeological evidence confirms this description of overcrowding. In Nos. 73 and 75 Horstley Street appropriation of the narrow passage as living space provides an explanation for relatively large amounts of domestic debris that were inexplicably found concentrated under the floorboards, against the back wall.

Even before the war there had been pressure for the removal of Africans from the town, but before 1901 nothing had come of such moves. Clause 15 of the 1897 Public Health Act, however, gave the authorities the power to effect removals in the name of sanitation. Within days of the first identification of the disease, a plague hospital, a contact camp and an African location had all been established in Uitvlugt forest station, beyond the municipal boundaries. The following year a Locations Act was passed, legalising the location, now renamed 'Ndabeni'.[35]

There is no doubt that Africans in Horstley Street were particularly vulnerable to plague since many of them worked at the South Arm of the harbour where the disease was first identified. Thirty-five Horstley Street residents died (Fig. 4.9). Almost all were African men, and the victims were scattered through the street.[36] There is one intriguing feature. Amongst the victims were Annie Kacholie (25 years old) at No. 13, 60-year-old Witbooi Kocholie and 15-year-old William Kochobe at No. 18, and 5-year-old Sophie Kocholie at No. 8. Given the errors abounding in the sources, especially when names were not British, it would appear that most of an African family was wiped out in the epidemic. Such families were

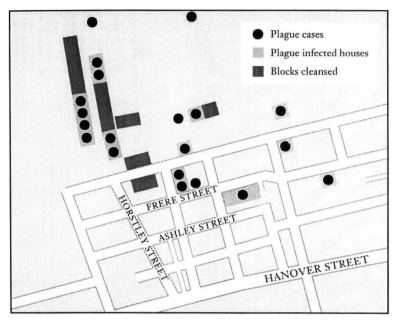

Fig. 4.9 The plan annexed to the Report of the Medical Officer of Health in 1901 showing evidence for plague in upper Horstley Street, probably including the houses on erf *7702.*

fairly rare in Cape Town but their first names suggest that this may have been a mission-educated group, possibly permanent residents of the District rather than migrant labourers.

For the owners of the infected properties, the plague was a mixed blessing. Although they lost rent, plague control included the fumigation, whitewashing and repair of houses in which plague victims were found. Not only did owners rid themselves of possibly undesirable tenants, but the improvements carried out also enabled them to increase their rents after the plague. Unfortunately, it has been impossible to ascertain whether this was the case at the Horstley Street site. Patterns in the coin dates and distribution, however, were interpreted by archaeologists as evidence of correlation between the addition of the new service area at the back of No. 75 and a change in the role of the passage.[37]

Living and working in Horstley Street

Horstley Street may not have been the insanitary slum depicted in the press at the turn of the century. Endemic poverty, however, was a characteristic of the area almost from its inception.[38] Work in Cape Town centred on the harbour, fishing, and small independent artisans and craftsmen: tailors, builders, furniture makers and the like. As late as 1900 Cape Town was still a pre-industrial city in its employment patterns, with only the Salt River railway works as an industry of any size. By that time dock labour had been taken over by the Harbour Board, ending the reign of docks contractors like A. R. McKenzie (whose name was enshrined in McKenzie Street in District Six). By this time, too, the immigration of Italian fishermen with more capital was driving the local fishermen to the wall. Essentially, however, work in Cape Town was still characterised by casual labour.[39]

The twentieth century saw the slow industrialisation of the city. In Horstley Street women benefited most, since inner-city industry consisted largely of the manufacture of garments, cigarettes and sweets, all of which employed young women. While wages were low, women's opportunities were widened beyond the single option of domestic service. The situation was bleaker for men. Established artisans and fishermen were marginalised by the expansion of factory production and the emergence of modern fishing companies. Young men, poorly educated and excluded from apprenticeship, suffered most. Unemployment was their usual fate and it is hardly surprising that the interwar period of the 1920s and 1930s saw the formation of a gang culture.[40]

The economic plight of the country during the Great Depression produced the first modern social welfare initiatives in South Africa, pioneered in the Western Cape. Professor Edward Batson, professor of the newly established department of sociology at the University of Cape Town, conducted the first social survey of the town in 1939. The results confirmed the grim poverty of Cape Town's coloured people. Three houses in Horstley Street were included in Batson's survey, all with coloured tenants. No. 40, a four-roomed cottage, was occupied by three families, each inhabiting 1⅓ rooms. The main tenant, a 59-year-old factory hand, was a woman who lived with her 9-year-old grandson. Her wages of 15s a week hardly covered her rent of £3 10s a month, so she sublet to a family of five – a machine assistant earning £2 a week, his wife who charred for about 10s 6d a week, and a young brother-in-law (26), unemployed and suffering from tuberculosis. The couple had two teenage daughters, having lost their first three children. The third family, independent tenants, consisted of a 35-year-old South African Railways labourer, his 21-year-old wife, a domestic servant, and two small daughters (2 and 1 years). The earnings of both were wretched, he getting £1 7s a week and his wife earning about 7s a week.[41] These families were all Christian and most came from Cape Town's immediate hinterland.[42] For all of them Horstley Street had one great advantage, for all could walk to work. These were Cape Town's 'respectable' poor, struggling to maintain standards on pitiful incomes.

Archaeological excavations give texture to these bare bones. On *erf* 7702 the landlord had improved the row by adding service areas to the back of the houses (Fig. 4.10). Behind the original core structure in Nos. 73 and 75, additions followed the same design, so were probably made to upgrade the block as a whole. Each service area comprised a kitchen at the end of the original passage, a yard and an outside toilet with water-borne sewerage. Both kitchens and yards had cement floors, with linoleum in the kitchen. The addition of a rear service area would double the surface area of the dwelling. The kitchen at No. 73 had three successive layers of linoleum; the one at No. 75 had more than twenty. Informants suggested that linoleum was replaced annually at Eid or New Year.

What is interesting for the archaeologist is the 'cultural landscape': the relationship between the public domain of the street front and what went on behind Horstley Street, on the 'undeveloped' land alongside the watercourse.[43] Unlike official maps and plans that are often idealised, the archaeological record includes evidence of manipulation of their material world by inhabitants that resulted in subversion of the intended purpose of social housing. The addition of rear service rooms and access routes would also undermine the intentions of the designer by enabling the occupants to avoid surveillance from the upslope 'home' dwelling. While the streetscape depicted in photographs of Horstley Street may have remained virtually unchanged until it was demolished, the back parts were areas of movement: informal visits, cooking, workshops, ablutions, dumping of refuse and unregulated building alterations.

At No. 73 Horstley Street a vehicle ramp had been built into the back yard for access from the undeveloped land behind the tenement. The linoleum floor surface continued through the kitchen door into the yard, suggesting that this had been roofed with a lean-to structure. At No. 75 there was a pedestrian entrance into the back yard area. In both houses toilet fittings had been roughly recessed into existing walls, suggesting that the sewerage line was a later, *ad hoc*, addition to the rear service areas. Documentary evidence confirms this picture. O. M. Parker illegally inserted a connecting door between his two houses, converting them into a single dwelling.[44] Louis Spolander was ordered to remove unauthorised roofing over his yard, which deprived the bedroom of light and ventilation.[45] Other people built walls and sheds or constructed verandahs. At Stuckeris Street there was extensive remodelling of the original structure and archaeologists found evidence for boot and shoe repairs being carried out in the back yard.

Despite the poverty, Horstley Street offered a lively environment. The Liberman Institute was the centre of a vigorous cultural life. The Moravian and Ebenezer churches and the mosques provided solace and hope. Cheap fish – *snoek* and crayfish – could be bought from the itinerant fishmongers or from the fish market in nearby Hanover Street. The corner stores were adapted to the local economy.[46] For those with a few pennies to spare, there was the local cinema. District Sixites were notable movie-goers.[47] In Horstley Street there was the Union Bioscope, sternly guarded by Esther Bailen. In the days of silent movies the ten Bailen children were called upon to provide the music.[48]

The cultural diversity of the District was equally enriching. As the Jews moved out, Indian residents became more common, many of them recent migrants from India. Ameer Camroodeen, the general dealer who lived in William Street, married both his wives in India. After his death in May 1931, his widow and their young son returned to live there.[49] It was the loss of this diversity and communal support that was so mourned by the people of District Six when they were summarily moved to the bleak townships of the Cape Flats.

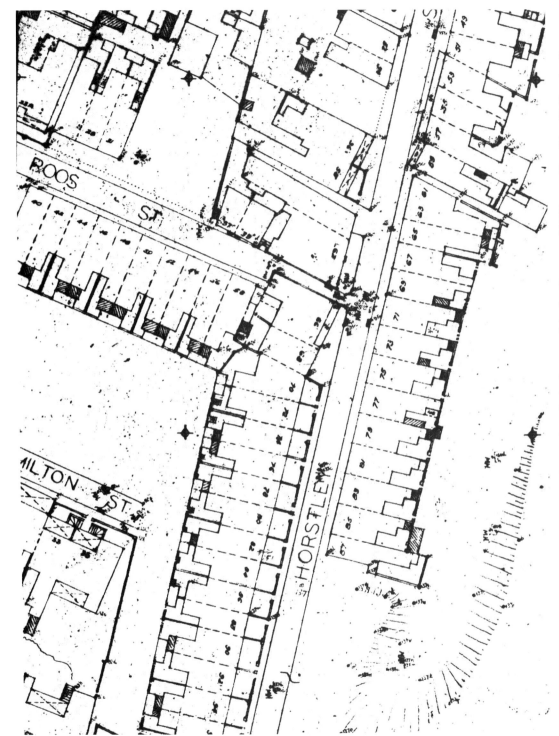

Fig. 4.10 Detail from a Municipal Survey, c. 1954, showing how the back parts of the dwellings on erf 7702, now Nos. 67 to 87 Horstley Street, have been modified and enclosed. The uphill house retains its relatively larger size.

The second removals

In post-war Cape Town, international and local ideas about planning and urban renewal intersected with Afrikaner nationalist theories on apartheid ethnic cleansing to provide a rationale for slum clearance.[50] From the mid-1930s, urban renewal consisted of slum clearance, plans for the reclamation of the foreshore to create a 'monumental gateway to southern Africa', and a fashion for planning routes for commuters and their motor cars into and through the city. In this way the distasteful red light district near the harbour – centred on the Dock Road Hotel – was obliterated by an elevated concrete highway, and De Waal Drive and Eastern Boulevard cut swathes through the edges of District Six. Even the most 'historic' colonial streetscapes came under threat from the wheels of Progress.

District Six residents were well aware of the threat which town planning schemes posed to their community. In 1939, when these plans were unveiled, residents rallied behind their charismatic emerging leader and municipal councillor, Cissie Gool, to protest.[51] The war saved the District for a time, as did conflict over post-war foreshore development schemes, but the Nationalist government's access to power in 1948 fundamentally altered the political context of planning.[52]

Once the decision was taken to remove the occupants of District Six, justification was easily found for destroying the buildings rather than upgrading or reusing them. Yet, although District Six did not escape demolition, removals occurred relatively late, beginning about 1976, continuing until about 1982. By this time resistance to *apartheid* had entered a new phase, starting with the rising of Soweto schoolchildren in 1976. District Six residents fought the evictions with all the legal weapons at their disposal. Segregation of people into their own boroughs facilitates community solidarity: class, work and family networks all overlap.[53] In Horstley Street, at least three residents are known to have signed a petition against their removal.[54] In 1978, when Lindy Wilson made a video publicising District Six protest, Horstley Street stood as the symbol for the whole District. *Last Supper at Horstley Street* depicted the final meal of a family in their home before they were moved to Belhar. Although Belhar had new houses, neighbours were strangers and the suburb lacked social amenities. Interviewed in their new home, the mother, Latiefa expressed her grief in one bitter sentence: 'I have lost my religion.'[55]

Since the 1980s, the initially all-white Cape Technikon has encroached on the open slopes of the District. A grid of new streets was sketched on the ground, then tarred and edged in concrete, deliberately obscuring the old layout of the district. In particular, Hanover Street was realigned and renamed and a famous local landmark, the Seven Steps, removed. From the ground, only a few historic structures remain: churches, schools and mosques. From the air a few more traces can be followed beneath the stunted bushes and rank grasses: for instance the cobbles of Horstley Street.

With so few traces remaining, it is only natural that the past which is recovered through memory and song should be one of a golden age, but unless we act soon and decisively in planning for integrated work in District Six we shall lose any opportunity to arrest the mythologising process. It is to be hoped that archaeological and historical research will provide a less romanticised framework which is ultimately more satisfying both for the residents of the District and for others who wish to understand that complexity, contradictions and ambiguity provide space for a more democratic society than dogma and bureaucratic planning. The more diverse the range of knowledge that is recovered about the people and the places they inhabited, the richer the choice of stories that will be left for their descendants. Once the remaining open areas have been developed, a source of archaeological information is removed.

Acknowledgements

Many thanks are due to Martin Hall, David Halkett and Tim Hart for providing access to materials and discussing interpretations of the Horstley Street site.

Notes

1 The District Six Museum is planning a new display on Horstley Street which is based on this chapter. The name 'District Six' derives from the voting districts of the municipality during part of the nineteenth century.

2 S. Jeppie and C. Soudien (eds.), *The Struggle for District Six: Past and Present* (Cape Town: Buchu Books, 1990). Reminiscences and biographies: H. Adams and H. Suttner, *William Street, District Six* (Diep River: Chameleon Press, 1988); L. Fortune, *The House in Tyne Street: Childhood Memories of District Six* (Cape Town: Kwela, 1996); A. La Guma, *Liberation Chabalala: The World of Alex La Guma* (Bellville: Mayibuye Books, 1993); N. Ngcelwane, *Sala Kahle, District Six: An African Woman's Perspective* (Cape Town: Kwela Books, 1998); A. Small, *Oos Wes Tuis Bes: Distrik Ses* (Kaapstad:

Human en Rousseau, 1973). Popular publications: G. Manuel and D. Hatfield, *District Six* (Cape Town: Longman Penguin, 1967); S. De Villiers, *A Tale of Three Cities* (Cape Town: Murray and Roberts Construction, 1985); T. Grogan, *Vanishing Cape Town* (Cape Town: D. Nelson, 1976). Photographic volumes: C. Breytenbach, *The Spirit of District Six* (Cape Town: Purnell, 1970); Chris Schoeman, *District Six: The Spirit of Kanala* (Cape Town: Human en Rousseau, 1994); A. Small and Jansje Wissema, *District Six* (Linden: Fontein, 1986). Thesis: C. Keeton, 'Aspects of material life and culture in District Six, c.1930–c.1950', BA thesis, University of Cape Town (1987). Novels: A. Brink, *Looking on Darkness* (London: W. H. Allen, 1974) including Abdullah Ibrahim's poem 'Blues for District Six'; A. Dangor, *Waiting for Leila* (Johannesburg: Ravan, 1981); R. Gool, *Cape Town Coolie* (Oxford: Heinemann International, 1990); A. La Guma, *The Stone Country* (London: Heinemann, 1974); A. La Guma, *A Walk in the Night* (Cape Town: David Philip, 1991); D. Muller, *Whitey* (Johannesburg: Ravan, 1977); R. Rive, *'Buckingham Palace', District Six* (Cape Town: David Philip, 1986); R. Rive, *Emergency* (Cape Town: David Philip, 1988). Videos: *Distrik Ses* (Starnet Television, 1991); Lindy Wilson, *Last Supper in Horstley Street* (Johannesburg: Film Resource Unit, 1989). Musicals by Taliep Petersen and David Kramer are *District Six: The Musical* and *Fairyland*.

3   *Cape Argus Weekly*, 20 March 1901, cited in C. Schoeman, *Portrait of a City* (forthcoming).

4   We are indebted to Martin Hall for permission to quote extensively from unpublished site reports: M. Hall, G. Cox, D. Halkett, T. Hart, K. Rubin and S. Winter, 'A shadow in stone: archaeology in Horstley Street, District Six' (1994); Archaeology Contracts Office, 'Excavations in District Six: a residential property at the corner of Stuckeris & Roger Streets' (1996); H. Clift, 'Excavation of a spoil heap in District Six: report on the RESUNACT Schools Programme prepared for the National Monuments Council' (1996). These reports are filed at the Department of Archaeology, University of Cape Town. The projects were supported by the Trustees of the District Six Museum Foundation. Financial assistance was received from the Centre for Science Development, but opinions expressed in reports and conclusions reached are those of the researchers and not to be attributed to the Centre for Science Development.

5   The trail of transfers is broken in places but after the estate was sold by Dieperman it was registered in the names of Nicolaas Gockelius in 1713, Steven Ten Holder in 1738, Rudolf Siegfried Alleman and his sons Nicolaas and Fredrik between 1739 and 1774, Jan Hendrik Munnik in 1774, Floris Brink in 1798, and George Hendrik Goetz and Alexander Tennant in 1800.

6   A. Malan, 'The Mount Nelson Project: unearthing houses and gardens in Hof Street, Cape Town', unpublished seminar paper, Department of Archaeology, University of Cape Town (September 1997).

7   A. Malan, H. Clift, O. Graf, M. Hall, J. Klose and E. Sealy, '"Between the castle and the stock pound": early nineteenth century developments at the corner of Tennant and Hanover Streets, Cape Town', unpublished report, RESUNACT, University of Cape Town (1999).

8   SG Dgm. 997/1897 filed with T4041, 19/5/1897, Deeds Office, Cape Town.

9   Possibly the rent collector, A. Stoffers, since the owner of *erf* 7702, William Pocock, lived elsewhere.

10 *Cape Times*, 11 March 1901.

11 External ornamentation of terrace houses separated – differentiated – classes in Britain. Thus the wood-framed *stoeps* shown on the plans for house façades lower down the street could be interpreted as 'embourgeoisement' for a better class of tenant. S. Muthesius, *The English Terraced House* (New Haven and London: Yale University Press, 1982), p. 26.

12 Stephen A. Mrozowski, 'Landscapes of inequality', in Randall H. McGuire and R. Paynter (eds.), *The Archaeology of Inequality* (Oxford: Blackwell, 1991), pp. 79–101, esp. pp. 80, 97.

13 K. Dumbrell, 'Working class housing in the nineteenth century: the impact of British planning trends and regulations on the British colonial settlements in the Cape Colony', theme paper, School of Architecture and Planning, University of Cape Town, (1998); K. Ström, 'Nineteenth-century working-class housing in Cape Town', MA thesis, University of Cape Town (in preparation); M. Bezzoli, R. Marks and M. Kruger, *Texture and Memory: The Urbanism of District Six* (Cape Town: Cape Technikon Urban Housing Research Unit, 1997).

14 E. B. van Heyningen, 'Public health and society in Cape Town 1880–1910', PhD thesis, University of Cape Town (1989), pp. 226–85; Vivian Bickford-Smith, *Ethnic Pride and Racial Prejudice in Victorian Cape Town: Group Identity and Social Practice, 1875–1902* (Cambridge: Cambridge University Press, 1995), pp. 10–38.

15 Muthesius, *The English Terraced House*, p. 37. Schotsekloof, in Cape Town's Bo-Kaap, is an example. There were remnants of double-storey single-roomed dwellings attached to the external wall of the back yard of a townhouse on Riebeeck Square, Cape Town: Archaeology Contracts Office, 'Archaeological excavations at Block 11, Cape Town', unpublished report for City Planner, Cape Town City Council (December 1990).

16 Van Heyningen, 'Public health and society', pp. 226–85.

17 Daniel Miller has argued that material culture researchers have emphasised production rather than consumption; however it is not what the things are but what people do with them that is significant. D. Miller, *Material Culture and Mass Consumption* (Oxford: Blackwell, 1987). See also A. Praetzellis and M. Praetzellis, 'Faces and façades: Victorian ideology in early Sacramento', in A. E. Yentsch and M. Beaudry (eds.), *The Art and Mystery of Historical Archaeology* (Boca Raton, FL: CRC Press, 1992), pp. 75–100.

18 'The Last Supper revisited', an installation by Sue Williamson at the Irma Stern Museum, Rosebank, Cape Town in May 1993; Clift, 'Excavation of a spoil heap in District Six'; A. Bohlin, 'The politics of locality: memories of District Six in Cape Town', in N. Lovell (ed.), *Locality and Belonging* (London: Routledge, 1998), pp. 168–88.

19 V. C. Malherbe, 'An East European immigrant makes good in Cape Town', *Studies in the History of Cape Town* 4 (1984), 135, 140. This interview is conducted with another branch of the Bailen clan.

20 T8619, 30/9/1913, Deeds Office, Cape Town.

21 T7226, 7/5/1920, Deeds Office, Cape Town.

22 Sophie Luck to the City Engineer, 24 June 1907, 3/CT 4/2/1/1/54–1084/9, Cape Archives.

23 'Malay' was the term commonly used for those Muslims who owed their religious origins to slaves and political prisoners brought by the Dutch from Batavia (Indonesia) in the seventeenth and eighteenth centuries. Nigel Worden, Elizabeth van Heyningen and Vivian Bickford-Smith, *Cape Town: The Making of a City* (Cape Town: David Philip, 1998), pp. 127–8.

24 T79, 10/1/1896; T4041, 19/5/1897; T8619, 30/9/1913, Deeds Office, Cape Town.

25 *Dictionary of South African Biography*, vol. 5, 599.

26 *Cape Argus Weekly*, 20 March 1901.

27 Financial records, W. Pocock papers, Box 24, MSC 18, South African Library.

28 W. Pocock to W. B. Jeffreys, 7 May 1902, Box 17, MSC 18, South African Library.

29 W. Pocock to W. B. Jeffreys, 26 January 1902, Box 17, MSC 18, South African Library; Steer & Co. to the City Engineer, 30 August 1901, 3/CT 4/2/1/1/92, Cape Archives.

30 Malherbe, 'An East European', pp. 135–7, 140, 141.

31 T4395, 27/5/1930, Deeds Office, Cape Town.

32 T9029, 25/11/1931; T3996, 21/2/1969, Deeds Office, Cape Town.

33 This was part of a pandemic which affected much of the world. See, for instance, P. Curson and K. McCracken, *Plague in Sydney: The Anatomy of an Epidemic* (Sydney: New South Wales University Press, n.d.).

34 *Cape Times*, 9 March 1901, 11 March 1901.

35 M. W. Swanson, 'The sanitation syndrome: bubonic plague and urban native policy in the Cape Colony, 1900–1909', *Journal of African History* 16:3 (1977), 387–410; C. Saunders, 'The creation of Ndabeni: urban segregation and African resistance in Cape Town', *Studies*, 1 (1984), 165–93; and E. van Heyningen, 'Cape Town and the plague of 1901', *Studies* 4 (1984), 66–107.

36 Cape Town, *Mayor's Minute for 1901*, Report of the Medical Officer of Health.

37 Hall *et al.*, 'A shadow in stone'.

38 Worden *et al.*, *Cape Town: The Making of a City*, pp. 68–9, 120–2, 248–9; S. Judges, 'Poverty, living conditions and social relations – aspects of life in Cape Town in the 1830s', MA thesis, University of Cape Town (1977).

39 Bickford-Smith, *Ethnic Pride and Racial Prejudice*, pp. 19–20.

40 Vivian Bickford-Smith, Elizabeth van Heyningen and Nigel Worden, *Cape Town in the Twentieth Century* (Cape Town: David Philip, 1999), pp. 44, 104–5, 188–9.

41 Stellenbosch University, Batson papers.

42 K. Ward, 'The road to Mamre: migration and community in countryside and city in the early twentieth century', *South African Historical Journal* 27 (1992), 198–224.

43 D. Upton, 'The city as material culture', in Yentsch and Beaudry, *Art and Mystery*, esp. p. 92.

44 3/CT 4/2/1/3/4131-B369, Cape Archives.

45 11 October 1906, 3/CT 4/2/1/1/30, Cape Archives.

46 District Six, Men, 1, 6 March 1990, BC 1004, Oral History Project, University of Cape Town.

47 B. Nasson, 'Oral history and the reconstruction of District Six', in Jeppie and Soudien, *The Struggle for District Six*, pp. 58–9.

48 District Six, Women, 39, 1 April 1980, BC 1004, University of Cape Town.

49 T4395, 27/5/1930, Deeds Office, Cape Town.

50 E. B. van Heyningen, 'A liberal town planner in Africa: L. W. Thornton White and the planning of Cape Town, South Africa, Nairobi, Kenya and Port Louis, Mauritius 1939–1950', 20th Century Urban Planning Experience Conference, 15–18 July 1998, University of New South Wales, Sydney; Bickford-Smith *et al.*, *Cape Town in the Twentieth Century*, pp. 144–56.

51 N. Barnett, 'Race, housing and town planning in Cape Town c.1920–1940: with special reference to District Six', MA thesis, University of Cape Town (1993).

52 Bickford-Smith *et al.*, *Cape Town in the Twentieth Century*, pp. 144 – 56.

53 R. H. McGuire, 'Building power in the cultural landscape of Broome County, New York 1880 to 1940', in McGuire and Paynter, *The Archaeology of Inequality*, pp. 102–24, esp. 108, 113.

54 Information from Dr Uma Mesthrie, University of the Western Cape. The residents were Abdulla Nakhwa, No. 40 Horstley Street, M. Parker and another Parker.

55 Wilson, *Last Supper in Horstley Street.*

5
Archaeology in the alleys of Washington, DC

BARBARA J. LITTLE AND
NANCY J. KASSNER

Introduction

In September 1998 the District of Columbia's Historic Preservation Review Board heard a presentation by the Shaw Community for designation of the U Street corridor of the Shaw neighbourhood as a historic district. This 'city within a city' was known as Black Broadway in the early twentieth century. During the presentation, Board members raised questions about the boundaries that were suggested for the district. In particular, the Board wanted to know why the district did not run all the way to Florida Avenue (also known historically as Boundary Street), which was the original boundary between the City of Washington and the County of Washington and which would have been a reasonable historical boundary. Based on National Register guidelines, however, many of the old buildings along Florida Avenue had lost their integrity, many modern buildings had been constructed, and there was a fair amount of vacant land, none of which would be eligible for listing in the National Register of Historic Places.[1]

Several of the Board members stated their concerns about the vacant lots: 'But we are concerned about what might happen to the community. We are concerned about the impact of development if this vacant land is not protected . . . we would like to have some input on the development they would put there, that it's not in conflict with the historic district.' In a final pitch to include the vacant lots within the historic district, a Board member questioned whether there would be important archaeological information in the lots: 'One could assume from some of the other things that we have seen before us that even though these sites are vacant that archaeology – like we

saw at the MCI Center – these could also reveal very significant revelations about working class Washington and its development patterns. It might yield the only significant archaeological finds given the fact that the rest of the historic district is intact.'[2]

As is evident from the above statements, the Board wanted larger boundaries in part to protect the neighbourhood from unwanted development. Archaeological resources were raised as something worth saving in the portion of the old neighbourhood where buildings were no longer intact. Unfortunately, a cursory archaeological survey had been conducted, but because the consultant could not get owner permission to excavate on the property, the status of archaeological resources was unknown. The Board made a final decision that did not include the area in question in the designated Historic District. When a new convention centre was proposed nearby, however, the National Capital Planning Commission required archaeology (under Section 106 of the National Historic Preservation Act) prior to licensing the new construction, which certainly had an impact on the Shaw neighbourhood, just as the community had predicted.

Such is the irony of the logistics of archaeology in Washington, and doubtless in other cities. There are few mechanisms to support archaeology. Even when archaeology is supported, there are impediments to conducting the level of work that needs to be done. In the meantime, development destroys resources. There is, therefore, very little opportunity for archaeology to become useful, to create a sense of place, or to enhance a sense of community.

The *Washington Post* offered an interpretation of the lessons of history in an article on the archaeological testing done in advance of licensing the new convention centre. The old Northern Liberties section of Shaw, the article surmised, 'might be considered a model for the 1990s. American-born and immigrant families, doctors and labourers, servants and those served all lived next to each other in the 1850s.'[3]

Lessons from the past vary. The harmony envisioned by the *Post* writer could not be said to characterise the city of Washington as a whole in the 1850s. During that decade the city's population rose by 50 per cent, from 40,000 in 1850 to over 61,000 in 1860. As in other North American cities, the 1850s saw sharp contrasts. Poverty, squalor, prejudice and violence were as much a part of Washington as wealth and taste.[4] During that decade, vandalism, arson, prostitution, theft, robbery and assault worsened every year. In 1858, a Senate Committee reported: 'Riot and bloodshed are of daily occurrence. Innocent and unoffending persons are shot, stabbed, and otherwise shamefully maltreated, and not unfrequently the offender is not even arrested.'[5] A sanitary committee was appointed in 1849 because of the high mortality in the city, especially of infants. The Board of Health reported: 'the larger proportion of these deaths are from among the children of negro, or foreign, and of destitute native parents who usually reside in alleys and in the suburbs'.[6]

The early history of life in Washington's alleys resides only in archaeology and in sporadic reports from Boards of Health. In the late nineteenth and early twentieth centuries, social reformers turned their attention to alleys to advocate housing reform. Their writings provide some detailed documentation. Historian James Borchert takes issue with the reformers. His analysis suggests that they found only what they intended to find. Reformers were devoted to social control, order and conformity to middle-class values. According to Borchert's analysis, their convictions led them to overemphasise disorder and pathology in their reports.[7]

From his study of alleys, Borchert contends that alley dwellers used their primary groups and folk experience to create strategies for surviving urban life rather than undergo periods of disorder. 'Folk migrants also "remade" their urban environment, both physically and cognitively, to fit their needs.'[8] Borchert might well agree with a challenge Henry Glassie made more than twenty years ago. Glassie writes that documentary history is 'superficial and elitist – a tale of viciousness, a myth for the contemporary power structure. Writing cannot be used to form the democratic, projective, quantifiable base for the study of past people. Artifacts can.'[9]

Borchert's historical work, along with that of the housing reformers whose work he critiques, provides detailed contexts for alley life. There is little archaeological evidence to corroborate or challenge such information. While there is little technical difference between archaeological work in alleys and elsewhere in the city, there have been relatively few opportunities for testing. The first excavations of alley dwellings in the city were done in 1983 at Quander Place, discussed in more detail below. The overall research objective of that project was to provide information about the quality of life that existed in an urban alley environment in DC in the late nineteenth and early twentieth centuries. Towards this end, the alley dwelling material was compared with the material retrieved from the street-facing lots to define any real economic differences between the ability of the respective households to participate in the 'mainstream of American culture'.[10]

We describe archaeological work in four alleys in the city and reconsider the premise of ethnic or racial distinc-

tions that tends to drive ethnicity studies in historical archaeology in the United States. We return to the community in our conclusion, as it may be the lack of community input that constrains archaeology in the city most insidiously. We believe that archaeology can contribute to the history of the District of Columbia and to the city's sense of itself in the present.

Archaeology in the alleys of Washington, DC

Alley housing in Washington is not very well documented. For example, because no city building permits were required before 1877, there is little documentary information on the buildings themselves. Census and city directories did not record alleys until 1858, when the City Directory listed 49 alleys with 348 heads of household. Earlier alleys, and those too small to be recorded in directories, as well as the conditions of alley life, require archaeological documentation.

Blagden Alley was one of the earliest alleys to be developed and was occupied until the 1940s. Three sites date from the original occupation of the lots in the early to mid-nineteenth century. Essex Court, located downtown, was occupied until the 1930s. Deposits date from the 1860s and 1880s. Slate Alley was an early alley in Northwest, the oldest part of the city. The deposits of particular interest here date from 1825 to 1855. Quander Place is a later alley in Southeast, the development of which lagged behind the rest of the city. These assemblages date from the 1880s to around 1910.

Blagden Alley and Naylor Court[11]

A grant from the Department of the Interior funded a survey for potential nomination of the Blagden Alley neighbourhood as an historic district. This survey included researching the historic and archaeological resources within the project area. The historic resources survey involved the investigation of the architectural, social and cultural history of the area encompassing Blagden and Naylor Alleys. Archival research included reviewing tax books, primary and secondary sources including building permits, historic maps, tax records, city directories, newspaper accounts, biographical sources, historic photographs and oral histories.

Squares 367 and 368,[12] in which Blagden and Naylor Alleys are located, retain a mixture of residential and commercial buildings that illustrate the historic evolution of land use in the City of Washington, particularly the independent development of property facing the public streets versus property facing the alleys. A rich variety of building types and architectural styles face the street.

There are textbook examples of the changing architectural fashions for the middle class in the last half of the nineteenth century. However, behind these buildings evolved a different world, the world of inhabited alleys. Entire alley communities developed which were completely isolated from the life on the street fronts.[13] This neighbourhood was one of the first in the city of Washington to be subdivided with lots that faced solely into an alley.[14] It seems that the H-Shape plan for alleys was an original platting for Squares 367 and 368 (see Fig. 5.2).

During the 1850s, the mix of black and white homeowners on the two squares seems to indicate that racial segregation before the Civil War was not as pronounced as it would later become. Census and tax assessment data indicate that in 1859 there were eighty-one property owners, twenty of whom were 'coloured'. These African American owners were clustered together, but only one was located in an alley. After the Civil War this neighbourhood developed a complex system of inhabited alleys behind the street façades. The population was largely African American working class that had migrated from the South. In addition to the alley dwellings there were also stables and shops that were part of the alley environment.

Before 1867 Blagden Alley and Naylor Court contained ten officially recorded lots which fronted onto the alley. Between 1871 and 1874, fifteen two-storey brick alley dwellings were constructed. In the 1880 census forty-two heads of household were recorded living in Blagden Alley and twenty-two were recorded in Naylor Court. All of these, according to the census records, were African Americans employed in unskilled or service occupations.

After the development of the historic context of the neighbourhood, a two-phased archaeological survey was conducted. Phase one was a visual examination of each lot to locate open areas and to evaluate the probability of intact subsurface remains with good context. The surface areas of the open lots were examined for artefacts. The second phase of the research design was then to test a sample of the areas that were determined to have probability of containing intact cultural resources. Open areas to be tested were limited to those lots where the property owner's permission to excavate could be acquired. The actual field testing strategy varied between lots, depending on the classification of the lot and the ground conditions. Each lot was tested either with shovel test pits to a depth of 3 feet, or with 3 foot test squares which extended into sterile subsoil. In the lots that were evaluated for their archaeological potential, three sites were identified. One is the site of an 1857 structure; another is the site of an

Fig. 5.1   Excavations in the parking lot at Essex Court, 1994.

undocumented house built in the early to mid-nineteenth century; the third contains mid-nineteenth century artefact deposits but no apparent structural foundations. These sites offer the potential for future community-oriented archaeology. At the time of writing, however, the sites have not yet been excavated.

Essex Court[15]

Alley dwellings were located in the Essex Court project area from the 1830s to the 1930s. In the 1830s two attached frame dwellings fronting Essex Court were constructed. A second construction phase occurred in the 1880s when two of the frame structures were replaced by two brick dwellings and divided into four units each. In 1934, the frame buildings were demolished. The brick ones were demolished a year later and the area became a parking lot (Fig. 5.1).

According to census research, the alley appears to have been occupied by non-foreign-born, non-black residents in the 1850s, and by black occupants by the 1880s. In the 1880 census, three African American households were located on Essex Court, headed by two laundresses and one labourer. In the 1900 census, the alley dwellers were a mixture of African Americans and Arabians. In 1920 whites, blacks and the foreign-born all lived in the alley. For example, at one address lived a white washerwoman, an African American government messenger and a man from Italy. At another address there was a white shoemaker and another African American government messenger.

The archaeological work focused on the area in the alley in which the brick and frame dwellings had been located. Of five trenches excavated, one contained *in situ* resources associated with the two frame dwellings (pre-1880s) and a small midden deposit associated with the post-1880 occupation.

A mean ceramic date (MCD) was calculated from the buried A horizon associated with the earlier occupation. The resulting date of 1833 appeared to be somewhat early for this site. However, because of the ambiguity of their manufacture date, 269 sherds of a ware type transitional between pearlware and whiteware were not counted in this initial calculation. When those sherds were added to the calculation using the whiteware date, the resulting MCD is 1848, which coincides more closely with the suspected occupation of the site. The glass was then studied for possible corroboration of the date, since glass is less likely to present the time lapse problem of ceramic artefacts. The glass dating places the majority of the collection before the 1860s. Both the MCD and the bottle analysis place the deposits between the 1830s, the first construction episode, and the 1880s when the buildings were razed. The ceramic assemblage highlights the flaw of our general assumption about the longevity of ceramic use. The use of inherited or out-of-date ceramics clearly can skew calculated dates.

Researchers conducted a Miller economic scaling analysis of the ceramic assemblages to determine the economic status of the individuals occupying the properties. The sherd index from the Essex Court assemblage was compared to two assemblages from a middle-class site located 'up the street', but the latter assemblages were not from alley dwellings and were known to be middle class. As mentioned above, 269 sherds were considered transitional. When they were included in the calculations (using the classification of ironstone, which, according to Miller, is at the same economic index as transfer-printed wares) the Essex Court assemblage was assessed to be somewhat lower middle class in comparison to the street dwellings. When the 269 transitional sherds were omitted the economic calculation was lower, placing the assemblage in a lower socio-economic stratum which is more in line with what is generally expected for alley dwellers.[16] In either case, ethnicity is not likely to be a factor in the difference between alley and street dwellings. In this earlier period it appears that whites occupied both.

The post-1880 occupation assemblage was retrieved from a trash pit. Economic scale was also assessed for this collection, using an index of values based on ceramic costs as reflected in the Sears/Roebuck catalogues after 1895. Researchers placed these occupants of Essex Court at the low, white-collar level, perhaps the level of a storekeeper, a clerk or a teacher. Some of the artefacts repre-

sent choices made by someone with disposable income. There were children's toys, cosmetics and a porcelain shirt stud from a man's dress shirt.

The economic scaling analysis for assemblages from both the pre-1880s and the post-1880s deposits reveal a higher-than-expected amount expended on material goods. However, the earlier assemblage of ceramics is also older than expected, perhaps indicating second-hand, or inherited, acquisition of household ceramics.

Slate Alley[17]

Slate Alley was so named because a slate yard was in operation here from 1843 to 1853 by James Parker on 'F' Street. The location of lots around the H-shaped alley afforded nearly every lot alley access (see Fig. 5.2). This square was in the core of the residential and commercial district of early Washington. In 1800 there were three houses; in 1853 there were forty houses. The square was first subdivided in 1835 after a sewer line was installed and the street graded and paved.

After performing documentary research, archaeologists selected the lot to be excavated. Researchers identified five phases of development but only the first two are of interest here. The first phase, beginning soon after the founding of Washington in 1790, dates from 1795 to 1825. The second phase, from 1825 to 1855, saw the subdivision of the lot and utility lines provided from the street.

During the first phase of occupation, a line of postholes marked a fence that divided the front of the property (facing the street) from the rear that was on the alley. There were distinct differences in the type of artefacts from each side of the fence, but the economic analysis of the ceramics indicates no economic difference, as there were relatively expensive tablewares on both sides. The alley-facing household contained more serving vessels and food storage vessels. Such evidence suggests that servants or slaves of the house fronting on 'E' Street may have occupied the rear yard.

In the second phase (1825–55) the lot was subdivided and utility lines were provided, at least for the street-facing dwellings. Documents indicate that, in addition to residences facing the street, at least one residence facing the alley was constructed. It was during this phase that alley residents dug a large oval pit, measuring 5 by 3.5 by 1.5 feet and filled it with 544 bottles of all types: 363 wine, 26 mineral water or beer and 2 pharmaceutical bottles. Makers' marks indicated that the source of the bottles was Philadelphia, Saratoga, New York and Washington, DC. Most of the bottles were whole. Also contained within the pit were iron hardware, window glass, bricks, marbles, nails and animal bones. This separation of glass

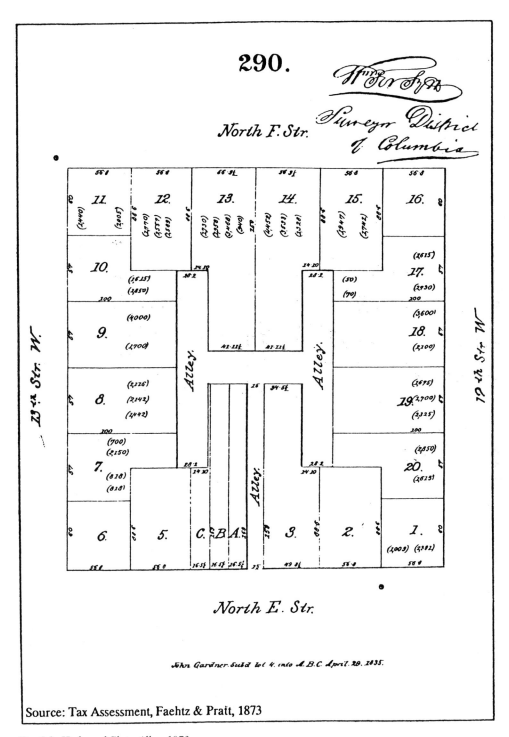

Fig. 5.2 H-shaped Slate Alley, 1873.

from the more general deposition may have occurred as a result of 'junking,' discussed in more detail below.

Quander Place[18]

In 1983 a study was conducted in the Southeastern Quadrant of the District of Columbia, in what is currently the Washington Navy Yard Annex. Historically this neighbourhood was racially mixed and working class, containing brick and frame row-houses with some industrial and commercial structures. The area to be effected by construction included dwellings that faced the street (streetface) and others that fronted onto the alley. The buildings on the streetface were constructed between 1830 and 1855, but the alley was not developed until late in the nineteenth century. The Navy Yard block was a racially mixed working-class neighbourhood. White skilled labourers lived on streets and black unskilled workers lived on the alleys and in the interior of the block. This difference held after the alley was created in the 1880s until around 1910 when most of the houses facing both street and alley were occupied by African Americans.

Researchers approached this first study of Washington, DC alleys with two major research goals. The first was to understand how people on the block lived their daily lives. The second was to see if there were real differences in material culture and behaviour between street- and alley-facing dwellings and therefore to test the accuracy of social reformers' and Borchert's views. The first phases of the archaeological research and excavation indicated that there were a number of rear yard midden deposits, some of which were related to the alley dwelling occupation of the block and others to the street-facing lots.

An economic scale for twentieth-century ceramics was created for the project in order to compare households' monetary investment in these wares. Researchers found no significant difference between alley and street in either cost or ceramic vessel form. There were some differences in the choice of glass tableware. There were fewer forms, just bowls and tumblers, in the alley components, while the street components contained these forms as well as plates, butter dishes, salts, wine glasses and pitchers. There was also a difference in food storage, with alley households apparently relying on the more modern system of canning jars while the street households used the older system of domestic stoneware.

One interesting difference was revealed in the flotation analysis of soil samples. Potential food plants were much more frequent in the alley than the street, and the street lots had more weeds considered useless as food. Amaranth and other edible plant seeds such as purslane and Cruciferae were numerous in the alley. There was also no difference in the types of meat consumed. The animal bone in the alley tended to be sawn, unlike the cleaver-cut street bone. There was also a higher percentage of pig's feet in the alley debris. The number of buttons also differed between the two contexts, with thirteen from the street and fifty-five from the alley.

The two groups were more alike than anticipated. Based on ceramic scale and foodways, researchers concluded that the distinct differences between alley and street populations were probably due to cultural or ethnic factors rather than economic differences.

What we don't learn from alleys

In 1880, only 8 per cent of the adult males in Borchert's sample of alley dwellers were skilled. Most of these men were carpenters, barbers, shoemakers, blacksmiths, plasterers or brick masons. Fewer than 7 per cent were white collar, proprietorial or professional, and of these 17 per cent were 'rag picker', 'rag gatherer', 'rag dealer', 'junk dealer', and 33 per cent were 'pedlar', 'jobber', 'huckster', and 'horse trader'.[19]

The reports of house interiors by alley reformers varied widely, but the condition of yards was universally described as 'filled with uncollected garbage, rubbish and filth'. Borchert confirmed this observation by analysing contemporary photographs. 'Junking' was a full-time occupation for some alley men and supplemented many families' incomes. Young boys junked too. Junking involved 'collecting of glass bottles and breaking them to be sold as broken glass by the hundreds of pounds; selling of old rags, paper, iron and tin, and any article of value which may be found among trash cans, or on the dumps. Thus the disorder in the backyard was often the alley family's savings account and insurance policy.'[20]

Junk dealers bought from people coming in or from pickers in the street. The most productive method of getting junk was working the streets for bottles, rags and junk. Paper was collected from lawyers' offices and printers for sale to merchants, especially butchers. Clothes were collected for resale or rags were sold to brokers who sold them to paper or cloth mills, where the rags were shredded, spun and rewoven into 'shoddy cloth'. Bones were collected to be ground into meal for fertiliser and to be processed into buttons. Bottles were resold to retailers or to brokers.[21] The higher number of buttons in Quander Place than in the neighbouring streets may indicate rag-picking as an economic sideline in the alley households. The pit of whole bottles in Slate Alley suggests that this may have been a storage area for these objects in anticipation of selling them.

Writing in 1890 in *Progress of the Colored People of Maryland since the War*, Jeffrey Brackett commented on the success of African American business in Baltimore. He thought the coal dealers, haulers and hod carriers more successful than store managers and wrote, 'the junk business – which, before the war, was the work of the Jews – is now done mostly by blacks'.[22] It is possible that a similar shift occurred in Washington.

The mass market of the late nineteenth and twentieth centuries would have excluded whole segments of society were it not for the second-hand trade which allowed cash-poor consumers to acquire higher-quality goods. Second-hand stores may have allowed barter in addition to cash sales. Junk stores were common in nineteenth- and early-twentieth-century American cities, but trade in second-hand goods is not well documented in the written record.[23] It is possible that an early entrepreneur was operating a junk shop in Slate Alley before the Civil War.

The researchers at Quander Place set out to test one of Borchert's propositions about alley dwellers: their adaptations resulted from a folk pattern born in rural slavery. Borchert writes: 'Drawing on a culture developed from the slave experience, alley dwellers were able to take advantage of their environment, creating physical and psychological barriers to isolate and protect their community as well as developing a strategy for survival in a hostile world.'[24] The patterns reflected a different set of values that may have had correlates in material culture. Therefore, behaviours reflecting ethnic difference may have remained strong in the alleys and thus able to be discovered in the archaeological record. In evaluating Borchert's hypothesis, Charles Cheek and Amy Friedlander had to attempt to factor out the economic variable to look for an ethnic difference in material culture. As discussed above, research indicated that the assemblages of the two groups were rather similar economically. Differences were interpreted as ethnic differences.[25]

Cheek and Friedlander state that 'common sense and recent studies' show that material culture functions as a signal of group membership.[26] But even if we could state that so unequivocally, it is necessary to question in which group or groups is membership being signalled. In keeping with most historical archaeology of ethnic and group behaviour, it is reasonable to suggest, or tacitly assume, that the African American alley dwellers of Quander Alley wished to signal their membership in the African American community. However, within the racially polarised society in which they lived, we ask to whom would they need to signal that membership? Such signalling appears redundant and unnecessary as well as,

in some cases, counterproductive. We do not raise this issue as a criticism of the original pioneering study, which is important in pointing out the economic similarity between African American households in alleys and those of European Americans facing the street. Instead we wish to point out that a shift is occurring in archaeological studies of ethnicity.

Many historical archaeologists have addressed issues of ethnicity, albeit often indirectly and implicitly through the study of various ethnically defined groups. The direct discussion of ethnicity itself as an organising construct has been somewhat more limited, and understandably so given its complexities.[27]

Consideration of 'ethnic processes' forces the realisation that there is a great deal of variability within the creation and maintenance of ethnic groups. Group structure and history vary according to cultural context, and economic, political, social and religious circumstances. Ethnicity, like ethnic groups themselves, is a changing construct. It is currently evolving, within historical archaeology, into a new methodological concept. Although ethnicity and race are not equivalent, most historical archaeologists have relied upon theoretical treatments of ethnicity to interpret the material culture of both ethnic and racial groups. Ethnicity does not operate alone but in conjunction with at least class and social position, and certainly with race.[28]

Archaeologically, the definition of ethnicity gets intertwined with consumption and the marketplace. However, we cannot expect to find predictable correspondence between the archaeological record and some imagined category of ethnicity or race. Several scholars have been critical of material culture studies of ethnicity. They warn about the use of conceptual methods that mislead analysis into predictable 'findings'.

Critiquing the way that archaeologists have analysed certain artefacts, Brackette Williams[29] questions whether an archaeologist can really use the concept of ethnicity. In a larger view of anthropological method, she questions the construction of a national people who are white and ethnic people who are not. She is critical of calling people 'ethnics' and 'minorities' and emphasises that ethnicity is not a natural result of contact but is created through power differentials.

Dell Upton argues that the core assumptions about ethnicity that have shaped interpretations of architecture and landscape also apply to historical archaeology. These are: (1) a positivistic notion of ethnicity wherein it is believed that a piece of research can list the values and attributes of an ethnicity; (2) stability of ethnic cultures as static and traditional and corrupted by contact with others; and

(3) ethnicity being invested in a material world wherein it is believed that some artefacts are more ethnic than others and that ethnicity is invested in these. Instead of this untenable, embedded view of static cultural and racial categories, Upton recommends a dynamic ethnicity: 'we can step away from the commodified notion of culture for a minute and understand ethnicity as a synthesis of imposed and adopted characteristics that is forged through contact and conflict'.[30] Studying 'invented traditions' may reveal the processes of ethnic groups choosing to commodify their identities and attach them to visible (or not) material culture. The connection is arbitrary, not 'authentic'.

Tightly wound with archaeological method that searches for 'ethnicity' is historical archaeology's methodology for analysing consumption and the contents of assemblages. It is far too simplistic to imagine that we know what the price of goods means in an assemblage. The economic evaluation of assemblages often misses the point that methods of acquisition vary considerably. There are second-hand shops, gifts, barter, theft and other sources of goods.

Traditional expectations about material culture and status, that high status translates into more or more-expensive household goods, are not always met. For example, Wade Catts and Jay Custer[31] find that there is no simple correlation between patterned variability in ceramic assemblages and socio-economic status, site function, layout, ethnicity or cultural geographic context. They explored the Thomas Williams site in New Castle County, Delaware. The most archaeologically visible occupation was that of an African American labourer and his family who bought the property in 1887 and lived there until 1922. This site and the few comparative sites demonstrated that there is a great variety in the assemblages of rural blacks, who, in spite of poor representation in the documentary record, participated fully in the consumer culture. In their study in South Carolina, Melanie Cabak and Mary Inkrot[32] also find that ethnicity is a poor indicator of material culture choices.

Given this change in perspective on ethnicity and material culture, we find it compelling both to question the assumption of ethnic signalling behaviour in the context of alley dwellers suggested by the Quander Place research and to ask the question, what other messages might consumption convey? To begin to address this latter question, the work of Paul Mullins in nearby Annapolis, Maryland, is invaluable.

In a study of African American dwellings in Annapolis, Maryland, Mullins finds not 'ethnic markers' – with the exception of a steel hair-straightening comb – but typical goods and differences among the households. This tellingly undermines the 'expectations' of racial difference brought to the study by standard historical archaeological method.[33] Mullins finds that African Americans explicitly used their purchasing power as a strategy to confront the racism that attempted to exclude them from American social and economic life.

In emphasising that assemblages are not inherently comparable simply because they are from African American sites, Mullins states that 'perhaps the most fundamental point of [his study of African Americans in Annapolis, Maryland] . . . is that the *monolithic Black caricature* constructed by genteel Whites was completely delusive [emphasis added]'.[34] We want to insist that a similar caricature should not come to characterise an archaeology of African Americans.

The work at Essex Court, albeit limited and inconclusive, suggests that the African American alley dwellers in the 1880s were using at least some of the accoutrements of middle-class display: cosmetics and dress shirts. Even the alley reformers found variety and the unexpected in spite of themselves. One Reformer writes: 'With all the notoriety, the alleys remain fundamentally unchanged; some of the homes are comfortable, some are fair and some are, to use an over-used adjective, "deplorable." The people who live there represent many different grades of culture; some are coarse migrants, some suspicious and bitter, and other gracious and poised.'[35]

In sum, what we do not learn from archaeology in alleys is anything conventional or 'expected' about the difference between black and white households, because unknown differences within black, white and mixed neighbourhoods make such comparisons premature and misleading.

What we might learn from alleys

So what *does* the archaeology of alleys in Washington, DC indicate? Archaeology needs to rework and continue to complicate its methodologies to address the reality of complex 'ethnic' behaviour. African Americans participated wholly in consumer culture, albeit perhaps through second-hand shopping and barter. African American alley dwellers continued various strategies of 'making do,' a practised way of life. One example of this is in the use of wild food resources at Quander Place. One alley reformer wrote, 'the people studied are admirably resourceful in their use of edible wild plants for food' – able to 'get a few of these plants from vacant lots and along the river bank'.[36] There was plenty of local wild food to be found. The Federal Writers Project reported in the 1930s that, 'Marshes of wild rice extend over much of the Anacostia River estuary, and, along the lower Potomac, wild celery, Peltandra, and various waterweeds.' Throughout the nineteenth century and early in the twentieth, the Potomac marshes feed many birds and waterfowl. 'Waterfowl, cranes, rails, pigeons, grouse, bobolinks, and blackbirds were sold in the Washington market as late as 1912; and, finally, with the draining and clearing of the land for real-estate development, many bird haunts ceased to exist.'[37]

Oral histories collected in neighbouring southern Maryland provide another complication in considering the lives of African Americans in Washington after Emancipation. People moved frequently between the city and rural areas. One family recounts an ancestor who worked as a hod carrier in construction to earn enough cash to move back to Charles County and eventually buy farmland. Land ownership was an important goal for African Americans and there is good reason to expect that some proportion of alley dwellers in the city were not as interested in 'status display' in their temporary home as they were in accumulating enough cash to fulfil their dreams outside of the city.[38]

David Babson[39] asks 'whether or not the data recovered by archaeology and the way they are presented to the public can help in changing the stereotyped views that many white Americans hold about black Americans'. Archaeology serving racist interests is 'highly likely to happen where members of descendant groups are excluded from all aspects of archaeology, including the conception of research questions, excavation, data analysis, and interpretation'.[40] Maria Franklin writes:

> History belongs to everyone ideally, perhaps, but in actuality it belongs to those who have access to its material remnants, to those who control its penning, and to those who pass the power to authorize and disseminate it. History should belong to everyone, and that is the goal archaeologists must reach for if we are intent on archaeology being relevant to non-archaeologists.[41]

In 1989, 70 per cent of the population of the city of Washington, DC was African American.[42] It is not too much to ask that a historical archaeology of the city attempt to formulate and address questions about black history, particularly about life in Washington after the Civil War, and to address questions about coping with racism and class prejudice.

Archaeology in Washington, DC is a study in contradictions. As the seat of the federal government, Washington did not develop as most urban places but was planned as a national capital. Although African Americans lived in Washington from its founding, the Civil War swelled the black population with those escaping slavery. Housing was in short supply as the city's population grew and the infamous alley dwellings of Washington developed in the later nineteenth century. White social reformers decried the dangerous, disease-ridden, crowded alleys but many of these alley neighbourhoods provided a sense of community to blacks and also to immigrants who could not afford or find acceptance in other neighbourhoods.

Only since the early 1980s has there been any systematic archaeological work on the development of the city. In this chapter we have summarised archaeological evidence in Washington that relates to alley dwellings. As should be evident, an archaeology of alley life in the city has barely begun, but it should have a powerful future. We are particularly hopeful that archaeology be done in the Blagden Alley and Naylor Court neighbourhood with the interest and participation of the local community. As Theresa Singleton writes, 'African-American archaeology should be seen primarily as a way of framing questions pertinent to the African experience in the Americas. It is not necessary to restrict such questions to sites with an identifiable or discrete black provenience, but to any site than can illuminate aspects of African-American history and culture.'[43] We believe that historical archaeology can help us uncover the silences of both documents and artefacts and offer a vehicle in which to examine our history and preconceptions of that history.

Notes

1 The National Register of Historic Places was established in 1966 by the National Historic Preservation Act. It is a list of places in the United States considered worthy of preservation. Listing in the National Register, however, is not a guarantee of preservation and assures only that federal projects will take the significance of historic places into account.
2 DC Government, 'Transcript of Proceedings', Government of the District of Columbia, Department of Consumer and Regulatory Affairs Historic Preservation Review Board. Excerpt from Public Hearing, October 22, 1998, Washington, DC, p. 34.
3 *Washington Post*, 30 October 1997, D3.
4 Constance McLaughlin Green, *Washington: Village and Capital, 1800–1878* (Princeton: Princeton University Press, 1962), p. 228.
5 *Ibid.*, p. 215.
6 *Ibid.*, p. 211.

7 James Borchert, *Alley Life in Washington: Family, Community, Religion, and Folklife in the City, 1850–1970* (Chicago: University of Illinois Press, 1982), p. 257.

8 *Ibid.*, p. xii.

9 Henry Glassie, 'Archaeology and folklore: common anxieties, common hopes', in Leland Ferguson (ed.), *Historical Archaeology and the Importance of Material Things*, Society for Historical Archaeology, Special Publications Series 2, pp. 23–35, p. 29.

10 C. D. Cheek, A. Friedlander, C. A. Holt, C. H. Lee Decker and T. E. Ossim, 'Archaeological investigation at the National Photographic Interpretation Center Addition, Washington, D.C. Navy Yard Annex' (Alexandria, VA: Soil Systems, Inc., 1983), p. 6.

11 Archaeological work at Blagden Alley was done under the Federal Grants Program. Every State Historic Preservation Office receives appropriated funds from the United States Department of the Interior. This money is used to fulfil certain requirements for the identification and evaluation of cultural resources, including both standing structures and archaeological resources. For a long time, in the District standing structures were recognised as the only resource to be surveyed. We were victims of 'urban mentality' that assumed archaeological resources were disturbed or destroyed in the urban environment because of the amount of construction. Because of this thinking, Washington has many historic districts with buildings that are protected under local law, but with archaeological resources that are unidentified and have not been surveyed and evaluated.

In the 1980s, survey of archaeological resources became part of grants that were given to communities to survey their standing structures with the potential of being designated historic districts. The archaeological portion of the survey is usually limited and consists of researching the historic context of the neighbourhood and doing a walkover survey to determine whether there has been any likely disturbance to any archaeological resources. However, it is not usually possible to conduct any field testing to determine if archaeological resources actually survive.

The work at Blagden Alley/Naylor Court is described in Elizabeth A. Myler and Richard J. Dent Jr, *Archaeological Survey and Evaluation of Squares 367 and 368, Washington, D.C.* (submitted to Traceries, Inc., Washington, DC, 1989).

12 Washington, DC was originally platted into squares, pieces of land that front on four streets. Squares are further divided into lots.

13 Katherine Grandine. Blagden Alley/Naylor Court, National Register of Historic Places Registration Form (Traceries, Inc., Washington, DC, 1989).

14 Borchert, *Alley Life*, p. 18.

15 Archaeological work at Essex Court was done under local DC law. The District of Columbia has a strong historic preservation law: the Historic Landmark and Historic District Protection Act of 1978, DC. Law 2–144. This Historic Protection Act provides for the official designation of Landmarks and Historic Districts. It also requires that certain types of work affecting designated properties be reviewed to ensure that historic characteristics are preserved. It provides for the protection of archaeological resources only if they are designated as landmarks. Under DC. Law, projects are presented to the Historic Preservation Review Board, an eleven-member board appointed by the Mayor, comprised of preservation professionals (including one archaeologist) and private citizens. The board discusses each case and then votes on how projects should proceed. Only a few times has archaeology been included in projects covered by DC. Law. In such cases the developers have had to use their own funds to finance the excavation. Since it is not realistic to expect the developer to pay for a full-scale excavation as is usually done under Section 106, a tight research design is necessary in order to maximise the retrieval of information. The philosophical approach is that getting some information, however limited, is better than nothing.

The work at Essex Court is described in William M. Gardner and Sally C. Anderson, *A Phase I Archeological Investigation of 51NW113* (prepared for Development Resources, Inc., Washington, DC, 1994).

16 This analysis was developed by George Miller in order to develop a consistent classification system for archaeological ceramic collections according to the original cost of the wares. Since the nineteenth century brought a reduction in the range of ware types from, for example, white salt-glazed stoneware and tin-glazed earthenware to primarily white earthenware, the classification of these wares by potters, merchants and people who used them was according to decoration (i.e. edged, painted, dipped). Miller developed index values from price lists, bills of lading and account books in order to study the expenditures on ceramics found in an archaeological assemblage. Miller divided the ceramics into four types based on increasing cost: undecorated or common creamware (CC) ware; minimally decorated wares; hand-painted

wares; and transfer-printed wares. See George L. Miller, 'Classification and economic scaling of 19th century ceramics', *Historical Archaeology* 14 (1980), 1–40. Also see Anne R. Brown, 'Historic ceramic typology with principal dates of manufacture and descriptive characteristics for identification' (prepared for Delaware Department of Transportation, Division of Highways, Location and Environmental Studies Office, Dover, 1982).

17   Excavations at Slate Alley and Quander Place were done through Section 106 of the National Historic Preservation Act of 1966, as amended (NHPA). Most of the archaeology done in the District has been done under this law. Under the NHPA, when a federal agency is planning a project such as new construction or demolition it must take into consideration the impact of the project on historic sites. This is when archaeology is conducted to its fullest extent, with identification, evaluative testing and, in some instances, data recovery as mitigation for the adverse effects of a project. The work at Slate Alley is described in E. Goodman, M. Walker, M. Pappas, C. Toulmin and E. Crowell, *Phase II and Phase III Investigations at Warner Theatre, Washington, DC* (prepared for the Kaempfer Company, Washington, DC, by Engineering-Science, 1990).

18   The work at Quander Place is described in Charles D. Cheek and Amy Friedlander, 'Pottery and pig's feet: space, ethnicity, and neighbourhood in Washington, D.C., 1880–1940', *Historical Archaeology* 24:1 (1990), 34–60 and Cheek *et al.*, 'Archaeological investigation'.

19   Borchert, *Alley Life*, pp. 167–8.

20   *Ibid.*, p. 96.

21   Mary Praetzellis and Adrian Praetzellis, *Junk! Archaeology of the Pioneer Junk Store, 1877–1908* (Papers in Northern California Anthropology 4, Rohnert Park, CA: Anthropological Studies Center, Sonoma State University, 1990), p. 396.

22   Brackett, quoted in Paul R. Mullins, 'The contradictions of consumption: an archaeology of African American and consumer culture, 1850–1930' (PhD thesis, University of Massachusetts Amherst, 1996), p. 271. Note that a hod is a trough carried over the shoulder for transporting loads such as bricks and mortar.

23   Praetzellis and Praetzellis, *Junk*, p. 394.

24   Borchert, *Alley Life*, p. 140. Borchert's argument that alley communities provided a sense of community makes sense to us, but we want to avoid sentimentality in structuring our understanding of alley life. We heed the warning of historian Patricia Limerick, who is critical of historians who have overused the concept of culture, making 'Culture' a sort of consolation prize for groups who are on the losing end of power and economic oppression. Limerick warns that 'By focusing on the culture of those who have been overpowered in history, we have allowed those who sought and exercised coercive power to avoid responsibility for their actions.' Patricia Nelson Limerick, 'The startling ability of culture to bring critical inquiry to a halt', *The Chronicle of Higher Education*, 24 October, 1997, p. 176.

25   Cheek *et al.*, *Archaeological Investigation*, pp. 158–9.

26   Cheek and Friedlander, 'Pottery and pig's feet', p. 30.

27   E.g., Randall H. McGuire, 'The study of ethnicity in historical archaeology', *Journal of Anthropological Archaeology* 1 (1982), 159–78; Barbara J. Little, 'Echoes and forecasts: group tensions in historical archaeology', *International Journal of Group Tensions* 18 (1988), 243–57; Edward Staski, 'Studies of ethnicity in North American historical archaeology', *North American Archaeologist* 11 (1990), 121–45.

28   See, for example, Charles E. Orser Jr., 'The challenge of race to American historical archaeology', *American Anthropologist* 100 (1998), 661–8.

29   Brackette F. Williams, 'Of straightening combs, sodium hydroxide, and potassium hydroxide in archaeological and cultural-anthropological analysis of ethnogenesis', *American Antiquity* 57 (1992), 608–12.

30   Dell Upton, 'Ethnicity, authenticity, and invented traditions', *Historical Archaeology* 30:2 (1996), 1–7, p. 4.

31   Wade P. Catts and Jay F. Custer, *Tenant Farmers, Stone Masons, and Black Laborers: Final Archaeological Investigations of the Thomas Williams Site, Glasgow, New Castle County, Delaware* (Delaware Department of Transportation Archaeology Series 82, 1990), p. 266.

32   Melanie A. Cabak and Mary M. Inkrot, *Old Farm: New Farm; An Archaeology of Rural Modernization in the Aiken Plateau, 1875–1950* (Savannah River Archaeological Research Papers 9, South Carolina Institute of Archaeology and Anthropology, University of South Carolina, 1997).

33   Mullins, 'Contradictions of consumption', p. 143.

34   *Ibid.*, p. 143.

35   Quoted in Borchert, *Alley Life*, p. 67.

36   Borchert, *Alley Life*, p. 178.

37   Federal Writers Project, *Washington: City and Capital* (Washington, DC: American Guide Series, 1937), p. 26.

38   George William McDaniel, 'Preserving the people's history: traditional black material culture in nineteenth and twentieth century southern Maryland' (PhD thesis, Duke University, 1979), pp. 200ff.

39 David W. Babson, 'Introduction', in *In the Realm of Politics: Prospects for Public Participation in African-American and Plantation Archaeology* (thematic issue), *Historical Archaeology* 31:3 (1997), 5–6, p. 5.

40 Maria Franklin, '"Power to the people": sociopolitics and the archaeology of black Americans', in *In the Realm of Politics: Prospects for Public Participation in African-American and Plantation Archaeology* (thematic issue), *Historical Archaeology* 31:3 (1997), 36–50, p. 40.

41 *Ibid.*, p. 41.

42 US Bureau of the Census, *1991 Statistical and Metropolitan Data Book* (Washington DC: US Government Printing Office, 1991).

43 Theresa A. Singleton, 'Facing the challenges of a public African-American archaeology', in *In the Realm of Politics: Prospects for Public Participation in African-American and Plantation Archaeology* (thematic issue), *Historical Archaeology* 31:3 (1997), 146–52, p. 148.

6
Small things, big pictures: new perspectives from the archaeology of Sydney's Rocks neighbourhood

GRACE KARSKENS

The reputed Rocks

From its first occupation by Europeans after 1788, the steep slopes on the west side of Sydney Cove were regarded by outsiders as an 'other' Sydney. The area grew riotously on the precipitous ground 'across the water' from the orderly civil precinct, its ground appropriated by convict women and men, who built houses, fenced off gardens and yards, established trades and businesses, and raised families. They created 'their town' there, with relatively little government intervention in their lives, much less official land grants or freehold titles. Orderly grid-patterned street layout was impossible on this terrain, and in any case was not a priority among the people there. Instead, they directed their considerable energies towards amassing goods and property, or at least a 'decent life', upon their own terms. Its name, the Rocks, was bestowed by the convicts, and survived in common parlance throughout the nineteenth and twentieth centuries despite numerous attempts to impose less infamous titles.[1] It was not officially named 'The Rocks' until 1975, by which time the convict past had gained a sort of picturesque respectability, as well as being a tourist drawcard.[2]

Throughout its history, though, and particularly over the second half of the nineteenth century, the Rocks was regarded by most outsiders, and by most historians, as a 'classic' slum, a fearful 'social cesspool' where poverty met disorder, dirt, disease and depravity. Its convict origins (the 'convict stain' which haunted emerging colonial society) and its disturbingly irregular landscape were the foundations of this reputation. Upon them was laid the landscape of rapid urban growth, particularly as a result of rising immigration from the 1840s onwards: close-packed, at first ill-serviced terrace houses, a multiplying maze of lanes and blind courts, severe problems of drainage, water supply, and rubbish and sewage disposal. As well, the Rocks was surrounded by water on three sides, and so was associated with seafaring and the maritime trades, with sailors from all over the world on shore leave, and with the constant movement of people and goods through the port city. The area had a higher proportion of Irish families than other parts of the city, and when Chinese immigration rose in the 1850s, Lower George Street, at the foot of the Rocks, became Sydney's first 'Chinatown'.[3]

These were the distinguishing elements – a foetid, crowded environment, mean and dirty houses and their poor, down-trodden tenants, drunken, brawling sailors, 'immoral' Chinese, the 'bad and dirty' Irish – which struck observers, and from which they constructed their written accounts. And there were those, indeed, drawn to the Rocks in search of just these elements: evangelical preachers like Nathaniel Pidgeon sought out drunks, prostitutes and Roman Catholics; the intrepid ladies of the Sydney Ragged Schools bent on dragging 'fallen people' out of darkness and into light; and later journalists searching for picturesque and pestilential stories about the city's 'rookeries' or 'warrens', as the homes of working people were called.[4]

Perhaps the best-known and most-quoted was early social scientist William Stanley Jevons, who wrote in the late 1850s. Taking the stance of the detached scientific observer, he dissected and analysed Sydney, arranging people and houses in classes of worth and status. His map of Sydney, recently reconstructed by historian Graeme Davison, showed that the Rocks had all 'classes' of houses, including those of genteel and professional ranks (first class), mechanics and skilled artisans (second class) and 'labourers and the indefinable lower orders' (third class).[5] But it was Jevons' description of the Rocks as a place of filth, vice and misery which became so well-known as to be unquestioned:

> It is in the lower streets . . . that the peculiar features of the Rocks are seen in all their horrible intensity. Small cottages constructed of stone or wood in convict days are here closely scattered almost without order, but practically formed in lines along the terrace of Rocks. Steep narrow passages . . . form the only cross streets . . . the streets are without even gutters except such as the drainage itself forms . . . In many places filthy water is actually seen to accumulate against the walls of the dwellings . . . In other places this accumulation of filth is prevented by a drain constructed beneath the floors

so as to lead the filth quite through the house. Many houses again are built but a few yards from a wall of rock over which various spouts and drains . . . continually discharge foul matter . . .

Nowhere have I seen such a retreat for filth and vice as the Rocks of Sydney . . . nowhere are the country and the beauty of nature so painfully contrasted with the misery and deformity which lie to the charge of man.[6]

When bubonic plague broke out in Sydney in 1900, all eyes turned to the waterfront areas, and to the Rocks in particular. Brought by fleas on rats which arrived with the ships, the plague was a disease which aroused ancient fears, horror and hysteria. It had a far worse effect on the city's psyche than its health, for other diseases such as diphtheria, whooping cough, tuberculosis, typhoid, dysentery and so on had taken a far heavier toll. Dysentery alone killed 8,522 people between 1875 and 1900; the plague carried off 103.[7] The victims of plague occurred more commonly in the areas on the waterfronts west and south of the city, where those who worked on the ships and at the markets lived, but cases were also found in Redfern, Surry Hills, Glebe, Woollahra and many other places. The Rocks itself had only five victims, but its 'slum' reputation meant that it was immediately assumed to be a central breeding ground for the disease. The whole of the waterfront area was resumed by the government in 1900, hundreds of houses were demolished, starting with the Rocks and neighbouring Millers Point, and moving outwards over the other inner city neighbourhoods over the next thirty-odd years.[8]

Much of the academic history written about the Rocks, usually a brief aside in a wider narrative, simply falls back upon the 'slumland' stereotypes, presented as either picturesque or pestilential, or both.[9] Most commonly quoted are the damning passages from Jevons: '[Jevons] deplored the over-concentration of working class population in the slum areas', wrote Birch and MacMillan in their compendium *The Sydney Scene* in 1962. 'Deserting seamen, criminal gangs, and all the hangers-on that find seaports congenial found refuge in the warrens around the Rocks . . . misery and disease . . . bred in such areas.'[10] Deformity was a key theme of early urban historian Bernard Barrett's blunt statement: '[The Rocks was] the rendezvous for the poorest – the birthplace of Australia's proletariat. Thus crippled, the Rocks was Australia's first slum.'[11] Until recently, historians have also constantly reinforced the earlier, unfounded association between the Rocks, rats and plague, with the result the demolitions and dislocations of the community are generally taken for granted, even cele-

brated, as long-overdue urban 'improvement' which 'had' to happen.

The slum images have also dominated much of the modern-day public presentation and understanding of the Rocks, now a historic tourist area visited by more than 7 million people every year. Popular booklets, guided tours, pamphlets and museum displays all incorporate the seedy, sick and sinful 'past'. More recently the idea of the Rocks as a close-knit, poor but proud working-class *community* has also made a tentative appearance in interpretative material. The deeply rooted slumland images are not easily challenged, however, and the two sit uneasily side by side in Max Kelly's *Anchored in a Small Cove*, a book which accompanies the historical and archaeological exhibition at the Sydney Visitors' Centre.[12] When the NSW Historic Houses Trust acquired a wonderfully intact 1840s terrace of four houses and a corner shop, 'Susannah Place', in Gloucester Street, its curators found no evidence of filth and deprivation, but layer upon layer of wallpaper, paint and linoleum, decades of domestic care and pride.[13] Domesticity and community are therefore key themes in the museum's presentation. But this evidence has been treated as exceptional. A video made recently for visitors still portrays the Rocks generally as a dirty slum, while Susannah Place 'was *not* one of these'.

Birthplace of a proletariat? Cultural identity by default and denunciation

As well as being a repository for historical stereotypes, the Rocks has been a place of possibilities for historians. With its convict pedigree and population of working people, the area has been dubbed, in Barrett's words, 'the birthplace of the proletariat', the heartland of authentic working-class culture. Robert Connell and Terry Irving agree, surmising

In some parts of the towns, like The Rocks at Sydney, a considerable social solidarity could develop against colonial respectability. Crowds often gathered for illicit sports like cockfighting and boxing . . . The magistrates attempted to control liquor and put down 'disorderly houses' . . . On occasions there were riots and minor disturbances, usually fired by drink. To the sanctimonious, such things were evidence of 'the Immorality and Vice so prevalent among the Lower Classes of this Colony'; to historians, they have usually represented light relief and colour. We should see them as signs . . . of the attempt by working men and women to carve out their space for living from a highly repressive environment.[14]

What 'their space' actually might have constituted is not actually further explored, apart from these stock-image references. But, despite the lack of actual investigation, this 'space' has nevertheless been filled with a certain set of values. The culture working people constructed for themselves there must have been utterly non-respectable: riotous, violent, illicit, immoral. It must have been, in short, the repudiation of the rules of authority, the exploitative bonds of nascent capitalism, and the hegemonic culture of the rising bourgeoisie.

This mirrors a number of wider assertions and assumptions about working-class culture and behaviour in Australia. Since class and class struggle have played such a fundamental role in Australian historiography, some historians have generally supposed that working-class beliefs, culture and attitudes must have been the opposite of those values and institutions defined as 'bourgeois'. Taken together, the latter make up an inordinate slab of social and cultural life, for the middle classes, although amorphous and notoriously difficult to define, were none the less apparently incredibly busy and powerful in nineteenth-century Australia. Constantly on the rise, here as everywhere else on the globe, they constituted, in David Cannadine's words, the 'soufflé of history'.[15]

In some accounts the middle class had a monopoly of 'respectability'.[16] The nuclear family, with its inherently exploitative gender relations, was recently invented bourgeois ideology 'imposed' upon the working classes as a 'main agency of cultural control', inimical to its interests and destiny.[17] The rise of the bourgeoisie has also been linked with the 'invention' of the 'child' as innocent, malleable, precious, in need of special care and training 'in the approved middle class way'; and of 'childhood' as a distinct period of life, separate from the world of adults.[18] Some historians argue that attitudes to contraception, abortion and the importance of infant life itself diverged radically along class lines. Middle-class women increasingly considered the embryo as human life, and, armed with means, knowledge and appropriate 'mental furniture', they alone forged the path towards artificial contraception.[19] Meanwhile working-class people, lacking these attributes, clung to so-called 'traditional', rather more callous and careless, attitudes to children.[20] Some say that they did not even regard the newborn child as a human being, so that infanticide 'fell inside the category of population control' and was a 'normal' even a routine measure, rather than one used by women in the most desperate of circumstances.[21] Judith Allen painted a grim picture of child neglect, abuse and murder, based on evidence from coroners' inquests, criminal records, and the evidence of doctors and police at the various inquiries.[22]

Springing from the allegedly bourgeois home-and-family-centred ideology is the 'cult of domesticity', the notion of the female-centred home as sacred, private haven from the workaday world of men.[23] The artefacts of domesticity revolve around physical comfort, decorative details and genteel distancing from the unpleasant or the crude: furniture of mahogany and rosewood, soft furnishings, cushions, carpet and rugs, pictures and wallpaper. Fire irons, grates and fenders tamed the old open fires, ornamental gardens further buffered the domestic sphere from the outside world. The increasing number of rooms, each with its own function, separated men from women, servants from masters and mistresses, parents from children, visitors from visited.[24] Poor labouring people who worked in manual occupations and lived in the congested cities were thus excluded from such refinements.

In her marvellous study of genteel culture in Australia, Linda Young recreates the world of the middle class in Australia, tracing out the intricate rituals of etiquette and the range of material goods they adopted to express social propriety. By demonstrating this 'social capital' via action, demeanour and things, they could recognise one another and exclude those of inferior quality, thus creating their own class. A whole world of new consumer goods was essential to this process, objects which, like houses, expressed individualisation and segmentation: elaborate dinner sets with a place setting for each person, and a particular vessel for each type of food; clothing and jewellery, worn in certain ways and combinations, which marked out the respectable from the unrespectable.[25] At a more general level, the middle class is credited with developing and spreading the values of cleanliness, godliness, hard work and temperance, in short the whole Victorian ideology of self-improvement and self-control. Several historians argue that these were exploitative ideologies which, once imposed, would ensure the sober, quiescent, reliable workforce needed by bourgeois capitalists. They too were, or must have been, opposed to the 'values' of working-class people.

The 'hegemonic offensive', as Jan Kociumbas terms it, was also launched by the bourgeoisie via institutions, large and small: 'schools, Mechanics' Institutes, churches, theatres and sports grounds; universities, houses of parliament and banks, asylums, hospitals and gaols', as well as various scientific endeavours.[26] The chief purposes of the education system, for example, were to 'reorganise the workforce for industrial capitalism' (though that was still decades away), and to 'defuse radicalism'.[27] In this scheme, working people were the victims or opponents of education, science, temperance movements and the censoring and gentrification of various amusements and sports. Either by default, or via the denunciations of policemen, churchmen, doctors and the like, people of the 'real' working class were, by force of circumstance or cultural outlooks, or both, uncommitted to family life and domesticity, neglectful of their children, forever drunk, fighting and engaging in bloody sports and lewd, noisy public behaviour, and always associated with poverty and hard times.

An archaeology of the 'slum'?

A major problem for the archaeologists who have undertaken excavations on the Rocks was that, despite its fame as a historic precinct, it had no scholarly history. There was no framework, besides that of the slum and the 'wicked waterfront', which they, as well as architectural historians and other heritage professionals, could use as an interpretative starting point. The author of the Archaeological Management Plan prepared for the Rocks and Millers Point in 1991 did not even include historical material and themes for the period after 1850, assuming that it was already well documented, and implying that later-nineteenth-century sites were not really worth excavating.[28]

My own historical research on the Rocks was partly aimed at providing such a contextual history. At the same time it had also become clear to me that archaeology offered one of the few paths *inside* the Rocks, allowing us to examine the 'space for living' which working people actually 'carved out' for themselves, so long hidden, and demonised by the writings of outsiders. Postmodernist writers had ably demonstrated the role of literary constructs and the discourses of class and masculinity by deconstructing the texts, but they were generally unwilling or incapable of dealing with the 'real people, living in real houses' about whom archaeology 'speaks'.[29] At the other end of the spectrum, however, were equally 'disembodied' artefacts, hundreds of thousands of them, earnestly counted, measured, weighed, and listed in long and inscrutable catalogues (Fig. 6.1).[30]

Recently archaeologists have begun to develop broader and far more sophisticated approaches to the sites and artefacts of the Rocks by conducting primary research on their historical, cultural and ethnographic contexts, and by posing appropriate research questions.[31] The Cumberland/Gloucester Street site, at the heart of the Rocks, was an opportunity to apply a new collaborative approach, one which sought to integrate history and archaeology, rather than maintain the artificial disciplinary boundaries which had bedevilled any real interpretation of urban archaeological sites.[32] The site was excavated in 1994 by a team assembled by Godden

Mackay Pty Ltd, directed by Richard Mackay and with myself as project historian. It was one of the largest sites excavated in Australia, occupying two half-city blocks where forty-two houses had stood. The site is an extraordinary material record of urban life and development in Sydney, for below the massive fills which raised and levelled the site after the demolition period in the early twentieth century were deposits documenting each phase of European occupation. The row-houses and shops of the mid- to late nineteenth century overlay larger freestanding houses, hotels and yards of the settled convicts and ex-convicts; beneath them were the postholes and trenches of the convicts who appropriated land here from the 1790s onwards (Fig. 6.2).[33]

Could the site, and the three-quarters of a million artefacts ultimately retrieved from it, throw new light on the stock portrayal of the Rocks as an unmitigated slum? Were all its occupants poor, depraved and condemned to live in shockingly crowded and dirty conditions? Located in the heart of the neighbourhood, our site would seem to be a prime example of 'slumland'. It had the back and side lane terraces so much reviled by observers as hidden pockets of fearful filth and depravity. Externally it even answers some of Jevons' descriptions: the rock walls behind some of the houses really were festooned with pipes and drains, they did glisten slimily with moisture, and drains did run under houses. The mid- to late-nineteenth-century houses were conjoined and often had small rooms, and few of the houses had any cesspits at all.[34] Yet, if we move inside, an entirely different scene materialises (Fig. 6.3).

The archaeology of the Rocks

It is important to note at the outset that the basic unit of social organisation and household structure on the Rocks was the nuclear family of mother, father and children, irrespective of whether the parents were legally married or not. This pattern was not 'imposed' at any stage, but dates from the earliest days of unregulated convict settlement and stretches unbroken to the 1900s. These were, however, rather 'porous' households in that they included convict servants in the early years (who were treated as members of the household), and numerous lodgers and other family members throughout the period. In many cases, the patterns of occupancy as well as the houses themselves – the very shape of the neighbourhood – were tied directly to family relationships, particularly those of women. Another important factor was the ethnic affiliation: Scandinavians, Portuguese and Irish in particular tended to live close by one another.[35]

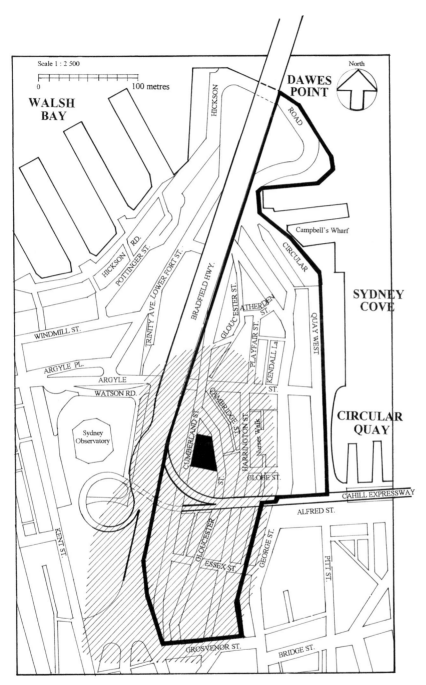

Fig. 6.1 The Rocks, Sydney, showing the original area, 1788–c. 1830 (shaded); the modern boundaries of the former Sydney Cove Authority in heavy line; and the Cumberland/Gloucester Street archaeological site, excavated in 1994.

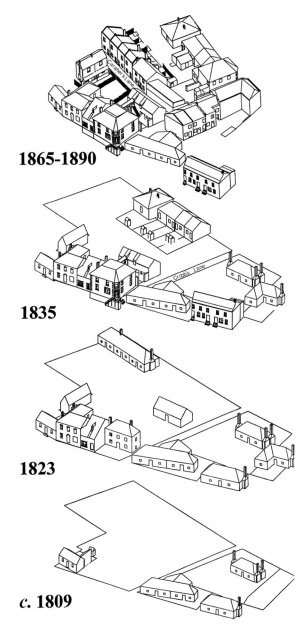

1865-1890

1835

1823

c. 1809

*Fig. 6.2 Wayne Johnson's bird's-eye view re-creation of
the site as it developed over the nineteenth century, views
to south-west.*

Looking over the thousands of nineteenth-century artefacts, the most obvious overall change in consumer patterns and culture from 1800 to 1900 is the slow, broad swing from partly pre-industrial, local and handmade, and objects with intrinsic worth and value, towards industrialised, machine-made and standardised commodities mass-produced at a distance and often single-use and disposable. The result was a greatly enlarged range of things from which to choose, commodities – everything from buttons to glass food bottles, bricks to tea sets – which were often cheaper, smoother, more readily available, easily replaceable and in a dizzying range of colours and patterns. Foodways are also deeply marked by the increase of pre-prepared, pre-packaged foodstuffs of great variety, and the concomitant reliance on external, commercial networks rather than household systems of food production and processing which had characterised part of the earlier assemblages.[36]

Yet the material record suggests that this was more a gradual shift in emphasis than a sharp break in habits and tastes over the nineteenth century. People continued to use salted meat, packed in barrels, and cooked in large iron pots over the hearth, just as the convicts and ex-convicts had done, until around the 1860s. Glass tumblers and simple blue- and green-edged ware were common from the earliest years of the colony and lasted well into the 1860s, although the glassware was increasingly machine-pressed rather than hand-blown, and became much more affordable. The site's convict residents had been keen consumers of ceramic tableware, both matched and individualised sets of English manufacture, as well as quasi-matched Chinese ware of widely varying quality. The interest in refined dining was expressed over the century in an extraordinary range of dinner, breakfast and tea sets, often of the best quality, in an explosion of colours and designs. Until around the 1860s the tableware included all the use-specific and refined pieces like butter dishes, gravy boats and the like.[37]

Nineteenth-century genteel consumerism was, as Linda Young has pointed out, a culture of aspiration. For working and 'middling' people (the distinction still very much blurred over the nineteenth century) that aspiration was expressed as striving for respectability and means. Amidst the older-established patterns, there were new streams of thought and behaviour, and new commodities for creating, expressing and demonstrating the respectable family, and some of these were indistinguishable from those of the comfortable to wealthy middle classes. Perhaps the most striking of these artefacts are what archaeologist Graham Wilson has called 'moralising china'. In a period when Christian philanthropists were

Fig. 6.3 Cribb's Lane, later called Cumberland Place, view to west, about 1900. This early lane bisected the site from east to west and by this stage was paved with sandstone blocks. On the left are gabled hotel stables, a walled yard and a substantial corner shop; on the right are an early house (c. 1810) and its yard, and a row of three flat-fronted terraces, with a corner hotel adjoining at the end. As in most of the photographs of this period, this one is constructed to suggest a 'crowded neighbourhood' scene, with local people carefully posed. The second woman on the right is hugging a large ceramic platter, typical of those found during the excavation.

launching the Ragged Schools to save 'slum' children from the terrible neglect of their brutal, uncaring, drunken parents, the wives of coal-lumpers and mariners living in the back-lane terraces were feeding their babies and children from mugs, plates and bowls designed especially for them. These items were embellished with educational and moral phrases and patterns. The letters of the alphabet set about the rims of soup plates and porridge bowls helped a child learn to read at the table. Others have pictures showing children behaving well, while mugs inscribed 'A Present for a Good Girl' underscore rewards for good behaviour. Still another mug bears the legend 'Lessons for Youth on Industry, Temperance and Frugality'. This moralising china reveals a clear interest in educating children, in inculcating them with moral principles of self-control, self-improvement and hard work.[38]

Rocks sites have also yielded a great collection of manufactured toys, many 'of fine and unusual quality': dainty tea sets, pretty dolls with glass eyes, lead figures such as horses, soldiers, boats and carriages, playing pieces from games, ceramic figurines and child-sized jewellery. An abundance of slate and slate pencils suggests that children were practising their letters at home. These things reveal that children were not regarded by working people as 'non-human' and unimportant at all; clearly they held modern cultural notions of childhood as a phase separate from adult life, a time of play and indulgence as well as education.[39] More intriguing is the discovery, in late-nineteenth-century underfloor deposits of a small back-lane terrace, of a plain bone ring. The ring matches descriptions of an 'occlusive pessary' available in this period, a modern contraceptive device made of 'membranes of rubber encircled by rings of bone'.[40]

Personal care and presentation were also extremely important. Cleanliness was evident in the wash-sets (basins, ewers, soap dishes), combs and brushes, while a love of dress and personal adornment established by the convicts was intensified by rising availability and variety of consumer goods.[41] The houses and yards of nineteenth-century working people have yielded thousands of buttons, in all manner of designs and fabrics, over 1,500 different types of beads, and a large collection of jewellery which, as Nadia Iacono concludes, 'attests to occupants of comfortable means'. Among the collection are high-quality earrings, including one of gold filigree and cloisonné enamelling, set with faceted beryl stones; handsome hat pins with glass balls, copper alloy leaves or disks of shell at their ends; rings (one of gold set with rubies) and good-quality jet mourning jewellery. Iacono's analysis of the scraps of surviving fabric revealed fine-quality silks, wool crepe, very fine weave silk crepe and organza.

Rebecca Bower's examination of the shoes from the site indicates that much of the residents' footwear was of good quality, including 'fashionable . . . high quality boots' and elegant slip-on or slipper-type women's shoes, finely made of calf, kid or fabric.[42]

While women wore jewellery, hair combs and perfume throughout the nineteenth century, it appears that, towards the end of the century, working men also began to take more interest in their appearance. There are rising numbers of men's jewellery, collar and cuff studs, handsome and even extravagant 'bachelor buttons' and so on. Men also seem to have taken a liking to wearing non-prescriptive spectacles which would have given them a sober, respectable, dignified appearance. On Sundays and holidays they put on their sober, best suits, looped gold or silver Albert chains through the waistcoat buttonholes, and tucked prized watches into the pockets, the 'special badge', as Graeme Davison puts it, 'of the self-regulated, provident, punctual workingman'. These were the men who joined the lodges and friendly societies, with their orderly, rational and hierarchical organisation, their glorious regalia and their public processions, their brotherly and patriotic aims.[43]

A tour of the interior of one of these small houses reveals spaces made warm, pleasant and comfortable by women. The walls were tinted from a wide palette of colours, and sometimes dado lines and wallpapers were added. The floors featured a great range of highly decorative and coloured tiles, or were covered with rugs or matting. The rooms were lit by glass lamps and some of the furniture was padded with kapok, decorated with buttons and tassels. Shell collections, with an example of each species, indicate that some Rocks people practised the same sort of rational scientific collecting as the genteel men and women in Tom Griffith's *Hunters and Collectors*. Shells were also placed on the mantelpieces for decorative purposes, alongside a great array of sentimental figurines of poodles, cottages, lambs, ladies, and angels sheltering little children under their wings. The bankruptcy inventories for such households list items such as clocks, pictures, blinds and valences, books, perhaps a ship in a bottle or a telescope. These were common in all but the most destitute of houses.[44]

What should we make of these unmistakable signs and patterns? If genteel culture is the defining hallmark of the middle classes, how can it appear in the homes of labourers, tradesmen and -women, coal-lumpers and other waterside workers? Was the material culture really indistinguishable from one class to another? Some historians and archaeologists would, conversely, see this plethora of genteel goods as manifestations of the same exploitation and manipulation of the proletariat which governed the production sphere of the industrial revolution. Stuart Ewan, for example, argued that 'the fantasy of consumption . . . served the important function of diverting the American working class from efforts to unite and exercise control over their work lives. Instead they were seduced by the essentially individualistic glamour of consumption.'[45] These artefacts are merely more evidence of the resounding success of the 'hegemonic offensive' in winning over hearts, minds and bodies of working people. Archaeologist Mark Leone argued, in the same vein, though for the eighteenth century, that domestic artefacts such as individualised place settings represent 'false consciousness', the imposition of dominant ideology through the alliance of capitalism and the ruling class. The rise of individual over corporate identity, and consumption itself, then, is really a cynical device to create a docile, divided workforce, to 'control wage labour and direct their workers to higher production goals'.[46] As Martin Hall remarks dryly: 'It is almost as if the possession of matched tableware turned the worker into an automaton, as if the capitalist had won the struggle for ideological control as soon as he had persuaded his laborer to adopt good table manners.' Or perhaps the dinner sets, shells and buttons, vases, teacups and jewellery represent the 'trickle down' model of culture, which Neil McKendrick implied in *Birth of a Consumer Society*. They are merely the cast-offs of slavish social emulation by which the working classes simply aped their 'betters' in order to display status or aspirations. In this model, once more, the hundreds of thousands of artefacts, particularly those which were mass-produced, would appear to be largely empty of genuine cultural meaning (Fig. 6.4).[47]

Dimensions of respectability: confluence and divergence

But if we interpret this large, consistent, and insistent, body of evidence as reflection of either exploitation, seduction or 'embourgeoisement', we surely run the risk of dismissing the most direct account we have concerning the conditions and aspirations of Rocks people themselves, of what mattered to them, and of what they were striving for in their everyday lives. For the material record to make sense in these terms, it is necessary to shift from the 'dominant ideology thesis', the 'either/or' model of culture, in which cultural identity was *exclusively* a battleground, a site for struggle and inevitable domination.[48] Archaeology demonstrates that some important cultural strands, in this case expressions of genteel culture, *were* shared across classes. Rather than a culture of repudiation, resistance and/or sheer brutal poverty, consumer

and popular material culture among the urban working classes ran parallel with, or was identical to, those of the suburban middle classes. They had similar inspirations in rising evangelicalism, with its emphasis on personal redemption, and in the culture of individual self-improvement through education, temperance and rational recreation. It did not automatically follow, however, that middle-class observers recognised this commonality, or heeded the demonstrations of respectability. At the same time, if we review the sites and assemblages as a whole – houses, yards, cesspits as well as artefacts – certain conditions, practices and tastes may be identified as other elements of a particular urban culture which was very different from that of the middle classes. And if we then reread these assemblages and the sites in their wider social contexts, important divergences in the use and meaning of some shared material culture emerge.

In the first place, a closer examination of the archaeological vista itself reveals a number of patterns of consumption and use which suggest that people there were actively choosing and shaping their material worlds, rather than being passive recipients of whatever goods manufacturers foisted upon them. From the 1850s, the range of ceramic tablewares available 'became far more extensive, though of a lesser quality' as a result of the increased mechanisation of the English potteries. But rather than their buying sets exactly as offered by the manufacturers, archaeologist Graham Wilson observed that residents of the Cumberland/Gloucester Street site often possessed sets of china in matching transfer-prints, but in different colours: blue, green, brown, grey, mulberry, purple, red and, more rarely, black. Wendy Thorp, writing about the Lilyvale site further south, noted a penchant for 'crazy' tea sets, made up of pretty unmatched china, a very personal creation of household assemblages. People also personalised common mass-produced tumblers by engraving their initials on them, and they reused, recycled, repaired and modified a great many other manufactured objects.[49]

While a large proportion of the assemblages have to do with respectability, self-improvement and control and so on, we can see that strands of more traditional pastimes also survived. The proportion of the glass assemblage relating to alcohol consumption, together with the hotels which stood on the site, indicate that drinking remained an important part of Rocks socialising, as it had been from the early days. The site's people drank wine, beer, champagne, schnapps and brandy from a great range of bottles, flasks and glasses. To outsiders, usually middle-class and evangelical people obsessed with the drinking habits of working people, the mere sight of these bottles,

Fig. 6.4 Cribb's Lane during the excavation of the site, view to west, 1994. The stone flagging on the left (above middle) was the floor of the stables shown on the left in Fig. 6.3 (where the man is standing); on the right are the remains of the early house and yard, and a glimpse of 4 Cribb's Lane, as excavated.

decanters and hotels was enough to confirm their worst suspicions of hopeless and widespread alcoholism.[50] But as historian Richard Waterhouse points out, towards the end of the nineteenth century 'there is considerable evidence to suggest that the working classes applied a high degree of discipline to their drinking'. Though there would always be some men and women for whom drinking was a debilitating problem, generally it is likely that working people distinguished between the pleasures of drinking, and drunkenness, between sobriety and teetotaling (the avoidance of drink altogether). For them sobriety, in the older sense, meant moderation, not the loss of the pleasures of drinking together.[51]

Gambling remained a popular pastime among working people, one which also continued the traditions of pleasure for its own sake, but which was marked, in horseracing at least, by small wagers and disciplined betting. The Rocks sites – Lilyvale and Cumberland/Gloucester Street – have yielded many gaming pieces manufactured from lead, or 'home-made' out of sherds of broken crockery and slate. These may well have been used in 'innocent' games, children's or adults'; equally they may have been used as counters for games involving wagering.[52]

Hidden below the floorboards, too, were some of the thirty spent cartridges from .22 and .45 calibre guns, lead shot and gun flints. The presence of such weapons and their potential for violence seem at odds along with the lamps, shell collections and figurines; they make us consider the limits of domesticity and moral order in some houses, in some lives. In the nineteenth century, guns of many types were widely available and completely unregulated. A number of .22 cartridges from No. 1 Caraher's Lane also suggest that women as well as men were gun owners and users, for they are likely to have come from the small, easily concealed 'Ladysmith', also known as the 'prostitute's favourite'.[53]

Respectable culture amongst tradespeople, labourers and housewives of the Rocks dominates the archaeological record, but there are also these concurrent signs of older cultural streams – less polite, less inhibited, not entirely pious and proper – which, like their neighbourhoods and workplaces, marked them out from middleclass people. As Waterhouse argues in his study of Australian popular culture, urban culture was a lively, complex and distinctive *blend* of traditional pastimes, new and old institutions, and rising interest in the 'private pleasures' of domestic life and 'respectable' culture. In her intimate portrait of the working-class community of the Melbourne suburb of Richmond, Janet MacCalman also outlined the importance of 'respectable' and 'unrespectable' culture as the division clearly understood and

felt among working people themselves.[54] The maintenance of respectability could not always be taken for granted. At times, and for some, it was more a struggle, fought on many fronts: in some ways between men and women, in other ways between old and new cultures; but always against the searching, accusing eyes of outsiders.

There were also undeniable economic differences in the lives of working and middle-class people. The most obvious of these, as Shirley Fitzgerald has well demonstrated, was the far more precarious financial situation of many working people, and the lower down the social scale, the more precarious was the getting of a living.[55] Much work was seasonal, irregular and on a day-to-day basis, and in many households there was little or no margin for illness, accident or strikes. Bills or fees unpaid in lean times often remained unpaid when things improved, because income only covered weekly outgoings, and could not easily cope with accumulated debts. Thus, while the notion of the male breadwinner and dependent wife and children appears to have grown stronger over the nineteenth century, many Rocks women none the less did all kinds of work to contribute to the family income.[56] Women's work – sewing, piecework, laundry work, baking, taking in lodgers – was often tied to the home so that they could also run their households and care for children.[57] This in turn meant that the idea of separate and symbolic spaces, such as the middle-class halls, drawing rooms and separate bedrooms, was an impossible luxury for most. A parlour, the equivalent of the drawing room, was a highly desired aim, and those who were better off – artisans, people who had successfully invested in real estate, the bigger shopkeepers – could maintain this room where the family's finest furniture and decorative items were displayed in pristine, glorious isolation. But with the arrival of children, and the taking in of lodgers and work, the parlour was often compromised with beds, sewing machines and work tables, and there was nothing to be done about it.[58]

We cannot ignore the stark differences in the housing conditions of the middle classes and working people. Though the interiors were characterised by comfort and domesticity, the conjoined houses of the city lined streets and lanes, not suburban avenues. Their condition depended on their age and on the conscientiousness of their owners, the landlords. Some were quite solid, comfortable and roomy, others were appalling. The houses were not swathed by calming gardens, but by the public footpaths at the front and small patch at the rear, crowded with washing and tools, rubbish and even a few chooks. Archaeology has revealed that some of these were neatly paved and regularly swept, but that others were damp, muddy patches full of rubbish pits and strewn with debris.[59] Not every house was connected to the sewer when it arrived in the 1850s, cesspits often leaked and overflowed, and people without even these threw their night soil in the street to mingle with the mud, horse droppings and rubbish. Street-making, paving and drainage were carried out constantly from the 1850s but progress seems to have been slow and the results quickly worn down or blocked up. By the end of the century, however, considerable improvements had been made to these amenities.[60]

Until late in the century, too, garbage collection was erratic, and this is probably the reason archaeologists found that rubbish – broken glass and ceramics, food scraps including meat bones – was deliberately thrown under the floorboards, choking the underfloor spaces. Alarmingly, it seems that dead dogs and cats were also sometimes disposed of in this way. The remains of two medium-sized dogs were found stowed underneath the cottage-cum-shop at 128 Cumberland Street. Another lay entombed below No. 5 Caraher's Lane.[61] What this suggests is an 'out of sight, out of mind' mentality, a culture of disguise, aimed at hiding the problems of high-density living. MacCalman suggests that respectable working-class culture and domesticity were somewhat 'obsessive', the fruits of low self-esteem and status and reactions against widespread prejudice. While the archaeology from Rocks sites suggests a much more positive and assertive cultural stance, that working people were in fact active participants in modern cultural practices, the determined efforts at domestic comfort and cleanliness among working people may also have been a kind of response, or defence, against an external urban world which was not always pleasant, just as the best suit or dress, jewellery and shoes were the repudiation of the dirty weekday work clothes that went with much manual labour.[62]

In this context we can see that certain aspects of material culture – pictures, pianos, showerbaths, thimbles – had different meanings according to who was choosing and using them.[63] The artefacts of sewing are good examples. While the association of sewing with women was practically universal in the mid- to late nineteenth century, middle-class women tended to regard needlework and embroidery as a leisured activity with which to produce goods to embellish homes, to provide and mend clothing, as presents or to do good works for charity. The sheer numbers of items of sewing equipment found on urban working people's sites, though, strongly suggests that the women there were working as seamstresses and dressmakers as well as sewing for their families. Sewing for them was work, not leisure, although, as Jane Lydon has observed, this pragmatism did not rule out the style and sentiment of Victorian domesticity. She found metal thimbles inscribed with various mottoes and messages, 'Esteem', 'Remember Me', 'Contentment', 'The Queen Forever', and some incised with floral, tendril and line motifs. For these women, paid work was *fused* with the cult of domesticity, rather than its anathema.[64]

Observations

Still, stepping back from the houses, we can see that consumer culture, and the aspirations which drove it, meant that there were many common strands between the working and middle classes, between city and suburbs. Such a common language of things, together with the many solid and neat homes, the lace-curtained windows, those yards which were tidy and neatly swept, should have allowed recognition, dialogue, sympathy and acceptance. The lone social investigators, the energetic Christian women, the parties of frock-coated gentlemen who ventured into places like the Rocks, saw and even noted many things, manners and habits which would have been familiar to them. But these observations were usually made with some *puzzlement*: they did not fit the images and rhetoric about working people and city spaces these outsiders carried about in their heads. Stanley Jevons spent a rather uneventful evening perambulating around the Rocks in search of vice in the 1850s, and noted instead people gossiping quietly on street corners or seated comfortably in their front rooms, reading, talking and sewing. Yet it did it not occur to him that his portrayal of the area as a stinking sink of the purest evil and the people as possessing 'dirty clothes, slovenly manner and repulsive countenance' might be just a little exaggerated.[65] The indefatigable Miss Danne, a teacher for the Ragged Schools, admitted in her daily journal that, after all, 'It is true very few are starving. The visitor finds houses apparently better furnished than the London garrets or cellars.' She found people not brutish, but polite and kind (if rather bemused at her self-invitation into their homes; the middle class seemed to think the sanctity and privacy of the home applied only to them). Why did she and the men who wrote the impassioned reports of the Schools' work year after year fall back on the same fearful stereotypes of drunken, loutish parents, and children who were 'polluted in heart and imagination, and corrupt and wicked of tongue'?[66] Why did the vases of flowers, the spick-and-span rooms, the soft furnishings and little ornaments make no impression on the frock-coated professional men when they barged into homes, covering their noses and making demolition orders (Fig. 6.5)?[67]

*Fig. 6.5 Rockswoman Jane Neal (*left*), wife of mariner William Kitchen Neal, with the youngest of her five sisters, Margaret. The Neals lived in Gloucester Street just south of the Cumberland/Gloucester Street site. Note their genteel clothes, the tea set on the table, and the tea cups in their hands, which, archaeology shows, were quite familiar objects to them.*

These reports, 'eyewitness' accounts and official actions were based, as Alan Mayne has argued, on pre-existing cultural assumptions and literary devices.[68] They were often aimed at fascinating and horrifying readers, or persuading them to renew subscriptions, or to convince them that official parties, committees and scientific gentlemen knew what was best for the city. And what they wrote then provided much of the 'history' of working people and their environments. Difference, poverty, poor housing, social and urban problems which did exist, were drawn out, magnified, demonised, while the obvious day-to-day fabric, the homes, families, communities and the things with which most lives were constructed and defined, remain largely invisible, unremarked. And so people continued to talk of 'the great unwashed', the ignorant and

beast-like working class, the unmitigated misery of the anonymous 'faces in the street',[69] hapless dwellers of the irredeemable 'slums'.

Acknowledgements

This chapter is based partly on the extensive and detailed collaborative work of the Cumberland/Gloucester Streets archaeological team, including Richard Mackay, Graham Wilson, Nadia Iacono, Dominic Steele, Martin Carney, Kate Holmes and Kevin Barnes, who are all to be acknowledged for their skills and scholarship, and thanked for their generosity. I also want to acknowledge the essential contribution – the conversation, inspiration and guidance – of colleagues and friends Susan Lawrence,

Linda Young and Wayne Johnson, and of the editors Alan Mayne and Tim Murray. Richard Waterhouse sustained and supported me all through the project from which this chapter springs.

Notes

1 Grace Karskens, *The Rocks: Life in Early Sydney* (Melbourne: Melbourne University Press, 1997); and 'The dialogue of townscape: the Rocks and Sydney 1788–1820', *Australian Historical Studies* 108 (1997), 88–112.

2 *Sydney Morning Herald*, 22 February 1975.

3 Max Kelly, 'Picturesque and pestilential: the Sydney slum observed 1860–1900', in Max Kelly (ed.), *Nineteenth Century Sydney: Essays in Urban History* (Sydney: Sydney University Press, 1978); Terry Kass, 'A socio-economic history of Miller's Point', report prepared for the New South Wales Department of Housing (Sydney, 1987); Wayne Mullens, 'Just who are the people in your neighbourhood? The archaeology of "the neighbourhood" in the Rocks and Millers Point', BA thesis, University of Sydney (1993); Jane Lydon, *Many Inventions: The Chinese in the Rocks, 1890–1930* (Clayton: Department of History, Monash University, 1999).

4 Kass, 'A socio-economic history', p. 14; Nathaniel Pidgeon, *The Life, Experience and Journal of Nathaniel Pidgeon* (Sydney, Smith and Gardener, 1852); Sydney Ragged Schools, *Annual Reports* (Sydney, 1861–1918); see newspaper articles reproduced in Alan Mayne, *Representing the Slum: Popular Journalism in a Late Nineteenth Century City* (Melbourne: University of Melbourne, 1990), Part 2.

5 Graeme Davison, 'The unsociable sociologist – W. S. Jevons and his survey of Sydney, 1856–8', *Intellect and Emotion: Essays in Honour of Michael Roe*, Special issue, in *Australian Cultural History* 16 (1997/8), 127–50.

6 W. S. Jevons, 'Notes for a social survey of Australian cities – The Rocks'; and 'Remarks upon the social map of Sydney', 1858–9, manuscripts, Mitchell Library, Sydney.

7 See Peter Curson and Kevin McCracken, *Plague in Sydney: The Anatomy of an Epidemic* (Sydney: New South Wales University Press, n.d.), pp. 90ff; Shirley Fitzgerald, *Sydney 1842–1992* (Sydney: Hale & Iremonger, 1992), pp. 220–2; Kelly, 'Picturesque and pestilential', p. 78.

8 Bubonic Plague Register, X647, State Records New South Wales (hereafter SRNSW); Peter Curson, *Times of Crisis: Epidemics in Sydney 1788–1900* (Sydney: Sydney University Press, 1985), p. 144; Shirley Fitzgerald, *Chippendale: Beneath the Factory Wall* (Sydney: Hale & Iremonger, 1990), pp. 75ff.

9 For example, Portia Robinson, *Women of Botany Bay: A Reinterpretation of Women in Australian Society*, revised edition (Ringwood: Penguin, 1993), p. 214; Michael Cannon, *Who's Master? Who's Man?* (Melbourne: Viking O'Neil, 1971), pp. 22–5.

10 Alan Birch and David S. MacMillan, *The Sydney Scene 1788–1960* (Sydney: Hale & Iremonger, 1962), p. 92.

11 Bernard Barrett, *The Inner Suburbs: The Evolution of an Industrial Area* (Melbourne: Melbourne University Press, 1971), pp. 3–4.

12 Max Kelly, *Anchored in a Small Cove: A History and Archaeology of The Rocks, Sydney* (Sydney: Sydney Cove Authority, 1997), pp. 66–9, 84.

13 Pers. comm., Ann Toy, Robert Griffin, Gary Crockett, Curators, Susannah Place Museum.

14 R. W. Connell and T. H. Irving, *Class Structure in Australian History* (Melbourne: Longman Cheshire, 1980), pp. 57–8. See also Frank Broeze, 'Militancy and pragmatism: an international perspective on maritime labour, 1870–1914', *International Review of Social History* 36 (1991), 165–200.

15 David Cannadine, *The Pleasures of the Past* (London: Penguin, 1989), p. 219.

16 Connell and Irving, *Class Structure*, p. 56.

17 *Ibid.*, pp. 123–5; Anne Summers, *Damned Whores and God's Police*, first published 1975 (Melbourne: Penguin, 1982), p. 166; Lynette Finch, *The Classing Gaze: Sexuality, Class and Surveillance* (Sydney: Allen & Unwin, 1993), pp. 28–9, 51.

18 Jan Kociumbas, *Possessions: The Oxford History of Australia*, vol. 2, *1770–1860* (Melbourne: Oxford University Press, 1992), pp. 223–34; Finch, *Classing Gaze*, pp. 86–7, 92.

19 Lynette Finch and Jon Stratton, 'The Australian working class and the practice of abortion 1880–1939', *Journal of Australian Studies* 23 (1988), 45–64; Judith Allen, 'Octavius Beale re-considered: infanticide, babyfarming and abortion in NSW 1880–1939', in Sydney Labour History Group, *What Rough Beast? The State and Social Order in Australian History* (Sydney: George Allen & Unwin, 1982), p. 112.

20 Connell and Irving, *Class Structure*, p. 126.

21 Finch and Stratton, 'Practice of abortion', pp. 48ff.

22 Allen, 'Octavius Beale', pp. 113–16.

23 Finch, *Classing Gaze*, p. 40; Connell and Irving, *Class Structure*, p. 126.

24 Linda Young, 'The struggle for class: the transmission of genteel culture to early colonial Australia', PhD thesis, Flinders University of South Australia (1997), esp. chap. 6; Leonore Davidoff and Catherine Hall, *Family Fortunes: Men and Women of the English Middle Class 1780–1850* (London: Hutchinson, 1987); Mary P. Ryan, *Cradle of the Middle Class: The Family in Oneida County, New York 1790–1865* (Cambridge: Cambridge University Press, 1983); Stuart Blumin, *The Emergence of the Middle Class: Social Experience in the American City 1760–1900* (New York: Cambridge University Press, 1989), pp. 155–7, 182–91.

25 Young, 'Struggle for class', esp. chap. 3.

26 Kociumbas, *Possessions*, pp. 316–17; see also Finch, *Classing Gaze*, p. 95.

27 Kociumbas, *Possessions*, pp. 209, 237.

28 E. Higginbotham, with Terry Kass and Meredith Walker, 'Archaeological management plan for the Rocks and Millers Point', report prepared for the Sydney Cove Authority and the New South Wales Department of Planning, 1991.

29 For example Finch, *Classing Gaze*, p. 2.

30 For discussion, see Grace Karskens and Wendy Thorp, 'History and archaeology in Sydney: towards integration and interpretation', *Journal of the Royal Australian Historical Society* 78:3–4 (1992), 52–75; Grace Karskens, 'Crossing over: archaeology and history at the Cumberland/Gloucester Street Site, the Rocks, 1994–1996', *Public History Review* 5/6 (1996–7), 30–48.

31 See Wendy Thorp, 'Report on the excavation at Lilyvale', draft report prepared for CRI, Sydney, 1994; Lydon, *Many Inventions*.

32 See Godden Mackay Pty Ltd in association with Grace Karskens, 'The Cumberland Street/Gloucester Street site archaeological investigation: archaeological assessment and research design', report prepared for the Sydney Cove Authority and others, Sydney, 1994. This approach was greeted with great scepticism, dire predictions and much wailing and gnashing of teeth from some senior academic and consultant archaeologists.

33 For a full account, see Grace Karskens, *Inside the Rocks: The Archaeology of a Neighbourhood* (Sydney: Hale & Iremonger, 1999).

34 Godden Mackay Heritage Consultants, *The Cumberland/Gloucester Streets Site, the Rocks: Archaeological Investigation Report*, vol. 3, 'Trench reports' (Sydney: Sydney Cove Authority, 1996). See especially Dominic Steele, 'Trench G report', pp. 287–334

35 See Karskens, *Inside the Rocks*, chap. 4.

36 This section is based on the combined findings of the archaeological team, namely Graham Wilson (ceramics), Martin Carney (glass), Dominic Steele (bone), Nadia Iacono (miscellaneous artefacts), Kate Holmes (metal) and Kevin Barnes (building materials). See Godden Mackay Heritage Consultants, *The Cumberland/Gloucester Streets Site, the Rocks: Archaeological Investigation Report*, vol. 4, 'Specialist artefact reports' (Sydney: Sydney Cove Authority, 1996).

37 Graham Wilson, 'Artefact report – ceramics' in *ibid.*

38 Young, 'Struggle for class', pp. 66ff; Wilson, 'Artefact report – ceramics', pp. 94–5.

39 Nadia Z. Iacono, 'Artefact report – miscellaneous', in Godden Mackay, *The Cumberland/Gloucester Streets Site*, vol. 4, pp. 61, 78, 80ff; see also Thorp, 'Draft report on Lilyvale site', section 4.3; compare with Neil McKendrick, John Brewer and J. H. Plumb, *The Birth of a Consumer Society: The Commercialization of Eighteenth Century England* (Bloomington: Indiana University Press, 1982), chap. 7.

40 Iacono, 'Artefact report – miscellaneous', pp. 85, 109; Alain Corbin, 'Intimate Relations', in Michelle Perrot (ed.), *A History of Private Life IV: From the Fires of Revolution to the Great War* (Cambridge, MA: Harvard University Press, 1990), p. 600. For further discussion, see Karskens, *Inside the Rocks*, chap. 5.

41 *Ibid.*, chaps. 2 and 3; Wilson, 'Artefact report – ceramics', p. 102; Iacono, 'Artefact report – miscellaneous', pp. 83–5; compare with Young, 'Struggle for class', p. 86.

42 Iacono, 'Artefact report – miscellaneous', pp. 46ff, 59ff, 71ff; Rebecca Bower, 'Artefact report – leather', in Godden Mackay, *The Cumberland/Gloucester Streets Site*, vol. 4, pp. 5–8.

43 Iacono, 'Artefact report – miscellaneous', pp. 76–7; Graeme Davison, *The Unforgiving Minute: How Australia Learned to Tell the Time* (Melbourne: Oxford University Press, 1993), pp. 66–70. For a list of the twenty-three lodges and other organisations already in existence in Sydney in 1844, see *Lowe's Directory* (Sydney, 1844), pp. 146–53.

44 Kevin Barnes, 'Artefact report – building materials', in Godden Mackay, *The Cumberland/Gloucester Streets Site*, vol. 4, pp. 11–13, 57–8; see Dominic Steele,

'Artefact report – animal bone and shell collections', in *ibid.*, pp. 13–14, 15–17, 90, 114 and pers. comm.; compare with Tom Griffiths, *Hunters and Collectors: The Antiquarian Imagination in Australia* (Melbourne: Cambridge University Press, 1996); vases and figurines see Wilson, 'Artefact report – ceramics', pp. 97, 101; lamps and metal fittings see Martin Carney, 'Artefact report – glass', in Godden Mackay, *The Cumberland/Gloucester Streets Site*, vol. 4, pp. 106–7, 133, 134 and Type Series list; and Kate Holmes, 'Artefact report – metal', in *ibid.*, pp. 26, 98ff, 136; kapok, buttons etc. see Iacono, 'Artefact report – miscellaneous', pp. 57, 59, 71; see also inventories of household goods attached to Bankruptcy Files, 1842–1922, SRNSW.

45 Stuart Ewan, *Captains of Consciousness* (New York: McGraw Hill, 1976), cited in James Carrier, *Gifts and Commodities: Exchange and Western Capitalism since 1700* (London: Routledge, 1995), p. 6.

46 Mark P. Leone, 'The Georgian order as the order of merchant capitalism in Annapolis, Maryland', in Mark P. Leone and Parker B. Potter (eds.), *The Recovery of Meaning: Historical Archaeology in the Eastern United States* (Washington, DC: Smithsonian Institution Press, 1988), pp. 235–61.

47 Martin Hall, 'Small things and the "mobile, conflictual fusion of power, fear, and desire"', in Anne E. Yentsch and Mary C. Beaudry (eds.), *The Art and Mystery of Historical Archaeology: Essays in Honor of James Deetz* (Boca Raton, FL: CRC Press, 1992), p. 384; Mary C. Beaudry, Lauren J. Cook and Stephen A. Mrozowski, 'Artifacts and active voices: material culture as social discourse', in Randall H. McGuire and Robert Paynter (eds.), *The Archaeology of Inequality: Material Culture, Domination and Resistance* (Oxford: Blackwell, 1991), pp. 156–9; McKendrick *et al.*, *Birth of a Consumer Society*, p. 11.

48 Compare with Beaudry *et al.*, 'Artifacts and active voices'.

49 Wilson, 'Artefact report – ceramics', p. 100; Thorp, 'Report on Lilyvale', section 4.3; for detailed discussion see Grace Karskens, 'Main report', in Godden Mackay, *The Cumberland/Gloucester Streets Site*, vol. 2, pp. 130–2.

50 Carney, 'Artefact report – glass', pp. 97–9.

51 Richard Waterhouse, *Private Pleasures, Public Leisure: A History of Australian Popular Culture since 1788* (Melbourne: Longman, 1995), p. 82.

52 *Ibid.*, pp. 80–1; Wilson, 'Artefact report – ceramics', p. 105; Iacono, 'Artefact report – miscellaneous', p. 82; Barnes, 'Artefact report – building materials', p. 59.

53 Holmes, 'Artefact report – metal', pp. 144ff; Simon Cook, 'Violence and the body: methods of suicide, gender and culture in Victoria, 1841–1921', paper given at the Australian Historical Association Biennial Conference, Melbourne, 1996.

54 Waterhouse, *Private Pleasures*, chap. 3. Janet MacCalman, *Struggletown: Public and Private Life in Richmond 1900–1965* (Melbourne: Melbourne University Press, 1984), pp. 20ff. Finch insists that these were merely middle-class constructs, *Classing Gaze*, pp. 14, 28.

55 Shirley Fitzgerald, *Rising Damp: Sydney 1870–1890* (Melbourne: Oxford University Press, 1987).

56 Marilyn Lake, 'Intimate strangers', in Verity Burgman and Jenny Lee (eds.), *Making a Life: A People's History of Australia since 1788* (Melbourne: Penguin, 1988), pp. 152–65.

57 For detailed discussion, see Karskens, *Inside the Rocks*, chap. 5.

58 Young, 'Struggle for class', p. 66; interview with Daphne Toni, 20 March 1996.

59 Graham Wilson, 'Trench A report', in Godden Mackay, *The Cumberland/Gloucester Streets Site*, vol. 3, pp. 16, 17, 25; Kate Holmes, 'Trench B report', in *ibid.*, pp. 10, 12, 15–19; Martin Carney, 'Trench C report', in *ibid.*, pp. 14, 19; Nadia Z. Iacono, 'Trench E report', in *ibid.*, p. 12; Dominic Steele, 'Trench G report', in *ibid.*, pp. 11, 12–13.

60 *Australian*, 16 November 1842; Richard Seymour, Inspector of Nuisances, 'Report on sanitary condition of Gipps Ward', 8 September 1868, no. 887, 26/887, Sydney City Council Archives (hereafter SCCA); for street-making and drainage see indexes and letter-books of the Sydney Corporation 1842–c. 1900, SCCA.

61 Henry Graham, Quarterly Report of the City Health Officer, 9 June 1862, no. 624, 26/57, SCCA; Holmes, 'Trench B report', pp. 17–19, and 'Artefact report – metal', p. 86; Steele, 'Artefact report – bone', pp. 84, 90; Thorp, 'Report on Lilyvale', section 4.3.

62 MacCalman, *Struggletown*, p. 28; Thorp, 'Report on Lilyvale', section 4.3.

63 Compare with Matthew Johnson, *An Archaeology of Capitalism* (CA, Mass: Basil Blackwell, 1996), p. 2; and Beaudry *et al.*, 'Artifacts and active voices', p. 166.

64 Iacono, 'Artefact report – miscellaneous', pp. 45–6; Jane Lydon, 'Task Differentiation in historical archaeology: sewing as material culture', in Hilary Du Cros and Laurajane Smith (eds.), *Women in Archaeology: A Feminist Critique* (Canberra: Australian National University, 1993), pp. 129–33.

65 Jevons, 'Notes for a social survey – Sydney by night'; see also Davison, 'Unsociable sociologist', p. 135.

66 Sydney Ragged Schools, *Annual Report:* for 1862, pp. 4, 9, 11; for 1863, pp. 6ff; and for 1881.

67 See for example 'The rookeries of the city', *Daily Telegraph* 7 January 1881; City of Sydney Improve-

ment Board, Annual Returns of Buildings and Minute Book, 1879–92, SRNSW.

68 Mayne, *Representing the Slum.*

69 Henry Lawson, 'Faces in the street' (1888), in Henry Lawson, *Poems of Henry Lawson* (Sydney: Ure Smith, 1973).

PART II

Applications and conclusions

7
Imaginary landscapes: reading Melbourne's 'Little Lon'

TIM MURRAY AND ALAN MAYNE

Background

The site which has since become known as 'Little Lon', the greater part of a city block (3,000m^3) in the centre of Melbourne, Australia, was excavated by consulting archaeologist Justin McCarthy between December 1987 and May 1988. The excavation was followed by approximately five months of artefact analysis, with the report being completed during 1989.[1] At this point the ownership of the site records, artefacts and photographs was transferred to the Museum of Melbourne (see Fig. 7.1).

McCarthy's account, which tended to support conventional historical accounts of 'Little Lon' as a slum that was occupied by people who lived at the margins of social respectability, remained unexamined for seven years despite the fact that 'Little Lon' captured the public's attention more than any of the other sites in Melbourne's core. One explanation for the lack of interest in taking analysis of the 'Little Lon' assemblage further than the construction of a descriptive catalogue was the difficulty of getting access to the assemblage, which was housed in a variety of abandoned factories and warehouses all over Melbourne. This dispersal has since been proved to have had a major (and deleterious) impact on the collection, but for most of the early 1990s it was simply an impediment to conducting serious research on 'Little Lon'.

Notwithstanding issues such as low profile or difficulty of access, the most significant explanation for this lack of interest is linked to the almost mythic quality of life at 'Little Lon', something which McCarthy's synthesis had perpetuated. In essence, urban archaeologists and historians had been given a narrative account which to all intents and purposes confirmed what they already knew

about the place. 'Little Lon' was uncontroversial, unproblematic and largely forgotten except by those who had the responsibility for curating the collection.

Two factors changed this situation. The first was disquiet, arising especially from experience in Sydney, that although many urban sites had been excavated and massive collections accumulated, archaeological analysis rarely proceeded beyond the level of descriptive catalogues.[2] For those of us involved in teaching historical archaeology outside Sydney this activity was frustrating, in that it was producing few in-depth publications of sites, contexts or artefacts. This was a much more severe case of the problems noted at 'Little Lon'. Although consultants' reports contained much valuable stratigraphic and contextual information, by the late 1980s it was becoming evident that no clear sense of the nature of such sites had emerged. It was evident, too, that there was no sustained engagement in the basic tasks of comparison and contrast, which are important parts of our search for an archaeological understanding of urbanisation in Australia and in the modern world.

Although undergraduate students completed research projects during the early 1990s based on the holdings of the Historic Houses Trust of New South Wales (NSW) – the repository of collections from sites such as the Hyde Park Barracks and First Government House in Sydney – it was by then clear that if we were to advance our understanding then a great deal more pure research had to be undertaken, both for its own sake and also to help archaeologists to avoid two serious consequences. The first of these had to do with the perpetuation of approaches to the interpretation of sites, contexts or artefacts which have not had their efficacy assessed by a thorough engagement with the material they purport to interpret or explain. The second consequence related to a need to increase radically the interpretative and explanatory output of urban archaeology in order to support arguments that urban sites, contexts and collections are significant beyond the level of media interest in the public performances of excavation and artefact cataloguing. Those authorities with the primary responsibility for managing the collections from such sites (such as the Historic Houses Trust of NSW) had begun to point out that lack of interest in the analysis of collections made it more difficult to justify the expense of curating those collections.

The second factor grew from discussions about the theoretical issues that were raised by seeking a more comprehensive integration of archaeological and historical perspectives in doing the archaeology of the modern city. We have not been alone in seeking a more convincingly materialist history of the city. Apart from the significant work of Rebecca Yamin (among others in North America),[3] Australian archaeologists – such as Grace Karskens and Richard Mackay,[4] and Jane Lydon[5] – writing about 'the Rocks' in Sydney, have been developing approaches which go beyond simple dichotomies between empirical and theoretical, and which do not dissolve the city, or indeed the neighbourhood, as categories of analysis.

With 'Little Lon' we had the chance to begin the analysis of a collection which had been to all intents and purposes ignored by historians and archaeologists. We also had the opportunity to re-evaluate McCarthy's seamless synthesis of archaeology and history, which drew so heavily upon highly problematic notions about slums.[6] In our view, even though McCarthy's methodology was right within the mainstream of Australian historical archaeology, such a methodology tended to produce conventional historical narratives larded with pots and pipes – histories which carefully avoided the disparities between such diverse sources of information and perspective. In our view, those disparities presented significant challenges to historical archaeologists, making it possible more thoroughly to explore unexamined assumptions about slums and the lives of the urban poor.[7]

From 'slum' to archaeological site

Little Lonsdale Street gained notoriety in Melbourne for much of the nineteenth and twentieth centuries as a place of vice, disease and grinding poverty. *The Age* newspaper characterised it in 1931 as 'the heart of slumdom'.[8] 'Little Lon', as the neighbourhood was locally known, had gained fame outside Melbourne from the time of the First World War, through the best-selling works by poet and journalist C. J. Dennis, *The Songs of a Sentimental Bloke* (1915) and *The Moods of Ginger Mick* (1916). Created by Dennis' verse into a place where his popular characters the Sentimental Bloke and Ginger Mick could frolic as they might, 'Little Lon' was, to use Dennis' version of the local slang, a place of 'scowlin' slums' that were the haunts of 'low, degraded broots'. Dennis' verses enabled readers to imagine 'Little Lon' as a place where the respectability of the suburbs was sharply divided from the slums of the inner city. Reworked as Slumland, Dennis' 'Little Lon' became a place of disreputable behaviour and even of violence: a place where low-life brutes 'deals it out wiv bricks an' boots'.[9]

Although Dennis' slumland was tough, it was also a place of humour. This sense of humour was noticeably absent in the longer-running discourse of moral reform-

ers. 'Little Lon' was appropriated by them as a symbol of the urban wastelands that needed to be reclaimed for decency. Representations of 'Little Lon' as an example of moral laxity were pioneered by evangelists. The Church of England's Mission to the Streets and Lanes began here in 1885, with the establishment of a mission house run by lay sisters in Little Lonsdale Street. This was the origin of the mission convent of the Sisters of the Community of the Holy Name. The Roman Catholic Church was also active in the neighbourhood. Sister Mary McKillop (who may shortly become Australia's first saint) started a slum mission in La Trobe Street in 1891, and opened the St Joseph's elementary school nearby on Little Lonsdale Street in 1897. A St Vincent de Paul Home also operated in Little Lonsdale Street. From 1927, the headquarters of the Melbourne City Mission were located on the corner of Little Lonsdale and Exhibition Streets. On the opposite corner, the Salvation Army had, since 1897, run Hope Hall as a women's shelter and – as a large sign on the pavement outside announced – the 'Headquarters of Army Slum Work'. In 1910 the Army opened a Home for Women in Little Lonsdale Street, as a citadel from which its 'Slum Sisters' could mobilise their rescue missions to slumland's fallen women. The 'Little Lon' slum stereotype thus came to overlap with the precinct's reputation as Melbourne's chief red-light district.[10]

That fame grew at the turn of the century as moral crusaders led by evangelist Henry Varley and Colonel James Barker of the Salvation Army focused their indignation upon Madame Brussels, a brothel owner in the neighbourhood since 1876. The resulting publicity ensured that, by the time of her death in 1908, Brussels was widely known as 'one of the most notorious harlot-house keepers that Australia has ever seen or heard of'.[11] The conflation of slum and brothel in common-sense understandings of 'Little Lon' owed much to the sensationalism of city newsmakers. The mass-circulation *Truth* newspaper saw the place and its moral laxity as being one and the same, and newspaper crusades against the slum as the source of vice and disease continued unabated through the 1930s and 1940s. Out-sensationalising its sensationalist newspaper rivals, the *Truth* characterised 'Little Lon' as 'the Street of Evil'.[12]

In 1948 the Commonwealth Government compulsorily acquired the blocks on either side of Little Lonsdale Street, from La Trobe Street in the north to Lonsdale Street in the south, and from Spring Street in the east to Exhibition Street in the west. Most of the northern block to La Trobe Street was bulldozed in the late 1950s and 1960s to make way for government offices. The rest of the

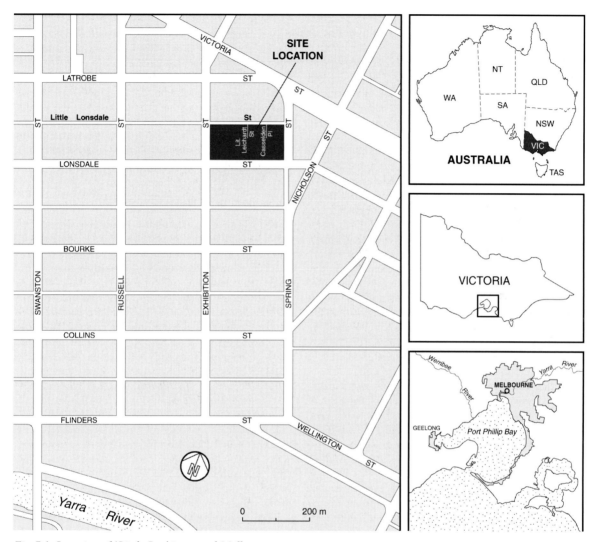

Fig. 7.1 Location of 'Little Lon' in central Melbourne.

block was cleared in the 1970s for a telephone exchange. To the south of Little Lonsdale Street, demolition and redevelopment made further inroads. This process was capped by the construction in the 1990s of two tower blocks at Little Lon's eastern and western ends: Casselden Place Commonwealth Government Offices, and the new Telstra headquarters. The excavations at the site of 'Little Lon' that we discuss in this chapter were undertaken to mitigate the impact of these last developments.

The mythology of the slum destroyed the neighbourhood of 'Little Lon'. A cluster of distorting stereotypes, the slum myth was none the less 'real' in so far as it became entrenched in the common-sense associations upon which public knowledge was built, and informed the public policies which flowed from such certainties. Today, apart from an incomplete shell of late-nineteenth-century buildings along the southern side of Little Lonsdale Street, and around the perimeter formed by Spring, Lonsdale and Exhibition Streets, the physical markers of this former community have (at least upon the surface) been obliterated. The internal laneways, and the entire block north from Little Lonsdale Street to Latrobe Street, have disappeared. Redevelopment and changing landuse from a mosaic of houses, shops, pubs and factories to office towers has created a single community of office workers in place of the great diversity that had survived in 'Little Lon' for over a century.

It is a straightforward matter to establish the consequences of all that bad press which 'Little Lon' had received since the mid-nineteenth century. It is also not particularly difficult to accept that C. J. Dennis and the social campaigners of the period were not making it all up. 'Little Lon' was indeed a place of brothels, itinerants and poor-quality housing, but it is equally true that 'Little Lon' was not *just* these things, and that the community which attracted so much attention numbered amongst its residents people who, although poor, were far removed from the stereotype of criminal, whore, degraded foreigner or itinerant pauper.

Notwithstanding half a century of 'renewal', traces of this vanished community and of its forgotten history remain. Documentary and archaeological research have provided a counterpoint to the prevailing perception of 'Little Lon' as a slum, revealing instead a working-class and immigrant community that was complex, self-reliant, and constantly changing. Our object is to tell something of the lives of the actual residents of these two central-city blocks, in place of the phantoms and caricatures that have hitherto clouded understanding of 'Little Lon'.

Writing the history of that community requires imagination, grounded in turn on the convincing integration of archaeological and historical evidence.[13] At 'Little Lon' we have based our integration on matching precise places with the historical records of such places, and then developing the analysis of place and people in tandem. Making interconnections has not been easy. Not that meshing archaeological and historical evidence ever is, as one moves backwards and forwards between particular contexts and broader frameworks. However, at 'Little Lon' the interplay between hermeneutics and imagination was especially potent, because the loss of many of the photographs and some key elements of the paper records (such as level books and contexts sheets) from the excavation has severely limited the quality of the data we have to work with, thereby restricting our analysis to an establishment of artefact frequencies and to exploring the meaning of the counter-intuitive patterns which are discussed in this chapter. Thus we have had to fall back on the grosser analytical scales of quadrants within barely glimpsed historical sites, that we have painstakingly reconstructed from incomplete excavation notes and surviving historical plans.

In this chapter we will focus discussion of our reanalysis of the archaeological and documentary evidence on the period between 1850 and 1880, with particular emphasis

on the remains of houses located in Casselden Place (see Figs. 7.1 and 7.2). The reanalysis, focused initially on the object of deriving archaeologically useful information from the excavations, has allowed us to detect counter-intuitive patterns in the archaeology of Casselden Place and elsewhere at 'Little Lon'. Making sense of those patterns, in the context of the clear limits set by the structural properties of the Casselden Place record as it has been reconstructed by us, has emphasised the need to work towards new ways of writing the historical archaeology of the modern city.

Archaeological and historical analysis

The following discussion reports the results of the reanalysis of the excavated houses in Casselden Place (which had been known until the mid-1870s as Whelan's Lane), and concentrates on reporting the archaeology of two home sites: locations 74B and 69 (Fig. 7.2). We have selected these two sites because their documentary and archaeological records allow us to explore whether different patterns of residential occupancy create archaeological records which have different structural properties. Archival research indicated that location 74B had been occupied by many short-term tenants during the course of the second half of the nineteenth century. Location 69 was the exact opposite, being occupied by the same family for over forty years.

It is possible to identify 19 similar locations along the lane as it evolved between 1850 and 1900, together with some 300 principal tenants (not including spouses, children, and sub-tenants) and 50 owners who were associated with them. Integrated archaeological and documentary data are available for nine of these sites: a collection of cottages along the western side of Casselden Place (one of which is Location 74B) and, on the opposite side, the Moloney–Neylan site (Location 69) and a house site adjoining it.

Five two-roomed wooden cottages were erected along the western side of Whelan's Lane in 1851. On the basis of municipal documents and maps we have inferred that each house had a yard. Probably each had a cesspit as well. We only have clear evidence of cesspits at the house sites of No. 7 and No. 9, but it is possible that others were located in the unexcavated portions of No. 11 and No. 15.[14] At least one of the houses is recorded as having a shed for a workshop. John Casselden, a local newsagent, bought the properties in 1871. He submitted a building application in 1876 to erect six brick cottages on the site of the five wooden cottages and an adjoining unoccupied block (No. 17, at the northern end of his property). By

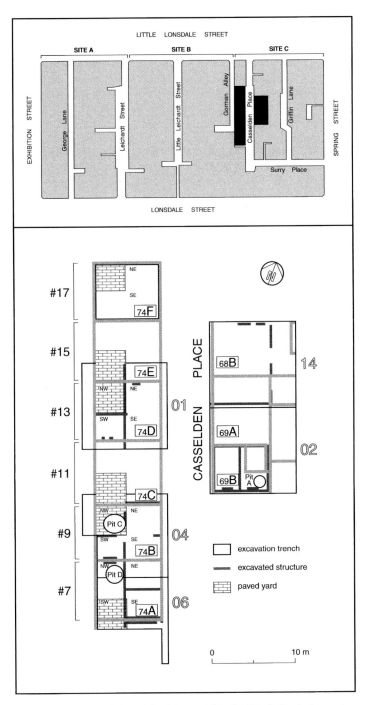

Fig. 7.2 Location of Casselden Place within the 'Little Lon' site, and the excavated areas discussed in the text.

1878 these had been built: each consisting of three small rooms and a yard. The layout of these houses remained substantially unaltered until they were demolished (with the exception of No. 17) in the 1960s.

The bluestone foundations of these later brick buildings were uncovered by McCarthy's excavation in 1987–8, and provide the framework within which the material finds have been analysed. The excavators did not identify the foundations of the earlier wooden structures, although two cesspits (which we argue date back to this earlier period) were revealed. Excavation located these cesspits in the north-west quadrant of house No. 7 and the north-west quadrant of house No. 9 (marked as pit D and pit C in Fig. 7.2). The City Council had since the early 1870s phased out cesspits in favour of a municipal pan service, and follow-up legislation in 1876 allowed municipalities to prohibit the construction of new cesspits. A comprehensive sewerage system was established from 1897 onwards.[15] It is therefore highly likely that the cesspits in Casselden Place date to the wooden house period. As we will discuss, the artefacts recovered from the cesspits are generally consistent with these dates, with the exception of some more modern material (such as a plastic ballpoint pen and pieces of vinyl) that may have been introduced when the site was levelled.

Figure 7.2 illustrates the location of the trenches excavated in Casselden Place, the historical locations that they correspond to, the foundations revealed by their excavation, and the layout of the brick houses as recorded on the Melbourne Metropolitan Board of Works plans of 1896. Excavation trenches across the site were based upon a grid system that had been laid across the area by the Australian Survey Office. These are shown as numbers (01, 04 etc.) in Fig. 7.2. Most excavation trenches were 10 × 10 metres. These were sometimes truncated by the edges of the site and extant buildings, or extended where items of interest were recovered or to meet site/building boundaries. Overlaying this trench system are historically defined locations which roughly correspond to the location of individual blocks (and their subdivisions) as recorded in Board of Works plans. These are shown as letters (74A, 74B, etc.) in Fig. 7.2. There is no direct correlation between the placement of trenches and historical locations, and therefore a single trench may include portions of a number of different historical locations (and vice versa). The street numbers of the brick houses (Nos. 7–17) are marked on Fig. 7.2.[16] It is worth reiterating that the loss of crucial elements of the excavation records has meant that artefact provenance cannot be made more specific than this, and that our reconstruction to this level relies on some (we think reasonable) assumptions.

Excavations from the row of houses along the western side of Casselden Place yielded 50,777 individual items. This area was not completely excavated, with three excavation trenches (01, 04 and 06) uncovering the complete foundations of houses No. 7, No. 9 and No. 13, while houses No. 11 and No. 15 remained unexcavated. At the time of excavation most of the area where this row of houses had stood was covered by a bitumen car park. However house No. 17, at the northern end of the row, was still standing. In 1995 an excavation of the immediate below-floor surface of two of the rooms in No. 17 was undertaken by the consultants Du Cros and Associates. The information obtained from this excavation has also been recorded by our project.

No. 9 Casselden Place

No. 9 Casselden Place stood towards the southern end of the row of houses that Casselden built along the western side of the lane. The foundations recovered during excavation demonstrate that the basic plan of the house was exactly the same as that of No. 7 next door, which we have described in detail elsewhere.[17] However, surviving plans from the period indicate that the internal layout of No. 9 was in fact the reverse of No. 7. The yard of No. 9 was located in the north-west quadrant, where a cesspit was also found. The bluestone foundation of a fireplace was identified along the southern wall of the south-east quadrant. In 1851–2 the structure was described in the Melbourne City Council valuation books as a wooden two-roomed house with a value of £16. After the erection of Casselden's brick buildings along this strip it was described in 1878 as a brick house of three rooms, with a rateable value of £18. This house is covered by excavation Trench 04 and its historical location designation is 74B.

A total of 9,788 items were recorded at 74B and, after closely examining the excavation records, we could assign almost 80 per cent of these to rooms within the brick house (the footings of the interior walls being used by the excavators as recovery units) (see Fig. 7.3).

Just over 45 per cent of the items were glass, but relatively high proportions of bone and ceramic were also recorded. Most of the lithic items are roofing slate and the miscellaneous items are predominantly charcoal, coal and building materials.

Only 880 items were recovered from the cesspit located in the north-west quadrant (Fig. 7.4). The cesspit contained a lower proportion of glass than was found across the rest of the site, and a higher percentage of ceramic. A high proportion of the miscellaneous items were also identified in the cesspit contents (Fig. 7.5).

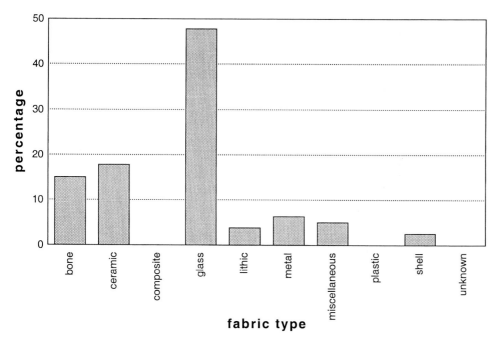

Fig. 7.3 9 Casselden Place: percentage of each fabric type present.

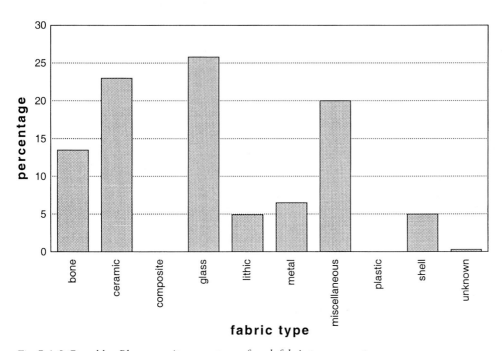

Fig. 7.4 9 Casselden Place cesspit: percentage of each fabric type present.

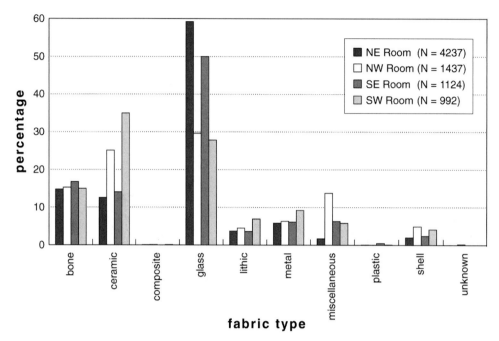

Fig. 7.5 9 Casselden Place: percentage of each fabric type present per room (calculated as percentage of total number of items per room).

Almost half of the assemblage was recovered from the north-east quadrant, with the lowest amounts of materials coming from the two southern quadrants. About 60 per cent of the items recovered from the north-west quadrant came from the cesspit. The highest proportion of glass was located in the north-east quadrant, which also had the lowest proportions of bone and ceramic. The south-east quadrant also contained a low proportion of ceramic and a relatively high proportion of glass and bone. The highest proportion of ceramic was in the south-west quadrant, which contained little glass, while the north-west quadrant had a relatively high proportion of ceramic and a high proportion of the miscellaneous items and shell (Fig. 7.6).

The highest proportion of domestic items was in the south-west quadrant, which had the lowest proportion of items associated with recreational activities. The highest proportion of recreational items was in the north-east quadrant, which, conversely, had the lowest proportion of domestic items.

The majority of cup fragments were located in the north-east quadrant, as were most of the marbles, pieces of oval platter, saucers, clay pipes, and beer and alcohol bottles. There were no cup fragments and few plates in the south-east quadrant. All the pieces of plant pot were from

the north-west quadrant (the yard), which also contained a relatively high proportion of saucers but few plates. The bone and shell assemblage was very similar to that recorded at 7 Casselden Place.[18]

Over half of the glass assemblage was dark green and about a quarter clear (most of which was window glass). Medium-green glass used for champagne and wine bottles was relatively uncommon. Several pieces that conjoined to form a single Codd-style ball stopper were identified. This is one of only two bottles of this type that have so far been located across the entire 'Little Lon' site. However, many small glass and ceramic marbles that would have formed the stoppers of this form of bottle have been recovered. Codd's ball stoppers were patented in the USA in 1870 and therefore this item must post-date that time.

Over 78 per cent of the ceramic assemblage is earthenware, 14 per cent porcelain and 7 per cent stoneware. Decorative styles include a similar range to those identified at 7 Casselden Place.[19] Over half of the ceramics are transfer-printed, but 3 per cent are flow wares, 5 per cent hand-painted, 28 per cent plainwares and 5 per cent salt-glazed. Ten pieces are gilt, five are Rockingham, one is transfer-printed with flow, and three are transfer-printed with paint. Some pieces of porcelain and stoneware were clearly from Chinese items. A fragment of 'moralising

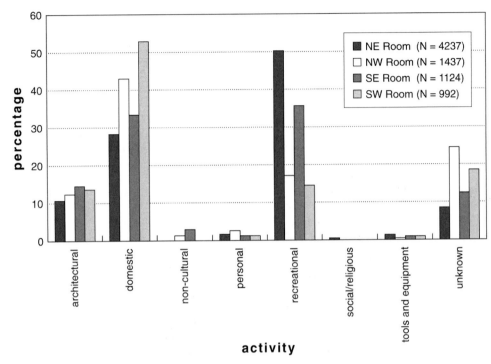

Fig. 7.6 9 Casselden Place: percentage of different activities represented in each room (calculated as percentage of total number of items in each room).

china' was also identified.[20] The most common transfer-print colour was blue (at 77 per cent, although a range of other colours were also present); 85 different transfer-print patterns were identified on 789 pieces.

Among the inevitable clay pipe fragments, bottle glass, coins and tokens and pieces of flatware were objects that expressed the great variety of material culture used and disposed of by the people of Casselden Place. A fly button from the uniform of a Victorian Police Officer and a small figurine of a naked Lady Godiva lie in the same contexts as (among other things) a complete porcelain figurine of a child seated on a dog, a piece of stocking with a brass suspender attachment, thirty-two dressmaker's pins, and a pair of small sewing scissors.

No. 9 in the context of Casselden Place

Generally the Casselden Place houses have similar assemblages that exhibit similar spatial patterns. In all the houses, the vast majority of items were recovered from the north-east quadrant, with a significantly lower proportion being recovered from those to the south. In the later brick buildings the yards were adjoining between sets of houses so that the yard at No. 7 was in the south-west, No. 9 in the north-west, No. 11 in the south-west, No. 13 in the north-west, and so on. While it might be expected that houses No. 9, No. 13 and No. 17 would all show a similar pattern owing to their comparable layouts, with the yard in the north-west quadrant, it is surprising that this pattern of artefacts is also observed at house No. 7, where the layout is different and the yard is in the south-west quadrant. It is also unclear why the cesspit at house No. 7 is in the north-west quadrant and not in the yard. It is likely that the patterning of the artefacts and the location of cesspits reflects the layout of the earlier two-roomed wooden houses, when the yard may have covered the entire western side of the block and the cesspit was always located in the north-west corner, rather than the layout of the later brick structures. The overall low number of artefacts in the north-west (if the items recovered from the cesspits are excluded from analysis) and south-west quadrants may support the suggestion that this area was once part of the yard. It is also possible that the layout of house No. 7 has changed over time from that depicted on the 1896 plan, where the yard is clearly in the north-west, though this seems an unlikely explanation.

It may be that the high number of items in the north-east quadrant in each house reflects the type of flooring in this room. The Du Cros consultants noted wooden flooring in the north-east and south-east rooms of 17 Casselden Place, whereas the kitchen (the south-west room) had a concrete floor. The concrete would have been a twentieth-century addition, disturbing any deposits associated with the earlier wooden or earthen floor. This would explain the presence of more small items that fell between the floorboards of the north-east and south-east rooms, but it does not explain the presence of larger items such as crockery, unless these were deposited by residents pulling up the floorboards as has been noted in 'the Rocks'.[21] It also does not explain the large disparity in the number of items recovered from the north-east and south-east quadrants in all the houses. Given the repeated nature of this pattern, we find ourselves in something of a quandary, because the bulk of the artefacts are thought to reflect occupation of the earlier wooden houses, rather than the later brick ones.

In our view this problematic data set is most reliably interpreted as representing a palimpsest. At all levels of the site, older items are interspersed with material from later periods. Even in the supposedly *in situ* deposits, tokens from the 1850s, ceramics manufactured no later than 1862 and pre-1870-style bottles intermingle with pieces of plastic and a 1951 penny.

The inhabitants of Location 74B
To whom did these artefacts from 9 Casselden Place belong? The documentary record allows us to establish that the two houses on this site were occupied by a succession of short-term tenants. Like much of the rest of Victoria at this time, the Casselden Place neighbourhood was one of young families with small children.

Ellen Connell from Dublin and her husband James Hart, a labourer from County Sligo, lived in the wooden house on the site of 9 Casselden Place from 1862 to 1866–7. The couple and their three surviving children had moved from around the corner in Little Lonsdale Street, not long after the death of their 10-month-old son. Another daughter and son were born in Whelan's Lane (Casselden Place). After their second son died aged 6 months in 1866, the family moved again, to West Melbourne. Michael Cummings, a young Irish butcher, his Adelaide-born wife Mary Alphey, and their two infant daughters lived in the wooden house during the early 1870s.[22]

Thereafter, until its demolition to make way for the brick cottage row, the house was tenanted by another young couple, William Taylor and Elizabeth Hall.

William, an English immigrant, laboured for a living. Elizabeth was Victorian born. She was the niece of Mary Atkins and her husband Richard, who were long-time local residents. The Atkins lived in Whelan's Lane/Casselden Place from 1868 to 1886, and thereafter around the corner in Little Lonsdale Street for the remainder of the century. Elizabeth and William Taylor may have stayed briefly with the Atkins family before moving into their own home in Whelan's Lane. They had moved from nearby Bouverie Street in south Carlton, after the death of their 13-week-old daughter late in 1871. A son was born in the new home in December 1874.

When the wooden house was demolished, the Taylors moved into the southernmost of Casselden's new cottages (No. 7, adjoining the site of their previous residence), and they lived there until the mid-1880s. Leonard Frewer, a young Victorian-born man, who worked variously as a storeman and a labourer, lived next door to them between 1879 and 1885 in the new brick house that had been built at 9 Casselden Place. In 1881 he married Margaret Bogle, a dressmaker. The newlyweds became friends with the Atkins, and the Cunningham family who lived at the end of the lane. Leonard and Richard Atkins acted as witnesses for David Cunningham's will in 1879. When the Frewers moved into another of Casselden's row-houses, Michael Carney, a newsagent, rented No. 9 until almost the end of the century.

The overall similarity of patterns of residence in the Whelan's Lane/Casselden Place cottages might help account for the similarity in the overall structure of the assemblages recovered from those sites. This assumption can be tested by comparison with the assemblage derived from Location 69, on the opposite side of the lane, which is a site with a very different residential history.

Location 69
From the historical records it appears that a structure had existed on Location 69A (Trench 02 north) since 1851 (as marked in Fig. 7.2). This building was described in Melbourne City Council valuation books as a wooden house of three rooms. Between 1857–63 it is further described as having a cowshed or shed. A three-roomed brick house was built in the yard in 1887, and the older wooden house was demolished *c.* 1891.

No remains of the wooden house were uncovered by excavation. However bluestone foundations were found in the southern portion of Trench 02 on Location 69B. These presumably belong to the brick house that was built in the yard during 1887. A wood-lined cesspit is located in the south-eastern corner of Trench 02 (marked as A in Fig. 7.2), placing it within Location 69B (and also within

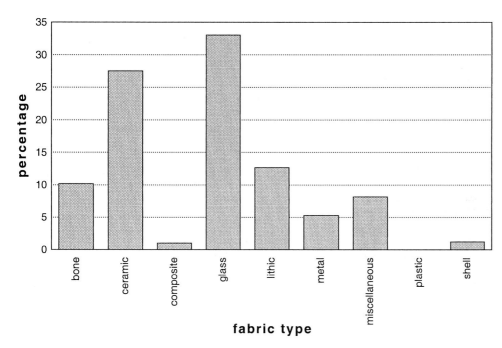

Fig. 7.7 *East Casselden Place Trench 2: percentage of each fabric type present.*

the bluestone foundations of the 1887 house). This cesspit must date to a period before the brick house was built, given that the use of cesspits was wound back by the City of Melbourne after 1870.[23] It is probable that this cesspit was once in the backyard of the house on 69A. For the purposes of this paper we will focus our discussion on Trench 02 as the location which most directly corresponds to the home which the Moloney–Neylan family occupied between 1855 and 1901.

Trench 02
Excavation of this trench yielded 9,335 artefacts. While almost all of these were excavated from within the house foundations, only about one third could be located within any one of its rooms, and of these all but twelve came from the south-east quadrant of the house. 2,534 of the 3,561 items from this quadrant were identified from cesspit deposits, and the rest came from the small area of *in situ* demolition deposits in the south-east corner that immediately overlay the cesspit (Fig. 7.7).

Just under 35 per cent of the items recorded in Trench 02 are glass and just below 30 per cent are ceramic. Bone makes up about 10 per cent of the assemblage, and there is also a high proportion of lithics (predominantly slate roofing tiles). The miscellaneous items are mostly wood, charcoal, coal, mortar and plaster (Fig. 7.8).

Of the items recorded, 2,534 were recovered from the cesspit located in the south-east quadrant. Over 42 per cent of the material within the pit was ceramic, about 18 per cent glass, and about 14 per cent bone. Miscellaneous material made up 11 per cent, and other materials were a minor component. These percentages demonstrate that a higher proportion of the cesspit assemblage was ceramic and bone, and a lower proportion glass and lithic, compared to the overall pattern observed within the trench (Fig. 7.9).

The activities that are represented by the assemblage are predominantly domestic, with less than 20 per cent attributed to recreational pastimes such as smoking and consuming alcohol. Of these domestic items, 58 per cent are tablewares and 33 per cent are associated with food (such as animal bones and food containers). A large quantity of architectural materials – mainly building rubble, slate tiles, nails and bricks – was also recorded. The bone assemblage is a typical domestic assemblage, similar to those recorded at Casselden's houses on the opposite side of the lane. Sheep, cow and chicken were present, as well as rat and mouse. Shell species identified were oyster, mussel and turbo. Just under 45 per cent of the glass is from dark-green beer/wine bottles and case gin bottles, and there is also a large proportion of clear glass, mostly from windows. Medium-green champagne and

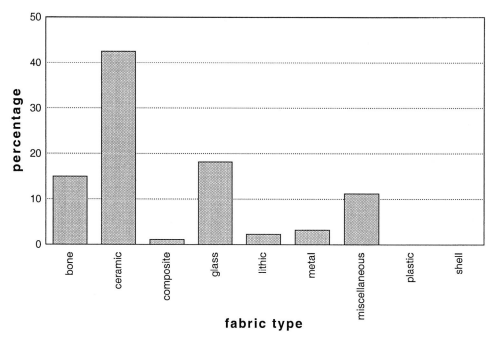

Fig. 7.8 East Casselden Place cesspit in Trench 2: percentage of each fabric type present.

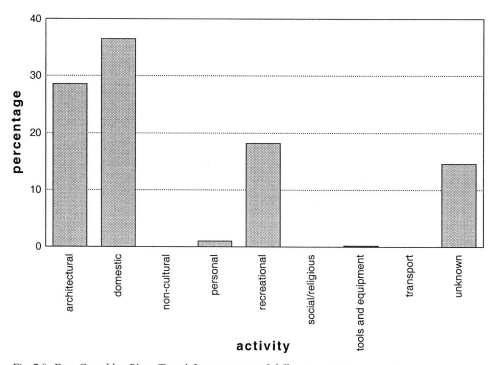

Fig. 7.9 East Casselden Place Trench 2: percentage of different activities present.

wine bottle glass, as at 9 Casselden Street, is relatively uncommon. None of the glass contained recognisable marks.

Most of the ceramics in the assemblage are earthenwares (81 per cent), with only 6 per cent porcelain and about 12 per cent stoneware. Ceramics demonstrate the same range of forms already noted at Casselden's houses (cups, plates, bowls, mugs, jugs, milk jugs, chamber pots, basins, oval platters, pitchers, serving bowls and small plates), as well as an almost complete large terracotta crock, partially glazed in black, that was found within the cesspit deposits. Five pieces of Chinese ceramic were identified: three pieces of a dark-coloured saltglazed container, one piece of hand-painted porcelain, and a piece from a green-glazed ginger jar. About 46 per cent of the ceramics are transfer-printed, 6 per cent are flow ware, 4 per cent hand-painted, 26 per cent plainware and 9 per cent saltglazed. Twenty items are gilt and one is Rockingham. Most of the transfer-printing is in blue, but other colours are also represented; 102 different transfer-print patterns were identified from 1,129 pieces.

The inhabitants of Location 69

We have noted that the excavators recovered over 2,500 artefacts from the cesspit that was used by the people who lived in the wooden house. This dwelling had been built in 1851 by a labourer named Lewis Hawkins. It was bought in 1855 by John Moloney, an Irish labourer who had arrived from County Clare in 1849, aged 24. John lived here until his death in 1882, along with his younger brother Edward and elder sister Hannah. They may also have taken in their younger sister Margaret after her partner Patrick Neylan died in 1866. Margaret had left Ireland with Hannah and their eldest brother Thomas in 1851. She lived in the cottage with Hannah after John died, and became its sole proprietor upon Hannah's death in 1886. Margaret built the three-roomed brick house over the filled-in cesspit during 1886–7, and later demolished the old wooden house. She lived here until her own death in 1901, aged 82.[24]

The information derived from the Melbourne City Council rate books and other documentary sources demonstrates that the Moloneys do not fit the slum image of rootless paupers. The Moloneys lived in Casselden Place for half a century. John Moloney was not a rich man, but he owned his house outright. He had worked successfully as a gold-miner on the diggings, and invested in property. So did his *de facto* brother-in-law, Patrick Neylan, who owned a hotel in the adjoining inner suburb of Carlton. Margaret piously left 10 pounds in her will 'to the Dean [of] . . . St Patrick's Cathedral for masses for the repose of

my soul'.[25] Patrick's will named her his wife, and Margaret in her turn bequeathed her house to the widow of her stepson. Like her brother and her partner, Margaret was not without means, and when the family home was condemned as a 'slum' by the City Council in 1886, she had it rebuilt in brick.

Analysis of the cesspit assemblage from the first Moloney house allows us to match domestic refuse with a particular family for a period of over thirty years. Therefore we can say, for example, that the Moloneys had several pieces of Spode china, some of it made between 1829 and 1833: in other words, it was either passed on from an earlier generation and brought with them from Ireland, or it was purchased second hand in Australia. They decorated their home with Staffordshire figurines, one commemorating the Death of Nelson and one a Shepherdess. A George III threepence was lost in the cesspit, in which was also found a military button and the remains of a cat. The items are mundane, but that is their interest: these are the remains from a poor home that was occupied by the same family for nearly fifty years. The fact that the structural properties of the deposits from 9 Casselden Place (a house with a very different pattern of occupancy from that of the Moloneys) were in essence so similar to the Moloney house allows us to begin to re-evaluate a simple correlation between slum dwelling and itinerant lifestyles. The richness of the deposits in places which were understood to be occupied by the poorest elements of Melbourne society opens other pathways for us to explore.

Integrating archaeological and documentary evidence

The excavation strategy adopted at 'Little Lon' by the consultants meant that not all the cottage sites along Casselden Place were excavated. None the less, we argue that a robust pattern exists across the majority of the cottage sites, including that occupied by the Moloneys. In general terms the preliminary results of our admittedly restricted reanalysis indicate that these sites have similar assemblages exhibiting similar spatial distributions within the foundations of the later brick cottages. In all the houses the vast majority of items were recovered from the north-east quadrant, with a significantly lower proportion being recovered from those to the south. Owing to the fact that there are many ambiguities in the spatial and temporal distribution of the artefacts, partly the outcome of the complex formation processes operating on urban archaeological sites, partly to the history of the excavation records, we have concluded that we must consider these sites to be palimpsests of occupation spanning both the wood and brick house phases.

In the case of the row of cottages on the western side of Casselden Place, this conclusion means that we cannot, with any degree of confidence, interpret the assemblages (either from the cesspits or the trenches) at the level of the individual occupants. Although this does not necessarily apply to our interpretation of Location 69 (the Moloney–Neylan site), there is a significant tension between the admittedly problematic generalisations of the archaeological analysis and the fine-grained specificity of the historical documents.

The *documentary evidence* about the house sites on both sides of the street confirms that Casselden Place was a poor neighbourhood. Its houses were small, and municipal rate assessors gave them a low rating. As such they formed the bottom of the rental housing market, places where newly arrived immigrants could find shelter for their families. Casselden Place was cheap. At a time when 'ordinary houses' were let for 12 to 15 shillings and more per week, two brick cottages of two rooms next door to the Moloney–Neylan house were let at 7 shillings per week in 1884, and Casselden's brick row-houses rented at 8 shillings each per week in 1888.[26] These small houses were crammed with people. In 1892 the principal tenant of the property next door to Margaret Neylan was fined 'for allowing twelve people to sleep in one room, seven in each bedroom, and three or four in two other rooms'.[27] The occupants were Indians.

But for much of the period between 1850 and 1900 the majority of the lane's residents – such as the Harts, the Cummings, the Taylors and the Moloneys – were Irish immigrants. Some of the houses were fully occupied by members of the same family; others offered space to single immigrants who were passing through, seeking work. Facilities for hygiene – running water, waste removal – were basic. Rear yards held overflowing cesspits, and rubbish was disposed of beneath the floors. Life here was consequently hazardous for infants, and deaths from diseases such as diarrhoea were common.

Casselden Place was poor and crowded, but it was not a homogeneous place of outcasts. The documentary evidence does not support the claims by anti-slum crusaders that violence and criminality were endemic to the lane. Indeed there is evidence of the reverse. In 1880 John Moloney and his brother (and neighbour) Thomas, together with Richard Atkins, Anne Cunningham, John Casselden and other local residents, wrote to the Commissioner of Police to complain about several brothels in Cunningham Place, which intersected with the end of Casselden Place:

These houses are inhabited by the lowest class of abandoned women who congregate on the footpaths using the most disgusting language openly and boldly soliciting prostitution from passers-by and rendering it unsafe and annoying for any of us to leave our residences during the evening.[28]

Prostitutes rubbing shoulders with families: the actuality of these laneways was pastiche, not slum. Documentary evidence shows that Casselden Place was populated by people with a wide diversity of manual occupations (both skilled and unskilled). Most were renters. Some – such as the Moloneys – were homeowners. A few – such as John Casselden – operated small businesses (in his case a newsagency), and accumulated sufficient capital to purchase multiple real estate in the area. Children from labouring families – if they survived childhood – often moved into skilled trades and the professions. Tenants lived alongside owner occupiers, and landlords lived in the street or close at hand. The documents also show that the children of Casselden Place and adjacent streets married each other, a few staying in the immediate area, the bulk moving into nearby suburbs to pursue their fortunes. Notwithstanding the fact that, with few exceptions such as the Moloneys and John Casselden, the majority of Irish immigrants gradually moved away from the area, a sense of community had been created and was long sustained. Probate papers, inquests and the correspondence files of the City Council and the Police Department attest to this neighbourliness.

The *archaeological record* of Casselden Place is very difficult to integrate into this fine-grained documentary analysis. The key point to emerge from our preliminary and quite rudimentary analysis is the remarkably low level of variability in assemblage structure and composition between houses occupied by the same people (such as the Moloneys at Location 69), and those (such as Location 74B: the Harts, the Cummings and the Taylors) which experienced a more rapid turnover of occupants. Although the houses were occupied by people of no great means, the archaeology reveals a wide variety of material culture being discarded in such places, ranging from tools of trade to dinner services. They purchased (and discarded) a great many material possessions associated with all aspects of everyday life. The working people of Casselden Place were avid consumers of a wide range of domestic material culture.

Rereading 'Little Lon'

The apparent homogeneity of the total Casselden Place assemblage (and the real possibility that spatial distribution is also homogeneous between the houses), in a context which the historical records clearly show to have been occupied by a number of different tenants over the period between 1850 and 1900, raises three obvious questions. Given the limitations placed on the sophistication of the analysis we have been able to undertake up to this time, how real are the patterns identified on the basis of simple percentages? How might we account for this counter-intuitive pattern, and how worthwhile was our initial expectation that there should be a strong distinction between the archaeological signatures of short-term and long-term residency?

It seems clear enough that, given the special problems raised by the Casselden Place record, we cannot convincingly answer the first question at this site. We will, however, get a much better idea of how real such patterns are by exploring domestic sites where such problems of data quality do not exist. Turning to the other questions we can observe that given the developing scale and power of mass production and mass consumption during the period covered by the Whelan's Lane/Casselden Place objects, it perhaps should not be surprising that there are clear patterns of similarity in assemblage composition which overlie the great diversity of items which were used and deposited by the residents. But it is also true to say that comparative studies from Australian sites which would help us to establish whether there is much value in this analysis are not yet numerous or published in an accessible fashion. On the other hand, the identity of Casselden Place as a community must also be understood through analysis of the singular, the different, the heterogeneous. Apart from observing that reconciling these differing perspectives is a task that awaits us, it is also worth noting that significant puzzles and problems thrown up here at 'Little Lon' are common enough in the archaeology of any modern city.

We can identify some of the more obvious puzzles raised by our initial work at 'Little Lon'. Is this homogeneity of assemblage structure a function of the economies of supply in a world shifting at great speed towards mass consumption during the last three decades of the nineteenth century? If this is so, in such a levelling or conventionalising environment is it possible (or indeed even worthwhile) to seek to establish linkages between place and identity, between uniqueness and specific histories? This is obviously a huge question, but we need to go a little further and understand that homogenisation may well be masking the kinds of heterogenising processes which reflect the establishment of identities which slum reformers in the late nineteenth and early twentieth centuries did so much to stamp out. We need to go deeper, past the descriptive statistics which talk of homogeneity, in order to tackle more difficult questions of value and meaning.

That these questions not only exist but have proved difficult to answer convincingly supports our overall goal of demonstrating that we need, as historical archaeologists, to rethink the viability of long-held totalising notions such as the 'slum'. We have had the chance at 'Little Lon' to begin what is going to be a long process of learning to link people, material culture and archaeological contexts at specific sites and within vanished communities. Certainly the documentary record holds out tremendous possibilities for delivering a level of information about the social history of 'Little Lon' which was hitherto considered to be either impossible or difficult to make archaeologically meaningful. It is also quite clear that the archaeology is far more equivocal. Selecting the appropriate scale of comparison and generalisation between and among archaeological records – be they an excavation quadrant, the remains of a house, a row of houses such as Casselden Place, a city block such as 'Little Lon' (or even wider still) – has proved to be a significant challenge (modelled in Fig. 7.10). It seems self-evident that we should want to range from the very specific analysis of place, such as 9 Casselden Place and all of its registered occupants, to a consideration of the depositional palimpsest which is the archaeological reality of such a place. Obviously this is situational, but in general we have begun to understand that, at its most inclusive, the archaeology of the modern city is the archaeology of the modern world.

It is a natural concern to many that, as one moves away from the specificities of place and the particular nexus between individuals, place and time, the sense and importance of those specificities (the things which make people real flesh and blood beings in the past) will be lost. It has been argued that in its place a levelling, conventionalising, dehumanising generalisation of human lives will grow up – an outcome which has previously characterised much social history of 'slums'. Acknowledging that there is an inevitable loss of detail and focus as one moves around the circle of increasing generalisation (refer to Fig. 7.10) does not mean that one cannot return to the specificities of place with new perspectives drawn from the wider world. In the case of 'Little Lon' we are only too aware that these important specificities of place, people and time are themselves the products of concepts, categories and units of analysis which are built from acts of comparison and generalisation. Indeed to argue otherwise would be to accept that, at all levels of discussion, every historical or archaeological observable must be unique. This is an

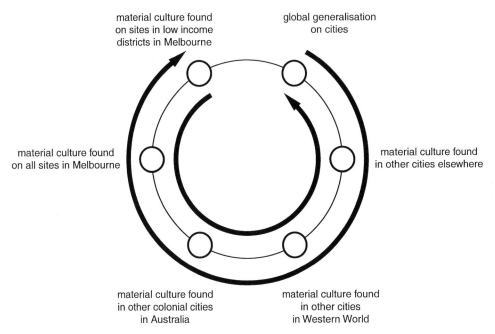

material culture found
on sites in low income
districts in Melbourne

global generalisation
on cities

material culture found
on all sites in Melbourne

material culture found
in other cities elsewhere

material culture found
in other colonial cities
in Australia

material culture found
in other cities
in Western World

Fig. 7.10 Modelling a research strategy into global material culture in urban settings, 1830–1950.

argument that would effectively spell the end of our search for understanding.

At 'Little Lon' we are faced with the pragmatic problem of attempting to integrate the archaeological and historical records of the site in ways which can give us a sense of working-class inner-city neighbourhoods during the mid- to late nineteenth century. In the absence of fundamental data about people and things in Melbourne (or for the greater part of Sydney), we cannot yet fully describe the specificities of Casselden Place. To do this we have to compare, generalise and contrast, but our goal of seeking such an intense engagement with people and place will mean that it will be vital for us to move back as well as to move forward in order to write our history of the modern city.

Acknowledgements

We owe a great deal to Christine Williamson (who undertook the re-analysis of the 'Little Lon' collection) and Kasia Zygmuntowicz (who researched the historical documents). Wei Ming drew the maps and the graphs (based on the work of Christine Williamson). We also thank Gary Pearson and John Scarce at the Victorian Registry of Births, Deaths and Marriages. Susan Lawrence read earlier drafts of this chapter, and shared

the results from parallel research on 'Little Lon'. We thank her.

Notes

1 Justin McCarthy, *Archaeological Investigation: Commonwealth Offices and Telecom Corporate Building Sites. The Commonwealth Block, Melbourne, Victoria*, 5 vols.

2 There are some notable exceptions, such as Godden Mackay Heritage Consultants, *The Cumberland/ Gloucester Streets Site, the Rocks: Archaeological Investigation Report*, 4 vols. (Sydney: Godden Mackay Logan 1999).

3 See Rebecca Yamin, 'Lurid tales and homely stories of New York's notorious Five Points', *Historical Archaeology* 32:1 (1998), 74–85; also Mary C. Beaudry, Lauren J. Cook and Stephen A. Mrozowski, 'Artifacts and active voices: material culture as social discourse', in Randall H. McGuire and Robert Paynter (eds.), *The Archaeology of Inequality: Material Culture, Domination and Resistance* (Oxford: Blackwell, 1991), pp. 156–9.

4 See Grace Karskens, 'Main report', in Godden Mackay, *The Cumberland/Gloucester Streets Site*, vol. 2. See also Grace Karskens, 'Crossing over: archaeol-

ogy and history at the Cumberland/Gloucester Street Site, the Rocks, 1994–1996', *Public History Review* 5/6 (1996–7), 30–48; Grace Karskens, 'The dialogue of townscape: the Rocks and Sydney 1788–1820', *Australian Historical Studies* 108 (1997), 88–112; Grace Karskens, *The Rocks: Life in Early Sydney* (Melbourne: Melbourne University Press, 1997); Grace Karskens, *Inside the Rocks: The Archaeology of a Neighbourhood* (Sydney: Hale & Iremonger, 1999). See also Grace Karskens and Wendy Thorp, 'History and archaeology in Sydney: towards integration and interpretation', *Journal of the Royal Australian Historical Society* 78:3–4 (1992), 52–75.

5 Jane Lydon, *Many Inventions: The Chinese in the Rocks, 1890–1930* (Clayton: Department of History, Monash University, 1999).

6 Alan Mayne, *The Imagined Slum: Newspaper Representation in Three Cities 1870–1914* (Leicester: Leicester University Press, 1993); Alan Mayne, 'A barefoot childhood: so what? Imagining slums and reading neighbourhoods', *Urban History* 22:3 (1995), 380–9.

7 See Alan Mayne, Tim Murray and Susan Lawrence, 'Melbourne's "Little Lon"', *Australian Historical Studies* 31:114 (2000), 131–51. Note also the hostile rejoinder by Chris McConville, and our response, in *ibid*. 31:115 (2000).

8 *The Age*, 3 January 1931, quoted in Alan Mayne and Tim Murray, '"In Little Lon . . . wiv Ginger Mick": telling the forgotten history of a vanished community', *Journal of Popular Culture* 33:1 (1999), 49–60. The broader social context is well described in Andrew Brown-May, *Melbourne Street Life: The Itinerary of Our Days* (Kew, Victoria: Australian Scholarly Publishing, 1998); Graeme Davison, David Dunstan and Chris McConville (eds.), *The Outcasts of Melbourne: Essays in Social History* (Sydney: Allen & Unwin, 1985); Graeme Davison, *The Rise and Fall of Marvellous Melbourne* (Melbourne: Melbourne University Press, 1978), pp. 236–9, 250–1.

9 C. J. Dennis, *The Moods of Ginger Mick* (Sydney: Angus & Robertson, 1916), p. 69. C. J. Dennis, *The Songs of a Sentimental Bloke* (Sydney: Angus & Robertson, 1916), p. 40.

10 Mayne and Murray, 'In Little Lon', pp. 50–1.

11 *Truth*, 18 July 1908, 5.

12 For example, *Truth*, 23 April 1932, 5; 7 May 1932, 1.

13 See Alan Mayne and Susan Lawrence, 'Ethnographies of place: a new urban research agenda', *Urban History* 26:3 (1999), 325–48. Note also Barbara J. Little, 'Compelling images through storytelling: comment on "Imaginary, but by no means unimagin-

able: storytelling, science, and historical archaeology"', *Historical Archaeology* 34:2 (2000), 10–13.

14 The house sites at Nos. 11 and 15 Casselden Place were not excavated by McCarthy's team.

15 David Dunstan, *Governing the Metropolis: Melbourne 1850–1891* (Melbourne: Melbourne University Press, 1984), pp. 233–88. Tony Dingle and Carolyn Rasmussen, *Vital Connections: Melbourne and Its Board of Works 1891–1991* (Ringwood, Victoria: Penguin, 1991).

16 Consistent street numbering in Casselden Place dates from the late 1870s, but the addresses were renumbered in 1893. We have adopted the 1893 numbering system, which remained unaltered throughout the twentieth century.

17 Mayne, Murray and Lawrence, 'Melbourne's "Little Lon"', pp. 144–7; Tim Murray and Alan Mayne, '(Re)-constructing a lost community: "Little Lon", Melbourne, Australia', *Historical Archaeology* (in press).

18 *Ibid*.

19 *Ibid*.

20 See Karskens, 'Main report', pp. 138–42.

21 Kate Holmes, 'Trench B Report', in Godden Mackay, *The Cumberland/Gloucester Streets Site*, vol. 3, p. 109.

22 Information about the Harts, and other inhabitants of Casselden Place, was collected by Kasia Zygmuntowicz in the Victorian Registry of Births, Deaths and Marriages, the Victorian Public Record Office (VPRO), City of Melbourne rate books and citizens' rolls, and post office directories.

23 Dunstan, *Governing the Metropolis*, p. 245.

24 Information about the Moloneys and Neylans was collected by Kasia Zygmuntowicz in the Victorian Registry of Births, Deaths and Marriages, the VPRO, City of Melbourne rate books and citizens' rolls, and post office directories.

25 Will of Margaret Neylan, 18 October 1900, in Victorian Public Record Series (VPRS) 7591/P2, unit 321.

26 T. A. Coghlan, *Labour and Industry in Australia* (Melbourne: Macmillan, 1969), vol. 3, p. 1,628 (first published 1918). John Franz, statement of assets and liabilities, 29 July 1884, VPRS 28/P0, unit 331, item 28/27. John Casselden, statement of assets and liabilities, 11 October 1888, VPRS 28/P2, unit 245.

27 Town Clerk's files, quoted in McCarthy, *Archaeological Investigation*, vol. 1, p. 80.

28 Petition to the Chief Commissioner of Police, 19 October 1880, in Inward Registered Correspondence to the Chief Commissioner of Police, VPRS 937, unit 303, bundle 3.

8

Work, space and power in an English industrial slum: 'the Crofts', Sheffield, 1750–1850

PAUL BELFORD

The modern 'crofts' is a place with no particular identity. A few older folk may remember the area as the setting for episodes of gang warfare in the 1920s; others may recall the clearance of old houses a decade later. To most people, this small area on the north-western side of Sheffield's old town is a forgotten place: it is rarely a destination, and it is not on the way to anywhere (Fig. 8.1). Only a small number of people actually live there. The place is defined not by its role in the modern urban landscape, which is literally unremarkable, but by its older identity as a slum. This identity was born in the second half of the nineteenth century, the product of Victorian and later perspectives which saw the narrow streets and filthy houses as a hotbed of drunkenness, laziness, prostitution and all manner of immoral behaviour. These views – the views of outsiders – have been used to colour in the blank space that is the modern 'crofts' in the collective memory of Sheffield. This chapter therefore will attempt to penetrate the late Victorian characterisations of the 'crofts' as a slum, in order to investigate the development of this suburb in the context of the growth of Sheffield and its industries. Discussion will focus on the ways in which various interests attempted to control and influence the developing landscape; the notion of 'resistance' amongst the slum dwellers and workers will also be explored.

Maps, myth and morality

The story of the 'crofts' began in the seventeenth century, when Sheffield was still very much a market town at the centre of a hinterland known as Hallamshire. The place was dominated by the medieval castle, church and water-mill, and the population numbered less than 3,500.[1] The principal industry of the region was the manufacture of cutlery, literally meaning 'that which cuts' and therefore encompassing axes, sickles, scythes, razors and forks, as well as knives. These metal-working industries were largely rural activities which took place in the numerous water-powered forges and grinding wheels on the outlying rivers. The first quarter of the seventeenth century saw considerable growth in this trade, and in 1624 a regulatory body was established: the Corporation of Cutlers in Hallamshire. This body was part medieval guild and part modern chamber of commerce; it controlled apprenticeships and trademarks throughout the seventeenth and eighteenth centuries.[2]

The establishment of the Cutlers' Company was the first in a series of events that resulted in a more self-governed town by the end of the seventeenth century. The castle was destroyed after the Civil War; although obsolete as a residence, it had continued to dominate the physical and social architecture of the town. The manorial deer park on the eastern side of the town was turned over to farming, charcoal burning, and later coal mining. Industry began to move into the town, tripling the population in a century and changing the character of the place. By 1672, 46 per cent of Sheffield houses had a forge or smithy attached.[3] The changes to the town were first depicted in 1736, when a surveyor named Ralph Gosling drew *A Plan of Sheffield from an Actual Survey*. The old medieval plan was still very much in evidence, the medieval town boundary still contained considerable areas of unbuilt ground, and the main focus of settlement was still the site of the old castle. However, Gosling's map shows one significant change in the urban design. The built area had encroached beyond the old township boundary and on to the Town Fields, formerly open fields or 'crofts' in the medieval sense of the word.

At about the same time as Ralph Gosling was undertaking his 'Actual Survey', Daniel Defoe was compiling notes on his *Tour through the Whole Island of Great Britain*. He thought Sheffield 'populous and large', but found that 'the streets [were] narrow, and the houses dark and black, occasioned by the continued smoke of the forges'.[4] In the 1730s the population of Sheffield stood at around 10,000. By the end of the eighteenth century, it was over 30,000, and the 'crofts' had developed into an ill-defined but densely packed suburb on the north-western edge of the town. The 'crofts' were the setting for a wide range of industrial activities: steelmaking and cutlery manufacture predominant amongst them. Such industries helped to create the distinct character of the 'crofts', where 'shops, warehouses and factories, and mean houses,

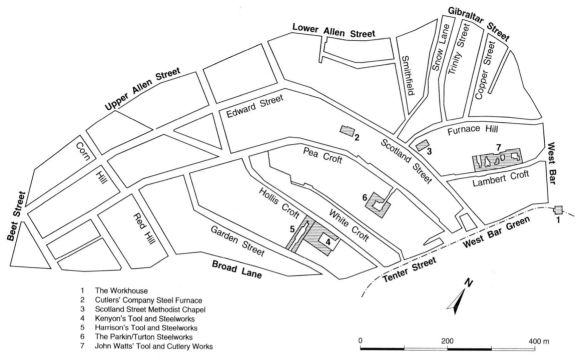

Fig. 8.1 Sheffield 'Crofts', 1820 (principal streets and sites mentioned in the text).

1 The Workhouse
2 Cutlers' Company Steel Furnace
3 Scotland Street Methodist Chapel
4 Kenyon's Tool and Steelworks
5 Harrison's Tool and Steelworks
6 The Parkin/Turton Steelworks
7 John Watts' Tool and Cutlery Works

run zig-zagging up and down the slopes'.[5] A visitor to the 'crofts' one hundred years after Defoe used almost identical words to describe what he saw. It was a place with 'numerous streets, which . . . are narrow and inconvenient: the houses, chiefly of brick, have obtained from the works a sombre appearance'.[6]

However, something had changed by the 1830s. The 'crofts' was no longer perceived as a setting for industrious activities, representative of the Malthusian 'productive body'.[7] Instead, for subsequent observers, this apparently haphazard mixture of working, living and meeting places was morally filthy, chaotic and rotten. By mid-century, Friedrich Engels was able to state that 'immorality among young people seems to be more prevalent in Sheffield than anywhere else'.[8] Such views were typical of those who read the reports of the various Royal Commissions into housing, sanitation and working conditions which were being published at that time. Indeed, the almost verbatim repetition of later written descriptions of the town suggests that very few of these morally offended Victorians had actually visited the place. Nevertheless, the geographical space defined by these writers has been used as the basis for this study. A local report of 1848 focused on the 'district bounded by Beet-

street, Upper and Lower Allen-street, Gibraltar-street, Westbar-green, Tenter-street and Broad-lane' and also 'Lee-croft, Hawley-croft, School-croft and Sims-croft' (Fig. 8.1).[9]

Of these, the former area was described in the report as 'more densely populated in relation to its extent than any district previously mentioned', and the latter was characterised by its poor housing and sanitation. On to both were grafted Victorian middle-class perceptions of immorality, vice and poverty. The 'crofts' image – a place where 'early, unbridled sexual intercourse, youthful prostitution . . . [was] extraordinarily frequent' and 'crimes of a savage and desperate sort [were] a common occurrence' – reflected the perceived anarchy which was the result of this disordered and polluted environment.[10] Such parallels were drawn again and again. Thus in the 1860s the 'crofts' was seen as being 'as devoid of the decencies of civilisation as it was in the Dark Ages'.[11] By the end of the century, the place was not merely medieval, it was literally diabolical, being 'suggestive of nothing so much as the popular conception of the infernal regions . . . the general darkness and dirt of the whole scene serves but to create feelings of repugnance and even horror'.[12] The 'crofts' consequently became an easy target for middle-class reformers keen to identify slum areas ripe for improvement.

The design of the landscape

The identification of the 'repugnant' landscape with social and moral decay was made explicit in the Sheffield Medical Officer's report of 1899. Although he acknowledged that some slum dwellers, when 'put into better surroundings . . . would soon make what was good into bad surroundings', he felt that for 'the vast majority the influence of better surroundings does . . . act in the most beneficial manner'.[13] But these 'bad surroundings' had not just come about of their own accord; they were the product of more than two hundred years of human activities within the landscape. Landowners, industrialists, workers, builders and tenants were all engaged in a process of defining who was being controlled and who was controlling, a struggle of resistance and domination. The landscape itself was the crucible of Bourdieu's 'alchemy' of personal action, reaction and interaction, which transformed 'the distribution of capital, the balance sheet of a power relation, into a system of perceived differences, distinctive properties'.[14] Moreover, the physical shape of that crucible was dynamic, for, as Anthony Giddens has suggested, shifts in social practices and structures were reflected in the material construction that was the urban landscape.[15] At each turn the landscape was modified, the creation and manipulation of space a necessary evolution of an arena in which social differences were displayed.

Significantly, the location of that arena was an important factor in the ability of various interests to manipulate it. For this land represented neither the town nor the country, it was a liminal place: both a physical space between the old town and its hinterland, and also a mental space within which the new industrial town could flourish beyond the confines of the medieval one. This liminality had already been made explicit by the Town Trustees, for the Sheffield Workhouse – an institution for those who were simultaneously 'parasites and victims'[16] – was located on the very edge on the town boundary, between 1733 and 1829, at the bottom of West Bar Green (Fig. 8.1). The name West Bar simply means 'western boundary'. The otherness of the 'crofts' was further reinforced by developments such as the innovative steel furnace erected by the Cutlers' Company in 1763 (the first and only time that organisation undertook a commercial venture), and the influx of Irish immigrants to Sims Croft and Tenter Street half a century later. The liminal status of the area was thus always apparent, enabling the 'crofts'

continually to generate new identities and new social relations, which in turn fuelled perceptions of it as a place apart.

Theoretically, the people with the most influence over the pattern and character of new development were the landowners, representatives of local authority. The area of the 'crofts' was owned by four major landlords: the Duke of Norfolk, the Town Trustees, the Church Burgesses and the Trustees of the Hollis Hospital.[17] The Dukes of Norfolk did not live in Sheffield, and management of their property was devolved to an agent. The other landowners were established oligarchic institutions, in which overall decisions were made by people who had never set foot on the 'crofts'. The ground plan of the new industrial suburb was determined, therefore, by the people on the ground: the existing leaseholders, the land agents and the surveyors. Significantly, one family dominated the surveying profession in eighteenth- and early-nineteenth-century Sheffield. William Fairbank started drawing maps in the 1720s, and three generations followed, often revisiting the same documents. The firm later expanded into quantity surveying and architectural design, and acted as agents for the building trade; they also assisted in disputes over boundaries and rights to light and air.[18] Their knowledge of the town and its inhabitants would have been impressive, and it seems likely that their independent opinions (as Quakers) would have been valued by those who commissioned them to redesign the landscape.

It would appear that the surveyors were aware of the liminality of the place. The streets are not quite straight, the lines a little too irregular to suggest confidence in the identity of the landscape. Older social practices had established 'locales' within the rural landscape which had a strong influence on the character of the new urban one.[19] At first the old strip fields which ran up and down the slope opposite the town guided the surveyors in the layout of new streets; later, new elements of the built environment had an impact. Christopher Tilley has argued – along with many others – that the memory of events, people and practices associated with such 'locales' was reinforced through the act of naming them.[20] The first phase of development in the 'crofts' included Lambert Croft, White Croft, Hawley Croft, Scargill Croft and Sims Croft: all named after the tenants of the fields in which they were created. Later streets were named for the landuse at the time of survey (Pea Croft, Corn Hill and Garden Croft); others for structures that had become landmarks in the new urban setting (School Croft, Workhouse Croft and Furnace Hill); and yet others apparently for fun (Scotland Street was so named for its length). Only one – Hollis Croft – was named for the land-owner.

The use of locally derived names in the 'crofts' was in marked contrast to later suburbs, devised around the turn of the nineteenth century in Sheffield and elsewhere.[21] One notable Sheffield example was a development at 'Alsop Fields' on the south-eastern edge of the town, which began in the 1790s (Fig. 8.1). This was designed to attract the same kind of industrial activity as the 'crofts', but here a conscious effort was made by the landowner to impose a certain character on the development. The grid-planned suburb had been laid out without reference to the earlier landscape and the 'locales' within it. The streets were named Duke, Norfolk, Earl, Arundel, Surrey (the landowner's titles); Charles (his first name); Howard, Furnival (older family names) and Eyre (the name of his estate manager). As one early-nineteenth-century writer observed, these 'newer parts [of the town] are laid out with more regularity'.[22] Urban life that was set in such regular frameworks could therefore be distinguished at a glance from the 'zig-zag' 'crofts', which enabled the development of later characterisations of the place as a slum.

In fact, the original design of the 'crofts' had been much more regular than nineteenth-century writers liked to admit. Unlike contemporary American cities, there was no 'republican' sense of equality motivating the subdivision of space between the streets into individual plots; nevertheless there was still an attempt at 'organising the otherwise chaotic juxtaposition of individual selves' into a rational framework.[23] On Hollis Croft and White Croft, for example, laid out in the two decades before 1750, neighbouring subdivisions were at first reasonably equal. Despite the irregular shape of White Croft – owing to its origins as a path between fields – the first twenty blocks backing onto it all measured between 309 and 387 square yards in area. On the south side of Hollis Croft the sub-divisions were more varied in size, from Samuel Marples' 271 square yards to Elizabeth Doe's 498 square yards, although most of the properties contained between 440 and 450 square yards. Smaller subdivisions tended to be made on the later streets, although the same sort of pattern was evident. Thus the first twelve blocks on Pea Croft were all either 160 or 192 square yards in area when first laid out in the 1760s, and the average size of blocks on the whole street was 182 square yards.

By the end of the eighteenth century much of this apparent equality had become obscured by the development of various properties (Fig. 8.2). Physical expansion took place in many directions. By the 1780s, John Kenyon's saw and steel works on Hollis Croft occupied 1,742 square yards along the street frontage, the equiva-

Fig. 8.2 Hollis Croft. This rare survival of early eighteenth-century architecture illustrates many aspects of the design of the 'crofts'. The building on the left is a typical two-storey workshop built around 1810 for cutlery manufacture. This is constructed in a vernacular style and placed at the back of a fairly open yard. About twenty years later the houses on the right were built along the street frontage to close off the yard, and with their rendering and architectural details, convey a different impression.

lent of four blocks of 435 square yards. Other businesses preferred to expand backwards, which enabled them to have entrances on two streets. Thus Kenyon's neighbour, John Harrison – also a sawmaker with a steel furnace – constructed new workshops and an additional furnace on a thin strip of ground between the back of his original property and Garden Street. Spaces were also created away from the streets, in new subdivisions created at nodal points in the complex web of property boundaries. This happened in several places, hence the creation of Widdle's Yard and Sambourne Place in the 1790s, and Thomas Turton's steelworks midway between Pea Croft and White Croft, built in the first decade of the nineteenth century.

The growth of the industrial urban landscape comple-mented the development of an industrial urban society in Sheffield. On the whole this new urban society had little to do with the old one, for the main impetus behind the growth of the 'crofts' in the second half of the eighteenth century was an increase in migration to the town. Amos Rapoport has argued that the spaces, or 'locales', within the urban landscape form a system of settings, within which the system of activities that is human action takes place. These systems were based within the physical landscape, but they were not dependent upon it; consequently the intended plan of the landscape could be subverted.[24] Thus, the design of the (urban) landscape was modified by the (rural) experience of those who moved into it. Hence the boundaries in the spaces between streets in the 'crofts' shifted over time as properties expanded and contracted. Similarly, the streets themselves, which had been intended as thoroughfares, became extensions of the house and workshop. The people who spent 'the whole of Sunday lying in the street tossing coins or dog-fighting'[25] were creating locales of their own. Streets were also used for negotiation between employers and employees, and for more formalised activities such as funerals, meetings and riots.[26] This role as public open space was critical, and it seems to have gained a greater meaning from the late eighteenth century as the relationship between the street and the buildings on either side of it began to change.

Spaces in common: the house and yard

In the eighteenth century each property in the 'crofts' generally comprised an open yard, with the principal buildings running down the sides, gable-end facing the street. Buildings were also constructed across the back of the yard. The basic functions of any one group of buildings could therefore generally be observed from the street. Some of the wider blocks may have had a low brick wall or fence, but the overall character of the landscape was open. The entrance onto the main street was the only one, for no back lanes were consciously incorporated into the design of the 'crofts'. From the 1790s these open-fronted yards began to disappear as leaseholders added an additional range of buildings along the street frontage. This would incorporate a through passage (locally called a 'ginnel') giving access to the yard, but the inhabitants were now separated visually from the street. An opportunity was therefore created for landlords to differentiate formally between different street frontages; moreover, it became easier to ensure what Stefan Muthesius has termed the 'inspectibility of the working classes'[27] (Fig. 8.2). This process of 'closure' was not only defined by the desires of the landlords and builders; it reflected ongoing changes in the nature of society. For the inhabitants, the creation of new spaces provided new settings for activities other than those which took place on the street.

The arrangement of the individual plots into a yard was almost ubiquitous, and even on unusually shaped plots an attempt was made to provide a single common entrance and a central common space. Yards formed the basic core of the ground plan of both industrial and domestic properties, and although in some cases the two functions were mixed on one site, the adoption of this layout enabled them to be separated. The use of the yard in the domestic sphere, where it was termed a 'court', was the particular focus of Victorian writers, who saw the enclosed space as a contributor to poor health, and consequently a major factor in the moral decline of the population. Thus in 1848 it was found that the houses on the slopes to the west of West Bar, *especially those erected in the yards . . . are ill constructed, badly lighted and ventilated; being built back-to-back, and generally of three storeys high, which of itself is an impediment to the free access of light and air . . . in many places the evil [smoke] is so extensive that the inhabitants find the greatest difficulty in maintaining personal or domestic cleanliness'.[28]

Earlier documentary sources suggest that the dislike of smoke, for example, was unheard of before the 1840s, whereas fifty years earlier very much the opposite feeling had prevailed. 'It has often been remarked', wrote the Sheffield *Iris* in 1794, 'that infectious distempers are not apt to spread in this place . . . [T]he smoke, produced by the manufactories, is thought by many persons to be serviceable in this view.'[29] Even in the 1840s there were still 'a number of persons who think the smoke healthy',[30] reflecting contemporary middle-class ambivalence about the relationship between disease and hygiene. Perhaps because of this attitude by no means all of the residents of the 'crofts' were the working-class poor. A number of manufacturers built their own residences adjacent to or on the same property as their works. The sawmaker John Harrison, for example, constructed an impressive three-storey four-bayed brick mansion at the Hollis Croft end of his works in the 1780s. The family lived there until the early nineteenth century.[31] Likewise the steelmaker Thomas Turton lived in a new house within sight of his furnaces on Pea Croft in the early part of the nineteenth century; as did Daniel Doncaster, who owned a house and orchards on the fringes of the 'crofts'.

The richer members of society owned their houses, but the majority of 'crofts' residents rented living space. The insecurity and short-term nature of tenancies was emphasised by Victorian writers, with the implication that tenants cared little about the quality of their environment. Although trade fluctuations meant that working-class wages were often irregular, an examination of eighteenth-century Poor Rate assessors' books suggests that most people stayed put for around ten years. Less than 3 per cent of a sample of 1,465 houses listed in the 1787–8 rate books had changed occupiers since the year before.[32] Substantial price and wage fluctuations during the Napoleonic Wars, and a series of depressions in 1818–20 and 1825–31, increased economic hardship and personal mobility, yet the 'crofts' was still characterised by the relatively stable juxtaposition of different social groups. This only began to change following a serious outbreak of cholera in 1832. The Master Cutler was among the 1,347 people affected, for 'the disease did not confine itself to the poor . . . [S]everal wealthy and respectable individuals were amongst its victims.'[33] The response of those who could afford to – which included many of the senior workers as well as their employers – was to move away; improved sanitation for those who stayed was not immediately forthcoming.

It is clear that the individuals and groups of people living around the yards had different relationships with the space around them than those who observed them. The Sheffield 'court' conformed to Roderick Lawrence's model of a 'transition space', which 'simultaneously linked and separated the private and public domains, and the interior from the exterior'.[34] The enclosed 'court' was separated from the street by the 'ginnel' and the street frontage. It therefore became a semi-private space, in which private activities such as going to the toilet and doing the laundry were undertaken alongside more public activities such as arguments and children's games. Later, the yard area also acted as what Oscar Newman has termed a 'defensible space'.[35] It was overlooked by all the tenants; consequently a stranger in the yard could be instantly detected and treated appropriately. This may explain why much of Sims Croft came to be 'inhabited principally by the Irish': as an immigrant community subject to racist attacks and official harassment, they chose places to live which had a relatively safe communal space.[36] Many social groups, therefore, continued to see the 'crofts' as a desirable place to live.

Just as the yard space reflected the social lives of the residents, so the house itself was both the medium and the outcome of social practices, enabling and constraining the dialectical relationship between people and their actions.[37] The typical back-to-back house had a single room on each of the three floors (Fig. 8.3). The main centre of household activity was the ground-floor 'living room'. This room contained the largest fireplace, and was used as 'kitchen, scullery, dining room, living room, [and] as wash-room and bathroom'.[38] The cellar below stored coal and meat; cellar dwellings as such were rare in Sheffield. The first-floor 'chamber' provided sleeping accommodation for the adults and younger children; the older children or a lodger slept in the 'attic' on the second. This use of space was not dissimilar to that found in late medieval houses. The 'living room' had a number of meanings. It was a liminal space between the outside and inside; it was a communal space where members of the household could get together; it was also a place 'on show' for visitors.

'Mystery and business': working spaces

The activities of the street, yard and house took place in a smoky atmosphere. Although the focus of Victorian attention, the smoke was only one of the sights, sounds, smells and vibrations produced by the variety of industries that inhabited the 'crofts'. These enterprises ranged from a single journeyman undertaking piecework in a rented room to relatively large steelworks and toolmaking firms employing tens of people. Perhaps the best known was the cutlery industry, which was not in fact a single entity but a collection of crafts ranging from forging, through various types of grinding, to 'buffing' and finishing. Related but separate industries included the manufacture of bone handles and buttons. Heavier trades that were attracted to the 'crofts' included steelmaking, and ferrous and non-ferrous founding. By the beginning of the eighteenth century, Sheffield already 'had a more specialised occupational structure than any other town in England'.[39] This picture of highly skilled industrial concerns, incorporating the latest technological innovations, is at odds with the stereotypical image of the 'crofts' as 'medieval' slum area full of listless idlers.

Even allowing for the very specific site requirements of certain industries such as steelmaking and tanning, the basic layout of most industrial sites was broadly similar. As with domestic accommodation, the buildings were grouped around a yard. The principal difference in appearance between the two was that on industrial sites a greater area was given over to a wider variety of buildings, and the entrance archway, or 'ginnel', was wide enough to admit wheeled traffic. Otherwise, the general level of architectural craftsmanship was much the same as for domestic buildings. The buildings in the yard, unseen from the street, continued to be constructed in a vernacular style appropriate to their use (Fig. 8.2). Such styles changed little (except in detail of materials) from the mid-eighteenth century to the end of the nineteenth. Until the mid-nineteenth century, the design of industrial premises was still very much 'the builders' domain'.[40] Some of the builders who lived in the 'crofts' specialised in industrial sites: the Taylor family, for example, built numerous

Fig. 8.3 Back-to-back housing. Although this particular example is located outside the 'crofts', this fragment of a row of ten houses built c. 1850 is typical of the type of housing that predominated there. Each house contains a single room on each floor, plus a cellar; this is the back row of houses that faced onto the yard.

eighteenth-century steelworks; and Margaret Taylor was still listed in 1825 as a 'bricklayer . . . and furnace builder'.[41]

The small-scale, domestic origins of the cutlery trade had considerable bearing on the layout of its sites in the nineteenth century. Frequently more than one firm shared the same property, and in such cases the relatively ornate street frontage provided a communal veneer of respectability. Thus the saw manufacturers Grayson and Cocker shared part of their frontage with the workshops of Thomas Makin, filemaker. The yard behind not only accommodated both firms, but also had room for Samuel Tingle's steel furnace.[42] Not all sites were shared by related businesses. The filemakers Jepson and Company, for example, shared a block of workshops on Furnace Hill

with W. and H. Guest, bone button makers.[43] At the other extreme, a single firm could occupy many yards. Firms that had expanded into adjacent properties often retained the mixed identity of the original buildings. John Watts' cutlery firm, for example, founded in 1765 in Lambert Croft, had expanded by the mid-nineteenth century to occupy ten adjoining properties[44] (Fig. 8.4). In the process the firm gained a reputation for the innovation and range of its products, which were advertised across the various frontages: 'Cutlery and Other Specialities . . . Safety Razors, Scissors, Skates etc'. Here the diversity and apparent specialisation of the buildings was used to emphasise the character of the organisation within.

John Watts' premises were the exception in the light trades; generally the most impressive sites were the steel-

Fig. 8.4 Lambert Croft. The frontage of John Watts' premises, a long-established cutlery and edge-tool manufacturer that originated in the eighteenth century. Most of the present buildings are of nineteenth-century date. There is a dichotomy between the apparent uniformity of the rendered frontage and the diversity of the various buildings which were occupied by the firm.

works, which required a greater investment in fixed capital and tended to remain in business for two or three generations. Until the second half of the nineteenth century, steelmaking involved the combination of two processes. The first – 'cementation' or 'converting' – involved the carburisation of wrought iron bars by packing them with charcoal in sandstone chests, and heating them with a coal or coke fire below. The furnace was surmounted by a conical chimney up to 30 m high. The nature of the process meant that steel quality varied throughout each bar, making it unsuitable for fine work. Hence the local invention in the 1740s of the second process – 'steel melting' or 'refining' – in which the bars of cementation steel were broken up and melted in a crucible over a coke

fire.[45] The first urban crucible steel furnaces were built in the 'crofts' in 1763, and by 1787 nine of the nineteen 'steel converters and refiners' listed in the Sheffield directory were located there.[46] The partnership deeds of the early concerns highlighted the enigmatic nature of the new technology. The firm of Love and Manson, for example, founded in 1766 on Gibraltar Street, was to be engaged in the 'art, trade, mystery and business of running or casting steel'.[47]

The elements comprising a steelworks varied according to the processes undertaken there; moreover, because of the relative permanence of steelmaking structures they were given a more formal architectural treatment than their counterparts in the lighter trades. Sites came in a wide range of shapes and sizes: some steelworks contained either cementation or crucible furnaces, some contained both, and some toolmaking sites added steel furnaces at a later date. Sites of all categories shared a common framework, again based around the enclosed yard. The mysterious glowing furnaces were potent symbols; the tall cementation cones in particular denoted the prosperity of the firm and industrial progress generally, and were therefore displayed prominently. In sites where steelmaking was the primary concern, cementation furnaces were typically used as a focal point, situated on the opposite side of the yard to the entrance; firms with only crucible furnaces used them in the same way. Even on sites where steelmaking was not the primary activity, the prestige of having furnaces was emphasised by their placement in dominant positions.

The steelmakers therefore appear to have arranged their sites so that, simultaneously, visitors could be mystified and impressed and employees observed and controlled. These meanings could be enhanced by the way in which the site was approached. One typical example was the steelworks built in Pea Croft in 1810 by Thomas Turton, which was approached along a narrow lane running back from the street. Two cementation furnaces were positioned opposite the site entrance and would have been prominent – but mysteriously distant – to the visitor coming down the lane. The mystery was retained until the visitor actually entered the yard, for only then was the crucible furnace revealed to provide a concentrated impression of the whole steelmaking process. For employees, however, this was reversed. There was no mystery in the site; instead, surrounded by the heat and smoke of their trade, dominated by the huge furnace structures and offices of their employer, the only escape was down a long alleyway. Furthermore, the demarcation between cementation and crucible furnaces was made explicit by their location on opposite sides of the yard.

'When the workman chooses'

As Dell Upton has remarked, the built environment was 'only the shell of the urban artifact'.[48] It is likely that the meanings intended by the designers of industrial premises were not always adopted by those who used them; however, the actuality of people's working lives has been obscured by the often contradictory perspectives of later observers. On one hand, industries were seen as contributors to the squalor of the Crofts, through the emission of smoke and the reputation for hard drinking during and after the working day. On the other, workers were portrayed as victims of harsh working conditions and long

hours. Such ambivalence was inherent in contemporary Malthusian notions of the 'productive body'.[49] The concept of the worker as a victim was surpassed in the later nineteenth century by what Jacques Rancière has termed the 'myth of artisanship'.[50] One famous proponent of artisanship was John Ruskin, whose words are written around the main dining room of Cutlers' Hall: 'In cutlers' iron work we have in Sheffield the best of its kind done by English hands, unsurpassable, when the workman chooses to do all he knows, by that of any living nation.' Ironically, notions of artisanship were most vigorously promoted by the large, mechanised cutlery factories of the later nineteenth century.[51]

The history of the cutlery industry has provided a rich seam for miners of social and economic history. Their work has perpetuated both myths by emphasising the worker's role as class warrior. It is true that the highly specialised and devolved nature of work in the 'Sheffield trades' enabled the workers to retain a 'special kind of independence'.[52] Indeed, by the mid-nineteenth century some branches of the industry were sufficiently well organised to practise overt forms of resistance. Moreover militant actions, albeit of a more spontaneous nature, had also occasionally occurred in the eighteenth century.[53] However, closer examination of the evidence suggests that most worker resistance in the eighteenth- and nineteenth-century light trades was more subtle. This was implied by Ruskin himself, in his phrase 'when the workman chooses', hinting towards what James Scott has termed 'everyday resistance'.[54] In Sheffield this was principally expressed in variations in the rate of work. Even in the mid-1860s it was still felt that grinders were 'not tied to any stated hours of labour . . . [A]uthority on one side and subjection on the other . . . scarcely exists in Sheffield'.[55] Perhaps the most blatant manifestation of this was the practice of not working at all on Monday, and sometimes Tuesday as well.

It is possible to find hints towards the practice of 'St Monday' and similar customs in the material culture. Excavations were recently undertaken in a rural grinding works to the south of Sheffield, in use from the mid-eighteenth century to around 1830.[56] One of the buildings on site contained a large quantity of discarded wine bottles and clay pipe fragments, of early-nineteenth-century date. The location of this building within the site suggested a secret place. From it, anyone approaching the site could be observed unseen; furthermore, after the initial sighting the visitor would have moved behind a dip in the ground, allowing two or three minutes to assume working positions or open another bottle. This would enable St Monday 'celebrations' to take place unobserved, although more prosaic interpretations of the site layout are equally plausible. Comparable examination of urban sites of that period has not been undertaken, and the survival of standing buildings is biased towards the later, larger examples. Nevertheless, building recording of a large cutlery factory in Sheffield of mid-nineteenth-century date found a subtle manifestation of workers' everyday resistance in the form of a cribbage board drilled into one of the workbenches, enabling covert games to be played during working hours.[57]

Older working patterns in the steel industry have been largely obscured by later-nineteenth- and twentieth-century impressions of a militant and resistant factory-based workforce. In fact, the cementation process always retained its essentially pre-industrial rhythm, characterised by 'alternate bouts of intense labour and idleness'.[58] The firing of the furnace, or 'heat', took about three weeks. Trial bars were examined during the 'heat' in order to assess when the steel was done; judgement of the right moment required experience and skill. The end of the 'heat' was celebrated with ale.[59] Eighteenth-century steelmakers were rare, and were highly valued by their employers. Thus the cementation steelmaker Henry Ball could raise an initial offer from his employer, Samuel Shore, of a seven-year contract on 10 shillings per 'heat' (about 3 shillings per week) to a more stable ten-year contract at a fixed rate of 6 shillings per week.[60] Steelmakers were managers of the whole process, being in charge of the hire of employees and the sale and purchase of materials.

The working day at the crucible furnace also consisted of short periods of intense activity and longer periods of inactivity, and the crucible steelmakers held a similar status to their colleagues at the cementation furnace. In 1786, for example, William Hague and John Parkin established a steelworks on Trinity Street. Under the terms of the partnership, John Parkin was given complete autonomy in the day-to-day running of the furnace, being paid 8 shillings per hundredweight (51 kg) of steel produced; out of which he paid his assistants' wages.[61] Later in the same decade, John Tingle was paid on a similar basis for steelmaking, but was also paid to employ assistants for the running and repair of the furnace and the manufacture of crucibles.[62] Demarcation and hierarchy were expressed more formally in the nineteenth century through pay scales. Typically the 'head melter' received three times the wage of his assistants. Individual promotion was therefore more attractive than the prospect of a better life obtained through resistance across the wider trade.[63] The steelmakers, more so than the cutlery workers, were perhaps the 'true metallurgists of Yorkshire'.[64] Even in 1864 it was still possible for a 'proper' metallurgist to state that 'the varieties of steel . . . are exceedingly numerous, but the causes of difference are in many cases unknown'.[65]

Conclusion

Clearly there was much more to life in the 'crofts' than the slum myth would suggest. Far from being a muddled mass of confusion, chaos and crime, the eighteenth- and early-nineteenth-century 'crofts' was a planned and ordered suburb, deliberately designed to provide a setting for new and innovative industries, and moreover remoulded by its inhabitants into an effective living environment. The residents of the 'crofts' came from a wide range of social backgrounds, and worked hard at a variety of trades. This is not to pretend that standards of housing and sanitation were high, or that working lives were long and healthy. Nevertheless, this analysis of the 'crofts' during the hundred years before 1850 invalidates the 'slum' identity of the place, with which this area of Sheffield is still associated. Earlier views of life in the 'crofts' were quite different, and emphasised the diversity of social groups that lived and worked there. The scope for archaeological investigation of this industrial suburb is huge – much of the area has remained undeveloped since the 1930s – and is worth attempting, for, as Dell Upton has pointed out, only by rigorous analysis of the material culture can we begin to understand the complexity of the early industrial 'city-artifact'.[66]

Acknowledgements

Without the invaluable help and support of Annsofie Witkin, this chapter would never have been completed. I must also thank the staff of the Sheffield Archives and Local Studies Library for their patience and resourcefulness. I would like to extend particular gratitude to James Symonds for assistance throughout this work; plus Glyn Davies, Anna Badcock, Jane Downes and Jo Mincher for doing other things and thereby preventing me from having to do them. Thanks also to David Crossley for introducing me to the magical world of historical archaeology. Bob, Linda, Anna, Sarah and Dot helped tremendously by providing fresh air and hot sunshine in the middle of a long and gloomy winter.

Notes

1 G. Scurfield, 'Seventeenth-century Sheffield and its environs', *Yorkshire Archaeological Journal* 58 (1986), 168.

2 R. E. Leader, *History of the Company of Cutlers in*

Hallamshire (Sheffield: J. W. Northend, 1905–6), vol. 1, pp. 8–39.

3 D. Hey, *The Fiery Blades of Hallamshire* (Leicester: Leicester University Press, 1991), p. 48.

4 *Ibid.*, p. 62.

5 S. Sidney, *Rides on Railways* (London, 1851), cited in *ibid.*, p. 45.

6 S. Lewis, *A Topographical Dictionary of England* (London: Macmillan, 1835), p. 267.

7 C. Gallagher, 'The body versus the social body in the works of Thomas Malthus and Henry Mayhew', in C. Gallagher and T. Laquer (eds.), *The Making of the Modern Body* (Berkeley: University of California Press, 1987), pp. 83–106.

8 F. Engels, *The Condition of the Working Class in England*, reprint of 1844 first edition (London: Penguin Books, 1987), p. 216.

9 J. Haywood and W. Lee, *Report on the Sanitary Condition of the Borough of Sheffield*, second edition (Sheffield, 1848), pp. 77–8.

10 Engels, *Condition of the Working Class*, p. 216.

11 'The condition of our chief towns – Sheffield', *The Builder*, 21 September 1861.

12 J. S. Fletcher, A *Picturesque History of Yorkshire* (London: Macmillan, 1899), p. 179.

13 H. Keeble Hawson, *Sheffield, the Growth of a City* (Sheffield: J. W. Northend, 1968), p. 104.

14 P. Bourdieu, *Distinction: A Social Critique of the Judgement of Taste*, trans. R. Nice (London: Routledge, 1989), p. 172.

15 A. Giddens, *The Constitution of Society: Outline of a Theory of Structuration* (London: Polity Press, 1984), p. 17.

16 G. Lucas, 'The archaeology of the workhouse: the changing uses of the workhouse buildings at St. Mary's, Southampton', in S. Tarlow and W. West (eds.), *The Familiar Past: Archaeologies of Later Historical Britain* (London: Routledge, 1999), p. 135.

17 D. Hey, *A History of Sheffield* (Lancaster: Carnegie Publishing, 1998), pp. 27–8.

18 R. E. Leader, *Surveyors of Eighteenth Century Sheffield* (Sheffield, privately published lecture transcript, 1903), pp. 2–4.

19 Giddens, *Constitution of Society*, pp. 20–1.

20 C. Tilley, *A Phenomenology of Landscape* (Oxford: Berg Publishing, 1994), pp. 18–19.

21 E. Blackmar, *Manhattan for Rent 1785–1850* (Ithaca and London: Cornell University Press, 1989), pp. 96–8.

22 J. Smith, 'A report on the condition of the town of Sheffield', in the *Report of the Royal Commission on the Health of Towns* (London, 1841), p. 27.

23 D. Upton, 'The city as material culture', in Anne E. Yentsch and Mary C. Beaudry (eds.), *The Art and Mystery of Historical Archaeology* (Boca Raton, FL: CRC Press, 1992), p. 56.

24 Amos Rapoport, 'Systems of activities and systems of settings', in Susan Kent (ed.), *Domestic Architecture and the Use of Space* (Cambridge: Cambridge University Press, 1990), pp. 16–19.

25 Engels, *Condition of the Working Class*, p. 216.

26 F. K. Donelly and J. L. Baxter, 'Sheffield and the English revolutionary tradition', in S. Pollard (ed.), *Economic and Social History of South Yorkshire* (Sheffield: South Yorkshire County Council, 1976), pp. 103–10.

27 S. Muthesius, *The English Terraced House* (New Haven and London: Yale University Press, 1982), pp. 114–15.

28 Haywood and Lee, *Sanitary Condition of Sheffield*, p. 80.

29 Sheffield *Iris*, 4 December 1794.

30 J. C. Symonds, *Report into the Sanitary Conditions of the Working Classes in Sheffield* (Sheffield: J. W. Northend, 1841), p. 222.

31 M. Olive (ed.), *Central Sheffield* (Stroud: Chalford Publishing, 1994), p. 119.

32 Sheffield Archives, *Rate Book, Sheffield Upper and Lower Divisions*, vol. 1 (1787–8).

33 J. Stokes, *The History of the Cholera Epidemic of 1832 in Sheffield* (Sheffield: J. W. Northend, 1921), p. 32.

34 R. J. Lawrence, 'Public collective and private space: a study of urban housing in Switzerland', in Kent (ed.), *Domestic Architecture*, p. 89.

35 O. Newman, *Defensible Space: People and Design in the Violent City* (London: Architectural Press, 1973), pp. 3–66.

36 Haywood and Lee, *Sanitary Condition of Sheffield*, pp. 82–3; S. Pollard, *History of Labour in Sheffield* (Liverpool: Liverpool University Press, 1959), pp. 91–3.

37 A. Giddens, *Central Problems in Social Theory: Action, Structure and Contradiction in Social Analysis* (London: Macmillan, 1979), pp. 206–10.

38 Pollard, *Labour in Sheffield*, p. 18.

39 Hey, *History of Sheffield*, p. 60.

40 V. A. Beauchamp, 'The workshops of the cutlery industry in Hallamshire 1750–1900', PhD thesis, University of Sheffield (1996), p. 149.

41 R. Gell, *A New General and Commercial Directory of Sheffield and Its Vicinity* (Sheffield: privately published, 1825), pp. 139–40.

42 Sheffield Archives, Fairbank Collection, M.B.392.

43 D. Smith, 'The buttonmaking industry in Sheffield', in

M. Jones (ed.), *Aspects of Sheffield 1* (Barnsley: Wharncliffe Publishing, 1997), p. 98.

44 G. Tweedale, *The Sheffield Knife Book: A History and Collector's Guide* (Sheffield: Hallamshire Press, 1996), p. 289.

45 K. C. Barraclough, *Steelmaking before Bessemer*, 2 vols. (London: The Metals Society, 1984) vol. 1, *Blister Steel*; vol. 2, *Crucible Steel*.

46 Gales and Martin, *Commercial Directory of Sheffield* (Sheffield: privately published, 1787), p. 38.

47 Sheffield Archives, Tibbitts Collection, T.C.200.

48 Upton, 'The city as material culture', p. 59.

49 Gallagher, 'The body versus the social body', pp. 88–100.

50 Jacques Rancière, 'The myth of the artisan: critical reflections on a category of social history', in S. L. Kaplan and C. J. Koepp (eds.), *Work in France: Representations, Meaning, Organisation and Practice* (Ithaca and London: Cornell University Press, 1986), pp. 217–19.

51 Tweedale, *Sheffield Knife Book*, pp. 61, 261.

52 J. Rule, *The Experience of Labour in Eighteenth-Century Industry* (London: Croom Helm, 1981), p. 36.

53 Donelly and Baxter, 'English revolutionary tradition', pp. 90–118.

54 J. C. Scott, *Weapons of the Weak: Everyday Forms of Peasant Resistance* (New Haven and London: Yale University Press, 1985), p. 29.

55 R. D. Storch, 'The problem of working-class leisure. Some roots of middle-class moral reform in the industrial north: 1825–50', in A. P. Donajgrodzki (ed.), *Social Control in Nineteenth Century Britain* (London: Croom Helm, 1977), p. 146.

56 P. J. Belford, 'Archaeological excavations at Foxbrook Furnace, Derbyshire', *Historical Metallurgy* 19 (1999), 32.

57 P. J. Belford, *Standing Building Recording of 'Cornish Place', Sheffield*, ARCUS, Research School of Archaeology, University of Sheffield, Report 414 (forthcoming).

58 E. P. Thompson, *Customs in Common* (London: Penguin Books, 1991), p. 373.

59 P. J. Belford, 'Converters and refiners: the archaeology of Sheffield steelmaking 1700–1850', MA thesis, University of Sheffield (1997), pp. 27–31.

60 Sheffield *Independent*, 6 January 1876.

61 Sheffield Archives, Parker Collection, P.C.740.

62 Sheffield Archives, M.D.5246.

63 Pollard, *Labour in Sheffield*, pp. 84–5.

64 F. LePlay, 'Mémoire sur le fabrication de l'acier en Yorkshire', *Annales des Mines*, 4th series, 3 (1843), 655–6.

65 J. Percy, *Metallurgy – Iron and Steel* (London: John Murray, 1864), p. 764.

66 Upton, 'City as material culture', p. 3.

9
Cultural space and worker identity in the company city: nineteenth-century Lowell, Massachusetts

MARY C. BEAUDRY AND
STEPHEN A. MROZOWSKI

Introduction

Lowell, Massachusetts, is remembered today as North America's classic nineteenth-century mill city. With the twentieth-century decay of New England textile production, the city also became infamous for an urban landscape that was scarred by the parking lots of demolished mill sites, and blighted by virulent 'slums'. Lowell originated in 1825, however, as a planned industrial city. Its founders attempted – through urban planning and careful oversight of workers' lives, housing and amenities – to create ideal conditions for profit through textile production. The space they created would serve as a model for mill communities throughout New England. Yet within little more than a century of its founding, the identification of 'slum' landscapes in the city would stand as a stark reminder of the vagaries of industrial capitalism's cycles of prosperity and poverty. By the 1880s, the lure of cheaper labour and no unions enticed the city's mill owners to invest their capital in the American South. The workers left behind saw family traditions of jobs in the mills severed, with no real alternative on the landscape.[1]

The question that Lowell's history begs is how a community planned and conceived to succeed could have been so quickly transformed into a landscape of neglect. And what of its workers? Was the sudden silence of the mills after generations of bustle the final humiliation, or just the predictable end of a capitalist experiment? Or are these both perhaps merely presentist interpretations that see Lowell's failure out of context. Did Lowell fail?[2] Can it be said that the corporations so dominated the lives of their employees that there was little opportunity for working people to forge their own identities? And if they

did, how are we to interpret the evidence of such action? Is it enough that workers had the freedom to configure parts of their material world, pursue activities outlawed by the company, and express their political views through protest and display? Or do we misrepresent the situation by highlighting what some consider to be efforts 'to cope with a degrading and largely intolerable condition'?[3]

Just who is a working-class 'hero'?

These important interpretative questions go to the heart of class analysis in historical archaeology.[4] In his critique of our study of Lowell mill workers Charles Orser questioned whether the 'subaltern can speak', noting that our Lowell study 'made the workers' actions seem unheroic because the workers were simply building a culture, not fighting oppression'.[5] We contend that the notion of heroism is not a particularly useful historical concept to impose on others' lives. It creates a standard, one derived from bourgeois treatments of history, that working-class people are required to uphold retroactively or not be considered valid as a class. The narrow construct of 'heroism' restricts us to examining only a small part of working-class lives, the part in which working-class people express resistance to authority, to capitalism. Using 'heroism' as a litmus test for whether people's lives are worth studying overlooks in particular what working-class people, when asked, consider important.[6]

By requiring working-class people of the past to meet the bourgeois standard of 'heroism', Orser is led to argue against the 'inside-out perspective' he correctly attributes to our work by stating 'I do not believe that archaeologists can ever obtain this viewpoint, even when confronted by a large body of written and archaeological information'.[7] On the whole we agree with Orser's call for a more dialectical approach that gives voice to all who participated in the dialogue.[8] Indeed, our approach explicitly aims to give voices to the voiceless and to provide for multiple voices, although we have chosen to focus more on how people construct power and identity in their everyday lives rather than on highly visible and organised political struggles. We argue that archaeological evidence recovered from the sites indicated on Fig. 9.1 speaks best to the practices of everyday life and that 'heroism' does not exist solely in the arena of overt political resistance to capitalist domination.[9] In addition we acknowledge that, in some instances, those in positions of power can dominate the tenor and dynamics of the discourse. This goes without saying, we believe, and to emphasise the point is merely to restate the obvious. We disagree, however, that a dialectical approach requires us to abandon attempts to develop a 'bottom-up'

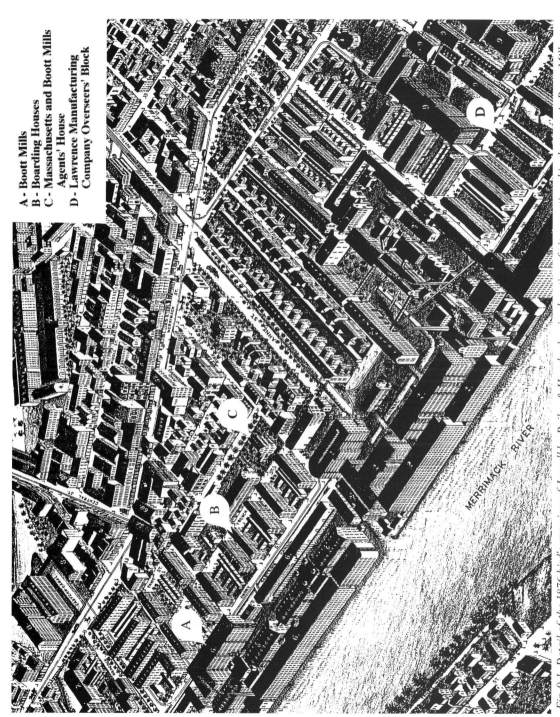

A - Boott Mills
B - Boarding Houses
C - Massachusetts and Boott Mills
    Agents' House
D - Lawrence Manufacturing
    Company Overseers' Block

Fig. 9.1 Detail of the 1876 bird's-eye view of Lowell by Bailey & Hazah, showing location of sites mentioned in the text: A. Boott Mills complex; B. Boott Mills boardinghouses; C. Kirk Street Agent's House; D. Lawrence Manufacturing Company Overseer's Block.

or 'inside-out' perspective.[10] Whether the workers felt oppressed or saw their living conditions as intolerable are historically contingent questions that are and will remain open to debate.[11] Less debatable, we believe, is the assertion that real political action first required a sense of cultural cohesiveness, a sense of class identity. The challenge is understanding the dialectical interplay of cultural and political action and its impact on the course of Lowell's history.

Multiple ways of seeing and interpreting urban space

We believe that the multifaceted material record we have inherited can provide answers to these sorts of questions, but only if we exploit all that is available to us. Multidimensional and malleable, the material world writ large served as one of the chief mediums of negotiation and mediation as the social relations of production were being forged. In Lowell's case, the documentary and cartographic sources are just as important as the architectural and archaeological record. This is particularly true if the goal of our research is to understand Lowell in the broader context of nineteenth-century industrial capitalism. What makes Lowell such a wonderful laboratory is the conceptual, self-conscious record of its history expressed in the planning documents, architecture and landscape. Still another manifestation of that record is the archaeological deposits that have accumulated during the city's history. In and of itself, this is a rich and diverse record that has demanded interdisciplinary interrogation.[12] Set against the evidence of what Lefebvre calls representations of space,[13] the archaeological record presents compelling testimony of that same space as social space, the locus of spatial practices. At times during the life of the city, these same spaces have also served as representational spaces, arenas for social expression such as protests or marches.[14]

Lefebvre's notions of space offer a useful framework for examining multidimensional space that served many purposes. It also helps to articulate the interwoven character of the urban landscape. Lefebvre describes three different moments of space, the *perceived*, the *conceived* and the *lived*.[15] This triad of constructs form the central core of Lefebvre's thinking about the production of space and its meaning. *Space as perceived* refers to material space and material spatial practices, the concrete world in which work is conducted, goods are produced and transported, and daily life is lived.[16] *Space as conceived* refers to planned space as envisioned in the abstract by the architect or planner. This takes the form of architectural renderings, plans, and the thought behind them. Lowell is

a most fertile community in which to explore these 'representations of space' because of its history of planning.[17] The final moment of Lefebvre's triad is what he terms *representational space* or, to employ Harvey's terminology, 'spaces of representation', which are places like museums, squares or streets, which become the locus of social expressions such as theatre, riots or demonstrations.[18]

The urban landscape of Lowell

When the founders of Lowell planned the community they conceived of the space they were to produce in terms of economies of scale, or the spatial practices surrounding industrial production. Lowell was a planned city only in part, however. The site chosen in 1825 by the Boston Associates, the group of capitalists who founded the city, promised abundant power for industry from the dramatic 30-foot drop of the falls of the Merrimack River. The falls posed a hazard to navigation that had been partly overcome through construction of the Pawtucket Canal around the falls. The existing canal was seen as an advantage in that it could readily be converted for use by industry through the construction of feeder canals leading to the water wheels and, later, turbines that powered thousands of spinning machines and looms installed in the multi-storey, monolithic red brick mills that would be built alongside them.[19] The route of the existing canal, therefore, dictated the form the city was to take. Lowell's planners imposed a modified grid plan on the land lying within a network of feeder canals; the result was a city in which each mill complex and its housing existed as a separate enclave.

Developers of other New England mill cities lacked Lowell's 'accidental' canal system and built according to a rigidly gridded plan. They constructed power canals parallel to the river from which water for power was drawn, and created in cities such as Lewiston, Maine, a solid corridor of industry between the river and canal, with worker housing forming yet another band of settlement beyond the industrial zone.[20] Beyond the boarding-house rows, developers permitted the growth of a business district by selling off the 'industrially useless' land to commercial interests.

The companies attempted to dictate the nature and composition of the urban environment; Lowell's planners *intended* that the structure of the city – street plan, mills, worker housing, and urban parks or 'greenways'[21] – would serve as an agent of social control.[22] Lowell developed into a series of zones through which workers moved on their way to work, to church, to shops and so on (Fig. 9.2).

VIEW OF THE BOOTT COTTON MILLS AT LOWELL, MASS.

Fig. 9.2 An 1852 view of the Boott Mills from Gleason's Pictorial *illustrates the attention given in Lowell's early days to the creation of carefully landscaped 'greenways' through which residents and visitors could promenade.*

Mill complexes hence dominated much of the townscape, separating the realm of work and home life from amenities like stores and taverns for the majority of the workforce. One deliberate result of company policy was to push establishments serving alcohol to the periphery of the urban centre. Since worker access to company housing was subject to a fairly high level of monitoring, drinking behaviour was ever subject to scrutiny. Whether this effort to control drinking away from company premises contributed to clandestine drinking in the boardinghouses and the boardinghouse backlots is not clear, but archaeological excavations revealed that in the latter half of the nineteenth century, drinking in the boardinghouses was quite common despite its being prohibited.[23] Large numbers of alcoholic beverage containers were recovered from sheet middens in the backlots as well as from accumulated deposits along fence lines and against sheds and outbuildings (Fig. 9.3). Fill of wells and privies likewise produced

liquor bottles, and one well also contained wine goblets and a beer mug, indicating consumption not just of distilled spirits but also of wine and beer. A most tell-tale find was a cache of liquor bottles in a spot that must once have been a hiding place beneath the steps leading into the woodshed that housed a privy. This deposit evokes the image of clandestine drinkers perched on the steps of the woodshed, smoking, perhaps playing cards, defying company rules but doing so in relative privacy.[24]

Here then is an image, albeit a fleeting one, of workers finding both the time and space to be themselves. Despite the rhetoric to the contrary, it appears that the companies cared more for appearances than for substance in such matters. Public drinking received great condemnation, as did public smoking. Any expression of working-class culture, working-class identity, posed a threat to the carefully constructed bourgeois façade that was Lowell's built environment as well as to the capitalist social construction

Fig. 9.3 Lewis Hine photograph of a backlot scene of a boardinghouse, at Homestead, Pennsylvania, used as an illustration in Margaret Byington's classic study, Homestead: The Households of a Mill Town *(Philadelphia: W. F. Fell Co., 1910). Here liquor bottles have accumulated against the rear of the building much as they had done in the backlots of the Boott Mills boardinghouses in Lowell.*

that required that a vast labouring class should remain largely invisible outside the workplace. As long as the workers were restricted to a space designed to maintain their anonymity, it seems they were free to live as they chose.

Lowell as cultural space

The evidence of secreted alcoholic beverage containers illustrates just how ephemeral the archaeological traces of working-class and ethnic identity can be. Despite the fact that the formation of ethnic identity among workers was a passionately contested arena in nineteenth-century

Lowell, involving as it did politics, strikes and public demonstrations, all very public activities, archaeology tends to reveal only the private, clandestine or small-scale evidence of everyday resistance.[25] This evidence cannot be divorced from the larger picture of the community as a whole, just because it represents private behaviour. To do so would be to limit artificially the purview of archaeology. The spaces that served as the contexts for daily social interaction among workers are no less 'our territory' than the representational spaces that would later be the media for more overt forms of working-class expression; they, too, are part of the urban landscapes archaeologists explore.

By the third quarter of the nineteenth century, for instance, Lowell's Irish community demonstrated its identity and solidarity by marching, through the public ritual of the annual St Patrick's Day parade.[26] Begun in 1841, at first the parade was the sole province of a group of conservative and assimilation-minded Irish, much to the resentment of other segments of Irish community. Gradually, resistance to discrimination and continued alienation from full participation in republican America forced the Irish to abandon their regional animosities – in public, at least – and to present a unified front as an established ethnic group with valid claims on power in Lowell. The parade route extended well beyond the Irish neighbourhoods to encompass the main commercial arteries, passing 'the corporate boardinghouses, City Hall, the mills, the edges of the Yankee residential areas'.[27] Marchers also made their parades ever noisier, so that their passage, indeed their very presence and numbers and insistent claims on power, could be heard beyond the parade route by those at whom these public demonstrations of identity and ethnic unity were aimed.

The material signature of these public acts, if there was one, is not the stuff of traditional archaeology. Instead, our work in Lowell explored backlots of boardinghouses and tenements, where we recovered such scrappy and mundane and fragmentary evidence as bits of clay pipe, broken glass and ceramics, buttons and other personal effects, seeds, pollen and so on. These leavings are the sorts of things historical archaeologists find: they are what we have to work with. Traditionally the approach has been to use such finds to date site strata, to make statements about trade networks, socio-economic status, and so on. These are perfectly appropriate and even necessary questions, of course, but not what we were most interested in for the Lowell study. We sought to make use of the scrappy bits and pieces of everyday life in our attempt to understand how workers constructed and expressed identity within the tightly structured and controlled physical and social environment of a company city such as Lowell.

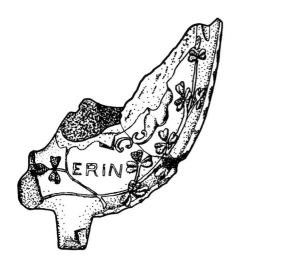
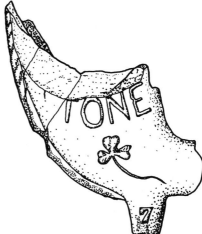

Fig. 9.4 A fragment of a white ball clay smoking pipe bowl from the Boott Mills boardinghouse backlots bearing slogans and symbols of Irish republican sentiments.

This led to close consideration of activities like smoking and drinking, using documentary sources to recover the action contexts in which the artefacts figured and the multiple meanings these actions had in both their expected and unexpected contexts and for user or performer as well as for others. Smoking pipes – cheap, abundant, highly disposable as well as highly breakable – embodied and conveyed powerful messages.[28] This is because smoking, like drinking, is entangled in a complex and emotional web of associations linked to class, ethnicity and gender (and, of course, now, to health, though health concerns were far from the nexus of contestation over smoking in the nineteenth century). As emblems of working-class identity, clay pipes became ready signifiers in contemporary illustrations. The viewer received the message that the person depicted was a member of the working class as readily from the clay pipe in his or her mouth as by his or her clothing and posture and surroundings. Some pipes were targeted at specific ethnic markets, such as those that bore the Gaelic term *Dhudeen*; others bore political legends, *Home Rule* being the most common, while others displayed shamrocks and the name of the great Irish republican martyr Wolf Tone (Figs. 9.4 and 9.5).

Only a person of the most limited imagination could insist that smokers were wholly insensible to the sentiments the decorations on such pipes conveyed, or would deny that some sort of choice was exercised in selection of one style of pipe over another. Likewise the very act of smoking could be an act of defiance of middle-class

mores when it was done in public, or on the streets or the front stoops of the boardinghouses. Pipe fragments were found in abundance in the backlots, but this does not mean that smoking was always clandestine: we did not dig in the streets or public spaces of the town but have only the written testimony of newspaper accounts drawing attention to the menacing and unsavoury practice of working people who appeared in public not just in their shirt sleeves but smoking as well.[29]

Other items such as buttons, hair combs, brooches and the like testify to the presence of women, of course, but they offer far less explicit expressions of identity.[30] Close readings of such fragments, however, reveal the pride workers took in their appearance. The tendency is to view purchase of such items in light of theories about consumerism and emulation, but we choose to twist things a bit and see in the conversion of earnings into items of personal adornment the active process of the construction of selfhood and of identity.[31] Among the young female operatives in Lowell, a penchant for costume jewellery appears to have been a clear marker of working-class cultural identity. In some instances these items were less expensive black glass imitations of the jet pieces that were popular among middle-class women of the period (Fig. 9.6).[32] Other examples included the numerous combs that were used to keep women's hair up when working. Their utilitarian service notwithstanding, these items were as carefully chosen as were the items of costume jewellery worn by working-class women in Lowell. Artefacts of personal adornment served as one element of 'appearential ordering' through which

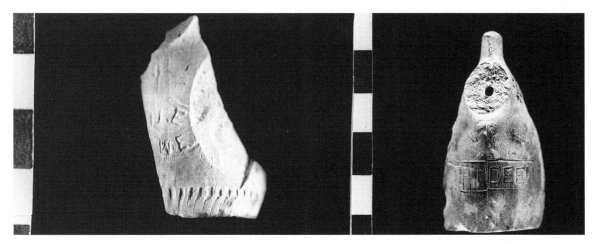

Fig. 9.5 *White ball clay pipe bowls with Irish associations.* Left, *a pipe bowl with a cartouche bearing the legend '*HOME RULE*'; right, a pipe bowl marked with the Gaelic word* Dhudeen, *a term referring to inexpensive short-stemmed clay pipes marketed to Irish workers.*

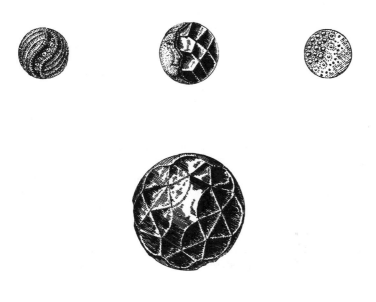

SCALE 1:1

Fig. 9.6 *Imitation jet buttons from the Boott Mills boardinghouse backlots.*

women made statements about their earning power and aspirations to middle-class status.[33]

This concern for appearance seems to have involved yard space as well. The presence of planting holes and flower pot fragments can be seen as evidence of efforts to rework the unembellished, utilitarian stage set for their lives that the companies erected into more viable and personalised living spaces. In some instances archaeobotanical and palynological data provide precise detail of the use of the yards associated with the company-supplied boardinghouses. Evidence of elderberry (*Sambucus canadensis*), for example, was found in association with a planting hole in the rear yard of a boardinghouse. The discovery of postholes and grape seeds (Vitus spp.) in the rear yard of another boardinghouse may also indicate the presence of grape arbours in the latter stages of the nineteenth century.[34] Both plants would have provided fresh fruits to the diet as well as pleasant vegetation for the yards.

The yard space provided for the boardinghouses was designed with the same efficiency as the factories themselves. With no front or side yards, the boardinghouses had only rear yards, surrounded by fencing and opening onto back alleys. Only the end units, where skilled workers and their families lived, had gated fences opening to the street. This subtle but significant difference was part of a community-wide pattern in which yard space was used to mark status within the company hierarchy. The block built expressly for the Lawrence Manufacturing Company overseers (Fig. 9.1 shows its location), in contrast to the workers' boardinghouses, included both rear and front yards. Although the front yards were small, this is in itself important because it points to their primary use as ornamental space. This was confirmed archaeologically by the presence of planting holes.[35] The same was true of the rear yards, although the presence of postholes thought to have once held clothes-line posts indicates that the space also served utilitarian purposes.

The importance of ornamental yard space as an expression of status is most visible at the Massachusetts/Boott Mills Agent's House (see Fig. 9.1). This well-appointed duplex was elaborately landscaped: fill was used to raise the level of the house well above street level. Such terracing set the Agent's House apart from both the boardinghouses and the Overseer's Block, which were at street level; here granite curbs and wrought iron fencing added to the finished character of the agent's front yards. The side yards were also raised, with loam brought to the site expressly for that purpose.[36] Palynological research confirmed that turf was used to complete the landscaping of the Agent's House in 1845.[37] Although archaeological

and contextual analysis indicated that the rear yard of the Agent's House served as utilitarian space, the front and side yards were purposely designed as extensions of the façade of the building.[38]

These differences in the allocation of space also extended to domestic technology, especially that relating to waste and water management. As originally envisioned, Lowell appears to have been relatively democratic in terms of sanitation. In part this resulted from available technology: when the city was first established in the early stages of the nineteenth century, wells and privies were still the chief facilities relied upon for water and waste management. As the century progressed and sanitary technology improved, company employees were not all provided with equal access to such advances. The company agents were the first to be provided with the benefits of indoor plumbing, followed some years later (1870s) by mid-level employees like overseers.[39] Not surprisingly, the evidence of sanitary change at the boardinghouses indicates that wells and privies were still in use in the first two decades of the twentieth century. This was nearly thirty years after the companies were instructed to rid themselves of these vestiges of a bygone era.[40]

Despite the discomfort or inconvenience this may have meant for boardinghouse residents, its one benefit was an archaeological record that had not been compromised by large-scale excavation resulting from the addition of water and waste piping. At the same time, the physical evidence of late nineteenth-century construction that brought water directly into the home, and indoor toilets, attests to a major shift in the nature of cities. For thousands of years, yard space had been the chief locus of facilities for water and waste management.[41] During much of this time, private responsibility for the construction and maintenance of these facilities was the norm. Starting in the late nineteenth century, this began to change as municipalities took over this function. There were several reasons for this, but growing population density, limited space and the need for improved sanitation were paramount.

The changing face of capitalism

Large companies like those in Lowell fell somewhere between the city and small property owners. In most instances, the companies paid to have the work carried out, although the overall system for municipal sanitation was being developed at the expense of the taxpayer. Given this company involvement, it made sense to focus first on managers like the Lawrence Manufacturing Company's overseers. These were, after all, the most important employees in the eyes of the company owners. They had been entrusted with the task of increasing profits and maintaining production without the benefit of more workers. Overseers were part of the changing face of capitalism in the mid-nineteenth century, what business historian Alfred Chandler has called 'managerial capitalism'.[42] Before 1840, growth among even the largest industrial enterprises was limited by scarce labour and reliance upon what still amounted to traditional technologies.[43] Improvements in machine technology and the development of railroads provided the conditions for rapid growth. In fact the increased scale of operations after 1840 owed much to company diversification into railroads and communications technology.[44] The result was a new, highly structured, hierarchically organised enterprise that was the precursor of the modern industrial giants that we know today.[45]

A key element of this transformation was the growing need for a class of professional managers. Unlike the early agents and treasurers of the Lowell mills, managers and overseers were seldom company stockholders. They were salaried employees whose success was based on their ability to improve profits by pushing workers they supervised to be more productive. The people who filled such management positions were part of a new group of workers whose very existence was linked to the development of managerial capitalism. Situated between the agents, for whom they worked, and the workers they supervised, the overseers were not only a new group of employees, they were part of a new social class as well. This status was not preordained; it was constructed over time. The company's contribution to the construction of this new identity came in the form of new housing units with ornamental front yards, as we have already discussed. Housing was not the only source of information concerning the class-consciousness of the overseer's households, however. Other classes of material culture such as ceramics, pipes and personal items suggest the dialectical character of the transformational process as people began constructing new identities: new in the sense that these were new positions in the company hierarchy and with that the process of negotiating a new status began.

The material culture recovered from around five units of the Lawrence Manufacturing Company's Overseer's Block indicates a dynamic social arena.[46] Census and directory information for the period 1850–90, the period best represented archaeologically, indicates that the Lawrence Block was home for a variety of company employees. Early in its history, the block included some boardinghouses. This practice ended quite quickly, and by 1860 the block housed primarily overseers and their fam-

ilies. This pattern remained fairly consistent until the end of the century, although there appear always to have been skilled workers such as machinists and carpenters as well as an occasional dyer, bleacher or watchman boarding on the block.[47]

The five units investigated archaeologically were those of overseers. Still the possibility of post-depositional mixing and the presence of servants in some overseer households mean that social interpretations are subject to reconsideration. Assuming that the material recovered is most representative of overseer households, the following observations can be offered. The ceramics and other evidence of dining habits reveal practices that place the overseers directly between the agents and the skilled and unskilled workers. In general the ceramic assemblages from the Overseer's Block reflect the higher status of the overseers compared with those from the Boott Mills boardinghouses and tenements. Slightly higher percentages of hand-painted and transfer-printed wares, for example, indicate subtle differences that may best reflect the greater buying power of the overseer's households.[48] The salary of an overseer was commonly twice to three times what a mill operative was paid. Among the ceramics were several fragments of a small plate decorated with the 'Texian Campaigne' pattern (Fig. 9.7).[49] The importance of this discovery is that the same pattern appears to have graced the table of Massachusetts Mill agent Homer Bartlett. This is based on its association with a large ceramic assemblage found on the Agent's House site attributed to the Bartlett household.[50] Bartlett and his wife Mary Starkweather Bartlett, along with three servants, lived at the Kirk Street Agent's House between 1846 and 1858, when Mary Bartlett died.[51] Bartlett remained in the house, where he was joined by his married daughter and her husband, until 1861.

Although the plate fragments represent only a small part of the larger assemblage they nevertheless point to the subtle ways that class consciousness can be read. In this instance it points to a sharing of tastes that helped to define social position. Other classes of material culture reflected similar sharing of tastes, but often mostly in subtle form, as in the case of the ceramic patterns. Examples include plastic pipe mouthpiece fragments at both sites. Although small in number, they also point to a similarity in tastes between the overseers and the agents. The small finds reflect the fact that overseer's households were upwardly mobile, embracing through their consumption patterns the middle-class values so comfortably exhibited by the possessions of the agent's families. Moderation in tobacco use and indulging in tobacco by smoking pipes that were more costly than the cheap white

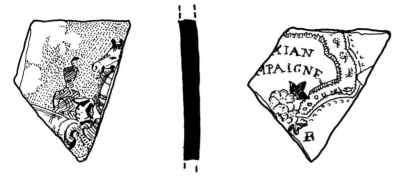

Fig. 9.7 Fragment of a white earthenware plate printed with the 'Texian Campaigne' pattern recovered from the rear lot of the Kirk Street Agent's House; sherds from plates in this romantic Staffordshire pattern were also found in the backlots of the Lawrence Mills Overseer's Block.

ball clay pipes favoured by working-class smokers are behaviours that speak to the social and economic aspirations that led overseers and their families to imitate the lifestyle of the agent's households.

The assemblage of personal items recovered from the Overseer's Block is similar to that found at the Boott Mills boardinghouse.[52] It comprises items from clothing like buttons and fasteners as well as a few pieces of jewellery. The buttons were manufactured from a variety of materials including bone, shell, metal, porcelain, glass, plastic and glass imitations of jet. The shell and bone buttons recovered from the site included two- and four-hole types that were probably covered by cloth. These artefacts are difficult to date because the design remained unchanged for centuries. They served a variety of purposes in dresses, waistcoats and shirts. The presence of white porcelain buttons could represent a diachronic change in tastes given that these later replaced bone and shell buttons. Porcelain buttons were durable and attractive enough to be used plain. In some instances they could be decorated with pie-crust edging. These porcelain buttons were often larger than their bone or shell counterparts and served a variety of purposes. They could also be used for both utilitarian, everyday clothing or fancier items for special occasions.

Porcelain buttons of this kind represented the majority of the collection from the Overseer's Block, along with those made of glass. Of these the jet examples were the most interesting. Included among these were several dress buttons similar to examples recovered from the Boott Mills boardinghouses.[53] Jet buttons like those recovered from the Overseer's Block normally served as fasteners for women's clothing. They represent some of the clearest evidence of women's status and consumer choices recovered from the block. In her discussion of personal effects from the Boott Mills boardinghouses, Ziesing argues that imitation jet items are best interpreted as inexpensive substitutes for real jet pieces. Whether the same interpretation applies to the women who resided at the Overseer's Block remains unclear because of the possible presence of servants. In several of the overseer's households the demographic structure consistently included a mother and father in their mid- to late thirties, an array of children, and a single female in her twenties or thirties. Besides the information on the demographic structure of the households, the 1870 and 1880 censuses provide some evidence of ethnicity in the form of names. Based on this, the block appears to have remained completely American born during this time, a pattern also reflected in the earlier directories as well. This suggests that the women could have been domestic servants and perhaps governesses.

Changing notions of class and of working-class culture

In his early discussion of working-class communities, E. P. Thompson cautioned against generalising about either the morals or the manners of such groups.[54] Today this has given way to a new awareness that class can no longer be accorded causal primacy.[55] The importance of class consciousness is not being questioned so much as being tempered by the reality that it is just one of many factors that shape the dynamics of social interaction. Issues of age, gender, ethnicity and race all converge to contribute to social discourse.[56] There is also a growing recognition that the concept of class as a rigid, objective social category is flawed and that class should rather be viewed as a discursive object.[57] The archaeological evidence from Lowell tends to support the latter formulation. In comparing the material culture recovered from around the Massachusetts Mills Agent's house with that from the Lawrence Overseer's Block and the Boott Mills boardinghouses and tenements, we clearly see the expression of class differences. Furthermore there seems little doubt that artefacts served as active expressions of class consciousness tempered with other variables such as occupation and gender. In the case of the Lawrence Overseer's Block, for example, it seems possible that the women of these households were not participating in the construction of a new class identity on an equal footing with their husbands. This observation is based on the similarities in women's personal items among the various sites. And yet even here, the presence of dinner wares identical to those found at the agent's house indicates a point of class identity.

We have chosen to interpret these various classes of material culture as evidence of an extremely dynamic situation, in which identities were actively being forged. The company agents and overseers were negotiating their new status through material culture that complemented the space created for them by the companies. The same was true of skilled and unskilled workers for the Boott Mills. They too were actively engaged in the construction of their own identities. In the case of the Irish workers of the latter stages of the nineteenth century, the factor of ethnicity contributed to the equation. Their St Patrick's Day celebrations were an important example of the manner in which rituals can serve political ends.[58] Contradicting the view that ritual serves primarily to maintain tradition, Comaroff and Comaroff argue that it also serves as 'a means of experimental practice, of subversive poetics, of creative tension and transformative action'.[59] The space chosen to frame such action is critical. In the case of the Irish paraders in Lowell, marching, not only through their own neighbourhoods or down the streets designed to channel operatives to their workplaces, but also along the routes of power and wealth within the city, added to the political purpose of the act. They could have chosen to celebrate in individual homes or in small groups, but instead they chose the streets as the arena in which to express their emerging class and ethnic solidarity. Its seems hard to imagine that the point was lost on the mill owners and those they paid to oversee the workers.

Although the founders of Lowell had made every effort to design their city with economy and efficiency in mind, their control over the space they had created was not total. The struggle against the ideological hegemony of the ruling class was a battle fought on many fronts 'on the basis of tensions and contradictions which are present in the actual structures of work and life'.[60] In the yards of the boardinghouses, workers found a haven where they could relax and express their feelings beyond the gaze of the factory. Was it like the workers of today, supported by unions who fought for more than a century to establish an awareness of workers' rights? No, but the genesis of such power can be traced to these same backyards.

In our study of Lowell we have taken a variety of perspectives and used a range of analytical scales from the grand to the minute. Our chief concern has been to look beyond the brittle carapace of the built environment and its accompanying straitjacket of company policy and company control of workers' lives at all levels, in and out of the workplace, to glimpse the ways in which workers created their lives and identities. We see Lowell's workers as individuals who claimed for themselves the right to decide how to spend their money or their leisure time. Most often we can best see how Lowell's workers created their own cultural space by looking at how they manipulated the public and private presentation of self through use of seemingly trivial archaeological finds, the lost fragments of everyday life. We argue that, more often than not, what was important for working-class people, the values upon which their notions of 'success' were based, had more to do with home, family and better lives for their children than with workplace issues. To adopt a notion that people can only be 'heroes' in the public arena, when they are resisting the forces of capitalism, misses this important point and limits our ability to examine working-class lives on their own terms. We are saying not that we want to 'de-heroise' members of the working class, but that, rather than impose from without a bourgeois concept of 'heroism', our goal should be to broaden the notion of what is considered 'heroic' to include what working-class people themselves would find important.

The construction and constitution of cultural space is an important element in the formation of working-class identity; private acts begun in private find public expression as working-class identities are forged. Workers attempt first to control life in the spaces where, to expand upon Lefebvre,[61] space is experienced and life is lived.

Acknowledgements

Thanks to Alan Mayne for inviting us to participate in his session 'Archaeologies of Slumland' at the World Archaeology Congress in Cape Town in January 1998, and to him and Tim Murray for including us in this book. We're flattered to be in such great company! We also thank Alan and Tim in their capacity as editors for their constructive advice on revising our chapter. Heartfelt thanks to all of the many scholars and researchers who participated in the interdisciplinary study of the Lowell Boott Mills, most particularly to Lauren Cook, for his useful insight and helpful suggestions regarding the present manuscript.

Notes

1 See Mary H. Blewett, *The Last Generation: Work and Life in the Textile Mills of Lowell, Massachusetts 1910–1960* (Amherst: University of Massachusetts Press, 1990).

2 See, e.g., Laurence F. Gross, 'The game is played out: the closing decades of the Boott Mill', in Robert Weible (ed.), *The Continuing Revolution: A History of Lowell, Massachusetts* (Lowell: The Lowell Historical Society, 1991), pp. 281–99.

3 Charles E. Orser Jr, *A Historical Archaeology of the Modern World* (New York: Plenum Press, 1996), p. 178.

4 For an explicit reformulation of the treatment of issues of class in historical archaeology, see the essays in a special issue of the journal *Historical Archaeology*: LuAnn Wurst and Robert K. Fitts (eds.), *Confronting Class*, special issue, *Historical Archaeology* 33:1 (1999).

5 Orser, *Modern World*, pp. 178–9; Orser critiques Mary C. Beaudry, Lauren J. Cook and Stephen A. Mrozowski, 'Artifacts and active voices: material culture as social discourse', in Randall McGuire and Robert Paynter (eds.), *The Archaeology of Inequality* (Oxford: Blackwell, 1991), pp. 150–91. For further discussions of our approach, again based on the Beaudry, Cook and Mrozowski essay, see LuAnn Wurst and Robert K. Fitts, 'Introduction: Why confront class?', in Wurst and Fitts, *Confronting Class*, p. 3, and LuAnn Wurst, 'Internalizing class in historical archaeology', in Wurst and Fitts, *Confronting Class*, p. 11.

6 See, e.g., Mary C. Beaudry, 'Public aesthetics versus personal experience: archaeology and the interpretation of 19th-century worker health and well being in Lowell, Massachusetts', *Historical Archaeology* 27:2 (1993), 90–105.

7 Orser, *Modern World*, p. 181.

8 *Ibid.*, p. 182.

9 See Beaudry *et al.*, 'Active voices', pp. 158–9, 163–5.

10 E. P. Thompson, 'The poverty of theory or an orrery of errors', in E. P. Thompson (ed.), *The Poverty of Theory and Other Essays* (New York: Monthly Review Press, 1978), p. 157; see also E. P. Thompson, *The Making of the English Working Class* (New York: Vintage Books, 1963), pp. 17–25; Henry Glassie, *Passing the Time in Ballymenone: Culture and History of an Ulster Community* (Philadelphia: University of Pennsylvania Press, 1982), p. 86.

11 Barrie Trinder has made this point effectively in discussing the industrial landscape of Britain, noting that we should not 'assume without evidence that the creation of such a horrific landscape was a deeply deliberated act committed by unnamed exploiters, or that to live there was of necessity dehumanizing'. Barrie Trinder, *The Making of the Industrial Landscape* (Gloucester: Alan Sutton, 1987), p. 1.

12 Mary C. Beaudry and Stephen A. Mrozowski (eds.), *Interdisciplinary Investigations of the Boott Mills, Lowell, Massachusetts: A Preliminary Report*, Cultural Resources Management Series 18 (Boston: National Park Service, North Atlantic Regional Office, 1987); Mary C. Beaudry and Stephen A. Mrozowski (eds.), *Interdisciplinary Investigations of the Boott Mills, Lowell, Massachusetts*, vol. 2, *The Kirk Street Agent's House*, Cultural Resources Management Series 19 (Boston: National Park Service, North Atlantic Regional Office, 1987); Mary C. Beaudry and Stephen A. Mrozowski (eds.), *Interdisciplinary Investigations of the Boott Mills, Lowell, Massachusetts*, vol. 3, *The Boardinghouse System as a Way of Life*, Cultural Resources Management Series 21 (Boston: National Park Service, North Atlantic Regional Office, 1987); Stephen A. Mrozowski, Grace H. Ziesing and Mary C. Beaudry, *'Living on the Boott': Historical Archaeology at the Boott Mills Boardinghouses, Lowell, Massachusetts* (Amherst: University of Massachusetts Press, 1996).

13 Henri Lefebvre, *The Production of Space* (Oxford: Blackwell, 1994).

14 *Ibid.*, p. 33.

15 *Ibid.*, p. 46.

16 *Ibid.*, pp. 40–6; see also David Harvey, *The Urban Experience* (Baltimore: Johns Hopkins University Press, 1989), pp. 261–3.

17 Lefebvre, *Space*, pp. 38–9.

18 *Ibid.*, pp. 39–46; Harvey, *Urban Experience*, p. 261.

19 Patrick Malone, *Canals and Industry: Engineering in Lowell, 1821–1880* (Lowell: Lowell Museum, 1983); Weible (ed.), *Continuing Revolution*; John S. Garner, *The Model Company Town* (Amherst: University of Massachusetts Press, 1984); John S. Garner (ed.), *The Company Town: Architecture and Society in the Early Industrial Age* (New York: Oxford University Press, 1992); Richard M. Candee, 'Architecture and corporate

planning in the early Waltham system', in Robert Weible (ed.), *Essays from the Lowell Conference on Industrial History 1982/1983* (Lowell: Lowell Historical Society, 1985), pp. 17–43.

20 Richard M. Candee, pers. comm., 1998.

21 See Patrick M. Malone and Charles A. Parrott, 'Greenways in the industrial city: parks and promenades along the Lowell canals', *IA: The Journal of the Society for Industrial Archeology* 24 (1998), 9–18.

22 Mary C. Beaudry, 'The Lowell Boott Mills complex and its housing: material expressions of corporate ideology', *Historical Archaeology* 23 (1989), 19–32; Stephen A. Mrozowski and Mary C. Beaudry, 'Archaeology and the landscape of corporate ideology', in W. M. Kelso and R. Most (eds.), *Earth Patterns: Essays in Landscape Archaeology* (Charlottesville: University Press of Virginia, 1990), pp. 189–208; Stephen A. Mrozowski, 'Landscapes of inequality', in McGuire and Paynter (eds.), *The Archaeology of Inequality*, pp. 79–101.

23 Kathleen H. Bond, 'Alcohol use in the Boott Mills boardinghouses: tension between workers and management, a documentary and archaeological study', MA thesis, Boston University (1988); Kathleen H. Bond, '"That we may purify our corporation by discharging the offenders": the documentary record of social control in the Boott boardinghouses', in Beaudry and Mrozowski (eds.), *Interdisciplinary Investigations*, vol. 3, pp. 23–36.

24 Kathleen H. Bond, 'The medicine, alcohol, and soda vessels from the Boott Mills boardinghouses', in Beaudry and Mrozowski (eds.), *Interdisciplinary Investigations*, vol. 3, pp. 121–39.

25 James Scott, *Weapons of the Weak: Everyday Forms of Peasant Resistance* (New Haven: Yale University Press, 1985); Martin Hall, 'Small things and the "mobile, conflictual fusion of power, fear, and desire"', in Anne E. Yentsch and Mary C. Beaudry (eds.), *The Art and Mystery of Historical Archaeology: Essays in Honor of James Deetz* (Boca Raton, FL: CRC Press, 1992), pp. 373–99.

26 Sallie A. Marston, 'Contested territory: an ethnic parade as symbolic resistance', in Weible (ed.), *Continuing Revolution*, pp. 213–33.

27 *Ibid.*, p. 226.

28 Lauren J. Cook, 'Descriptive analysis of tobacco-related material from the Boott Mills boardinghouses', in Beaudry and Mrozowski (eds.), *Interdisciplinary Investigations*, vol. 3, pp. 187–207; Lauren J. Cook, 'Tobacco-related material culture and the construction of working-class culture', in

Beaudry and Mrozowski (eds.), *Interdisciplinary Investigations*, vol. 3, pp. 209–29.

29 *Ibid.*

30 Grace H. Ziesing, 'Analysis of personal effects from the excavations of the Boott Mills boardinghouse backlots in Lowell, Massachusetts', in Beaudry and Mrozowski (eds.), *Interdisciplinary Investigations*, vol. 3, pp. 141–68.

31 Cf. Lauren Cook, Rebecca Yamin and John P. McCarthy, 'Shopping as meaningful action: toward a redefinition of consumption in historical archaeology', *Historical Archaeology* 30:4 (1996), 50–65.

32 Mrozowski, *et al.*, 'Living on the Boott', pp. 77–80.

33 Cf. Ziesing, 'Personal effects'; Beaudry *et al.*, 'Active voices'.

34 *Ibid.*

35 Stephen A. Mrozowski, 'Interdisciplinary perspectives on the production of urban industrial space', in Geoff Egan and R. L. Michael (eds.), *Old and New Worlds* (Oxford: Oxbow Books, 1999), pp. 136–46.

36 Beaudry and Mrozowski (eds.), *Interdisciplinary Investigations*, vol. 2, pp. 145–6.

37 Gerald K. Kelso, Stephen A. Mrozowski and William F. Fisher, 'Contextual archeology at the Kirk Street Agent's House', in Beaudry and Mrozowski (eds.), *Interdisciplinary Investigations*, vol. 2, pp. 97–130.

38 Mrozowski, 'Landscapes of inequality'; Mrozowski *et al.*, 'Living on the Boott'.

39 Stephen A. Mrozowski, 'Managerial capitalism and the subtleties of class analysis in historical archaeology', in James A. Delle, Stephen A. Mrozowski and Robert Paynter (eds.), *Lines that Divide: Historical Archaeologies of Race, Class, and Gender* (Knoxville: University of Tennessee Press, 2000).

40 Edward L. Bell, 'A preliminary report on health, hygiene, and sanitation at the Boott Mills boarding houses: an historical and archeological perspective', in Beaudry and Mrozowski (eds.), *Preliminary Report*, pp. 57–68; Edward L. Bell, '"So much like home": the historical context of the Kirk Street Agent's House', in Beaudry and Mrozowski (eds.), *Interdisciplinary Investigations*, vol. 2, p. 9.

41 Mrozowski, 'Landscapes of inequality', pp. 79–80.

42 Alfred D. Chandler, *The Visible Hand: The Managerial Revolution in American Business* (Cambridge, MA: The Belknap Press of Harvard University, 1977); Alfred D. Chandler, *Scale and Scope: The Dynamics of Industrial Capitalism* (Cambridge, MA: The Belknap Press of Harvard University, 1990).

43 Chandler, *Visible Hand*, pp. 62–3.

44 *Ibid.*, pp. 81–203.

45 Chandler, *Scale and Scope*, pp. 51–89.

46 Mrozowski, 'Managerial capitalism'.

47 George Adams, *The Lowell Directory* (Lowell, MA: Oliver March, 1851); Adams, Sampson, and Company, *The Lowell Directory* (Lowell, MA: Joshua Merrill and B. C. Sargeant, 1861); Sampson, Davenport, and Company, *The Lowell Directory, 1871* (Lowell, MA: Joshua Merrill and Son and B. C. Sargeant, 1871); Sampson, Davenport, and Company, *The Lowell Directory, 1881* (Lowell, MA: Joshua Merrill and Son, 1881); Sampson, Murdock, and Company, *The Lowell Directory, 1891* (Lowell, MA: Joshua Merrill and Son, 1891); United States Bureau of the Census, *Ninth Census of the United States*, Massachusetts, Middlesex County, Lowell, Ward 2. Microfilm, Roll 627 (Washington, DC: National Archives, 1870); United States Bureau of the Census, *Tenth Census of the United States*, Massachusetts, Middlesex County, Lowell, Enumeration District 453. Microfilm, Roll 544 (Washington, DC: National Archives, 1880).

48 Mrozowski, 'Urban industrial space'.

49 S. Laidecker, *Anglo-American China Part 1* (Bloomsburg, PA: Keystone Printed Specialties Co., 1954), p. 34.

50 Lorinda B. Rodenhiser and David H. Dutton, 'Material culture from the Kirk Street Agent's House', in Beaudry and Mrozowski (eds.), *Interdisciplinary Investigations*, vol. 2, p. 75; *ibid.*, p. 144.

51 Bell, 'Historical context', in *ibid.*, pp. 19–20.

52 Ziesing, 'Analysis of personal effects', pp. 141–68.

53 *Ibid.*, p. 149.

54 Thompson, *English Working Class*, p. 409.

55 E. O. Wright, 'Class analysis, history and emancipation', *New Left Review* 202 (1993), 15–35.

56 See, e.g., Elizabeth M. Scott (ed.), *Those of Little Note: Gender, Race, and Class in Historical Archaeology* (Tucson: University of Arizona Press, 1994), pp. 7–9; Anne McClintock, *Imperial Leather: Race, Gender, and Sexuality in the Colonial Contest* (London: Routledge, 1995); Delle *et al.*, *Lines that Divide*.

57 Lynn Hunt, 'Introduction: history, culture, and text', in Lynn Hunt (ed.), *The New Cultural History* (Berkeley: University of California Press, 1989), pp. 7–16; see also Wright, 'Class analysis', pp. 28–9; Jacques Revel, 'Microanalysis and the construction of the social', in Jacques Revel and Lynn Hunt (eds.), *Histories: French Constructions of the Past. Postwar French Thought*, vol. 1 (New York: The New Press, 1995), pp. 492–502; Mrozowski, 'Managerial capitalism'.

58 John D. Kelly and Martha Kaplan, 'History, structure, and ritual', *Annual Reviews in Anthropology* 19 (1990), 119–50; Jean Comaroff and John L. Comaroff, 'Introduction', in Jean Comaroff and John L. Comaroff (eds.), *Modernity and Its Malcontents: Ritual and Power in Postcolonial Africa* (Chicago: University of Chicago Press, 1993), pp. xi–xxx.

59 Comaroff and Comaroff, 'Introduction', p. xxix; see also Jean Comaroff and John L. Comaroff, *Of Revelation and Revolution: The Dialectics of Modernity on a South African Frontier* (Chicago: University of Chicago Press, 1997).

60 Ralph Miliband, *Marxism and Politics* (Oxford: Oxford University Press, 1977), pp. 53–4.

61 Lefebvre, *Space*, p. 46.

10

The archaeology of physical and social transformation: high times, low tides and tourist floods on Quebec city's waterfront

REGINALD AUGER AND WILLIAM MOSS

Introduction

This article is an examination of the recent restoration of Quebec City's Lower Town as seen through archaeological data. The Historic District spans a period of four centuries which have seen a sequence of economic growth and collapse. Lower Town can be viewed as having gone through three stages and, over the past century, it has been transformed from an 'imagined slumland' into a prime tourist attraction. What underlies this development, and how does historic site development fit in with the process of urban renewal or the creation of a national identity? And what has been learned about the city in the process, and what has archaeological research been able to contribute to the narrative?[1]

We wish to demonstrate in this chapter that, although there was an interest to develop Quebec City's Lower Town as early as the 1930s in order to tap into the growing tourist trade, what effectively drove the restoration of Place-Royale was the development of a national consciousness and the recognition of an identity which has been at the core of Quebec politics for the last century. Historians have taught us that Place-Royale prospered at the end of the eighteenth century and during the nineteenth century, but the decline of its financial district, caused by reduced activities at the port and the construction of the railroad which bypassed Quebec City, resulted in a shift of the economic development west in favour of Montreal. In addition to those overarching external factors, we witnessed, locally, a migration of people to the Upper Town at the end of the nineteenth century. Then, the Lower Town became an amalgamation encumbered with rundown tenements and warehouses: an urban

quarter which left the visitor with an impression of poverty where Irish immigrants and French Canadian labourers and craftsmen had residence. As a result, we suggest that the first ideas about restoring the Lower Town to its heyday, the French period, were born out of a sense of national identity, and what has transpired is that, through a series of political decisions, very little is known archaeologically of the history of Quebec during the eighteenth and nineteenth centuries.

The Historic District, commonly known as Old Town, encompasses the walled city on Upper Town plateau, which overlooks the St Lawrence River and its tributary, the St Charles, and Lower Town, which extends along three sides of the fortified headland (Figs. 10.1 and 10.2). At the heart of Lower Town lies *Place-Royale*, a narrow strip of land contained between the river and Cap Diamant, chosen by Samuel de Champlain as the site of a trading post and settlement in 1608.[2] Royal Square (*place Royale*) must be clearly differentiated from Place-Royale. The former, a clearly defined city square laid out in the seventeenth century, sits in the middle of the latter, an arbitrarily defined part of the lower town, created by governmental decree in 1967.[3] Neither the former nor the latter can or should be seen as representative of Lower Town, though the two are often confused. Lower Town itself had a clear identity until the end of the nineteenth century, although its official definition and boundaries have always shifted. It has rarely corresponded to one parish or administrative unit, and over time its physical limits changed dramatically with urban development. This territorial confusion has frequently caused methodological problems for historians, as data sets such as census units rarely cover a uniform territory from one period to the next.[4] For us, Lower Town stretches from the foot of the cliff below the Citadel (*Anse-des-mères*) northwards to the head of the Princess Louise Basin. As we intend to demonstrate, the above-mentioned confusion has been reinforced by recent research and has helped to cloud a full understanding of the nature of Lower Town.

Université Laval's research programme and the city's archaeological monitoring of urban development projects have helped to shed new light on lesser-known aspects of Lower Town's history. The university and the city have developed an approach of contextual archaeology[5] using an ecosystemic model. This model, elaborated by Paul-Gaston L'Anglais following Odum's definition of an ecosystem, considers the city as an ecosystem supplied by exterior sources.[6] The model sets the guidelines for research on individual sites, considering the city as a whole rather than as a conglomerate of separate and independent archaeological sites. This approach specifies that

Fig. 10.1 Place-Royale *and the Lower Town in 1998 seen from the same perspective as Fig. 10.3. The massive transformation of the waterfront is evident, as are the additions of tourist facilities such as the* Musée de la Civilisation *and the restored houses and the reconstructed battery of* Place-Royale. *The Hunt Block is immediately south of the museum.*

data be collected from all phases of a site rather than concentrating on the identification of spectacular events such as the oldest or the most politically noteworthy components. At the Hunt Block, this has allowed us to trace the development of the site and to understand how the city has encroached on the marine environment, through a detailed study of the urbanisation of the waterfront.[7]

The Historic District's Lower Town

Quebec today is a medium-sized city with a regional population of some 700,000. Fifth in size in Canada, the city's relative size and importance have gradually declined over the past 150 years as industrialisation, urbanisation and demographics shifted the economic heart of Canada westward.[8] Quebec City's apogee was reached during the 1830s, when the city, with a population of some 28,000, was Canada's largest urban centre and North America's

third most important port, coming after New York and New Orleans. Seventy years earlier, just before New France was ceded to England in 1763, the town was home to 7,000 and was the centre of the French colony. A century before that, when royal government was proclaimed in 1663, the town of only 550 souls was beginning to be recognized as an urban society.[9] Place-Royale was at the heart of that emerging economic centre. By 1900, the city's population had grown to 68,000, but Quebec had been overshadowed in both size and importance by Montreal and Toronto. Place-Royale had itself been eclipsed as the heart of the urban agglomeration.

The area of Lower Town along the St Lawrence River was a bustling port district and home to merchants and craftsmen, whereas even as early as the mid-seventeenth century Upper Town housed numerous religious communities and colonial administrative functions. In the context of the colony, Lower Town was extremely

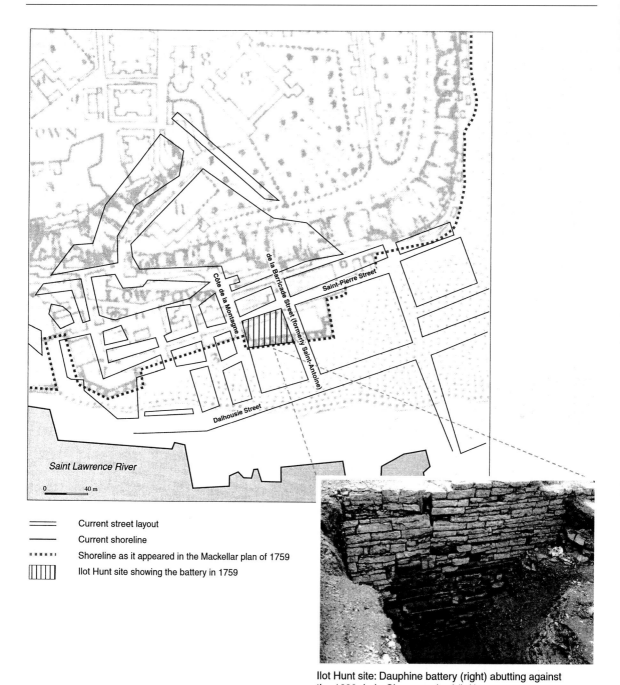

Current street layout

Current shoreline

Shoreline as it appeared in the Mackellar plan of 1759

Ilot Hunt site showing the battery in 1759

Ilot Hunt site: Dauphine battery (right) abutting against the 1699 de-la-Chenaye wharf (left).

Fig. 10.2 General plan of the Historic District superimposed on a c. 1750 plan.

Fig. 10.3 The Duberger Scale Model built in 1808. This view, which takes the same perspective as Fig. 10.1, shows the configuration of Lower Town just before the construction boom of the mid-nineteenth century.

wealthy, and somewhat ostentatious. Charles Aubert de la Chesnaye, the wealthiest merchant in New France, built his *hôtel particulier* fronting his wharves on the foreshore of the St Lawrence. Numerous other merchants had their houses, storehouses and wharves nearby. The area of Lower Town expanded continually between 1699, when Aubert de la Chesnaye built his first wharf, and the turn of the nineteenth century, by which point it had doubled (Fig. 10.3). The waterfront expansion continued until the end of the nineteenth century, with the locked Princess Louise Basin being built from 1877 to 1890.[10] More work was carried out in the 1980s to adapt the all-but-abandoned ocean-going port to modern cruise ships.

The population of Lower Town,[11] which totalled 3,243 in 1818, rose to a high of 8,303 in 1861 (23 per cent of the city's population) and then fell to 3,177 in 1921. Lower Town was home to only 3 per cent of the city's residents in 1947. Massive immigration during the nineteenth century changed the ethnic profile of the city's popula-

tion, which had remained entirely French until 1763. By 1830, 51 per cent of the Lower Town population was Irish and 39 per cent French Canadian, whereas the English and Scots were mostly in Upper Town. There was ethnic segregation within Lower Town itself. Merchants, mostly English, were concentrated around the *place Royale*, whereas the French and the Irish were on either extremity, between the foot of the cliff and the waterfront.

According to Laframboise, the Lower Town population in 1820 was composed of merchants, innkeepers and port-related workers.[12] For the period 1820–60, half of the resident population were merchants, traders, wholesalers or grocers, whereas the other half were tradesmen, labourers or unskilled workers.[13] There appears to have been a spatial segregation by trade: merchants were on Saint-Pierre and Sous-le-Fort streets, woodworking trades on Sault-au-Matelot Street, while watchmakers were on Notre-Dame Street.[14] The last cooper in Quebec City closed his shop on Sault-au-Matelot Street in 1940.[15]

Saint-Pierre Street became the city's financial district with the founding of the Bank of Quebec in 1818, followed by several more banks and financial institutions, including Canada's first Stock Exchange.[16] The last of these institutions was active until the 1950s.

The segregation observed for the first half of the nineteenth century progressively took on a new expression during the second half of the nineteenth century, as the wealthier merchants moved to Upper Town, then to suburbs outside the walls of the city. Lower Town became home to the Irish population, then to French Canadian workers, craftsmen and labourers. Most authors, beginning with Dahl *et al.* in 1975,[17] state that the wealthier residents began moving to Upper Town as a result of the cholera epidemic of 1832 and the massive arrival of Irish immigrants in the following decades. However, Provencher claims to the contrary, that there is no real evidence to confirm that the wealthy residents of Place-Royale actually moved out of this area before the 1860s; indeed, available evidence strongly suggests the continued presence of a wealthy population well into the second half of the nineteenth century.[18]

Place-Royale was the hub of regional land and water travel until the present century. Steam travel became increasingly frequent following the 1830s; the railroad reached the South Shore town of Lévis in 1854 and the city itself in 1879.[19] Travellers from the city took the ferry from Place-Royale to the train station on the opposite shore until the early 1900s. Improved travel corresponded with the arrival of tourists, all of whom had to transit via Lower Town because of transportation infrastructures. Beginning in the 1870s, local chroniclers published numerous picturesque texts intended for visitors.[20] Picturesque imagery appeared at the same time, and an icon frequently reproduced on postcards was Lower Town's narrow Sous-le-Cap Street, a mere alleyway spanned by numerous walkways and seemingly always filled with laundry hanging out to dry (Fig. 10.4).[21] Either photographers always came on Monday (washing day) or the residents were particularly fastidious about personal hygiene! By the 1940s, an English sign reading, 'Notice. Please refrain from giving money to children in order to avoid accidents. By order of Police' graced the walls of the alleyway.[22] A perception of poverty and the presence of English-speaking tourists are evident in Lower Town at this time. By then, Lower Town had a very small resident population (qualified as 'unstable'), numerous commercial and legal offices, and wholesalers' warehouses and outlets.[23]

Thus, during the 1950s, Lower Town – its commercial and industrial interests all but gone and most of the resident population having moved elsewhere – looked much more like an early-twentieth-century town, with its brick-faced and flat-roofed buildings standing five to six storeys high over most of the available land. Hidden in the back streets and alleys were run-down tenements and decrepit warehouses. In 1946, Maurice Lamontagne described Lower Town as the worst slum in Quebec City: '*la basse-ville n'a presque pas d'habitants fixes, sauf quelques essaims de familles très pauvres loties dans les pires taudis de la ville en des ruelles collées à la falaise*'.[24] That observation was followed in the early 1960s by a commission of inquiry into housing conditions which constituted the first step in a series of major urban renewal projects touching Lower Town and the adjacent Saint-Roch district. At the same time (1962), the Old Town Historic District was created under the terms of the provincial Cultural Properties Act.

Though several different groups had been promoting the restoration of Place-Royale and of specific buildings deemed of particular interest as early as the 1930s, the housing commission was the first to propose the consolidation of the tourism-related development of Lower Town.[25] The urban renewal movement gained importance in the post-war years and, in Lower Town, it culminated in the Place-Royale Project, begun in 1967.[26] Probably inspired by other major open-air museums sprouting throughout America, the Place-Royale Project essentially proceeded at a pace leaving little time to take stock. Conservation choices were made with one objective in mind: restore the site to its presumed heyday during the French regime. As a result, very little is known about the evolution of the Old Town during the nineteenth century.

Parallel to the launching of the Place-Royale Project, a general urban development concept was drawn up for the Historic District. This study, which included a chapter on historical sites and vestiges,[27] euphemistically stated that, in 1970, Lower Town was in a state of transition: 'certain residents still want to live here, whereas others would move away immediately if they had the chance'. Paradoxically, according to the same study:

> The resident population, comprised mostly of families, manifests a strong social cohesion and consequently a strong attachment to its milieu . . . The lower town presents a very deteriorated image of its buildings and shows the characteristics of a sector in transition insofar as its population is concerned but also with regard to its commerces, its institutions and its administrative structure. In want of a vocation, this sector is presently unfit for living in and its commerces are gradually leaving . . . Lodgings of more than four rooms should be concentrated in specific sectors in order to meet the needs of family households. Two

Fig. 10.4 A postcard view of Sous-le-Cap Street in the early 1900s.

sectors currently used for this end, Lower Town and the Palace, appear to be totally inadequate for this purpose and their population should be relocated.[28]

This same study obliquely suggests a cause for the degradation of the urban environment of Lower Town: landfill and industrial development during the nineteenth century cut the domestic zone off from the waterfront and reduced its economic value![29] To these authors, the economic importance of the port itself and the effects of its development on the urban landscape are entirely overshadowed by the high value placed upon French regime domestic architecture.

Although several individual rehabilitation projects were undertaken as early as 1955, the official commence-

ment of the restoration of Place-Royale did not occur until 1967, under the auspices of the provincial Ministry of Cultural Affairs with the financial support of the federal government. The beginning of the project was marked by a series of expropriations and demolitions, often contested by City Hall and by the few remaining residents, who in some cases had to be forcibly relocated.[30] The philosophy behind the urban renewal of Place-Royale in the 1970s is now recognised as having been ideologically based: proponents of the project wanted to create a representation of the eighteenth-century French regime to the exclusion of all other periods, which were deemed unsuitable.[31] Ironically, the argument invoked to justify total or partial demolition of certain buildings and additions constructed later than the eighteenth century was their perceived decrepitude![32] Elsewhere, for example in the neighbouring Saint-Roch district, where no symbolic value was attributed to the urban fabric by planning authorities, urban renewal projects proceeded with the wholesale demolition of entire neighbourhoods.[33]

The composition of the urban landscape and that of its inhabitants went through equally dramatic changes (Fig. 10.2). Place-Royale and other Lower Town attractions such as the Musée de la Civilisation have been turned into major poles in the complex of the city's tourist infrastructure, which supports the second most important industry in Quebec City. The region is now host to 4 million visitors annually, a good number of whom visit Lower Town. Only forty years ago, this same Lower Town had all the attributes that Mayne identifies in the literature as describing a slum: poverty and poor hygiene were rampant; poor-quality housing was prevalent.[34] This definition would indeed seem to apply to Quebec City's Lower Town, but for a period perhaps fifty to one hundred years later than that observed elsewhere.[35] This difference in timing has had consequences in terms of research on the city and our understanding of processes of transformation. This has been important for archaeologists, particularly when they have strived for an understanding of the evolution of the city.

Archaeological research on Lower Town

Old Town was declared a UNESCO World Heritage Site in 1985. This distinction recognises the historical character of the city, particularly as a fortified colonial city – whence Quebec's picturesque reputation in the nineteenth century as the 'Gibraltar of North America' – and also as the cradle of French civilisation on the continent. With its recently restored houses and reconstructed battery, today's Place-Royale resembles a French colonial city of the mid-eighteenth century. It is thus similar in appearance to what it would have been like during the French regime, when it was the port of entry to the Great Lakes watershed, which covers a large portion of North America. The waterfront, now extending several hundred metres downstream, is adapted to luxury cruise liners. Whereas the size and configuration of the waterfront have changed dramatically over the past four centuries, the restored core of Lower Town – Place-Royale – has been frozen in time. North of that sector, at the mouth of the St Charles River, remnants of the industrial port are still present in the form of a locked basin, now a marina protecting pleasure craft, pilot boats and tugs from the maximum 7 m tidal range. Warehouses converted into modern housing units, as well as a new farmers' market

and an historical interpretation centre built over the remains of factories and rail beds, line the city side of the basin; still-functioning grain elevators line the other side of the basin.

The recognition of Old Town as a UNESCO World Heritage Site followed several decades of research and heritage conservation projects and heralded concerted programmes to pursue these efforts further; archaeological research was one of these undertakings, particularly in Lower Town. An extensive research programme was carried out in the context of the Place-Royale restoration project, though virtually no historic research and no archaeological research was done on Lower Town for the period following 1860 in the context of the limited studies of Place-Royale during the 1960s.[36] Knowledge of the period from 1860 up until the undertaking of the restoration project in the 1960s is thus incomplete; research was restricted to the arbitrarily defined administrative limits of Place-Royale. This in turn has resulted in a truncated portrait of a complex social system[37] or, as L'Anglais has justly pointed out, we have so far failed to consider the city as a whole but have investigated Lower Town as a series of independent archaeological sites.[38]

Archaeological monitoring of demolition work was carried out during the first restoration projects at Place-Royale in the late 1960s and early 1970s. Fundamentally, this consisted of the emptying of basements by labourers hired by a general contractor under the supervision of an archaeologist. The result was that almost all context was lost.[39] This methodological approach was later modified and a research programme was defined in the early 1980s in order to answer the needs of the public interpretation programme.[40] A large series of publications studying topics such as commerce, lifeways, the urban environment and population dynamics has resulted from this programme. However, we lack information on the broad system in which these existed. Ironically, the archaeological material analysed to illustrate the 1820 to 1860 period comes from two sites in the block on which the Museé de la Civilisation stands rather than from the heart of Place-Royale itself as the project name would lead one to believe, and despite the effects of marked spatial segregation by trade within Lower Town.[41]

All in all, Place-Royale has imprinted its strong image on the archaeology of Quebec City: one third of all titles identified in a 1992 bibliography on archaeological research on the city were produced in the context of the Place-Royale Project, related either to the first phase of data collection in the 1970s or to the second-phase research programme of the 1980s.[42] The restoration of several remaining buildings was carried out in the 1990s and an interpretation centre recounting the history of this part of the city has opened for the new millennium. Four major themes will be treated in this new centre: commerce, transformation of the physical environment, daily life and social life. As well, 14,000 artefacts in the Place-Royale reference collection were given legal protection under the terms of the provincial Cultural Properties Act in 1998.

One other important Lower Town site was partially investigated during the construction of the Musée de la Civilisation in 1984 in the heart of the Historic District. Unfortunately, this important site, located immediately to the north of the Hunt Block, was only partially excavated archaeologically, the major portion of the block having been mechanically emptied during the construction of the museum complex. Once again, research results illustrate the eighteenth-century occupation, particularly the aspects related to the presence of abandoned ship hulls in the fill sequences.[43] Though first developed in the 1740s as a series of merchants' houses and adjacent wharves, the block seems to have been occupied essentially by warehouses, and then by offices, from the mid-nineteenth century until the massive demolition of the buildings in the 1960s and 1970s. Analyses of three closed contexts (latrines and rubbish pits) from this site confirm that the Musée block was inhabited by merchants up until the late 1840s. Further traces of domestic occupation were noted for the period ending *c.* 1870, but evidence is ambiguous.[44]

The Hunt Block, located at the heart of Lower Town's waterfront between Place-Royale and the Musée de la Civilisation (Fig. 10.2), is a microcosm of many aspects of the city's urban development, having at various times been commercial, residential, military, abandoned and tourist-orientated. The site did not exist prior to 1699, when the merchant Charles Aubert de la Chesnaye decided to build a wharf in front of his property on Saint-Pierre Street.[45] Up until that time, high tides reached the front of the property. Thus, the creation of the Hunt Block results from landfill, wharf construction and the erection of defensive works in times of war, each construction gaining ground from the river. As a dynamic port town, Quebec adopted various functions at short notice in response to rapidly changing political and economic situations. The block itself is quite small and, owing to the presence of a house and a recycled warehouse on the site, we were only able to excavate half of an area measuring approximately 18 m by 30 m. The site is none the less rich enough, and sufficient information is available from the city's monitoring and research projects on neigbouring sites, to allow us to reinterpret the general evolutionary sequence proposed for Place-Royale and to evaluate the current state of knowledge of Lower Town's archaeological heritage.

The proclamation of royal government in 1663 brought a wave of economic development that pushed the settlement of Lower Town north of Place-Royale. Beach lots were granted to merchants, who built wharves and warehouses along the new shoreline. In periods of crisis, their wharves were requisitioned and turned into defensive works such as the Royale and Hazeur batteries, built respectively in 1691 and 1692. After having been squeezed between the river and a point of land to the west of his property for a quarter of a century, the merchant Aubert de la Chesnaye decided in 1699 to enlarge his property by constructing a wharf 30 m long on the tidal flats. This impressive masonry structure was requisitioned in 1707, when the colonial authorities decided to fortify the waterfront. The wharf was then extended 15 m to the north between 1707 and 1709 and refitted as the first Dauphine battery. The battery did not last long and was converted back into a pier in 1719 after the signing of a truce between France and England. The ensuing period of peace brought renewed residential development of Lower Town, and a two-storey house was built by Maillou on the Hunt Block in 1721.[46] Five years of excavation have shown that these few square metres of Lower Town were used for commercial, military and domestic purposes, all within a twenty-year period!

The 1721 Maillou house covered almost half the area of the first battery. When a new battery was needed in the latter part of the 1740s, it was built farther out into the river, 15 m beyond the older battery. The second battery, like the first one, extended as far north as today's de la Barricade Street and its side wall turned to abut the vestiges of the earlier battery. The construction of a second battery was well advised, as Quebec was attacked after the fall of Louisbourg, the fortress located at the entrance to the Gulf of St Lawrence. Following a devastating siege, the city fell to the English after a brief but bloody battle on the Plains of Abraham on 13 September 1759.

A certain prosperity returned after the bombardment; commercial enterprises flourished and the residential sector of Lower Town boomed. Like most houses in Lower Town, the house built in 1721 on the site of the first battery had been destroyed during the bombardment and only the walls perpendicular to the river were left standing. Shortly thereafter a new three-storey house was built over the ashes of the first, using the still-upright end walls. The merchant who owned the new house built a wooden warehouse in his yard in 1783, and it was rebuilt in stone in 1815.

The density of the population attained a peak during the first quarter of the nineteenth century. The 1815 stone warehouse was transformed into a bakery in 1840 to feed the growing population. Meanwhile, two houses were built along de la Barricade Street (formerly Saint-Antoine Street), enclosing the yard on all sides; the only access to it was now through a passage leading into Saint-Antoine Street.[47] The overpopulation of Lower Town reached critical proportions; hygiene was probably the aspect that deteriorated the most. Excavation of the yard revealed the presence of a complex network of wooden drains and sewers linking the houses in the closed space available in the yard. This network drained into the St Lawrence River. The horrible smell that emanated when the sewers were cleaned forced authorities to legislate the time of year and day when people were allowed to empty their privies. Such legislation was probably easily accepted by the population, since a cholera epidemic had struck in that sector in 1832. The last event in this period of development in Lower Town is the construction of public water and sewage systems which occurred in 1852 and 1854 respectively. As a result of the new sewage system, the network of private drains and sewers built in the yard was abandoned and then gradually filled with domestic refuse over a twenty-year period.

Archaeoentomological research carried out on a deposit contained in latrines used before the construction of the city's sewage system has shed light on the poor hygienic conditions in which the Lower Town population lived during the middle of the nineteenth century. Although dietary conditions showed diversity, including meat, cereals and vegetables, the quality of food consumed and that of the ambient environment were questionable. Thus, the refuse pit in the yard contained manure and putrefying animal carcasses. Flour, dried fruits and other stored goods were infested with various species of Coleoptera. The presence of bed bugs (*Cimex lectularius*) is indicative of the state of personal hygiene, while remains tentatively identified as Spanish fly (*Lytta vesicataria*) give some indication of the medicinal practices of the time.[48]

The Hunt Block reached its maximum capacity in the middle of the nineteenth century. Wharf and warehouse expansion still progressed rapidly on the tidal flats of the St Lawrence, but new buildings are rare on the Hunt Block. In fact, the only new construction reported is a stable and hangar built in 1875 over the rotting remains of the abandoned sewer system in the yard. Overpopulation and poor hygiene seem to have created a split in the population living in the lower part of town. Those who could afford to leave Lower Town, the merchant class, bought residences in Upper Town.

The exodus of the merchant population was not the only factor triggering poverty in the sector; the larger political scene at the end of the nineteenth century had a great deal to do with it. Specifically, Quebec City lost its influence to Montreal, following the dredging of the St Lawrence River and the construction of a railway on the south shore. Lower Town changed from being the port of entry for approximately 30,000 immigrants a year during the 1830s to a waystation. The transfer of the seat of government to Ottawa in 1865 was another factor which contributed to the impoverishment of the population in general.

Research carried out on the Lymburner and Monro Site, two blocks to the north of the Hunt Block, when a 1911 firehouse was recycled as an experimental theatrical workshop, supplied graphic evidence of the massive investments made in improving the port during the English regime.[49] Beginning in the 1780s, wharves were built in the newly conquered port, later to be replaced by warehouses associated with the rapid expansion of the 1840 period. Archaeological research was carried out in the early 1990s prior to the restoration of the Aubert de la Chesnaye house, situated immediately to the west of the Hunt Block. Analysis of this extremely complex building revealed a progressive decline in the social standing of the site's inhabitants, as it went from being the home of New France's most prominent merchant at the time of its construction in 1669, to being turned into a warehouse in the 1860s.[50] Data from this site have shown that the wealth of the occupants decreased only slightly over the first half of the nineteenth century, before it was abandoned as a domestic site.

Archaeological research carried out in the nearby Saint-Roch suburb, inhabited by families of French origin employed in the shipyards before these collapsed in the 1850s and 1860s, indicated a dramatic downturn in the economic status of the working-class population in the second half of the nineteenth century. The phenomenon was quite marked in the 1880s. Archaeologists identified a noticeable drop in the quality of domestic ceramics during this period, as well as a change in consumer behaviour associated with meats: the preparation of more economical cuts, and indeed the butchery and probably the keeping of animals on the site, increased over the same period; all of these signs may be interpreted as a thrifty response to hard economic times.[51] Research carried out on a comparable site in the Saint-Jean-Baptiste suburb, in this case inhabited by families of Irish origin, suggests similar results, but full analysis of the material has yet to be carried out.[52]

Discussion

Five years of research on the Hunt Block have uncovered as many as fifteen different events from the end of the seventeenth century to the 1990s when the sector was renovated. Three distinct periods are evident: development (1660–1860), decline (1860–1960) and renaissance (1960–2000). The first is quite well documented both on the Hunt Block and elsewhere in Lower Town in so far as domestic occupations of bourgeois merchant sites are concerned. Other social classes and other aspects of the city's history, such as the evolution of the port itself, have scarcely been considered. The situation is more dramatic for the second period, which we have identified as that of decline (1860–1960), as only the Hunt Block project has contributed information on the subject, and this only for the period ending *c.* 1900. The final period, renaissance (1960–2000), is recent history and we are only now beginning to acquire critical knowledge of it. It is none the less clear that the approach taken at the beginning of recent restoration projects precluded an understanding of the city's history for the period of decline. A golden age – the French regime – was postulated and re-created.

It is possible to see the effect of ideologies behind the project for the urban renewal of Place-Royale, particularly when it comes to archaeological research in Quebec City. By focusing on a presumed golden age – the French regime – a crucial period in the evolution of the city, that of a certain decline between 1860 and 1960, was completely pushed aside. This has obscured any objective reference to the process of 'slumification'. The city and its partners have indeed made important efforts to prevent Old Town from turning into a museum by systematically maintaining a resident local population.[53] There is a strong desire to avoid one of the major pitfalls of heritage conservation, that is, allowing the city to become a parody of itself, as has occasionally occurred elsewhere[54] and as some have said has happened with Place-Royale.[55] But the abatement of this process will only succeed if based on accurate and objective knowledge of the city itself.[56]

That the restoration project of the 1960s and 1970s had an ideological basis should be no surprise, as this phenomenon has been abundantly observed elsewhere.[57] None the less, the manner in which fieldwork was carried out and the subsequent limitation of the research programme to pre-1860 have considerably hindered our knowledge of this fascinating area of Quebec City. A global view of Lower Town's history enables us to identify several evident periods in its evolution: creation, decline and renaissance. The creation period (1660–1860) is well documented both historically and archaeologically, whereas very little is known about the period of decline (1860–1960). The renaissance period corresponds, of course, to the very recent period during which historical and archaeological research was carried out and this

period has recently come under analytical scrutiny.[58] But what really happened during the period of decline, a century spanning the years from 1860 to 1960, is difficult to know. Indeed, we may view this decline period as a black box: we know what went into it and we are beginning to have a critical understanding of what came out. But what happened in this black box? We believe that the process of projecting the image of a slum onto the neighbourhood did indeed occur as described by Mayne, particularly in the middle of the twentieth century. If our evaluation is correct, what does this later timing mean when compared to similar phenomena in New York City beginning in the middle of the nineteenth century or elsewhere at the end of that century?

Conclusion

The decline period is a black box that has been created by an ideological bias towards certain research preferences and choices in site development. Interestingly, available evidence allows us to conclude that the 'slumification' process observable elsewhere also happened in Quebec City, but more than a half a century later. Recent scholarship has tended to portray the beginning of this process almost a full century earlier, notably for Australia and the United Kingdom, where it began in the 1830s.

Archaeology has begun to elucidate this period and this subject, but much more remains to be done. An agenda for research on Quebec City – historical, archaeological and ethnographic – has yet to be developed, though the contextual approach combined with the ecosystemic model presently used are useful instruments for identifying the precise contribution of archaeological research on this question. The Hunt Block has shown that this approach is particularly productive on a diachronic scale, analysing in detail the evolution of a single site. Research on varied contexts, particularly working-class neighbourhoods such as the Saint-Roch suburb or the O'Connell Site in the Saint-Jean-Baptiste suburb, which are of comparable date, is already providing interesting insights into life in the city far beyond what historians have written until now. Fascinating discoveries await us as we enlarge the database to embrace more sites on a synchronic perspective.

Acknowledgements

We would like to thank Jane Macaulay for her editorial suggestions and Jocelyn Beaulieu of the City of Quebec for his assistance in iconographic research. We also thank our colleagues Marcel Moussette and

Marc Vallières, both of Université Laval, for their comments and suggestions.

Notes

1 Alan Mayne, *The Imagined Slum: Newspaper Representation in Three Cities 1870–1914* (Leicester: Leicester University Press, 1993), p. 137.

2 Françoise Niellon and Marcel Moussette, *Le site de l'Habitation de Champlain à Québec, étude de la collection archéologique (1976–1980)*, Collection Patrimoines, Dossier 57 (Quebec: Les publications du Québec, 1981).

3 Isabelle Faure, *La conservation et la restauration des monuments historiques au Québec: étude des fondements culturels et idéologiques à travers l'exemple du projet de Place Royale* (Paris: Institut Français d'Urbanisme de Paris VIII, 1995), pp. 238–42.

4 This problem is well explained by Micheline Tremblay (Ethnotech inc.), *Etude de la population de Place-Royale 1660–1760*, Collection Patrimoines, Dossier 82 (Les Publications du Québec, 1993), pp. 9–55.

5 See Marcel Moussette, *Le site du Palais de l'intendant à Québec: genèse et structuration d'un lieu urbain* (Quebec: Septentrion, 1994), pp. 11–25, and William Moss, *Une archéologie du paysage urbain à la terrasse Dufferin à Québec*, Rapports et Mémoires de Recherche du CELAT 23 (Quebec: CELAT, Université Laval, 1994), pp. 3–13.

6 Paul-Gaston L'Anglais, *La recherche archéologique en milieu urbain: d'une archéologie dans la ville vers une archéologie de la ville*, Les Cahiers du CELAT, hors série 6 (Quebec: CELAT, Université Laval, 1994).

7 This process has been abundantly documented by recent archaeological research. See William Moss (dir.), *L'archéologie de la maison Aubert-de-la-Chesnaye à Québec*, Cahiers d'Archéologie du CELAT 3 (Quebec: CELAT, Université Laval, 1998); Myriam Leclerc, *Appropriation de l'espace et urbanisation d'un site de la basse ville de Québec: rapport de la première campagne de fouilles (1991)*, Cahiers d'Archéologie du CELAT 1 (Quebec: CELAT, Université Laval, 1998); Paul-Gaston L'Anglais, *Le site de l'îlot Hunt: rapport de la deuxième campagne de fouilles (1992)*, Cahiers d'Archéologie du CELAT 2 (Quebec: CELAT, Université Laval, 1998); Pierre Bouchard, 'Le site de l'îlot Hunt à Québec (CeEt-110): étude socio-économique des habitants d'après la collection archéologique, 1850–1900', Masters thesis, Ecole des Gradués, Université Laval (1998), and Manon Goyette, 'Des vestiges d'une arrière-cour à

8 See John Hare, Marc Lafrance and David-Thierry Ruddel, *Histoire de la ville de Québec, 1608–1871* (Montreal: Boréal/Musée des Civilisations, 1987).

9 Rémi Chénier, *Québec, ville coloniale française en Amérique: 1660 à 1690* (Ottawa: Environment Canada, Service des Parcs, 1991).

10 André Lemelin, 'Le declin du port de Québec et la reconversion économique à la fin du XIXe siècle,' *Recherches Sociographiques* 22:2 (1981), 180.

11 Population statistics are taken from Hare *et al.*, *Histoire*, pp. 325–8 and from Alyne Lebel, 'Les facteurs du développement urbain', in G. H. Dagneau (dir.), *La ville de Québec, histoire municipale. IV – De la Confédération à la charte de 1929* (Quebec: Société historique de Québec, 1983), pp. 31–47.

12 Yves Laframboise (Ethnotech inc.), *La fonction résidentielle de Place-Royale 1820–1860: Synthèse*, Collection Patrimoines, Dossier 70 (Quebec: Les Publications du Québec, 1991), p. 12, and Hare *et al.*, *Histoire*, p. 213.

13 Jean Provencher (Les Recherches Arkhis Inc.), *Les modes de vie de la population de Place-Royale entre 1820 et 1859: synthèse*, Collection Patrimoines, Dossier 66 (Quebec: Les Publications du Québec, 1990), p. 3.

14 *Ibid.*, p. 243.

15 Eileen Marcil, *Les tonneliers du Québec*, Collection Mercure 34 (Ottawa: Musées Nationals de l'Homme, 1983), p. 79.

16 Groupe Harcart, 'Etude d'ensemble des sous-secteurs Sault-au-Matelot et Saint-Paul', Service de l'Urbanisme, Ville de Québec (1988), p. 35.

17 Edward H. Dahl, Hélène Espesset, Marc Lafrance and Thierry Ruddell, *La ville de Québec, 1800–1850: un inventaire de cartes et plans*, Collection Mercure 13 (Ottawa: Musées Nationals de l'Homme, 1975), pp. 39, 410. See also Marc Lafrance and Thierry D. Ruddell, 'Physical evolution and socio-cultural segregation in Quebec City, 1765–1840' in G. A. Stelter and A. F. J. Artibise, *Shaping the Urban Landscape: Aspects of the Canadian City-Building Process* (Ottawa: Carleton, 1982), pp. 160–2.

18 Provencher, *Les modes de vie*, p. 169. See Hare *et al.*, *Histoire*, p. 215.

19 Hare *et al.*, *Histoire*, p. 292.

20 James MacPherson Lemoine, *L'album du touriste: archéologie, histoire, littérature, sport . . .* (Quebec: Imprimerie A. Côté, 1872), also published in

l'histoire de l'hygiène publique à Québec au XIXe siècle: la troisième campagne de fouilles archéologiques à l'îlot Hunt (1993)', Masters thesis, Ecole des Gradués, Université Laval (1998).

English as *The Tourist's Note-Book* (Quebec: F. X. Garant, 1876).

21 See the lithograph published in an 1882 edition of *Picturesque Canada* reproduced in Hare *et al.*, *Histoire,* p. 308.

22 Archives Nationales du Québec. Photo Gérard Morissette, E-6, S8, P11646-A-9.

23 Clément Brown in Alain Roy, 'Les grands traits de l'histoire de Place-Royale de 1860 à 1960', (Quebec: Musée de la Civilisation, 1998), p. 47.

24 Quoted from Roy, 'Les grands traits', p. 35.

25 'Rapport de la commission d'enquête sur le logement de la Cité de Québec', in Roy, 'Les grands traits', pp. 12, 39.

26 Alain Roy, 'Saint-Roch projeté, Saint-Roch inachevé: les schémas d'aménagement au XXe siècle', in Archithème, *Patrimoine du quartier Saint-Roch: études sectorielles* (Quebec: Ville de Québec, Service de l'Urbanisme, 1996), pp. 47–84; and Roy, 'Les grands traits', pp. 49–51.

27 Jules Blanchet, Pierre Talbot and Jean Rousseau, 'Concept général de réaménagement du Vieux-Québec', (Quebec: Ville de Québec, Service de l'Urbanisme, 1971), pp. 61–71.

28 *Ibid.*, pp. 84–6 (our translation).

29 *Ibid.*, p. 120.

30 Faure, *La conservation et la restauration*, pp. 232–4.

31 *Ibid.*, pp. 275–83; and Alain Roy, 'Le Vieux-Québec, 1945–1963. Construction et fonctions sociales d'un lieu de mémoire nationale', Masters thesis, Université Laval (1995).

32 Faure, 'La conservation et la restauration', pp. 288–92.

33 Roy, 'Saint-Roch projeté', pp. 60–2.

34 *Ibid.*, pp. 160, 170.

35 *Ibid.* and Rebecca Yamin, 'New York's mythic slum: digging Lower Manhattan's infamous Five Points', *Archaeology* 50:2 (1997), pp. 44–53.

36 Roy, 'Les grands traits', pp. 6, 7. See also Groupe Harcart, 'Etude des sous-secteurs', p. 1.

37 See Tremblay, *Etude de la population*, pp. 9–55, and Provencher, *Les modes de vie*, pp. 2–4.

38 L'Anglais, *La recherche archéologique*.

39 François Picard, *Les traces du passé* (Sillery: Québec Science–Les Presses de l'Université du Québec, 1979), pp. 151–7, and Françoise Niellon, Céline Cloutier, Catherine Fortin and Cathy Yasui, *Les modes de vie de la population de Place-Royale entre 1820 et 1859, Annexe 2* Collection Patrimoines, Dossier 66 (Les Publications du Québec, 1990), pp. 7, 8. See also Faure, *La conservation et la restauration*, pp. 248, 276.

40 Louise Décarie, 'Program de recherche en archéologie sur la Place-Royale, Québec', Quebec: Ministère des Affaires Culturelles du Québec (1982), and Marcel Moussette, 'La recherche en culture matérielle à la Place-Royale. Essai de redéfinition d'une orientation', Quebec: Ministère des Affaires Culturelles du Québec (1981).

41 Niellon *et al.*, *Les modes de vie*, pp. 8–20.

42 William Moss, 'Cent-vingt-cinq ans de découvertes. Une bibliographie sur l'archéologie de la ville de Québec', *Mémoires Vives*, 5 (1993), 20.

43 Daniel La Roche, 'Surveillance archéologique, Musée de la civilisation, Québec, 1984–1985', Québec: Société Immobilière du Québec (1986), and Daniel La Roche, 'L'archéologie des installations portuaires à Québec', *Mémoires Vives* 6 and 7 (1994), 31–5.

44 Niellon *et al.*, *Les modes de vie*, pp. 8–20.

45 Leclerc, *Appropriation,* and L'Anglais, *La recherche archéologique.*

46 Suzie Poulin, 'Etude architecturale de la maison Hunt', CELAT, Université Laval (1995).

47 Janic Dubé, 'Le site de l'îlot Hunt à Québec (CeEt-110). Rapport annuel d'activités, quatrième campagne de fouilles archéologiques', CELAT, Université Laval (1995).

48 Allison Bain, 'Analyse des restes archéoentomologiques de l'îlot Hunt (CeEt-110) dans la basse-ville de Québec', CELAT, Université Laval (1997).

49 Serge Rouleau, 'Les installations portuaires des marchands Lymburner, Monro et Bell (CeEt-536)', Quebec: Ville de Québec, Centre de Développement Economique et Urbain (1997).

50 Céline Cloutier, 'Hygiène privée, transferts culturels et mécanisation: le cas des latrines du site Aubert de la Chesnaye à Québec', in Louise Pothier, *L'eau, l'hygiène publique et les infrastructures* (Montreal: Groupe PGV–Diffusion de l'Archéologie, 1996), pp. 22–4; Serge Rouleau, 'Le site de la maison Aubert-de-la-Chesnaye XVIIe–XXe siècle: perspective archéologique', in Moss, *L'archéologie de la maison Aubert-de-la-Chesnaye*, pp. 11–233; Céline Cloutier, 'Les déchets des uns et des autres. Etude du contenu des fosses d'aisance du site archéologique de la maison Aubert-de-la-Chesnaye', in Moss, *L'archéologie de la maison Aubert-de-la-Chesnaye*, pp. 235–95.

51 Céline Cloutier, 'De l'aisance à la pauvreté. Etude d'une collection archéologique des ouvriers du quartier Saint-Roch à Québec au XIXe siècle', Quebec: Ville de Québec, Centre de Développement Economique et Urbain (1997), pp. 48, 49.

52 Dominique Lalande, 'Recherches archéologiques sur

le site de l'îlot O'Connell à Québec', Quebec: Ville de Québec, Centre de Développement Economique et Urbain (1996).

53 Francine Bégin, 'La gestion et la mise en valeur du patrimoine bâti à Québec', in Marie-Claude Rocher and André Ségal (dir.), *Le traitement du patrimoine urbain: intégration, intégralité, intégrité.* Actes du Colloque Mons-Québec 1996 (Quebec: Ville de Québec, Musée de la Civilisation, Patrimoine Canadien, 1997), p. 73.

54 Robert Hewison, *The Heritage Industry: Britain in a Climate of Decline* (London: Methuen, 1987), pp. 131–43.

55 See Faure, *La conservation et la restauration.*

56 See also Pierre Larochelle and Christina Iamandi, *Milieux bâtis et identité culturelle* (in press).

57 G. J. Ashworth and J. E. Tunbridge, *The Tourist-Historic City* (London: Belhaven, 1990), p. 255.

58 Faure, *La conservation et la restauration* and Roy, 'Le Vieux-Québec".

11
Values and identity in the 'working-class' worlds of late nineteenth-century Minneapolis

JOHN P. McCARTHY

Introduction

The term 'slum', since its emergence in the early nine-teenth century, has always been closely associated with the working people of densely populated urban districts and the often squalid and wretched conditions found there.[1] This chapter considers the results of archaeological investigations of two late-nineteenth-century sites associated with members of the 'working class' of Minneapolis, Minnesota. Working class in the sense used here refers to people who made their living in occupations involving manual labour of one sort or another. The archaeology of the home and work environments of these Minnesotans reflects material worlds that express cultural categories and principles, or values, that are essential elements in the representation, reproduction and manipulation of complex socio-cultural identities. Building on this understanding of the role of material culture, this chapter considers the behaviours, values and meanings reflected in the material record at these sites with respect to four topics: (1) sanitation, (2) consumer choice, (3) separation of work and home, and (4) investment in childhood relative to the construction of social identity and class structures more broadly.

Following this introduction, the sites and features investigated will be briefly described, and the historic context of each of the themes mentioned above and pertinent archaeological results from each site will then be reviewed and contrasted. While outwardly both of these communities may have been considered slums by some contemporary observers, what emerge are two distinctly different working-class worlds in nineteenth-century Minneapolis, reflecting different values and meanings.

The implications of these results for a clearer understanding of complex socio-cultural phenomena are then considered. It will be argued that terms such as 'working class' and 'middle class' are inadequate, if not misleading, when the complex sets of behaviours and values that comprised the fabric of everyday experience in the past are considered.

Minneapolis and the sites

Minnesota lies in the north central portion of the United States, and Minneapolis is its largest city. French explorers searching for the North-West Passage were the first Europeans to visit the region. In 1680, Father Louis Hennepin happened upon a magnificent waterfall on the upper Mississippi that he named for St Anthony.[2] One hundred and forty years later, when the United States government enforced its claim to the region by constructing Fort Snelling overlooking the confluence of the Minnesota and Mississippi rivers, the military erected saw and flour mills to take advantage of the power of the falls. By the 1840s, the village of St Anthony had been established on the east bank of the Mississippi at the falls. With the construction of a suspension bridge, the first to span the Mississippi, the village of Minneapolis was established on the west bank, and Minneapolis was first incorporated as a town in 1856. It was subsequently incorporated as a city in 1867. In 1872 Minneapolis and St Anthony were consolidated into a single city.[3]

Minneapolis' economic foundation was the milling of grain produced on Minnesota's rich farmlands to the south and west of the city and of lumber from the vast pine forests to the north and east. The tremendous power-generating capabilities of St Anthony Falls made these industries possible. Large mills were established along the river, and the city became an important transportation centre as railroads were built to service these industries.[4] The city remains a centre for the grain, timber and transportation industries, although its economy has diversified into other areas of manufacturing, banking and insurance.

In 1994 archaeological fieldwork was undertaken at two sites in downtown Minneapolis associated with the city's nineteenth-century working people. Historic features, including privy pits, were excavated prior to the construction of the new Federal Reserve Bank of Minneapolis in Area B of the Bridgehead Site, located just north of the site of the original suspension bridge, and named in its honour.[5] In addition, historic features, including cisterns and a privy pit, were excavated following their discovery during monitoring of the construction of a new Federal

Office Building/US Courthouse, several blocks south-east of the Bridgehead Site.[6]

The Bridgehead Site

At the Bridgehead Site a series of privy pits and other features were discovered arranged in a rough line at the approximate mid-point of four lots facing First Street North. This was an ethnically diverse riverfront neighbourhood of transient hotels, shops, mills, warehouses and foundries that included some residences. This portion of the block, designated Area B of the Bridgehead Site, had received approximately 12 feet of fill in 1907 or shortly thereafter, protecting the features from subsequent development impacts. These properties had been initially developed in the 1850s and included a mixture of commercial and residential uses in the late nineteenth century, including the following:

1. George Calladine's harness and saddle shop stood at No. 16 First Street North. This property included three features, of which Feature 15 was clearly a wood-lined privy vault, while Features 16 and 17 were shallow, unlined rectangular pits. These features have been interpreted as pits initially excavated for use as privy vault pits, but were abandoned and refilled without having been used as privy vaults, since no organic muck was present. This property was in use as a leather goods shop into the twentieth century. It was apparently not used as a residence during this time.

2. No. 22 First Street North was occupied by W. O'Donnell Boots and Shoes in the mid-1870s and subsequently by a barbershop until the turn of the century. A single privy vault, Feature 13, was excavated on this property. The recovered artefact assemblage appears to be associated with the barbershop.

3. No. 26 First Street North was a restaurant from the mid-1870s and subsequently housed a saloon until the 1920s. Three wood-lined privy vaults, Features 7, 11 and 12, were excavated on this property. It appears that this property may also have had a residential use, or other uses associated with entertainment.

4. Alan Knoblock, manufacturer of boots and shoes, occupied No. 28 First Street North. He apparently resided on the property as well. City building permits indicate that plumbing was installed in 1888 and in 1891, by which time Knoblock had been succeeded by L. E. Shoenberg, Boots and Shoes. Feature 10, an unlined privy pit, was excavated on this property and appears to be associated with Shoenberg's use of the property. It is suspected that Shoenberg, like Knoblock before him, resided above or behind his shop.

The Federal Courthouse Site

Historic features were also encountered during construction monitoring at the site of the new Federal Office Building/US Courthouse. The area monitored had been the site of several small rental houses in the late nineteenth century. City building permits indicate that plumbing was introduced into these buildings in 1886. The commercial building which replaced the houses in 1903 did not include a full basement, and portions of the back yards of two of the cottages, Nos. 326 and 328 Fourth Avenue South, were protected under a cement slab until excavations for the new Courthouse began.

Three significant refuse-bearing features were excavated. Features 2 and 5 were bowl-shaped cistern pits dug into the sandy subsoil, to which mortar was applied to create a waterproof vessel. Feature 3 was a wood-lined privy vault, apparently shared between at least two of the residences. Based on federal census data for the years 1880 and 1900, these properties were predominately occupied by skilled, first- and second-generation Irish workmen and their families.

Results

Project results addressing aspects of sanitation, consumer choice, separation of work and home, and investment in childhood are each put into historic context and described. These aspects of the results from these two sites were chosen for their ease of comparison and their association with, and sensitivity to, social identity in the late nineteenth century.

Sanitation

The late nineteenth century was a time of change in the understanding of disease transmission. While earlier miasmatic theories of disease associated illness with unclean conditions, personal health was often viewed as a product of one's moral character. The unhealthy state of the sick was often blamed on intemperance and other moral maladies. With the discovery of the germ theory of disease, science could demonstrate that health quality was directly related to one's physical environment. As one researcher has put it, 'Cleanliness, long associated with godliness, now became an end in itself as the equation of disease with dirt became more firmly entrenched.'[7]

A public health movement arose to spread the message of sanitary reform. Recent historical analysis has shown that middle-class Americans took the message of sanitary reform very seriously, investing considerably, as their individual means permitted, in sanitation improvements for their homes beginning in the middle of the nineteenth century, and later in sewer and water systems for their communities as well.[8] In contrast, the living conditions of working people generally, and in urban areas in particular, were characterised by inadequate and poorly maintained sanitation facilities from which disease was readily spread.[9] Such conditions are closely associated with the concept of the slum in the early nineteenth century. Archaeological evidence suggests that some members of the working class, including armoury workers living in Harper's Ferry, West Virginia, resisted middle-class efforts to impose sanitary reforms. In the social and political context of that town, where the rigid industrial hierarchy of federal armoury was reflected in numerous aspects of community life, the messages of the sanitary reform movement were reinterpreted and adapted in such a way as to render them apparently ineffective. Extensive levels of intestinal parasite infestation were documented into the twentieth century.[10]

At the Bridgehead Site, the installation of plumbing could be documented only for 28 First Street North. City building permits indicate that plumbing was installed on that property in 1888 and in 1891, although the precise nature of each of the improvements is undocumented. By those dates the property had passed from the hands of A. Knoblock to L. E. Shoenberg, Boots and Shoes, and the privy deposit associated with this property probably dates from this period. Archaeological evidence provides little additional indication as to when features were abandoned. Ceramic *terminus post quem* (TPQ) dates only indicated the earliest possible date for an assemblage, and accordingly, TPQ dates in the 1870s and 1880s only indicate that the features may have been in use at those dates. However, it is certain that all the Area B features had been abandoned by the time the central area of the block was filled, in the first decade of the twentieth century.

Accordingly, it is not possible to assess the extent to which the large quantities of refuse recovered in the Bridgehead privy-use deposits represent violations of city regulations instituted in 1897 forbidding the burial of wastes in privies.[11] In contrast, however, the Irish residents of the Courthouse Site at Fourth Avenue South discarded relatively little refuse when using their privy and cistern facilities. Only three buttons were recovered from the privy's use-related deposit and no artefacts appear to have been deposited in the cisterns during their use, although these features were abandoned in 1886, nearly a decade before the burial of waste was outlawed. Deposits used in closing and filling abandoned features at both sites, however, included considerable refuse.

Other evidence concerning the quality of sanitation practices at the Bridgehead Site is mixed. Analysis of soil samples for evidence of parasites found a low-density occurrence of roundworm eggs in a secondary refuse deposit from Feature 17 (which did not appear to have been a privy pit) at Calladine's shop at 16 First Street North. This result suggests that chamber pot slops may have been discarded into the fill of this feature along with other materials. Two of the features associated with the restaurant/saloon at 26 First Street North, Features 7 and 12, both contained evidence of parasite infestation. Feature 7 contained roundworm eggs in relatively low density in the uppermost layer of the privy fill and in high density in deeper use-related deposits. Feature 12 contained no evidence of roundworm parasitism, but eggs from two species of tapeworm were present. In contrast, the primarily privy use deposit from Feature 10, at 28 First Street North, Shoenberg's shop and residence, contained no evidence of parasites whatsoever.

The parasite infestations documented at the Bridgehead Site, while not extensive by contemporary standards, are in marked contrast to the results from the Courthouse Site, where soil samples from the privy use-deposit and from sediments which accumulated in the base of the cisterns revealed no evidence of parasite infestation, although there is every reason to believe that preservation of parasite eggs would have been excellent since pollen was well preserved in these soils. The absence of evidence of parasites in the privy is particularly unusual for a site associated with the nineteenth-century working class, and the absence of parasite eggs from the cistern deposits adds to the impression of high concern for sanitation, for chamber pot slops spilled or dumped in the vicinity of the cisterns could easily have contaminated the stored water supply.

Consumer choice

As mentioned at the beginning of the chapter, consumer behaviour is an important means of expressing socio-cultural identities. Objects and their uses express values and behavioural complexes central to socio-cultural identities such as ethnicity. Ceramics, for example, and their associated behaviours held an important place in class competition and social emulation from the end of the Middle Ages, when Chinese porcelain and tea consumption were first introduced to Europe. Ceramics came to symbolise and signal each step in social promotion.[12]

A distinctive middle class emerged in American cities in the nineteenth century. The rise of this class appears to be closely related to the rise of what has been termed romantic consumerism.[13] Consumerism, the demand for, and acquisition of, material non-essentials, is more than simple materialism; it represents the growth of modern, autonomous, imaginative indulgence. Individuals seek not so much satisfaction from products *per se* as self-illusory experiences from which they can construct meaning in their lives.

This trend was played out in the home, as middle-class women, as finances permitted, devoted themselves to household management and what some historians have referred to as the 'family consumer economy'.[14] Recently, Blumin's *The Emergence of the Middle Class: Social Experience in the American City, 1790–1900* made particular note of the importance of the role of women in creating and maintaining a genteel home.[15]

Household goods and the preparation and consumption of food became symbols of domesticity and a reflection of the growth of Romanticism. Ceramics, as objects of consumer choice and class identity, are closely related to their role in food consumption and the ritual entertainment of guests associated with the definition of the emergent middle class.[16] Specifically, Kasson has argued that the rituals of dining and the entertainment of business associates in the home served to distinguish the middle class in the nineteenth century.[17] Praetzellis and Praetzellis see ceramic use, in particular, as a form of didactic, meaningful communication of widely held Victorian values based on middle-class commercialism.[18] While these values and related patterns of consumer behaviour are widely documented for middle-class Victorians, they are less well understood in the context of working people's lives.

Complex patterns of consumer choice and related ritual behaviour and social display seem to have operated only to a very limited degree at the Bridgehead Site project area. The vast bulk of the ceramics recovered comprised undecorated white-bodied wares. However, banded, hand-painted and transfer-printed teawares were present in small numbers. That such wares are present at all is of interest, given the various commercial functions that the project area served. The ritual consumption of tea and other entertaining in the home provided a venue to express shared values. The meaning of such activities and their related material culture in a workshop or business environment is more ambiguous.

While ritual afternoon teas are unlikely to have taken place among the workers in Calladine's harness and saddle shop, teawares were perhaps used in other social contexts in the shop, since at least one piece of a relatively expensive ware was recovered from Feature 17, along with examples of more moderately priced wares. The ceramics used at the restaurant/saloon were, by and large, the very cheapest available, with the exception of a single valuable teaware recovered from Feature 7. It appears that the bar-bershop at 22 First Street North used ceramics similar in cost to many of those used in Calladine's shop, but only a single teaware was present. The results from Shoenberg's shop and residence are the most unusual, in that only the very cheapest ceramics were found. While kitchenwares dominated the assemblage, table and teawares were present, as well, in small numbers.

It seems likely that tea or coffee consumption was part of the routine of doing business in the two leather-working shops and perhaps to a lesser extent in the barbershop. Clients and customers may have been entertained when visiting the shop, and a tradesman's very success may have been linked to his ability to display appropriate ritual behaviours to his prospective middle-class customers and clients. In contrast, the customers of the restaurant/saloon do not appear to have been catered to at all in this regard and it is unlikely that they held any expectations regarding social ritual and Victorian gentility.

The situation at Shoenberg's shop and residence is less clear, given the documented multiple functions of the property. It is possible that the Shoenberg family resisted emerging consumerism and felt no need for costly ceramics for either family use or entertaining and social status display purposes. It also seems unlikely that the shop's customers would have been impressed by the cheapest ceramics.

At the Courthouse Site, the ceramic assemblage reflects complex consumer behaviour. Analysis of ceramic surface decoration revealed a reliance on undecorated plain whitewares and ironstone 'china'. However, nearly a quarter of the assemblage (23 per cent) consisted of relatively highly decorated teawares. The analysis of Miller ceramic index values revealed a mean value consistent with skilled to semi-skilled working-class households (1.74), but the range of values (1.00 to 5.06) is great, and reflects considerable investment in at least some of the most costly ceramic teawares available as well as purchase of the cheapest wares available, presumably for everyday use by family members.

This finding is of interest relative to Wall's research in which she found that professional members of the upper middle class in early-nineteenth-century New York purchased more expensive teawares for use in status maintenance entertaining, while cheaper wares were purchased for everyday family use. Wall believed this to have been less the case at the lower end of the middle-class spectrum where she noted there was 'less competition or need to impress one's peers'.[19] On the basis of the results from the Courthouse Site, it seems that Wall's conclusion is flawed, and in fact it is at the edges of categories, at the boundaries of social groups, that social competition is most keenly felt. None the less, it is clear that the Irish residents of the

Courthouse Site engaged in a pattern of ceramics consumption and use more generally associated with middle-class values and identity.

It is possible that traditional Irish culture may have influenced this result.[20] Henry Glassie's *Passing the Time,* an investigation of rural folklife in Northern Ireland, observed the importance of ceramics in social display and their role in the entertainment of visitors to the home.[21] Entertaining in the home was one of the important traditional forms of reciprocity which defined friendships and gave status in rural Ireland, and other researchers have recognised this trait as well.[22] In addition, among the rural Irish, real property and household goods often possess an emotional symbolism associated with family organisation and social power.

Investment in childhood

Parental involvement in and economic contributions to childhood increased in the nineteenth century, as childhood was recognised as a distinct stage of life.[23] These trends began in elite contexts in the late eighteenth century and quickly spread during the early nineteenth century so that values concerning childhood were embodied in Victorian ideals of morality and family life that defined the family as a 'haven in a heartless world'.[24] The home was where individuals were nurtured and received moral education. A prescriptive literature even arose to assist with child rearing, including such titles as *The Mother's Book*.[25]

While no children were noted in the Bridgehead Site project area from documentary sources, toys and other artefacts possibly associated with children, such as writing slates and graphite pencils, were recovered from features on at least three of the four properties studied: only the barbershop at 22 First Street North contained no materials clearly associated with children, and even there, Feature 13 contained materials with the potential to have been associated with children.

The forty-one items included in these classes of material comprise only a very tiny portion of the total artefact assemblage recovered from the Bridgehead Site features (just over 27,000 non-bone artefacts were recovered and the children's items represent 0.15 per cent of this assemblage). None the less, they are among the most evocative, creating a strong link to the past residents of the project area. As with costly ceramic tearwares, the interesting fact is their very presence in the Bridgehead Site project area.

Toys were recovered in workplace environments where children may have been present as labourers. At best, the presence of toys here raises new questions concerning the quality of working-class childhood. Previous considerations of working-class childhood paint a remarkably bleak picture of material privation that may be overstated given the presence of toys in the working environments of the Bridgehead Site.[26]

Human remains recovered at the Bridgehead Site perhaps reflect the value of children in those working environments. The recovery from Feature 7 of the partial skeletal remains of a 6-month-old foetus and a child's lower incisor, broken off at the root, however, suggests that children were present in the project area in an atmosphere that included violence and, perhaps, illegal activities. Some of these activities appear to have been directed against the children present. It seems unlikely that children at the Bridgehead Site were regarded as the 'innocent nestlings' of the Victorian middle class.

In contrast, children are well documented at the Courthouse Site. The residents of that project area are known from federal population census schedules to have included three male children, aged 6, 5 and 4 years, and three female children, aged 4, 2 and 1 years in 1880. In 1900 one male child, 8 years of age, and two females, aged 5 and 2 years, are documented.

A total of sixty toys and other objects associated with children were recovered from the cistern and the privy pit features, reflecting the presence of these children, and perhaps others as well. The artefacts included doll parts, toy dishes, marbles, other toys, and writing slate and graphite pencil fragments. These sixty items also represent a very small portion of the total assemblage (a total of 14,000 non-bone objects were recovered and the children's items represent 0.43 per cent of this assemblage). However, children's materials, proportionally, comprise nearly three times more of the overall assemblage at the Courthouse Site than at the Bridgehead Site. That these materials were much more numerous than at the Bridgehead Site suggests that the residents of the Courthouse Site made distinct investments in childhood. In so doing, they apparently recognised childhood as a distinct stage of life consistent with middle-class Victorian notions of family and home.

Work and home

At the Bridgehead Site the focus was clearly on work, although some workers appear to have called the site 'home' as well. Activity, clothing, tobacco and personal artefacts were found at the site, reflecting much of the documented work of the project and perhaps suggesting a form of 'work' undocumented, as well.

Artefacts recovered from the features at 16 First Street North, Features 15, 16 and 17, exhibit a significant predominance of items related to Calladine's harness and saddle making activity. These features, and especially Feature 15, contain extraordinarily high numbers of rivets, metal rings, hooks, buckles and leather fragments. These features also contained relatively large numbers of clay tobacco pipe bowl and stem fragments. Cook documented that such pipes were associated with working people in the late nineteenth century, as middle-class smokers adopted cigarettes.[27]

Feature 7, associated with the restaurant/saloon at 26 First Street North, appears to contain the greatest number and highest relative proportion of personal items, including jewellery, a musical instrument part, a pocketknife and combs. In addition, this feature also contains the highest number of buttons, beads, cloth and straight pins, not to mention scissors and a clothespin, and the largest number of smoking-related artefacts. While laundry or sewing may have been taken in, one does not generally expect this sort of domestic activity at a restaurant or saloon. These artefacts, artefacts indicating the presence of children on this property, and the recovery of foetal skeletal remains, clearly indicate the presence of women of childbearing age. In the context of a workingmen's restaurant or saloon, this result suggests the possibility that the oldest profession may have been being practised at 26 First Street North. This interpretation is supported by Seifert's analysis of the functional composition of artefact assemblages recovered from a documented 'red-light' district in Washington, DC.[28] She found a correlation between unusually large numbers of clothing artefacts, personal items, tobacco pipes and other activities artefacts and site function. The Feature 7 assemblage reflects this same functional profile seen at the Washington brothel. However, this profile may simply have resulted from a residence dominated by young women.

While teawares were used and children's toys lost, the Bridgehead Site was part of the working city. Artefacts recovered from features overwhelmingly reflect the commercial nature of the area and the types of work carried out day-to-day. However, the apparent widespread consumption of food and the presence of children clearly mark these work environments as different from those we think of today. The boundary between work and home was blurred and permeable. Work might stop at any time to permit attending to the needs of a child or to take a meal. Children may in fact have been workers. Tea rituals were observed, even if in a limited way that supported business activity, in the workplace. For Shoenberg and possibly others, home and work were, in fact, one and the same place.

As was mentioned above, the Victorian middle-class home became a comfortable haven from the outside world where guests were entertained and children reared. These were domestic settings, removed and separate from the workplace. The Courthouse Site, in contrast to the Bridgehead Site, represents a similar domestic environment with no archaeological reflection of work activities. While boarders may have been present in these rental properties, along with family members, they were single, detached houses located on a residential block adjacent to other single-family homes, not flats above or behind shops. Work, however, was probably located within a few blocks' distance in the city's industrial core along the Mississippi.

Implications of the working-class worlds of late nineteenth-century Minneapolis

The results from these two sites suggest two distinct working-class worlds in late-nineteenth-century Minneapolis. The Bridgehead Site reflects a working-class world where Victorian values of gentility, respectability, cleanliness and hygiene, and separation of home and work, did not really apply, or applied only to the extent that the sensibilities and tastes of the customers and clients of these businesses were accommodated. In contrast, the skilled Irish workers of the Courthouse Site on Fourth Avenue South exhibited a number of behaviours and values that might be considered 'middle class', especially in their totality: they resided in single-family homes, maintained unusually high standards of sanitation and hygiene (apparently readily accepting emerging concepts of public health), purchased at least some costly ceramics and engaged in their ritual use and display (while apparently using the cheapest wares available for everyday family use), and invested in toys for both male and female children, recognising childhood as a distinct stage of life.

These findings suggest several broad interpretations. First, it seems that young frontier cities such as Minneapolis may have been more socially open and may have offered greater opportunities for those with marketable skills than did eastern urban centres in this period. Ethnic background may have represented no real barrier to steady employment and social advancement in late-nineteenth-century Minneapolis.

Second, these findings have implications for our understanding of class and socio-cultural identity. One of the principal themes in the history of nineteenth-century America is the rise of a distinct middle class. By middle class, researchers have generally designated educated professionals and the white-collar office workers who made their living in the growing bureaucracies of American corporations and government, especially in the decades following the Civil War.[29] This group represents a group involved in neither manual labour nor ownership (in classic Marxist terms) of the means of economic production/social reproduction.

The nature of this group has been a focus of considerable theoretical and empirical attention.[30] Within this group there is a basic distinction between those who simultaneously own and work the means of production, sometimes employing others, typically relatives (petty bourgeoisie) and those employed in corporate or state organisations or whose position is based on personal credentials.[31] The skilled workers of the Courthouse Site may have approached this last definition on the basis of their marketable skills. Archer and Blau recognised that the middle class that emerged in nineteenth-century America was not a homogeneous group, but, rather, was fluid in its occupation and income composition.[32]

Even the very word 'class' has been the source of much confusion among both social scientists and the public at large. There has been no clear consensus as to its meaning, although it is generally understood to refer to a socio-cultural/economic division of society based principally on occupation and income.[33] In contrast, class in a strictly Marxist sense describes the structural relationships among social actors in relation to the control of and/or access to the means of economic production and social reproduction.

The examination of the working-class worlds of late-nineteenth-century Minneapolis presented here suggests that class relationships are operationalised in everyday life through a complex set of socio-cultural identities and related values and behaviours that often have little to do with the structural relationships of class in the Marxist sense *per se*, but that resemble class as more generally understood. These identities include, but are not necessarily limited to, place of birth, place of parents' and grandparents' birth, occupation, income, 'socio-economic status', religious affiliation, etc.

Socio-cultural identities are complexes of outward behaviours and associations and underlying, inward beliefs and values that are actively constructed in the course of everyday life. Material culture plays an important, if not central, role in the construction and explicit and implicit manipulation of these identities as they are 'performed' as part of everyday experience.[34] As Bourdieu has shown, the material expression of an aesthetic sense, or outlook, defines 'taste', which in class-bound contexts can become the basis for social differentiation and control.[35] 'Class struggle', then, emerges in everyday life, not as the struggle between classes for social power and the control of economic resources as argued by Marx, but

within classes and at the 'boundaries' of social categories where 'membership' is constructed, expressed and recognised in a process of negotiation. This process has the power to obscure the social relations of inequality that were the basis for Marx's notion of class struggle. Skilled Irish workers and their families in late-nineteenth-century Minneapolis 'struggled' to be part of the middle class, rather than to overthrow the robber barons of industrial America. It was by such means that America's pervasive ideology of middle-class identity arose. In this model, we are all members of the middle class, with the exception of a very small number of wealthy and poor individuals.[36] The results of the investigation at the Courthouse Site, in particular, suggest that by the close of the nineteenth century the definition of middle class should be broadened to include those whose behaviours and values, and perhaps identities, if not their occupations, were consistent with the middle-class ideals of home and family. Yet, the residents of the Courthouse Site relied on their manual labour skills to make their living. It seems that terms such as 'middle class' and 'working class' are often inadequate, if not patently misleading. Such aggregate terms mask the complex variability of the social matrix and deny individuals their distinctive identities, and do not do justice to the multifaceted socio-cultural identities that affect the values and behaviours of individuals, families and communities.

Notes

1 Encyclopedia Britannica Online Edition: city, urban planning, development, nineteenth century. http://members.eb.com/bol/topic?eu=109104&sctn=2.

2 Lucile M. Kane, *The Falls of St. Anthony: The Waterfalls That Built Minneapolis* (St Paul: Minnesota Historical Society Press, 1987).

3 William W. Folwell, *A History of Minnesota*, vol. 3. revised edition (St Paul: Minnesota Historical Society Press, 1969).

4 Charles R. Walker, *American City: A Rank and File History* (New York: Farrar and Rinehart, 1937).

5 Details of the investigation of the Bridgehead Site are presented in John P. McCarthy and Jeanne A. Ward, *Archaeological Investigations at the Bridgehead Site, Minneapolis, Minnesota, the 1994 Season*, vol. 2, *Site Area B, 19th-Century Residential and Commercial Occupations in the Vicinity of 1st Street North* (Minneapolis: Institute for Minnesota Archaeology Reports of Investigations 367, 1996).

6 Details of the investigation of the Courthouse Site are presented in John P. McCarthy, Jeanne A. Ward and

Karl W. Hagglund, *An Archaeological Evaluation and Data Recovery Investigation at the New Federal Building/United States Courthouse, Minneapolis, Minnesota: Material Insights into Working Class Life in the Late 19th Century* (Minneapolis: Institute for Minnesota Archaeology Reports of Investigations 369, 1996).

7   John Duffy, *The Sanitarians: A History of American Public Health* (Urbana: University of Illinois Press, 1990).

8   Maureen Ogle, *All the Modern Conveniences: American Household Plumbing, 1840–1890* (Baltimore: Johns Hopkins University Press, 1996).

9   David Ward, *Poverty, Ethnicity, and the American City, 1840–1925: Changing Conceptions of the Slum and Ghetto* (Cambridge: Cambridge University Press, 1989).

10 On the social context of sanitary reform in Harper's Ferry see Benjamin Ford, 'The health and sanitation of postbellum Harper's Ferry', *Historical Archaeology* 28:4 (1994), 49–61. On the analysis of intestinal parasites at Harper's Ferry see Karl J. Reinhard, 'Sanitation and parasitism at Harper's Ferry, West Virginia', *Historical Archaeology* 28:4 (1994), 62–7.

11 Frank Healy, L. A. Lydiard, W. H. Morse and Henry N. Knott (compilers), *Minneapolis City Charter and Ordinances, Court and Board Acts, Park Ordinances, Rules of City Council, Etc.* (Minneapolis, 1905), p. 716.

12 Neil McKendrick, John Brewer and J. H. Plumb, *The Birth of a Consumer Society: The Commercialization of Eighteenth Century England* (Bloomington: Indiana University Press, 1982), pp. 20–3.

13 Colin Campbell, *The Romantic Ethic and the Spirit of Modern Consumerism* (Cambridge, MA: Blackwell, 1987).

14 Louise A. Tilley and Joan W. Scott, *Women, Work, and Family* (New York: Holt, Rinehart, and Winston, 1978).

15 Stuart Blumin, *The Emergence of the Middle Class: Social Experience in the American City, 1790–1900* (New York: Cambridge University Press, 1989).

16 See for example, Clifford E. Clark Jr., 'The vision of the dining room: plan book dreams and middle-class realities', in Kathryn Grover (ed.), *Dining in America, 1850–1900* (Amherst: The University of Massachusetts Press, and Rochester: The Margaret Woodbury Strong Museum, 1987), pp. 142–72, and Diana di Zerera Wall, *The Archaeology of Gender: Separating the Spheres in Urban America* (New York: Plenum Press, 1994).

17 John F. Kasson, 'Rituals of dinner: table manners in Victorian America', in Kathryn Grover (ed.), *Dining in America, 1850–1900* (Amherst: The University of Massachusetts Press, and Rochester: The Margaret Woodbury Strong Museum, 1987), pp. 114–41.

18 Adrian Praetzellis and Mary Praetzellis, 'Faces and façades: Victorian ideology in early Sacramento', in Anne E. Yentsch and Mary C. Beaudry (eds.), *The Art and Mystery of Historical Archaeology: Essays in Honor of James Deetz* (Boca Raton, FL: CRC Press, 1992), pp. 75–100.

19 Diana di Zerera Wall, 'Sacred dinners and secular teas: constructing domesticity in mid-19th-century New York', *Historical Archaeology* 25:4 (1991), 79.

20 For an analysis of nineteenth-century Irish-American ceramic purchasing behaviour see John P. McCarthy, 'Material evidence of Irish-immigrant/Irish-American acculturation: traditional culture and the archaeology of the transition to the American "middle class"', paper presented at *The Scattering. Ireland and the Irish Diaspora: A Comparative Perspective*, University College Cork (1997).

21 Henry Glassie, *Passing the Time: Folklore and History of an Ulster Community* (Dublin: The O'Brien Press, 1982), pp. 361–6.

22 See for example, Conrad M. Arensberg, *The Irish Countryman: An Anthropological Study* (Garden City, NY: Natural History Press, 1968), p. 190.

23 Wall, *The Archaeology of Gender*, pp. 89–93.

24 Steven Mintz and Susan Kellogg, *Domestic Revolutions: A Social History of the American Family* (New York: The Free Press, 1988).

25 See for example Lydia M. Child, *The Mother's Book* (Bedford, MA: Applewood Books, n.d.), originally published in 1831.

26 See for example Morris Vogel, 'Urban play', in Brian Sutton-Smith (ed.), *Children's Play: Past, Present, and Future* (Philadelphia: The Please Touch Museum, 1985), pp. 8–9.

27 Lauren J. Cook, 'Tobacco-related material culture and the construction of working class culture', in Mary C. Beaudry and Stephen A. Mrozowski (eds.), *Interdisciplinary Investigations at Boott Mills, Lowell, Massachusetts*, vol. 3, *The Boarding House System as a Way of Life* (Boston: US Department of the Interior, National Park Service, North Atlantic Regional Office, 1989), pp. 209–30.

28 Donna J. Seifert, 'Within site of the Whitehouse: the archaeology of working women', *Historical Archaeology* 25:4 (1991), 82–108.

29 See for example Blumin, *The Emergence of the Middle Class*, and Wall, 'Sacred dinners and secular teas'.

30 See for example Pat Walker (ed.), *Between Labor and Capital: The Professional-Managerial Class* (Boston: South End Press, 1979); Michael Albert and Robin Hahnel, *Marxism and Socialist Theory: Socialism in Theory and Practice* (Boston: South End Press, 1991), pp. 190–5; Stephen Edgell, *Class* (London: Routledge, 1993), pp. 62–73; and Melanie Archer and Judith R. Blau, 'Class formation in nineteenth-century America: The case of the middle class', *Annual Reviews in Sociology* 19 (1993), 17–41.

31 Edgell, *Class,* pp. 63–6.

32 Archer and Blau, 'Class formation in nineteenth-century America'.

33 Martin J. Burke, *The Conundrum of Class: Public Discourse on the Social Order in America* (Chicago: University of Chicago Press, 1995).

34 See for example John P. McCarthy, 'Material culture and the performance of sociocultural identity: community, ethnicity, and agency in the burial practices at the First African Baptist Church cemeteries, Philadelphia, 1810–1841', in Ann Smart Martin and J. Ritchie Garrison (eds.), *American Material Culture, the Shape of the Field: Proceedings of the 34th Winterthur Conference* (Winterthur, DE: The Henry Frances du Pont Winterthur Museum, and Knoxville: University of Tennessee Press, 1997), pp. 359–79.

35 Pierre Bourdieu, *Distinction: A Social Critique of the Judgment of Taste* (Cambridge, MA: Harvard University Press, 1984).

36 See for example Richard Sennet and Johnathan Cobb, *The Hidden Injuries of Class* (New York: Vantage Books, 1972), and G. William Domhoff, *State Autonomy or Class Dominance?* (New York: Aldine De Gruyter, 1996).

12
Alternative narratives: respectability at New York's Five Points

REBECCA YAMIN

Colorless green ideas sleep furiously.
Noam Chomsky, *Syntactic Structures* 1957

Introduction

Old stories are easy to tell. It is the new ones that are diffi-cult. The old stories of Five Points – and there are many – are replete with images of the 'imagined slum':[1] 'dismal and repulsive alleys . . . whose ways were often ankle deep in mud';[2] 'sottish males, and half starved urchins perch-ing about the windows, stoops and cellar doors, like buz-zards on dead trees';[3] 'worse than even the Augean stable for filth and uncleanliness'.[4] No matter how much contra-dictory evidence is brought to bear, the narrative strength of the old stories wins out. Perhaps it is because the his-toric slum serves a purpose in the present,[5] but it may also be because the social historian's statistics and the archae-ologist's material evidence, presented as data, do not tell an alternative story. In fact, they tell no story at all. It is a little like Chomsky's nonsensical sentence about green ideas. You can begin to think about it because it is gram-matical, but you will never make it mean anything.

In an essay first published in 1974, Hayden White wrote, 'History is in bad shape because it has lost sight of its origins in the literary imagination. In the interest of appearing scientific and objective, it has repressed and denied to itself its own greatest source of strength and renewal.'[6] While archaeologists have never particularly identified with literary practice (although, thank good-ness, some archaeologists have proved themselves won-derful writers),[7] the nineteenth-century slum, Mayne's 'imagined slum', is the product of a nineteenth-century literary imagination, and if we are to counter its strength, or even begin to correct its inaccuracies, it will have to be with an equal amount of imagination. The interpretative approach to archaeological analysis begins the process,[8] but it may not go far enough to create an alternative nar-rative, a narrative strong enough to communicate agency in a way that does not seem trivial, or incidental.

Alternative narratives do not write themselves, even from very good data. In 1973, Carol Groneman Pernicone (hereafter referred to as Groneman) wrote a doctoral dis-sertation entitled '"The Bloody Ould Sixth": a social analysis of a New York City working-class community in the mid-nineteenth-century', that included Five Points. As a student of Herbert Gutman, Groneman was particu-larly interested in re-examining widely held assumptions about the effects of immigration.[9] She questioned the orthodox view that emigration necessarily produced dis-location and alienation, ultimately resulting in the loss of native cultures and the breakdown of the family.[10] To examine these assumptions, she did a statistical study of the 1855 New York State Household Census, a document that had previously been used to determine such factors as ethnicity and occupation. The census includes 25,000 residents of the Sixth Ward, a large percentage of them Irish, and at least a portion of them living at Five Points. Although its boundaries were never clearly defined, the intersection from which Five Points got its name was located within the central portion of the ward (Fig. 12.1).[11]

Groneman concluded that generally, 'despite the phys-ical deprivation which immigrants suffered, their life style was not the stereotypical one of moral depravity and social disintegration'.[12] She found that Irish household composition, in terms of age and marital status, did not differ from the rest of the city except for overcrowding;[13] that the majority of Irish emigrated in family groups and continued to live with kin, often in addition to boarders;[14] and that grown children remained in their parents' house-holds rather than living in boardinghouses.[15] A higher percentage of Irish were married than other adults in the city,[16] but there were also more female-headed house-holds. Her major conclusion from these data was that 'a quantitative analysis of a poor, working-class ward in New York City – one which should have been most affected by the "alienating" migration – has revealed the endurance of family ties and the stability of family com-position in the "wild Irish slums" of the mid-nineteenth century'.[17]

Groneman's chapter on the Irish worker none the less painted a pretty bleak picture. Only 34 per cent of Irish males had skilled jobs, with the majority depending on unskilled – and undependable – work.[18] Working men's

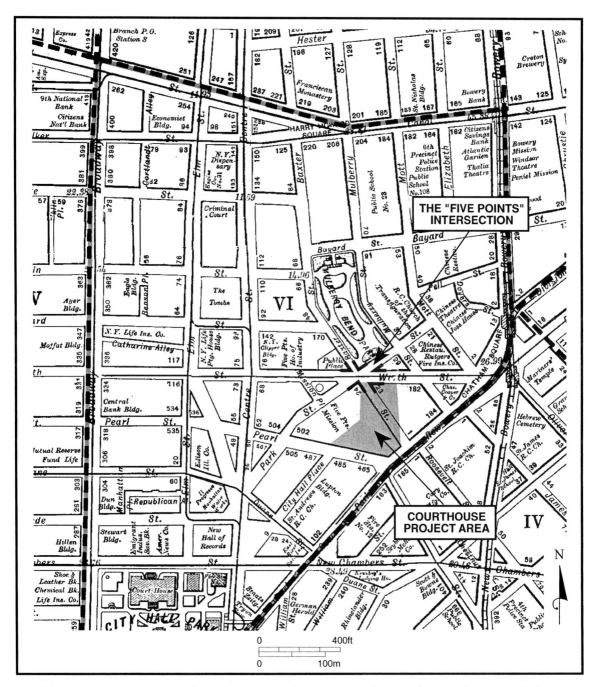

Fig. 12.1 Five Points was named for the points created at the intersection of Baxter (historically Orange), Park (historically Cross) and Worth (historically Anthony) Streets. The base map, taken from Jacob Riis' How the Other Half Lives, *shows the outline of the Sixth Ward in the late nineteenth century.*

wages ranged between 50 cents and $1.50 a day. Women, many working as seamstresses either at home or in shops, earned about 8 cents per shirt (sometimes as little as 4 cents), with three shirts being a hard day's work.[19] Women also worked as laundresses and many kept boarders who paid $1.50 per week. Two-room apartments, barely big enough for small families, often held one or two boarders in addition to three generations of a family. While Groneman stressed the respectability of family units, the acknowledged economic circumstances she described were indeed dire.

Groneman ended her dissertation on an optimistic note: 'With the help of the census records and our awareness of the distortions and contradictions of upper and middle-class observers, perhaps we can begin to rewrite the history of the mid-nineteenth-century urban poor.'[20] That has unfortunately not come to pass. In 1991, Luc Sante published what amounts to a journalistic (but well-referenced) updating of Herbert Asbury's classic, *The Gangs of New York*.[21] Sante's book, called *Low Life: Lures and Snares of Old New York*, and Asbury's before it, romanticise criminal activities at Five Points and repeat the very contemporary descriptions of the neighbourhood that Groneman hoped to refute. In the same year that *Low Life* was published, an archaeological excavation was conducted on the site of a new federal courthouse at Foley Square (Fig. 12.2). Fourteen historic lots were investigated by Historic Conservation and Interpretation (HCI) under contract to the General Services Administration. The site, which included tenement foundations and fifty truncated archaeological features, abutted the intersection for which Five Points was named (Fig. 12.1). It provided another perspective, and another opportunity, to investigate what life was really like in the 'wild Irish slums'.

The archaeological data

Twenty-two features were excavated on the courthouse block. They formed part of the built environment at Five Points, dating from *c.* 1790 to 1890, a hundred-year period in which the neighbourhood was transformed from an outlying industrial district into one of the most congested residential neighbourhoods in the city. Some of the early features were associated with artisans who lived and operated businesses along Pearl Street in the first quarter of the nineteenth century. Later features related to newly arrived German and Irish immigrants who rented apartments in the tenements that had replaced the artisans' houses by the middle of the century.

Of the fourteen historic lots in the project area, Lot 6 (472 Pearl Street) was the most intensively investigated

(Fig. 12.3). The lot included wood-lined privy features (C, D and E) dating to the beginning of the nineteenth century, when a series of carpenters and their families lived at 472 Pearl Street; a stone-lined privy (Feature B) that was filled in the early 1840s by Harris Goldberg, a rabbi and tailor, who lived there from 1839 to 1845 with his wife, children, and students or apprentices; and several features (J, Z and U) associated with the five-storey tenement that had replaced the original wooden structure on the lot by about 1848. The tenement was apparently constructed to receive refugees from the Irish potato famines of the late 1840s. Its owner, Peter McGloughlin, was himself an Irish immigrant, but one who was already well established in New York as a property holder and leader of the Irish Emigrant Society.

The features associated with the tenement produced the largest artefact assemblage (some 100,000 items) that could be indisputably connected to an Irish immigrant population. Feature J, the focus of this study, was a cesspool 11 feet in diameter containing two major artefact-bearing deposits separated by a thick, almost sterile, layer of fill. The upper artefact-bearing deposit (referred to as Analytical Stratum III or AS III) dated to about 1870, and the lower artefact-bearing deposit (AS V) dated to about 1854. The dates are based on the earliest manufacturing date for the most recent artefact (the *terminus post quem* or TPQ) in each deposit. The lower deposit could reasonably be associated with residents listed in the 1855 New York State Household Census (the same document that Groneman used for her study) and the upper one with residents listed in the 1870 federal census. Table 12.1 summarises the census data for 1855 and 1870.

Although much more detailed data were included in the 1855 New York State census than in the later federal census, some comparisons can be made. The increase in the number of residents may be attributed to the addition of a back tenement on the property by 1870 (Fig. 12.3). The back tenement appears on an 1875 Perris insurance map, but is not present on an 1867 map. More households were headed by men in 1870, fewer households included boarders, and fewer women listed occupations. These changes probably reflect the greater availability of local manufacturing jobs for men, keeping them at home;[22] fifteen out of the nineteen men who identified their occupations in 1870 were 'labourers'. Rather surprising is the fact that the heads-of-households and their spouses were born in Ireland in both periods; heads-of-households were, on the average, almost 40; and the average number of children per family was fewer than three. Hasia Diner has suggested that Irish women married late and therefore

Fig. 12.2 Historic Conservation and Interpretation, Inc., a New Jersey consulting firm, excavated the proposed location of a new federal courthouse (Block 160) at Foley Square in the Fall of 1991. The analysis was conducted by John Milner Associates, Inc. between 1992 and 1998 under contract to the General Services Administration.

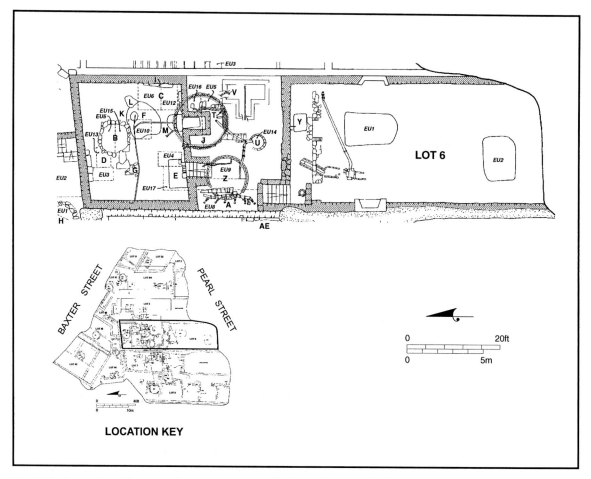

Fig. 12.3 A complex of features relating to sanitation fill the yard between the front and back tenements on Lot 6. Feature U served as a sump for Feature J, the 11-foot diameter cesspool, and Feature Z, a retired cistern, served as a cesspool for the school sink (Feature A) that ran along the west side of the yard. Earlier features – including wood-lined privies (Features C, D and E) and a stone-lined privy (Feature B) – were located further back on the lot, underneath the back tenement.

had less time to bear children.[23] Interestingly, there are several instances of children being born to women in their forties at 472 Pearl Street.

When compared, the archaeological data from the two major artefact-bearing deposits in Feature J suggest only subtle changes over time (Table 12.2). The difference in clothing may be accounted for by the larger number of outer garment buttons (162 out of 333 items), as well as shoes (15) and shoe parts (30) in the earlier deposit. The presence of so many buttons may relate to the recycling of old clothes into rags. The vast majority of sewing-related items in the early deposit (AS V) were scraps of cloth (181

out of 210 items), most of them wool rags that probably came from outer garments. The later deposit also included rags, but there were considerably fewer (76 out of 103 items). In addition to small wool rags (generally less than 10 cm in length) both deposits included long wool strips of cloth. The small rags were probably sold for recycling into shoddy,[24] but the strips may have been made into rugs. According to historian Richard Stott,[25] one of the things that amazed newly arrived immigrants were rugs in working-men's apartments.

Ornaments and flowerpots were recovered from both deposits, suggesting further attention to the aesthetics of

Table 12.1 *Occupants of 472 Pearl Street, 1855 and 1870*

| | 1855 | | 1870 | |
Occupants	No.	%	No.	%
No. of residents	57		91	
No. of households	12		18	
No. male-headed households	7	58.3	13	72.2
No. female headed households	5	41.7	5	27.8
No. household heads born Ireland	11	91.7	17	94.4
No. household heads born Germany	1	8.3	1	5.6
Average years in America	9		*	
Average age of household head	40		38	
Average no. of children	2		3	
Households with boarders	5	41.7	1	5.6
Average no. of boarders	2		1	
Average size of household	5		5	
Men with listed occupation	10		20	
Women with listed occupation	7		0	
No. different occupations	9		5	

Notes:
* Information not available.

Table 12.2 *Small finds by functional group from Feature J*

| | AS V | | AS III | |
Group	No.	%	No.	%
Clothing	333	35.1	145	25.2
Personal	60	6.3	84	14.6
Health and hygiene	31	3.3	22	3.8
Toys	34	3.6	34	5.9
Hardware	—	—	13	2.3
Sewing	210	22.2	103	17.9
Furniture	126	13.3	53	9.2
Tableware	2	0.2	4	0.7
Tobacco	152	16.0	118	20.5
Total	948	100.0	576	100.1

living spaces. Figurines included the canonical Staffordshire dog as well as pastoral shepherds and shepherdesses (Fig. 12.4). The figurines (more were found in the later deposit) attest to increasing participation in the consumer culture that made luxuries as well as necessities available even to people with limited incomes. They also reflect

working-class desires for material comforts – for a 'piece of the pie' – for something more than bare necessities in the midst of overcrowded, insanitary circumstances.[26] In addition to good clothes and such, figurines may have been useful sources of emergency money. As Christine Stansell has pointed out, 'through pawning, women made use of less-needed goods in the service of procuring necessities'. At the end of the week, they pawned what they could to get the rent money due on Saturday morning and redeemed the pawned items when wages were paid on Saturday night.[27]

The later deposit included more personal items such as coins (American and German), mirror fragments and keys, but such things as ornamental hair combs, eye glasses, flasks and slate pencils were equally represented in both strata. Artefacts relating to health and hygiene included more toothbrushes in the later deposit than in the early one, but neither produced more than three, a surprisingly low number considering the number of people living in the tenement in both periods. Twice as many (eight) lice combs were recovered from the earlier stratum and there were also more chamber pots and more wash bowls. Both strata included syringes. The quantitative differences in the personal and health and hygiene related artefacts suggest that sanitary practices may have been

Fig. 12.4 Staffordshire figurines recovered from Feature J.

slightly improved in the later period, but the evidence is not compelling.

More tobacco pipes were found in the early deposit although they made up a smaller proportion of the artefacts recovered than the proportion of pipes in AS III. Among the pipes from AS V were two made of porcelain in the German style, which presumably belonged to the German tobacco dealer on the premises, but most were fluted clays, the least expensive type you could buy. Although there were groups of unused pipes, again probably from the tobacco shop, a high percentage showed evidence (such as reused broken stems and mouthpieces, and tooth marks) of intense use. None was decorated with an Irish or American patriotic motif. The tobacco pipes from the later deposit were also predominantly fluted, the least expensive, and again, no Irish motifs were present although there were a few TD types with thirteen stars presumably representing the original thirteen colonies. Paul Reckner, who conducted the tobacco pipe analysis for the Five Points project, has suggested that the paucity of patriotic motifs relates to a disinclination on the part of Irish workers to identify with symbols used by Nativists. Nativists saw themselves as 'a race apart from those of the old world, imbued with a uniquely democratic nature by the very soil and institutions of their country of birth'.[28] Irish Catholics represented their antithesis and were subjected to vicious stereotyping and outright prejudice. In the public arena, where most smoking was presumably done, the Irish apparently distinguished themselves from the native born and at the same time did not advertise their Irish origins.

In private, they did something else. Table 12.3 summarises the ceramic sets recovered from the two deposits. Sets are defined conservatively here (three or more different forms in the same pattern) and do not include the many almost matching vessels that were probably purchased to replace broken items.

Two-thirds of the sets identified in the early deposit included only vessels associated with tea (assuming the 'deep dishes' were used as slop bowls), suggesting that matching tea sets were more highly valued than matching tablewares. Teawares (matching and non-matching) constituted about one half of the assemblage. There were many single tea cups with matching saucers, mainly decorated in blue scenic patterns (eighteen different Staffordshire printed patterns were identified), and a silver lustre decorated porcelain slop bowl and matching saucer. In addition to the two identified sets of tableware in the early deposit, many non-matching tablewares were recovered, including innumerable versions of edge-decorated and willow pattern plates. There were also serving pieces (a total of twenty-nine), many of them pitchers (Fig. 12.5).

Tea and tableware sets were differently distributed in the later deposit. Only one of the six sets identified was exclusively for tea, although the other sets included tea as well as tableware. Diana Wall[29] has argued that for the middle classes sets that included tea and tablewares were used within the family. Middle-class women at the upper end of the spectrum had fancier porcelain dishes for serving tea to guests, a luxury that middle-class women at the lower end of the spectrum did not have. The presence of matching tea and tableware in the upper deposit of Feature J suggests that the value placed on matching dishes for family meals by the middle class may also have been important to working-class residents at 472 Pearl Street. In addition, the shift from almost exclusively blue and white transfer-printed dishes in the early period to white granite ones is notable. The white granite sets were clearly valued by the later residents at 472 Pearl and they well may signal a turning away from the old Irish style in

Table 12.3 *Ceramic sets recovered from Feature J*

AS V	AS III

Whiteware, transfer-printed blue, 1820–34
  2 saucers
  1 slop bowl
  1 teapot or sugar bowl lid
	Whiteware, transfer-printed blue, 1820–47
	  1 saucer
	  1 tea cup
	  2 dinner plates
	  2 twifflers

Whiteware, transfer-printed blue, 1820
  1 tea cup
  1 deep dish
  1 twiffler
	Whiteware, transfer-printed blue, 1820
	  1 dinner plate
	  1 oval dish
	  2 saucers
	  1 teacup

Whiteware, transfer-printed blue, 1820
  9 soup plates
  2 dinner plates
  2 twifflers
  1 plate, unknown size
	White granite, panelled, 1840
	  5 tea cups
	  5 coffee/tea cups
	  6 saucers

Whiteware, spatter decorated, 1820
  2 tea cups (waisted)
  1 saucer
  1 slop bowl
	White granite, moulded, 1840–50
	  1 twiffler
	  3 dinner plates
	  1 soup plate
	  1 tea/coffee/chocolate pot

Whiteware, shell-edge blue, 1820
  1 dinner plate
  1 plate, unknown size
  1 deep dish
  1 oval platter
	White granite, moulded, 1855–6
	  1 saucer
	  1 teapot
	  2 dinner plates
	  2 soup plates

Whiteware, applied decoration, 1820
  1 deep dish
  1 slop bowl
  1 saucer
	White granite, moulded, 1840
	  1 tea cup
	  1 dinner plate
	  1 pitcher
	  1 cup plate

favour of the more fashionable dishes associated with genteel dining. It is also possible that the white gothic style was preferred for its clean lines and simplicity, a kind of antidote to the prevailing overcrowded, insanitary living conditions. In the later deposit about 45 per cent of all dishes were white as compared to only 13 per cent for the lower deposit, even though white dishes would have been as readily available to residents at mid-century as they were twenty or so years later.

Bottles of one sort or another made up the largest portion of the glass assemblage from both deposits. While the ratio of different types of alcohol bottles suggests a shift in preferences (Table 12.4), the most marked contrast appears between the percentage of medicine bottles in the two periods/deposits. The percentage of mineral/soda water bottles in the later deposit is also considerably larger. There is evidence that mineral water was used for medicinal purposes in the nineteenth century[30] and it may also have been used as a substitute for alcohol or as a cure for overindulgence.[31] Only eighteen glass tableware vessels were identified from AS V and thirty-two from AS III. Among the thirty-two in the upper deposit were three

Fig. 12.5 Among the decorated pitchers from Feature J was one for lemonade (far left), a common substitute for alcohol on the road to temperance.

wine glasses that matched tumblers. No such matches were found in the lower deposit.

Food remains from Feature J were numerous and well preserved. Tables 12.5 and 12.6 summarise the relevant finds for a discussion of diet. Although fish would have been less expensive, the residents of 472 Pearl Street clearly preferred meat. The larger proportion of fish in AS V, almost half of which was made up of porgies, may have been supplied by the resident fishmonger, Morris Callaghan (pers. comm., Claudia Milne). The relatively

Table 12.4 *Glass bottles recovered from Feature J*

Bottles	AS V	%	AS III	%
Wine	21	19.6	8	9.1
Whiskey	4	3.7	5	5.7
Case	—	—	1	1.1
Porter/ale	—	—	1	1.1
Undersized beer	2	1.9	—	—
Unknown alcohol	6	5.6	—	—
Medicine	65	60.7	42	47.7
Mineral/soda water	5	4.7	25	28.4
Pickles	2	1.9	5	5.7
Olive oil	2	1.9	—	—
Sauce	—	—	1	1.1
Total	107	100.0	88	99.9

small amount of poultry reflected either taste or cost. Middle-class assemblages from New York City sites dating to the same period include considerably more chicken.[32]

Pork was clearly the favoured food and came in all forms, from the most expensive to the least expensive: large hams, steaks, hocks and feet (a characteristically Irish dish called crubeen consisted of pigs' feet simmered for hours in white wine and spices).[33] Just over half (52.6 per cent) of all the meat bone recovered from both deposits was pork.[34] The residents of 472 Pearl Street apparently knew that pork (and other meat) had to be thoroughly cooked to avoid sickness. No parasitological evidence was found for beef or pork tapeworm, or for the cysts of the roundworm that causes trichinosis.[35]

The differences between the faunal remains in the early and late deposits are subtle. There is less fish in the later deposit and more pork, both of which suggest improved economic conditions, although there are other possible explanations. Differences in other categories of data may also be explained in various ways. When compared, however, as was fundamentally the purpose of this study, the two deposits from Feature J provide insights into life in an Irish tenement at Five Points over time. But like Groneman's statistical analysis of the 1855 census, the quantitative analysis of archaeological data does not rise to the level of narrative. It cannot counter previous descriptions of Five Points because there is no story line, no plot. To create a narrative requires what Carmel

Table 12.5 *NISP* faunal remains from Feature J*

NISP	AS V	%	AS III	%
Mammal	6,950	72.4	6,771	84.0
Bird	509	5.3	341	4.2
Fish	2,015	21.0	941	11.7
Reptile	119	1.2	4	0.0
Total	9,593	99.9	8,057	99.9

Note:

* NISP = number of identified specimens per taxon

Table 12.6 *Minimum number of meat cuts, Feature J*

	AS V	%	AS III	%
Beef	65	28.0	34	28.0
Lamb/mutton	63	27.2	24	19.8
Pork	104	44.8	63	52.1
Total	232	100.0	121	99.9

Schrire calls an 'act of imagination'.[36] Not to create narrative is to miss the opportunity to connect the data to real life. Narrative in this sense becomes a method of interpreting the data.

Narrative and historical archaeology

The following narrative weaves the archaeological and historical data just discussed into a vignette of daily life. It is written from the perspective of Mary Callaghan, a woman who lived at 472 Pearl Street in 1855 and was still there in 1870. The Mary Callaghan in the narrative is necessarily a composite character, a hermeneutic construction that makes it possible to imagine life in the tenement. This is the second narrative to be written about 472 Pearl Street.[37] The first described the physical features on the property, the tenement itself, its jerry-rigged sanitation system, and its well-meaning landlords. There is no way to know what life was really like at 472 Pearl Street in the middle of the nineteenth century, but there is an authenticity in the archaeological remains. Linked together using the same technique that historians use to link past events,[38] the archaeological remains make it possible to tell stories about Five Points that are different from the stories that have been told before.

Mary Callaghan: 1870

My Morris worked hard in the old days. When we first came to Pearl Street he had a fruit stand. Then he sold fish; the neighbours liked that. He would come home at the end of the day with a boxful of porgies and give them out to the housewives who didn't have a ham steak to cook or a pot of soup on the stove. They've all moved away now, left our little piece of Ireland behind. No matter, the new tenants are Irish too, families with young children: the Mangans and the Mahans, the Rileys and the Currys. And then, there's Bridget Kelly and us, with our big boys. They're all grown up now; been working for wages a long time, but they still come home every night to sleep where they did as wee ones. 472 has always been Irish except for the Germans downstairs. Used to be August Hendrick; a cigar maker, he called himself. Now it's Mr Henchall, Federich Henchall and his wife, Bertha, and their two sons. They keep a tidy tobacco shop, and doing good at it too, with Lysaight's saloon right next door.

Funny how some things change and some don't. In the 50s we'd sit out on the back steps sipping tea from the 'delph' brought from home – or bought to look just like it – and gossiping about one thing or another: where Timothy Lynch got all that money to put in the bank – Tammany, I suspect, probably in cahoots with his kinsman, the alderman – and then there were the pretty seamstresses living with Margaret Gillan and the handsome young men boarding with Mr Jones. We compared prices at Mr Crown's Store on the square and what you had to do when one of the littl'ns or someone else got sick. Wormseed, we used that for worms of course: it killed them off soon enough. And Udolpho Wolfe's Aromatic Schnapps was good for women's troubles. We complained about Father Varela and wished Father Mathew would pay a visit. We all wanted the tea cup that Eliza Burns kept on her mantle: the one with Father Mathew's picture; beautiful it was (Fig. 12.6). That never found its way to the pawn shop, not like so many other things. All the men, well just about, did labouring. They took what they could, some doing real well, working all the time, others not so much.

There was work to do at home too – shirts to sew, the halls to scrub – but nicest was to sit with the neighbours, laundry flapping overhead and children all about. When old clothes got too old to mend, we took off the buttons and tore them into rags for the ragman. Didn't venture much beyond the neighbourhood in those days. Mr Crown had everything: piles of cabbages, potatoes, squashes, egg-plants, tomatoes and turnips. You could get charcoal and nails and tobacco, all in one place. Since he's gone you have to go to Chatham for food, down Pearl

Fig. 12.6 Staffordshire brown printed teacup manufactured by William Adams and Sons (1800–64). Father Mathew is pictured preaching to his flock and administering the abstinence pledge. A legend on the inside of the cup's rim reads, 'Temperance and Industry – Industry Pays Debts'.

for those fancy white dishes everyone wants, and around the corner to the Jews on Baxter for clothes. The pawn shops are on Centre Street, and it's a good thing too. When there's no money, the china figurines on the mantle will bring a little, enough to put Sunday dinner on the table.

Sunday dinner, now that's a pleasure, with all the children sitting neatly in their church clothes. There's eight at the table these days, a good lot to feed, and my Morris so proud sitting up there at the head. He's still working, hard at it selling fruit instead of fish, and still bringing home the leftovers.

Comment

There could be no 'Mary Callaghan' without the recent historical scholarship on the Irish in New York,[39] and a variety of studies of working-class life in New York[40] and elsewhere.[41] And there probably would not be a 'Mary Callaghan' if Henry Glassie had not made such a strong case for studying people 'from the inside out, from the place where people are articulate to the place where they are not, from the place where they are in control of their destinies to the place where they are not'.[42] Beginning with the artefacts and their archaeological context, and staying as close to the data as possible,[43] this narrative vignette and the twenty-two others written for the Five Points report[44] provide a hypothetical picture of life on one block within the infamous Five Points. While this is far from the style of narrative discussed by Hodder in his 1989 article on 'writing archaeology',[45] it is another way to demystify archaeological interpretation and distinguish between the dry (and often obscure) recitation of technical data and what those data might mean. Much as the narrative report recommended by Hodder should be a 'process of argument',[46] narrative as it is used here becomes a process of understanding.

Through this process of constructing narratives for one block in Five Points, the complexity of the neighbourhood becomes visible. The saloons and brothels that take prominence in any description of the Points are still there, but even they differ from the stereotype. The remains associated with Lysaight's Saloon – next door to the tenement at 472 Pearl Street – included master ink bottles for decanting ink into the smaller umbrella types. The narrative could not just be about drinking and carousing; it had to include the saloon's other functions as a place to write letters home, make job contacts, sign up for the next political campaign. Even the brothel showed its human side. Artefacts associated with the private lives of the resident prostitutes were very different from the artefacts associated with their professional duties. The brothel narrative includes the daytime pleasures of female companionship, and the pain of venereal disease (and probable infanticide), as well as the rewards of well-paid work. Other narratives bring to life the ethnic divisions that created a mostly Irish enclave on Pearl Street and a mostly Polish/German one on Baxter. By the 1830s, Baxter, still known as Orange Street, was lined with tailor shops, shoemakers and second-hand clothiers. It was New York's first garment district. The contrast with Pearl Street – Mary Callahan's world – is revealed in the following portion of a narrative based on a feature at 22 Baxter Street, just two doors down from the infamous Five Points intersection.

Just like home

When the brick-lined cistern at 22 Baxter was finally retired in about 1860, thirteen people lived in the small frame house on the lot. Samuel Stone, a German-born (and almost certainly Jewish) clothier, lived with his wife, Rebecca, and 20-year-old son, also born in Germany, and six other New York-born children. Another German woman living with them may have been the house servant. Stone had been a clothier in the city since at least 1840, arriving in the wave of German Jews who emigrated to New York during the mid-1830s. In 1860 the Stones had no tenants, or at least none was listed in the census that year, although there had been several five years earlier. Samuel Lubra, another experienced German tailor, his wife and 11-year-old son, together with Lambert Blower, a Dutch tailor, his wife and three children, had rented from Stone in 1855. Lubra and Blower, and maybe even their wives, probably worked in Stones' second-hand clothing business, receiving food and housing as part of their wage. Throughout the Stones' stay on Baxter Street there were many mouths to feed and, much to the consternation of Jewish leaders, work was virtually continuous, leaving little time for the practice of religion. Only on the

high holy days (Rosha Shona and Yom Kippur) did the Jewish clothiers along Baxter Street lock their doors; the weekly Sabbath passed unobserved.

Bathed in the sour smells spewing forth from Pirnie's brewery behind Stone's shop, the tailors transformed tattered old clothes into 'good as new' garments for sale. They exchanged torn coat linings for new ones, replaced military buttons with civilian ones, and camouflaged tattered hems with seam binding. Working conditions were less than ideal, but the camaraderie of kinsmen, the familiar sound of the German language, and the pleasure of using skills honed in the old country to succeed in the new, made life on Baxter Street bearable.

Mrs Stone fed her houseful of men and children well. There were lamb roasts (leg o'lamb) or lamb chops and stews made of the less expensive neck and feet. Occasionally there was a pork roast (never mind the rules of kashrut, the rabbi wouldn't know), or beef steak, or ham steak, and even less often, a bit of chicken or turkey, perhaps for a holiday meal. And there was fish. The Stones ate cod and porgies, the cheapest fish you could get in mid-nineteenth-century New York. Meals were simple affairs, taken from well-used, blue, edge-decorated plates and, on special occasions, from a flow-blue set that Mrs Stone had bought as seconds. There were flow-blue cups and saucers to match the plates (or at least look like they matched), but less expensive cups were used every day: some of them hand-painted with flowers and berries, and others dipped in bands of different colours. Rebecca Stone's dishes were neither fancy nor fashionable. She was a practical woman who worked as hard as her husband, and when she wasn't tending the babies that came every year (four children were born between 1855 and 1860), she, too, made old clothes almost new.

Comment

The Stones lived differently from the Irish at 472 Pearl Street (and also differently from the brothel residents just six doors down the street). They spent less on food and tableware, although there was a maid in the household. They were probably better off than many of the tenement dwellers, but they lived more frugally. Their disregard for keeping kosher was not untypical. According to Grinstein's history of New York's Jewish community, immigration brought considerable laxity in Jewish practice.[47] However, other food preferences suggest that Jews maintained a different diet from the Irish, eating much more lamb and more fish. They were also more comfortable with patriotic imagery; a large proportion of the tobacco pipes associated with German families was decorated with the American patriotic motifs that the Irish eschewed. While the Irish and the German residents of Block 160 organised their lives differently, they shared the stigma of living at Five Points and a penchant for respectability in spite of it. Seen from the inside, through the narratives, respectability appears not as an imitation of middle-class behaviours but as an important value in working-class life.

Women and respectability

Women emerge as major players in the narratives mainly because so much of the material culture relates to their activities. The prominence of women and their domestic activities brings a kind of balance to previous scholarly descriptions of working-class life in nineteenth-century New York, which have emphasised men's roles and struggles.[48] Like the 'mothers' in London's East End described by Ellen Ross,[49] women at Five Points fed their families decent meals – including substantial amounts of meat despite limited incomes – and they set a respectable table. Meat had enormous symbolic significance in New York (as appears to have been the case in London) and was, according to Richard Stott, eaten twice, sometimes three times a day.[50] It was one of the reasons for being in New York. Much as they did in London, women also had to juggle finances in New York to make ends meet, and the china figurines found at 472 Pearl Street may well have been exchanged for cash when the need arose. In London similar ornaments from the mantle ('mother's altarpiece') went back and forth to the pawn shop.[51]

Respectability on Block 160 appears to have involved a combination of traditional practices and active participation in New York's consumer culture. Shopping, the social act of acquiring consumer goods, provided women with an opportunity to demonstrate their taste for goods appropriate to their status as members of the working class and their talent for acquiring such goods at a reasonable price. In his study of shopping in a small town in Trinidad, Daniel Miller found that people experienced shopping 'as the antithesis of their recent experience of sugar-cane estates and village life'.[52] The past seemed a kind of 'dark age of repetitive mundane daily tasks' compared to the delight of shopping. Similarly, shopping in New York – where goods were available from all over the world – must have been a new and wondrous experience for most immigrants. Work, of course, is what made it all possible.

In *Workers in the Metropolis*, Richard Stott describes a high-energy work environment in antebellum New York. Most workers laboured from seven in the morning until noon, took an hour for dinner, and then worked until six.[53] They drank on the job to keep up the pace and in some trades it was the bosses who provided the liquor.[54] Labourers, according to Stott, tolerated the pace and the pressure for the reward of higher wages than they had ever received in Europe and a higher standard of living.[55] The artefacts recovered on Block 160 complement that exuberant picture. They reflect active participation in consumer society, not in imitation of the middle class, but in celebration of what was available and what could be acquired with honestly earned wages. The shops at Five Points overflowed with food, and workers took advantage of the plenty. Shopping for food, as well as for fashionable household goods, expressed a working-class woman's membership in working-class culture. Although Stott sees working-class culture as fundamentally masculine,[56] the organisation of the very consumption that made work worthwhile was the domain of women. If the short-stemmed pipe was the worker's emblem of identity, the shopping basket may have been his wife's (Fig. 12.7).

The energetic work regimen identified by Stott is also evident in the archaeological remains, which include remnants of the second-hand clothing businesses on Baxter Street and of outwork done in the tenements along Pearl Street, much of it done by women. Work was not invisible in a working-class neighbourhood; it was everywhere. And home was not the quiet refuge from work that it had become for the middle class by the mid-nineteenth century. Using narrative, the archaeological strands of evidence suggest a working-class world that was distinct from the middle-class world. Working-class life was full of energy and struggle: to keep a steady job, to work at a breakneck pace, to make a living wage, to raise children in an unhealthy environment, to face sickness, and find pleasure. From the inside, that working-class world gains its respectability, in great part, through the acts of women who, except for prostitutes, are virtually invisible in nineteenth-century accounts of Five Points. It is not the artefact lists or statistics drawn from census records that make these women visible. It is the narrative process of imagining their lives.

A narrative response to a narrative image

The monolithic image of the imagined slum is difficult to dispute. The dignity of peoples' private lives was not visible to the nineteenth-century 'slummer', just as the causes of physical and economic deprivation were not visible to him. He saw what he wanted to see, the construct that was a useful foil for middle-class values (Fig. 12.8). That construct continues to be useful to modern writers looking for a backdrop for their tales of depravity (for example Caleb Carr's *The Alienist*, and E. L. Doctorow's

Fig. 12.7 Shopping on Baxter Street.

Waterworks). Actual remains of life at Five Points do not speak to the construct, but, like all archaeological remains, they do not speak at all. To make them speak we have borrowed the historian's narrative method, but with a difference. While historians create coherence by including some things and omitting others,[57] archaeologists seek to include as much of the data as possible. Coherence is measured by finding an explanation that makes sense of most of the data,[58] that uses the hermeneutic process of creating narratives to tuck in the loose ends.

The narrative vignettes of Five Points provide alternative images of New York's archetypal slum. They are no more real than Charles Dickens' mid-nineteenth-century description or Caleb Carr's more recent one, but they begin (and end) with the real stuff of everyday life. They attempt to do with material things what Greg Dening calls 'hearing the silences'.[59] To hear those silences takes imagination; not the imagination of fantasy, but an imagination that goes just beyond what is known, and yet is possible

because so much already is known.[60] Our stories are based on all we know: about the past we are attempting to understand and the present we cannot escape. The Five Points narratives take their coherence from the humanity of the people who lived at Five Points, and from what we can imagine about those people from the perspective of what we know about ourselves, and can glean about the physical, economic and political circumstances in which they lived. The alternative narratives reveal the respectable side of life in a working-class, immigrant neighbourhood, the part that is rarely glimpsed by outsiders.

Acknowledgements

I am grateful to Alan Mayne, first for his wonderful book, *The Imagined Slum*, and second for inviting me to participate in the symposium, 'Ethnographies of place: the historical archaeology of slumland' at the World Archaeological Congress 4 in Cape Town. I am grateful

Fig. 12.8 'Five Points 1827', lithograph published in Valentine's Manual of the Municipal Government of the City of New York in 1855. The edge of the excavated block is shown on the right of the image. The Stones lived several doors down from the intersection at 22 Baxter, and the Callaghans lived around the corner on Pearl Street (not shown).

to Alan and Tim Murray for including me in this volume, and to Alan again for his thoughtful comments on my contribution. Steve Patterson pointed me towards the relevant literature on narrative and Robin Stevens took time he didn't have to improve my script. I owe deepest thanks to my colleagues on the Foley Square project who did much of the tedious work while I had the fun of putting it all together. With Janet Spector (*What This Awl Means*, 1993) the writing of narratives has enabled me to recapture a feeling of connection with the past and to remember why the long analytical process is worth the effort.

Notes

1 Alan Mayne, *The Imagined Slum: Newspaper Representation in Three Cities 1870–1914* (Leicester: Leicester University Press, 1993).

2 Charles Dickens, *American Notes*, reprint of 1842 edn (New York: Fromm International, 1985).

3 William Bobo, *Glimpses of New York City* (Charleston, SC: J. J. McCarter, 1852).

4 *New York Transcript,* 4 June 1834.

5 Keith Gandal, *The Virtues of the Vicious: Jacob Riis, Stephen Crane, and the Spectacle of the Slum* (New York: Oxford University Press, 1997).

6 Hayden White, 'The historical text as literary artefact', in Hazard Adams and Leroy Searle (eds.), *Critical Theory since 1965* (Tallahassee: University Press of Florida, 1986), pp. 395–407.

7 See, for instance, Ivor Noel Hume's *Martin's Hundred* (New York: Alfred A. Knopf, 1988) or Anne E. Yentsch, *A Chesapeake Family and Their Slaves: A Study in Historical Archaeology* (Cambridge: Cambridge University Press, 1994).

8 Mary C. Beaudry, Lauren J. Cook and Stephen A. Mrozowski, 'Artefacts and active voices: material culture as social discourse', in Randall H. McGuire and Robert Paynter (eds.), *The Archaeology of Inequality* (Oxford: Blackwell, 1991), pp. 150–91; Yentsch, *A Chesapeake Family*.

9 Carol Groneman Pernicone, 'The "Bloody Ould Sixth": a social analysis of a New York City working class community in the mid-nineteenth century', PhD thesis, University of Rochester (1973), p. xviii.

10 Nathan Glazer and Daniel P. Moynihan, *Beyond the Melting Pot: The Negroes, Puerto Ricans, Jews, Italians, and Irish of New York City* (Cambridge, MA: MIT Press, 1970); Oscar Handlin, *The Uprooted: The Epic Story of the Great Migrations that Made the American People* (New York: Grosset's Universal Library, 1951).

11 The five points were created by the intersection of Orange (now Baxter), Cross (now Park), and Anthony (now Worth) Streets.

12 Groneman, 'The Bloody Ould Sixth', pp. iv–v.

13 *Ibid.,* chap. 3.

14 *Ibid.,* p. 59.

15 *Ibid.,* p. 82.

16 *Ibid.,* p. 209.

17 *Ibid.,* p. 83.

18 *Ibid.,* p.100.

19 *Ibid.,* p. 141.

20 *Ibid.,* p. 207.

21 *The Gangs of New York* by Herbert Asbury was first published in 1927 (New York: Alfred A. Knopf), but is still read avidly by New York history buffs. In addition to *Low Life* (New York: Farrar, Straus and Giroux, 1991), Sante also compiled photographs from police files in a volume entitled *Evidence* (New York: Farrar, Straus and Giroux, 1991).

22 Richard B. Stott, *Workers in the Metropolis: Class, Ethnicity, and Youth in Antebellum New York City* (Ithaca, NY: Cornell University Press, 1990).

23 Hasia R. Diner, *Erin's Daughters in America* (Baltimore: Johns Hopkins University Press, 1983).

24 Cheryl LaRoche and Gary McGowan, '"Material culture": conservation and analysis of textiles recovered from Five Points', in Rebecca Yamin (ed.), *Tales of Five Points: Working-Class Life in Nineteenth-Century New York*, vol. 2, draft on file (Philadelphia: John Milner Associates, 1998), pp. 276–88.

25 Richard B. Stott, *Workers in the Metropolis: Class, Ethnicity, and Youth in Antebellum New York City* (Ithaca, NY: Cornell University Press, 1990).

26 Pamela Fox, *Class Fictions: Shame and Resistance in the British Working-Class Novel, 1890–1945* (Durham, NC: Duke University Press, 1994).

27 Christine Stansell, *City of Women: Sex and Class in New York 1789–1860* (Urbana: University of Illinois Press, 1987).

28 Paul Reckner, 'Negotiating patriotism at Five Points: clay tobacco pipes and patriotic imagery among trade unionists and nativists in a nineteenth-century New York neighbourhood', in Yamin (ed.), *Tales of Five Points*, vol. 2, pp. 105–17.

29 Diana di Zerera Wall, *The Archaeology of Gender: Separating the Spheres in Urban America* (New York: Plenum Press, 1994).

30 David Armstrong and Elizabeth Metzger Armstrong, *The Great American Medicine Show* (Old Tappan, NJ: Prentice Hall, 1991).

31 Helen McKearin and Kenneth M. Wilson, *American*

Bottles and Flasks and Their Ancestry (New York: Crown Publishers, 1978).

32 Bert Salwen and Rebecca Yamin, 'The archaeology and history of six 19th century lots, Sullivan Street, Greenwich Village, New York City. CEQR#83-225M' (New York: New York University, 1990); Joan Geismar, 'History and archaeology of the Greenwich Mews Site, Greenwich Village, New York. CEQR No. 86–144M' (New York: Greenwich Mews Associates, 1989).

33 Theodora FitzGibbon, *Irish Traditional Food* (New York: St Martin's Press, 1968); Clare Connery, *In an Irish Country Kitchen* (New York: Simon & Schuster, 1992).

34 Claudia Milne and Pamela Crabtree, 'Revealing meals: ethnicity, economic status, and diet at the Five Points, 1800–1860', in Yamin (ed.), *Tales of Five Points*, vol. 2, pp. 138–205.

35 Karl Reinhard, 'Parasitic disease at Five Points: parasitological analysis of sediments from the Courthouse Block', in *ibid.*, pp. 391–404.

36 Carmel Schrire, *Digging through Darkness: Chronicles of an Archaeologist* (Charlottesville: University Press of Virginia, 1995), p. 5.

37 Rebecca Yamin, 'Lurid tales and homely stories of New York's notorious Five Points', *Historical Archaeology* 32:1 (1998), 74–85.

38 Hayden White, 'The value of narrativity in the representation of reality', in W. J. T. Mitchell (ed.), *On Narrative* (Chicago: University of Chicago Press, 1981), pp. 1–23; Laurel Thatcher Ulrich, *A Midwife's Tale: The Life of Martha Ballard, Based on Her Diary 1785–1812* (New York: Alfred A. Knopf, 1990).

39 See, for instance, Ronald H. Bayor and Timothy J. Meagher, *The New York Irish* (Baltimore: Johns Hopkins University Press, 1996).

40 Stansell, *City of Women*; Stott, *Workers in the Metropolis*.

41 Ellen Ross, *Love and Toil: Motherhood in Outcast London, 1870–1918* (New York: Oxford University Press, 1993); Fox, *Class Fictions*; Kevin C. Kearns, *Dublin Tenement Life: An Oral History* (Dublin: Gill & Macmillan, 1994).

42 Henry Glassie, *Passing the Time in Ballemenone: Culture and History of an Ulster Community* (Philadelphia: University of Pennsylvania Press, 1982), p. 86.

43 Joan M. Gero, 'Who experienced what in prehistory? A narrative explanation from Queyash, Peru', in Robert W. Preucel (ed.), *Processual and Postprocessual Archaeologies: Multiple Ways of Knowing the Past*, Occasional Paper 10 (Southern Illinois University at Carbondale, 1991), p. 127.

44 Rebecca Yamin, 'People and their possessions', in Yamin (ed.), *Tales of Five Points*, vol. 1, pp. 90–145.

45 Ian Hodder, 'Writing archaeology: site reports in context', *Antiquity* 63 (1989), 268–74.

46 *Ibid.*, 273.

47 Hyman B. Grinstein, *The Rise of the Jewish Community of New York 1654–1860* (Philadelphia: The Jewish Publication Society, 1945).

48 Paul A. Gilje, *The Road to Mobocracy: Popular Disorder in New York City, 1763–1834* (Chapel Hill: University of North Carolina Press for the Institute of Early American History and Culture, 1987); Sean Wilentz, *Chants Democratic: New York and the Rise of the American Working Class, 1788–1850* (New York: Oxford University Press, 1984); Stott, *Workers in the Metropolis*. An exception is Stansell's *City of Women*.

49 Ross, *Love and Toil*.

50 Stott, *Workers in the Metropolis*, pp. 176–7.

51 Ross, *Love and Toil*, p. 46.

52 Daniel Miller, 'Could shopping ever really matter?', paper presented at 'Consuming politics: how mass consumption has shaped and been shaped by political systems and cultures', a workshop sponsored by the Rutgers Center for Historical Analysis, New Brunswick, NJ, manuscript on file, John Milner Associates, Inc., Philadelphia, 1993, p. 3.; Lauren J. Cook, Rebecca Yamin and John P. McCarthy, 'Shopping as meaningful action: toward a redefinition of consumption in historical archaeology', *Historical Archaeology* 30:4 (1996), 50–65.

53 Stott, *Workers in the Metropolis*, p. 131.

54 *Ibid.*, p. 143.

55 *Ibid.*, p. 134.

56 *Ibid.*, p. 270.

57 White, 'On the value of narrativity', p. 10.

58 Ian Hodder, 'Interpretive archaeology and its role', *American Antiquity* 56:1 (1991), 7–18.

59 Greg Dening, 'Empowering imaginations', in Greg Dening, *Readings/Writings* (Melbourne: Melbourne University Press, 1998), p. 208.

60 *Ibid.*, p. 209.

Bibliography

Adams, George, *The Lowell Directory*, Lowell, MA: Oliver March, 1851.

Adams, H. and Suttner, H., *William Street, District Six*, Diep River: Chameleon Press, 1988.

Adams, Sampson, and Company, *The Lowell Directory*, Lowell, MA: Joshua Merrill and B. C. Sargeant, 1861.

Albert, Michael and Hahnel, Robin, *Marxism and Socialist Theory: Socialism in Theory and Practice*, Boston: South End Press, 1991.

Allen, Judith, 'Octavius Beale re-considered: infanticide, babyfarming and abortion in NSW 1880–1939', in Sydney Labour History Group, *What Rough Beast? The State and Social Order in Australian History*, Sydney: George Allen & Unwin, 1982, pp. 111–29.

Appadurai, A., *The Cultural Life of Things*, Cambridge: Cambridge University Press, 1986.

Archaeology Contracts Office, 'Archaeological excavations at Block 11, Cape Town', unpublished report for City Planner, Cape Town City Council, December 1990.

'Excavations in District Six: a residential property at the corner of Stuckeris & Roger Streets', unpublished site report, Department of Archaeology, University of Cape Town, 1996.

Archer, Melanie, and Blau, Judith R., 'Class formation in nineteenth-century America: the case of the middle class', *Annual Reviews in Sociology* 19 (1993), 17–41.

Archer, Thomas, *The Pauper, the Thief and the Convict: Sketches of Some of Their Homes, Haunts and Habits*, London: Groombridge and Sons, 1865.

Arensberg, Conrad M., *The Irish Countyman: An Anthropological Study,* Garden City, NY: Natural History Press, 1968.

Armstrong, David and Armstrong, Elizabeth Metzger, *The Great American Medicine Show*, Old Tappan, NJ: Prentice Hall, 1991.

Asbury, Herbert, *The Gangs of New York*, New York: Alfred A. Knopf, 1927.

Ashworth, G. J. and Tunbridge, J. E., *The Tourist-Historic City*, London: Belhaven, 1990.

Babson, David W., 'Introduction', in *In the Realm of Politics: Prospects for Public Participation in African-American and Plantation Archaeology* (thematic issue), *Historical Archaeology* 31:3 (1997), 5–6.

Bagwell, Beth, *Oakland: The Story of a City*, Novato, CA: Presidio Press, 1982.

Bain, Allison, 'Analyse des restes archéoentomologiques de l'îlot Hunt (CeEt-110) dans la basse-ville de Québec', CELAT, Université Laval, 1997.

Barnes, Kevin, 'Artefact report – building materials', in Godden Mackay, *The Cumberland/Gloucester Streets Site*, vol. 4, pp. 125–206.

Barnett, N., 'Race, housing and town planning in Cape Town c.1920–1940: with special reference to District Six', MA thesis, University of Cape Town, 1993.

Barraclough, K. C., *Steelmaking before Bessemer*, 2 vols., London: The Metals Society, 1984.

Barrett, Bernard, *The Inner Suburbs: The Evolution of an Industrial Area*, Melbourne: Melbourne University Press, 1971.

Barshay, Shirley F., *One Meaning of 'Citizen Participation': A Report on the First Year of Model Cities in Oakland California*, Office of Economic Opportunity, Western Region, 1968, on file in Environmental Design Library, University of California, Berkeley.

Bayly, [Mary], *Ragged Homes and How to Mend Them*, Philadelphia: American Sunday School Union, 1864.

Bayor, Ronald H. and Meagher, Timothy J., *The New York Irish*, Baltimore: Johns Hopkins University Press, 1996.

Beauchamp, V. A., 'The workshops of the cutlery industry in Hallamshire 1750–1900', PhD thesis, University of Sheffield, 1996.

Beaudry, Mary C., 'The Lowell Boott Mills complex and its housing: material expressions of corporate ideology', *Historical Archaeology* 23 (1989), 19–32.

'Public aesthetics versus personal experience: worker health and well-being in 19th-century Lowell, Massachusetts', *Historical Archaeology* 27:2 (1993), 90–105.

Beaudry, Mary C. (ed.), *Documentary Archaeology in the New World*, Cambridge: Cambridge University Press, 1988.

Beaudry, Mary C., Cook, Lauren J. and Mrozowski, Stephen A., 'Artefacts and active voices: material culture as social discourse', in McGuire and Paynter (eds.), *The Archaeology of Inequality*, pp. 150–91.

Beaudry, Mary C. and Mrozowski, Stephen A. (eds.), *Interdisciplinary Investigations of the Boott Mills, Lowell, Massachusetts: A Preliminary Report*, Cultural Resources Management Series 18, Boston: National Park Service, North Atlantic Regional Office, 1987.

Interdisciplinary Investigations of the Boott Mills, Lowell, Massachusetts, vol. 2, *The Kirk Street Agent's House*, Cultural Resources Management Series 19, Boston: National Park Service, North Atlantic Regional Office, 1987.

Interdisciplinary Investigations of the Boott Mills, Lowell, Massachusetts, vol. 3, *The Boardinghouse System as a Way of Life*, Cultural Resources Management Series 21, Boston: National Park Service, North Atlantic Regional Office, 1987.

Bégin, Francine, 'La gestion et la mise en valeur du patrimoine bâti à Québec', in Marie-Claude Rocher and André Ségal (dir.), *Le traitement du patrimoine urbain: intégration, intégralité, intégrité*. Actes du Colloque Mons-Québec 1996, Quebec: Ville de Québec, Musée de la Civilisation, Patrimoine Canadien, 1997.

Behlmer, George, *Friends of the Family: The English Home and Its Guardians, 1850–1940*, Stanford: Stanford University Press, 1998.

Belford, P. J., 'Archaeological excavations at Foxbrook Furnace, Derbyshire', *Historical Metallurgy* 19 (1999), 14–25.

'Converters and refiners: the archaeology of Sheffield steelmaking 1700–1850', MA thesis, University of Sheffield, 1997.

Standing Building Recording of 'Cornish Place', Sheffield, ARCUS, Research School of Archaeology, University of Sheffield, Report 414 (forthcoming).

Bell, Edward L., 'A preliminary report on health, hygiene, and sanitation at the Boott Mills boardinghouses: an historical and archeological perspective', in Beaudry and Mrozowski (eds.), *Preliminary Report*, pp. 57–68.

'"So much like home": the historical context of the Kirk Street Agent's House', in Beaudry and Mrozowski (eds.), *Interdisciplinary Investigations*, vol. 2, pp. 5–28.

Benjamin, Walter, *Baudelaire: A Lyric Poet in the Era of High Capitalism*, trans. Harry Zohn, London: New Left Books, 1973.

Bezzoli, M., Marks, R. and Kruger, M., *Texture and Memory: The Urbanism of District Six*, Cape Town: Cape Technikon Urban Housing Research Unit, 1997.

Bibby, Miss, Colles, Miss, Petty, Miss and Sykes, Dr, *The Pudding Lady: A New Departure in Social Work*, London: The St Pancras School for Mothers [1910].

Bickford-Smith, Vivian, *Ethnic Pride and Racial Prejudice in Victorian Cape Town: Group Identity and Social Practice, 1875–1902*, Cambridge: Cambridge University Press, 1995.

Bickford-Smith, Vivian, van Heyningen, Elizabeth and Worden, Nigel, *Cape Town in the Twentieth Century*, Cape Town: David Philip, 1999.

Biles, Roger, 'Thinking the unthinkable about our cities thirty years later', *Journal of Urban History* 25 (1998), 57–64.

Birch, Alan and MacMillan, David S., *The Sydney Scene 1788–1960*, Sydney: Hale & Iremonger, 1962.

Birmingham, Judy and Murray, Tim, *Historical Archaeology in Australia: A Handbook*, Sydney: Australian Society for Historical Archaeology, 1987.

Blackmar, E., *Manhattan for Rent 1785–1850*, Ithaca and London: Cornell University Press, 1989.

Blanchet, Jules, Talbot, Pierre and Rousseau, Jean, *Concept général de réaménagement du Vieux-Québec*, Québec: Service de l'Urbanisme, Ville de Québec, 1971.

Blewett, Mary H., *The Last Generation: Work and Life in the Textile Mills of Lowell, Massachusetts 1910–1960*, Amherst: University of Massachusetts Press, 1990.

Blumin, Stuart, *The Emergence of the Middle Class:*

Social Experience in the American City, 1760–1900, New York: Cambridge University Press, 1989.

Bobo, William, *Glimpses of New York City*, Charleston, SC: J. J. McCarter, 1852.

Bohlin, A., 'The politics of locality: memories of District Six in Cape Town', in N. Lovell (ed.), *Locality and Belonging*, London: Routledge, 1998, pp. 168–88.

Bond, Kathleen H., 'Alcohol use in the Boott Mills boardinghouses: tension between workers and management, a documentary and archaeological study', MA thesis, Boston University, 1988.

'"That we may purify our corporation by discharging the offenders": the documentary record of social control in the Boott boardinghouses', in Beaudry and Mrozowski (eds.), *Interdisciplinary Investigations*, vol. 3, pp. 23–36.

'The medicine, alcohol, and soda vessels from the Boott Mills boardinghouses', in Beaudry and Mrozowski (eds.), *Interdisciplinary Investigations*, vol. 3, pp. 121–39.

Booth, Charles, *Life and Labour of the People in London, First Series: Poverty*, London: Macmillan, 1902 (first published 1889, 1891).

Life and Labour of the People in London, Third Series: Religious Influences, London: Macmillan, 1902.

Borchert, James, *Alley Life in Washington: Family, Community, Religion, and Folklife in the City, 1850–1970*, Chicago: University of Illinois Press, 1982.

Bouchard, Pierre, 'Le site de l'îlot Hunt à Québec (CeEt-110): étude socio-économique des habitants d'après la collection archéologique, 1850–1900', Masters thesis, Ecole des Gradués, Université Laval, 1998.

Bourdieu, Pierre, *Distinction: A Social Critique of the Judgment of Taste*, Cambridge, MA: Harvard University Press, 1984.

Bourdieu, P., *Distinction: A Social Critique of the Judgement of Taste*, trans. R. Nice, London: Routledge, 1989.

Bower, Rebecca, 'Artefact report – leather', in Godden Mackay, *The Cumberland/Gloucester Streets Site*, vol. 4, part 2, pp. 121–36.

Boyer, M. Christine, *The City of Collective Memory: Its Historical Imagery and Architectural Entertainments*, Cambridge, MA: MIT Press, 1996.

Bradford, Armory, *Oakland's Not for Burning*, New York: David McKay Company, 1968.

Breytenbach, C., *The Spirit of District Six*, Cape Town: Purnell, 1970.

Brink, A., *Looking on Darkness*, London: W. H. Allen, 1974.

Brockway, Fenner, *Bermondsey Story: The Life of Alfred Salter*, reprinted, London: Stephen Humphrey, 1995.

Broeze, Frank, 'Militancy and pragmatism: an international perspective on maritime labour, 1870–1914', *International Review of Social History* 36 (1991), 165–200.

Brown, Anne R., 'Historic ceramic typology with principal dates of manufacture and descriptive characteristics for identification', prepared for Delaware Department of Transportation, Division of Highways, Location and Environmental Studies Office, Dover, 1982.

Brown-May, Andrew, *Melbourne Street Life: The Itinerary of Our Days*, Kew, Victoria: Australian Scholarly Publishing, 1998.

Buck-Morss, Susan, 'The flâneur, the sandwichman, and the whore: the politics of loitering', *New German Critique* 39 (Fall 1986), 99–140.

Burke, Martin J., *The Conundrum of Class: Public Discourse on the Social Order in America*, Chicago: University of Chicago Press, 1995.

Cabak, Melanie A. and Inkrot, Mary M., *Old Farm, New Farm: An Archaeology of Rural Modernization in the Aiken Plateau, 1875–1950*, Savannah River Archaeological Research Papers 9, South Carolina Institute of Archaeology and Anthropology, University of South Carolina, 1997.

California Department of Transportation, *EIR* 5–18. *Final Environmental Impact Statement/Report*, vol. 1, *I-880/Cypress Replacement, Alameda County, California*, 1991.

Privy to the Past, co-produced with Alpha Spectrum Educational Films, Oakland, and the Anthropological Studies Center, Sonoma State University, Rohnert Park, CA, 1999.

Calvert, Karin, *Children in the House: The Material Culture of Early Childhood, 1600–1900*, Boston: Northeastern University Press, 1992.

Campbell, Colin, *The Romantic Ethic and the Spirit of Modern Consumerism*, Cambridge, MA: Blackwell, 1987.

Candee, Richard M., 'Architecture and corporate planning in the early Waltham system', in Robert Weible (ed.), *Essays from the Lowell Conference on Industrial History 1982/198*3, Lowell, MA: Lowell Historical Society, 1985.

Cannadine, David, *The Pleasures of the Past*, London: Penguin, 1989.

Cannon, Michael, *Who's Master? Who's Man?* Melbourne: Viking O'Neil, 1971.

Carney, Martin, 'Trench C Report', in Godden Mackay,

The Cumberland/Gloucester Streets Site, vol. 3, pp. 133–92.

'Artefact report – glass', in Godden Mackay, *The Cumberland/Gloucester Streets Site*, vol. 4, pp. 15–125.

Carrier, James, *Gifts and Commodities: Exchange and Western Capitalism since 1700*, London: Routledge, 1995.

Catts, Wade P. and Custer, Jay F., *Tenant Farmers, Stone Masons, and Black Laborers: Final Archaeological Investigations of the Thomas Williams Site, Glasgow, New Castle County, Delaware*, Delaware Department of Transportation Archaeology Series 82, 1990.

Chandler, Alfred D., *The Visible Hand: The Managerial Revolution in American Business*, Cambridge, MA: The Belknap Press of Harvard University, 1977.

Scale and Scope: The Dynamics of Industrial Capitalism, Cambridge, MA: The Belknap Press of Harvard University, 1990.

Cheek, Charles D. and Friedlander, Amy, 'Pottery and pig's feet: space, ethnicity, and neighbourhood in Washington, D.C., 1880–1940', *Historical Archaeology* 24:1 (1990), 34–60.

Cheek, C. D, Friedlander, A., Holt, C. A., Lee Decker, C. H. and Ossim, T. E., 'Archaeological investigation at the National Photographic Interpretation Center Addition, Washington, D.C. Navy Yard Annex', Alexandria, VA: Soil Systems, Inc., 1983.

Chénier, Rémi *Québec, ville coloniale française en Amérique: 1660 à 1690*, Ottawa: Environment Canada, Service des Parcs, 1991.

Child, Lydia M., *The Mother's Book*, Bedford, MA: Applewood Books, n.d. (originally published 1831).

City Manager of Oakland California, 'Application for planning grant, model cities program, City of Oakland', City of Oakland, 1966.

Clark, Clifford E., Jr, 'The vision of the dining room: plan book dreams and middle-class realities', in Kathryn Grover (ed.), *Dining in America, 1850–1900*, Amherst: University of Massachusetts Press, and Rochester: The Margaret Woodbury Strong Museum, 1987, pp. 142–72.

Clift, H., 'Excavation of a spoil heap in District Six: report on the RESUNACT Schools Programme prepared for the National Monuments Council', Department of Archaeology, University of Cape Town, 1996.

Cloutier, Céline, 'De l'aisance à la pauvreté. Etude d'une collection archéologique des ouvriers du quartier Saint-Roch à Québec au XIXe siècle', Quebec: Ville de Québec, Centre de Développement Economique et Urbain, 1997.

'Les déchets des uns et des autres. Etude du contenu des fosses d'aisance du site archéologique de la maison Aubert-de-la-Chesnaye', in Moss, *L'archéologie de la maison Aubert-de-la-Chesnaye*, pp. 235–95.

'Hygiène privée, transferts culturels et mécanisation: le cas des latrines du site Aubert de la Chesnaye à Québec', in Louise Pothier, *L'eau, l'hygiène publique et les infrastructures*, Montreal: Groupe PGV–Diffusion de l'Archéologie, 1996, pp. 22–4.

Coghlan, T. A., *Labour and Industry in Australia*, 4 vols., Melbourne: Macmillan, 1969 (first published 1918).

Collins, Willie R., 'Jazzing up Seventh Street: musicians, venues, and their social implications', in Stewart and Praetzellis (eds.), *Sights and Sounds*, pp. 295–324.

Comaroff, Jean and Comaroff, John L., 'Introduction', in Comaroff and Comaroff (eds.), *Modernity and Its Malcontents: Ritual and Power in Postcolonial Africa*, Chicago: University of Chicago Press, 1993, pp. xi–xxx.

Of Revelation and Revolution: The Dialectics of Modernity on a South African Frontier, Chicago: University of Chicago Press, 1997.

Connell, R. W. and Irving, T. H., *Class Structure in Australian History*, Melbourne: Longman Cheshire, 1980.

Connery, Clare, *In an Irish Country Kitchen*, New York: Simon & Schuster, 1992.

Cook, Lauren J., 'Descriptive analysis of tobacco-related material from the Boott Mills boardinghouses', in Beaudry and Mrozowski (eds.), *Interdisciplinary Investigations*, vol. 3, pp. 187–207.

'Tobacco-related material culture and the construction of working-class culture', in Beaudry and Mrozowski (eds.), *Interdisciplinary Investigations*, vol. 3, pp. 209–29.

Cook, Lauren J., Yamin, Rebecca, and McCarthy, John P. 'Shopping as meaningful action: toward a redefinition of consumption in historical archaeology', *Historical Archaeology* 30:4 (1996), 50–65.

Cook, Simon, 'Violence and the body: methods of suicide, gender and culture in Victoria, 1841–1921', paper given at the Australian Historical Association Biennial Conference, Melbourne, 1996.

Corbin, Alain, 'Intimate relations', in Michelle Perrot (ed.), *A History of Private Life IV: From the Fires of Revolution to the Great War*, Cambridge, MA: Harvard University Press, 1990, pp. 549–613.

Council of Social Planning, 'Statement on low income housing in Oakland', typescript, 27 April 1966, in vertical file 'Oakland Housing (1960–1969)/ Peralta Villa Housing I', at Oakland Public Library, Oakland History Room.

Courtney, Janet E., *The Women of My Time*, London: Lovat Dickson, [1934].

Crary, Jonathan, *Techniques of the Observer: On Vision and Modernity in the Nineteenth Century*, Cambridge, MA: MIT Press, 1990.

Crouchett, Lawrence P., Bunch, Lonnie G., III and Winnacker, Martha Kendall, *Visions toward Tomorrow: The History of the East Bay Afro-American Community 1852–1977*, Oakland: Northern California Center for Afro-American History and Life, 1989.

Curson, Peter, *Times of Crisis: Epidemics in Sydney 1788–1900*, Sydney: Sydney University Press, 1985.

Curson, Peter and McCracken, Kevin, *Plague in Sydney: The Anatomy of an Epidemic*, Sydney: New South Wales University Press, n.d.

Cypress Freeway Replacement Oral History Project, transcript on file at Anthropological Studies Center, Sonoma State University, Rohnert Park, California.

D'Agostino, Mary E., Prine, Elizabeth, Casella, Eleanor and Winer, Margot (eds.), *The Written and the Wrought: Complementary Sources in Historical Anthropology*, Kroeber Anthropological Society Papers 79, Berkeley: Department of Anthropology, University of California at Berkeley, 1995.

Dahl, Edward H., Espesset, Hélène, Lafrance, Marc and Ruddell, Thierry, *La ville de Québec, 1800–1850: un inventaire de cartes et plans*, Collection Mercure 13, Ottawa: Musées Nationals de l'Homme, 1975.

Dangor, A., *Waiting for Leila*, Johannesburg: Ravan, 1981.

Davidoff, Leonore and Hall, Catherine, *Family Fortunes: Men and Women of the English Middle Class 1780–1850*, London: Hutchinson, 1987.

Davison, Graeme, *The Rise and Fall of Marvellous Melbourne*, Melbourne: Melbourne University Press, 1978.

The Unforgiving Minute: How Australia Learned to Tell the Time, Melbourne: Melbourne: Oxford University Press, 1993.

'The unsociable sociologist – W. S. Jevons and his survey of Sydney, 1856–8', in *Intellect and Emotion: Essays in Honour of Michael Roe*, special issue, *Australian Cultural History* 16 (1997/98), 127–50.

Davison, Graeme, Dunstan, David and McConville, Chris (eds.), *The Outcasts of Melbourne: Essays in Social History*, Sydney: Allen & Unwin, 1985.

Décarie, Louise, 'Program de recherche en archéologie sur la Place-Royale, Québec', Quebec: Ministère des Affaires Culturelles du Québec, 1982.

de Certeau, Michel (trans. Steven F. Rendall), *The Practice of Everyday Life*, Berkeley: University of California Press, 1984.

Deetz, James, *In Small Things Forgotten: The Archaeology of Early American Life*, New York: Doubleday, 1977.

Dellums, C. L., 'International president of the brotherhood of sleeping car porters and civil rights leader', typescript, Berkeley: Regional Oral History Office, Bancroft Library, 1973.

Dening, Greg, *The Death of William Gooch: A History's Anthropology*, Melbourne: Melbourne University Press, 1995.

Performances, Melbourne: Melbourne University Press, 1996.

Readings/Writings, Melbourne: Melbourne University Press, 1998.

Dennis, C. J., *The Moods of Ginger Mick*, Sydney: Angus & Robertson, 1916.

The Songs of a Sentimental Bloke, Sydney: Angus & Robertson, 1916.

Department of Urban Renewal, *Workable Program*, Oakland, 1959.

Desai, A. R. and Pillai, S. Devadas (eds.), *Slums and Urbanization*, Prakashan: Bombay Popular, 1970.

De Villiers, S., *A Tale of Three Cities*, Cape Town: Murray and Roberts Construction, 1985.

Dickens, Charles, *American Notes*, reprint of 1842 edn, New York: Fromm International, 1985.

Dickens, Roy S. Jr (ed.), *Archaeology of Urban America: The Search for Pattern and Process*, New York: Academic Press, 1982.

Diner, Hasia R., *Erin's Daughters in America*, Baltimore: Johns Hopkins University Press, 1983.

Dingle, Tony and Rasmussen, Carolyn, *Vital Connections: Melbourne and Its Board of Works 1891–1991*, Ringwood, Victoria: Penguin, 1991.

Domhoff, G. William, *State Autonomy or Class Dominance?* New York: Aldine De Gruyter, 1996.

Donelly, F. K. and Baxter, J .L., 'Sheffield and the English revolutionary tradition', in S. Pollard (ed.), *Economic and Social History of South Yorkshire*, Sheffield: South Yorkshire County Council, 1976, pp. 103–10.

Dubé, Janic, 'Le site de l'îlot Hunt à Québec (CeEt-110). Rapport annuel d'activités, quatrième campagne de fouilles archéologiques', CELAT, Université Laval, 1995.

Duffy, John, *The Sanitarians: A History of American Public Health*, Urbana: University of Illinois Press, 1990.

Dumbrell, K., 'Working class housing in the nineteenth century: the impact of British planning trends and regulations on the British colonial settlements in the Cape Colony', theme paper, School of Architecture and Planning, University of Cape Town, 1998.

Dunstan, David, *Governing the Metropolis: Melbourne*

1850–1891, Melbourne: Melbourne University Press, 1984.

Edgell, Stephen, *Class,* London: Routledge, 1993.

Engels, F., *The Condition of the Working Class in England*, reprint of 1844 first edition, London: Penguin Books, 1987.

Ewan, Stuart, *Captains of Consciousness*, New York: McGraw Hill, 1976.

Faure, Isabelle, *La conservation et la restauration des monuments historiques au Québec: étude des fondements culturels et idéologiques à travers l'exemple du projet de Place Royale*, Paris: Institut Français d'Urbanisme de Paris VIII, 1995, pp. 238–42.

Federal Writers Project, *Washington: City and Capital*, Washington, DC: American Guide Series, 1937.

Finch, Lynette, *The Classing Gaze: Sexuality, Class and Surveillance*, Sydney: Allen & Unwin, 1993.

Finch, Lynette and Stratton, Jon, 'The Australian working class and the practice of abortion 1880–1939', *Journal of Australian Studies* 23 (1988), 45–64.

Fitzgerald, Shirley, *Chippendale: Beneath the Factory Wall*, Sydney: Hale & Iremonger, 1990.

Rising Damp: Sydney 1870–1890, Melbourne: Oxford University Press, 1987.

Sydney 1842–1992, Sydney: Hale & Iremonger, 1992.

FitzGibbon, Theodora, *Irish Traditional Food*, New York: St Martin's Press, 1968.

Fletcher, J. S., *A Picturesque History of Yorkshire*, London: Macmillan, 1899.

Folwell, William W., *A History of Minnesota*, vol. 3, revised edition, St Paul: Minnesota Historical Society Press, 1969.

Ford, Benjamin, 'The health and sanitation of postbellum Harper's Ferry', *Historical Archaeology* 28:4 (1994), 49–61.

Fortune, L., *The House in Tyne Street: Childhood Memories of District Six*, Cape Town: Kwela, 1996.

Fox, Pamela*, Class Fictions, Shame and Resistance in the British Working-Class Novel, 1890–1945*, Durham, NC: Duke University Press, 1994.

Franklin, Maria, '"Power to the people": sociopolitics and the archaeology of black Americans', in *In the Realm of Politics: Prospects for Public Participation in African-American and Plantation Archaeology* (thematic issue), *Historical Archaeology* 31:3 (1997), 36–50.

Fritzsche, Peter, *Reading Berlin 1900*, Cambridge, MA: Harvard University Press, 1996.

Frye, Northrop, *Anatomy of Criticism*, Princeton: Princeton University Press, 1957.

Gales and Martin, *Commercial Directory of Sheffield*, Sheffield: privately published, 1787.

Gallagher, C., 'The body versus the social body in the works of Thomas Malthus and Henry Mayhew', in C. Gallagher and T. Laquer (eds.), *The Making of the Modern Body*, Berkeley: University of California Press, 1987, pp. 83–106.

Gandal, Keith, *The Virtues of the Vicious: Jacob Riis, Stephen Crane, and the Spectacle of the Slum*, New York: Oxford University Press, 1997.

Gans, Herbert J., *People and Plans: Essays on Urban Problems and Solutions*, New York: Basic Books, 1968.

Gardner, William M. and Anderson, Sally C., *A Phase I Archeological Investigation of 51NW113*, Washington, DC: Development Resources, Inc., 1994.

Garner, John S., *The Model Company Town*, Amherst: University of Massachusetts Press, 1984.

Garner, John S. (ed.), *The Company Town: Architecture and Society in the Early Industrial Age*, New York: Oxford University Press, 1992.

Gaskell, S. Martin, *Slums*, Leicester: Leicester University Press, 1990.

Gates, G. Evelyn (ed.), *The Woman's Year Book 1923–24*, London: Women Publishers, 1924.

Geertz, Clifford, *After the Fact: Two Countries, Four Decades, One Anthropologist*, Cambridge, MA: Harvard University Press, 1995.

Local Knowledge: Further Essays in Interpretive Anthropology, New York: Basic Books, 1983.

Geismar, Joan, 'History and archaeology of the Greenwich Mews Site, Greenwich Village, New York. CEQR No. 86–144M', New York: Greenwich Mews Associates, 1989.

Gell, R., *A New General and Commercial Directory of Sheffield and Its Vicinity*, Sheffield: privately published, 1825.

Gero, Joan M., 'Who experienced what in prehistory? A narrative explanation from Queyash, Peru', in Robert W. Preucel (ed.), *Processual and Postprocessual Archaeologies: Multiple Ways of Knowing the Past*, Occasional Paper 10, Southern Illinois University at Carbondale, 1991, pp. 126–39.

Giddens, A., *Central Problems in Social Theory: Action, Structure and Contradiction in Social Analysis*, London: Macmillan, 1979.

The Constitution of Society: Outline of a Theory of Structuration, London: Polity Press, 1984.

Gilje, Paul A., *The Road to Mobocracy: Popular Disorder in New York City, 1763–1834*, Chapel Hill: University of North Carolina Press for the Institute of Early American History and Culture, 1987.

Glassie, Henry, 'Archaeology and folklore: common anxieties, common hopes', in Leland Ferguson (ed.), *Historical Archaeology and the Importance of Material Things*, Society for Historical Archaeology, Special Publications Series 2 (1977), pp. 23–35.

Material Culture, Bloomington and Indianapolis: Indiana University Press, 1999.

Passing the Time in Ballymenone: Culture and History of an Ulster Community, University of Pennsylvania Press, 1982.

Passing the Time: Folklore and History of an Ulster Community, Dublin: The O'Brien Press, 1982.

Glazer, Nathan and Moynihan, Daniel P., *Beyond the Melting Pot: The Negroes, Puerto Ricans, Jews, Italians, and Irish of New York City*, Cambridge, MA: MIT Press, 1970.

Godden Mackay Heritage Consultants, *The Cumberland/Gloucester Streets Site, the Rocks: Archaeological Investigation Report*, 4 vols., Sydney Cove Authority, 1996. Published with different pagination by Godden Mackay Logan, Sydney, 1999.

Godden Mackay Heritage Consultants, *The Cumberland/Gloucester Streets Site, the Rocks: Archaeological Investigation Report*, vol. 3, 'Trench reports', Sydney: Sydney Cove Authority, 1996. Published with different pagination by Godden Mackay Logan, Sydney, 1999.

Godden Mackay Heritage Consultants, *The Cumberland/Gloucester Streets Site, the Rocks: Archaeological Investigation Report*, vol. 4, 'Specialist artefact reports', Sydney Cove Authority, 1996. Published with different pagination by Godden Mackay Logan, Sydney, 1999.

Godden Mackay Pty Ltd in association with Grace Karskens, 'The Cumberland Street/Gloucester Street site archaeological investigation: archaeological assessment and research design', report prepared for the Sydney Cove Authority and others, Sydney, 1994.

Goodman, E., Walker, M., Pappas, M., Toulmin, C. and Crowell, E., *Phase II and Phase III Investigations at Warner Theatre, Washington, DC,* prepared for the Kaempfer Company, Washington DC, by Engineering-Science, 1990.

Goodman, Ruth, 'The housing problem in Oakland', photocopy of typescript, dated 10 March 1966, in vertical file 'Oakland Housing (1960–1969)/Peralta Villa Housing I', Oakland Public Library, Oakland History Room.

Gool, R., *Cape Town Coolie*, Oxford: Heinemann International, 1990.

Goyette, Manon, 'Des vestiges d'une arrière-cour à l'his-toire de l'hygiène publique à Québec au XIXe siècle: la troisième campagne de fouilles archéologiques à l'îlot Hunt (1993)', Masters thesis, Ecole des Gradués, Université Laval, 1998.

Green, Constance McLaughlin, *Washington: Village and Capital, 1800–1878*, Princeton: Princeton University Press, 1962.

Griffiths, Tom, *Hunters and Collectors: The Antiquarian Imagination in Australia*, Melbourne: Cambridge University Press, 1996.

Grinstein, Hyman B., *The Rise of the Jewish Community of New York 1654–1860*, Philadelphia: The Jewish Publication Society, 1945.

Grisgsby, William, 'Slum clearance: elusive goals', reprinted in Desai and Pillai (eds.), *Slums and Urbanization*, pp. 255–60.

Grogan, T., *Vanishing Cape Town*, Cape Town: D. Nelson, 1976.

Groneman Pernicone, Carol, 'The "Bloody Ould Sixth": a social analysis of a New York city working class community in the mid-nineteenth century', PhD thesis, University of Rochester, 1973.

Gross, Laurence F., 'The game is played out: the closing decades of the Boott Mill', in Weible (ed.), *Continuing Revolution*, pp. 281–99.

Groupe Harcart, 'Etude d'ensemble des sous-secteurs Sault-au-Matelot et Saint-Paul', Quebec: Ville de Quebec, Service de l'Urbanisme, 1988.

Hall, Martin, 'Small things and the "mobile, conflictual fusion of power, fear, and desire"', in Yentsch and Beaudry (eds.), *The Art and Mystery of Historical Archaeology*, pp. 373–99.

Hall, M., Cox, G., Halkett, D., Hart, T., Rubin, K. and Winter, S., 'A shadow in stone: archaeology in Horstley Street, District Six', unpublished site report, Department of Archaeology, University of Cape Town, 1994.

Handlin, Oscar, *The Uprooted: The Epic Story of the Great Migrations That Made the American People*, New York: Grosset's Universal Library, 1951.

Hare, John, Lafrance, Marc and Ruddel, David-Thierry, *Histoire de la ville de Québec, 1608–1871*, Montreal: Boréal/Musée des Civilisations, 1987.

Harrington, Michael, 'Old slums, new slums', reprinted in Desai and Pillai (eds.), *Slums and Urbanization,* pp. 82–90.

Harvey, David, *The Urban Experience*, Baltimore: Johns Hopkins University Press, 1989.

Hausler, Donald, 'Blacks in Oakland, 1852–1987', manuscript on file at the Oakland Public Library, Oakland History Room, 1987.

'The Cypress structure and the West Oakland black community', *From the Archives*, Northern California Center for Afro-American History and Life, 1, 1990.

Hawson, H. Keeble, *Sheffield, the Growth of a City*, Sheffield: J. W. Northend, 1968.

Hayden, Dolores, *The Power of Place: Urban Landscapes as Public History*, Cambridge, MA: MIT Press, 1995.

Haywood, J. and Lee, W., *Report on the Sanitary Condition of the Borough of Sheffield*, second edition, Sheffield, 1848.

Healy, Frank, Lydiard, L. A., Morse, W. H. and Knott, Henry N. (compilers), *Minneapolis City Charter and Ordinances, Court and Board Acts, Park Ordinances, Rules of City Council, Etc.*, Minneapolis, 1905.

Heasman, Kathleen, *Evangelicals in Action: An Appraisal of Their Social Work in the Victorian Era*, London: Geoffrey Bles, 1962.

Heath, G. Louis, *The Black Panther Leaders Speak: Huey P. Newton, Bobby Seale, Eldridge Cleaver and Company Speak Out through the Black Panther Party's Official Newspaper*, Metuchen, NJ: Scarecrow Press, 1976.

Hewison, Robert, *The Heritage Industry: Britain in a Climate of Decline*, London: Methuen, 1987.

Hey, D., *The Fiery Blades of Hallamshire*, Leicester: Leicester University Press, 1991.

A History of Sheffield, Lancaster: Carnegie Publishing, 1998.

Higginbotham, E., with Kass, Terry and Walker, Meredith, 'Archaeological management plan for the Rocks and Millers Point', report prepared for the Sydney Cove Authority and the New South Wales Department of Planning, 1991.

Hillard, David and Cole, Lewis, *This Side of Glory: The Autobiography of David Hillard and the Story of the Black Panther Party*, Boston: Little, Brown, 1993.

Hilton, John Deane, *Marie Hilton: Her Life and Work 1821–1896*, London: Isbister and Company, 1897.

Hodder, Ian, 'Interpretive archaeology and its role', *American Antiquity* 56:1 (1991), 7–18.

'Writing archaeology: site reports in context', *Antiquity* 63 (1989), 268–74.

Hodson, A. L., *Letters from a Settlement*, London: Edward Arnold, 1909.

Hollis, Patricia, *Ladies Elect: Women in English Local Government 1865–1914*, Oxford: Clarendon Press, 1987.

Holmes, Kate, 'Trench B report', in Godden Mackay, *The Cumberland/Gloucester Streets Site*, vol. 3, pp. 89–132.

Holmes, Kate, 'Artefact report – metal', in Godden Mackay, *The Cumberland/Gloucester Streets Site*, vol. 4, pp. 369–450.

Housing Authority of the City of Oakland, *Fourth Annual Report*, Oakland 1942–3, on file, Oakland Public Library, Oakland History Room.

Hume, Ivor Noel, *Martin's Hundred*, New York: Alfred A. Knopf, 1988.

Hunt, Lynn, 'Introduction: history, culture, and text', in Lynn Hunt (ed.), *The New Cultural History*, Berkeley: University of California Press, 1989, pp. 7–16.

Iacono, Nadia Z., 'Trench E report', in Godden Mackay, *The Cumberland/Gloucester Streets Site*, vol. 3, pp. 215–48.

'Artefact report – miscellaneous', in Godden Mackay, *The Cumberland/Gloucester Streets Site*, vol. 4, part 2, pp. 13–120.

Israel, Kali, *Names and Stories: Emilia Dilke and Victorian Culture*, New York: Oxford University Press, 1999.

Jeppie, S. and Soudien, C. (eds.), *The Struggle for District Six: Past and Present*, Cape Town: Buchu Books, 1990.

Jevons, W. S., 'Notes for a social survey of Australian cities – the Rocks', manuscript, 1858–9, Mitchell Library, Sydney.

'Remarks upon the social map of Sydney', manuscript, 1858–9, Mitchell Library, Sydney.

Johnson, Matthew, *An Archaeology of Capitalism*, Cambridge, MA: Basil Blackwell, 1996.

Jones, Sian, *The Archaeology of Ethnicity*, London: Routledge, 1997.

Judges, S., 'Poverty, living conditions and social relations – aspects of life in Cape Town in the 1830s', MA thesis, University of Cape Town, 1977.

Kane, Lucile M., *The Falls of St. Anthony: The Waterfalls That Built Minneapolis*, St Paul: Minnesota Historical Society Press, 1987.

Kaplan, Carla, *The Erotics of Talk: Women's Writing and Feminist Paradigms*, New York: Oxford University Press, 1996.

Karskens, Grace, 'Crossing over: archaeology and history at the Cumberland/Gloucester Street Site, the Rocks, 1994–1996', *Public History Review* 5/6 (1996–7), 30–48.

'The dialogue of townscape: the Rocks and Sydney 1788–1820', *Australian Historical Studies* 108 (1997), 88–112.

Inside the Rocks: The Archaeology of a Neighbourhood, Sydney: Hale & Iremonger, 1999.

'Main report', in Godden Mackay, *The Cumberland/ Gloucester Streets Site*, vol. 2, pp. 53–226.

The Rocks: Life in Early Sydney, Melbourne: Melbourne University Press, 1997.

Karskens, Grace and Thorp, Wendy, 'History and archaeology in Sydney: towards integration and interpretation', *Journal of the Royal Australian Historical Society* 78:3–4 (1992), 52–75.

Kass, Terry, 'A socio-economic history of Miller's Point', report prepared for the New South Wales Department of Housing, Sydney, 1987.

Kasson, John F., 'Rituals of dinner: table manners in Victorian America', in Kathryn Grover (ed.), *Dining in America, 1850–1900,* Amherst: University of Massachusetts Press, and Rochester: The Margaret Woodbury Strong Museum, 1987, pp. 114–41.

Kearns, Kevin C., *Dublin Tenement Life: An Oral History*, Dublin: Gill & Macmillan, 1994.

Keeton, C., 'Aspects of material life and culture in District Six, c.1930–c.1950', BA thesis, University of Cape Town, 1987.

Kelly, John D. and Kaplan, Martha, 'History, structure, and ritual', *Annual Reviews in Anthropology* 19 (1990), 119–50.

Kelly, Max, *Anchored in a Small Cove: A History and Archaeology of the Rocks, Sydney*, Sydney: Sydney Cove Authority, 1997.

'Picturesque and pestilential: the Sydney slum observed 1860–1900', in Max Kelly (ed.), *Nineteenth Century Sydney: Essays in Urban History*, Sydney: Sydney University Press, 1978, pp. 66–80.

Kelso, Gerald K., Mrozowski, Stephen A. and Fisher, William F., 'Contextual archeology at the Kirk Street Agent's House', in Beaudry and Mrozowski (eds.), *Interdisciplinary Investigations*, vol. 2, pp. 97–130.

Kent, Susan (ed.), *Domestic Architecture and the Use of Space*, Cambridge: Cambridge University Press, 1990.

Kociumbas, Jan, *Possessions: The Oxford History of Australia*, vol. 2, *1770–1860*, Melbourne: Oxford University Press, 1992.

Koven, Seth, 'Culture and poverty: the London Settlement House movement 1870 to 1914', PhD thesis, Harvard University, 1987.

'Dr. Barnardo's "artistic fictions": photography, sexuality, and the ragged child in Victorian London', *Radical History Review* 69 (Fall 1997), 6–45.

'From rough lads to hooligans: boy life, national culture and social reform', in Andrew Parker, Mary Russo, Doris Sommer, and Patricia Yaeger (eds.), *Nationalisms and Sexualities*, New York: Routledge, 1992, pp. 365–91.

'Henrietta Barnett 1851–1936: the (auto)biography of a late Victorian marriage', in Susan Pedersen and Peter Mandler (eds.), *After the Victorians: Private Conscience and Public Duty in Modern Britain*, London: Routledge, 1994, pp. 31–53.

Lady Resident, A, 'Sketch of Life in Buildings', in Booth, Charles, *Life and Labour, First Series: Poverty*, London: Macmillan, 1902, vol. 3, pp. 37–41.

Laframboise, Yves (Ethnotech Inc.), *La fonction résidentielle de Place-Royale 1820–1860: synthèse*, Collection Patrimoines, Dossier 70, Quebec: Les Publications du Québec, 1991.

Lafrance, Marc and Ruddell, Thierry D., 'Physical evolution and socio-cultural segregation in Quebec City, 1765–1840', in G. A. Stelter and A. F. J. Artibise, *Shaping the Urban Landscape: Aspects of the Canadian City-Building Process*, Ottawa: Carleton, 1982, pp. 160–2.

La Guma, A., *Liberation Chabalala: The World of Alex La Guma*, Bellville: Mayibuye Books, 1993.

The Stone Country, London: Heinemann, 1974.

A Walk in the Night, Cape Town: David Philip, 1991.

Laidecker, S., *Anglo-American China Part 1*, Bloomsburg, PA: Keystone Printed Specialities Co., 1954.

Lake, Marilyn, 'Intimate strangers', in Verity Burgman and Jenny Lee (eds.), *Making a Life: A People's History of Australia since 1788* (Melbourne: Penguin, 1988), pp. 152–65.

Lalande, Dominique, 'Recherches archéologiques sur le site de l'îlot O'Connell à Quebec', Québec: Ville de Québec, Centre de Développement Economique et Urbain, 1996.

L'Anglais, Paul-Gaston, *La recherche archéologique en milieu urbain: d'une archéologie dans la ville vers une archéologie de la ville*, Les Cahiers du CELAT, hors série 6, Quebec: CELAT, Université Laval, 1994.

Le site de l'îlot Hunt: rapport de la deuxième campagne de fouilles (1992), Cahiers d'Archéologie du CELAT 2, Quebec: CELAT, Université Laval, 1998.

Laqueur, Thomas, 'Bodies, details, and the humanitarian narrative', in Lynn Hunt (ed.), *The New Cultural History*, Berkeley: University of California Press, 1989, pp. 176–204.

LaRoche, Cheryl and McGowan, Gary, '"Material culture": conservation and analysis of textiles recovered from Five Points', in Yamin (ed.), *Tales of Five Points*, vol. 2, pp. 276–88.

La Roche, Daniel, 'L'archéologie des installations portuaires à Québec', *Mémoires Vives* 6 and 7 (1994), pp. 31–5.

'Surveillance archéologique, Musée de la civilisation,

Québec, 1984–1985', Quebec: Société Immobilière du Québec, 1986.

Larochelle, Pierre and Iamandi, Christina, *Milieux bâtis et identité culturelle* (in press).

Lawrence, Emmeline Pethick, *My Part in a Changing World*, London: Gollancz, 1938.

Lawrence, R. J., 'Public collective and private space: a study of urban housing in Switzerland', in Kent (ed.), *Domestic Architecture*, pp. 73–91.

Lawson, Henry, *Poems of Henry Lawson*, Sydney: Ure Smith, 1973.

Leader, R. E., *History of the Company of Cutlers in Hallamshire*, 2 vols., Sheffield: J. W. Northend, 1905–6.

Surveyors of Eighteenth Century Sheffield, Sheffield, privately published lecture transcript, 1903.

Lebel, Alyne, 'Les facteurs du développement urbain', in G. H. Dagneau (dir.), *La ville de Québec, histoire municipale*, vol. 4, *De la Confédération à la charte de 1929*, Quebec: Société Historique de Québec, 1983, pp. 31–47.

Leclerc, Myriam, *Appropriation de l'espace et urbanisation d'un site de la basse ville de Québec: rapport de la première campagne de fouilles (1991)*, Cahiers d'Archéologie du CELAT 1, Quebec: CELAT, Université Laval, 1998.

Lefebvre, Henri, *The Production of Space*, Oxford: Blackwell, 1994.

Lemelin, André, 'Le declin du port de Québec et la reconversion économique à la fin du XIXe siècle', *Recherches Sociographiques* 22:2, 1981.

Lemoine, James MacPherson, *L'album du touriste: archéologie, histoire, littérature, sport . . .*, Quebec: Imprimerie A. Côté, 1872 (also published in English as *The Tourist's Note-Book*, Quebec: F. X. Garant, 1876).

Leone, Mark P., 'The Georgian order as the order of merchant capitalism in Annapolis, Maryland', in Mark P. Leone and Parker B. Potter (eds.), *The Recovery of Meaning: Historical Archaeology in the Eastern United States*, Washington DC: Smithsonian Institution Press, 1988, pp. 235–61.

LePlay, F., 'Mémoire sur le fabrication de l'acier en Yorkshire', *Annales des Mines*, 4th series, 3 (1843).

Lewis, Donald M., *Lighten Their Darkness: The Evangelical Mission to Working-Class London, 1828–1860*, New York: Greenwood Press, 1986.

Lewis, Jane, *Women and Social Action in Victorian and Edwardian England*, Stanford: Stanford University Press, 1991.

Lewis, S., *A Topographical Dictionary of England*, London: Macmillan, 1835.

Limerick, Patricia Nelson, 'The startling ability of culture to bring critical inquiry to a halt', *The Chronicle of Higher Education*, 24 October 1997, p. 176.

Little, Barbara J., 'Compelling images through storytelling: comment on "imaginary, but by no means unimaginable: storytelling, science, and historical archaeology"', *Historical Archaeology* 34:2 (2000), 10–13.

'Echoes and forecasts: group tensions in historical archaeology', *International Journal of Group Tensions* 18 (1988), 243–57.

Little, Barbara J. (ed.), *Text-Aided Archaeology*, Boca Raton, FL: CRC Press, 1992.

Lowenthal, David, *The Past Is a Foreign Country*, Cambridge: Cambridge University Press, 1985.

Lucas, G., 'The archaeology of the workhouse: the changing uses of the workhouse buildings at St. Mary's, Southampton', in S. Tarlow and W. West (eds.), *The Familiar Past: Archaeologies of Later Historical Britain*, London: Routledge, 1999.

Lydon, Jane, *Many Inventions: The Chinese in the Rocks, 1890–1930*, Clayton: Department of History, Monash University, 1999.

'Task differentiation in historical archaeology: sewing as material culture', in Hilary Du Cros and Laurajane Smith (eds.), *Women in Archaeology: A Feminist Critique* (Canberra: Australian National University, 1993), pp. 129–33.

MacCalman, Janet, *Struggletown: Public and Private Life in Richmond 1900–1965*, Melbourne: Melbourne University Press, 1984.

McCarthy, John P., 'Material culture and the performance of socio-cultural identity: community, ethnicity, and agency in the burial practices at the First African Baptist Church cemeteries, Philadelphia, 1810–1841', in Ann Smart Martin and J. Ritchie Garrison (eds.), *American Material Culture, the Shape of the Field: Proceedings of the 34th Winterthur Conference*, Winterthur, DE: The Henry Frances du Pont Winterthur Museum, and Knoxville: University of Tennessee Press, 1997, pp. 359–79.

'Material evidence of Irish-immigrant/Irish-American acculturation: traditional culture and the archaeology of the transition to the American "middle class"', paper presented at *The Scattering. Ireland and the Irish Diaspora: A Comparative Perspective*, University College Cork, 1997.

McCarthy, John P. and Ward, Jeanne A., *Archaeological Investigations at the Bridgehead Site, Minneapolis, Minnesota, the 1994 Season*, vol. 2, *Site Area B, 19th-Century Residential and Commercial Occupations in the Vicinity of 1st Street North*, Minneapolis: Institute for Minnesota Archaeology Reports of Investigations 367, 1996.

McCarthy, John P., Ward, Jeanne A. and Hagglund, Karl W., *An Archaeological Evaluation and Data Recovery Investigation at the New Federal Building/United States Courthouse, Minneapolis, Minnesota: Material Insights into Working Class Life in the Late 19th Century*, Minneapolis: Institute for Minnesota Archaeology Reports of Investigations 369, 1996.

McCarthy, Justin, *Archaeological Investigation: Commonwealth Offices and Telecom Corporate Building Sites. The Commonwealth Block, Melbourne, Victoria*, 5 vols., Melbourne: Commonwealth Department of Administrative Services and Telecom Australia, 1989.

McClintock, Anne, *Imperial Leather: Race Gender, and Sexuality in the Colonial Contest*, London: Routledge, 1995.

McDaniel, George William, 'Preserving the people's history: traditional black material culture in nineteenth and twentieth century southern Maryland', PhD thesis, Duke University, 1979.

McGuire, Randall H., 'Building power in the cultural landscape of Broome County, New York 1880 to 1940', in McGuire and Paynter (eds.), *The Archaeology of Inequality*, pp. 102–24.

'The study of ethnicity in historical archaeology', *Journal of Anthropological Archaeology* 1 (1982), 159–78.

McGuire, Randall H. and Paynter, Robert (eds.), *The Archaeology of Inequality: Material Culture, Domination and Resistance*, Oxford: Blackwell, 1991.

McIlroy Jack, 'The Cypress Archaeology Project', paper presented at the California Preservation Federation Conference, Berkeley, California, 8 May 1998.

Major, Reginald, *A Panther is a Black Cat*, New York: William Morrow and Company, 1971.

McKearin, Helen and Wilson, Kenneth M., *American Bottles and Flasks and Their Ancestry*, New York: Crown Publishers, 1978.

McKendrick, Neil, Brewer, John and Plumb, J. H., *The Birth of a Consumer Society: The Commercialization of Eighteenth Century England*, Bloomington: Indiana University Press, 1982.

MacKenzie, Norman and Jeanne (eds.), *The Diary of Beatrice Webb*, vol. 1, *1873–1892*, Cambridge, MA: Harvard University Press, 1982.

McKibbin, Ross, *Ideologies of Class: Social Relations in Britain 1880–1950*, Oxford: Clarendon Press, 1990.

Malan, A., 'The Mount Nelson Project: unearthing houses and gardens in Hof Street, Cape Town', unpublished seminar paper, Department of Archaeology, University of Cape Town, September 1997.

Malan, A., Clift, H., Graf, O., Hall, M., Klose, J. and Sealy, E., '"Between the castle and the stock pound": early nineteenth century developments at the corner of Tennant and Hanover Streets, Cape Town', unpublished report, RESUNACT, University of Cape Town, 1999.

Malherbe, V. C., 'An East European immigrant makes good in Cape Town', *Studies in the History of Cape Town* 4 (1984), 135–44.

Malone, Patrick, *Canals and Industry: Engineering in Lowell, 1821–1880*, Lowell, MA: Lowell Museum, 1983.

Malone, Patrick M. and Parrott, Charles A., 'Greenways in the industrial city: parks and promenades along the Lowell canals', *IA: The Journal of the Society for Industrial Archeology* 24 (1998), 9–18.

Manuel, G. and Hatfield, D., *District Six*, Cape Town: Longman Penguin, 1967.

Marcil, Eileen, *Les tonneliers du Québec*, Collection Mercure 34, Ottawa: Musées Nationals de l'Homme, 1983.

Marston, Sallie A., 'Contested territory: an ethnic parade as symbolic resistance', in Weible (ed.), *Continuing Revolution*, pp. 213–33.

May, Judith V., *Two Model Cities: Negotiations in Oakland*, Department of Political Science, University of California, Davis, 1970.

Mayne, Alan, 'A barefoot childhood: so what? Imagining slums and reading neighbourhoods', *Urban History* 22:3 (1995), 380–9.

The Imagined Slum: Newspaper Representation in Three Cities 1870–1914, Leicester: Leicester University Press, 1993.

'A just war: the language of slum representation in twentieth-century Australia', *Journal of Urban History* 22 (1995), 75–107.

'On the edge of history', *Journal of Urban History* 26:2 (2000), 249–58.

Representing the Slum: Popular Journalism in a Late Nineteenth Century City, Melbourne: University of Melbourne, 1990.

Mayne, Alan and Lawrence, Susan, 'Ethnographies of place: a new urban research agenda', *Urban History* 26:3 (1999), 325–48.

Mayne, Alan and Murray, Tim, '"In Little Lon . . . wiv Ginger Mick": telling the forgotten history of a vanished community', *Journal of Popular Culture* 33:1 (1999), 49–60.

Mayne, Alan, Murray, Tim and Lawrence, Susan, 'Melbourne's "Little Lon"', *Australian Historical Studies* 31:114 (2000), 131–51.

Merwick, Donna (ed.), *Dangerous Liaisons: Essays in Honour of Greg Dening*, Melbourne: University of Melbourne, 1994.

Meyer, Mrs Carl [Adele] and Black, Clementina, *Makers of Our Clothes*, London: Duckworth, 1909.

Miliband, Ralph, *Marxism and Politics*, Oxford: Oxford University Press, 1977.

Miller, Daniel, 'Could shopping ever really matter?', paper presented at 'Consuming politics: how mass consumption has shaped and been shaped by political systems and cultures', a workshop sponsored by the Rutgers Center for Historical Analysis, New Brunswick, NJ, manuscript on file, John Milner Associates Inc., Philadelphia, 1993.

Material Culture and Mass Consumption, Oxford: Blackwell, 1987.

Miller, George L., 'Classification and economic scaling of 19th century ceramics', *Historical Archaeology* 14 (1980), 1–40.

Milne, Claudia and Crabtree, Pamela, 'Revealing meals: ethnicity, economic status, and diet at the Five Points, 1800–1860', in Yamin (ed.), *Tales of Five Points*, vol. 2, pp. 138–205.

Mintz, Steven, and Kellogg, Susan, *Domestic Revolutions: A Social History of the American Family*, New York: The Free Press, 1988.

Moss, William, *Une archéologie du paysage urbain à la terrasse Dufferin à Québec*, Rapports et Mémoires de Recherche du CELAT, 23, Quebec: CELAT, Université Laval, 1994.

'Cent-vingt-cinq ans de découvertes. Une bibliographie sur l'archéologie de la ville de Québec', *Mémoires Vives*, 5 (1993).

Moss, William (dir.), *L'archéologie de la maison Aubert-de-la-Chesnaye à Québec*, Cahiers d'Archéologie du CELAT 3, Quebec: CELAT, Université Laval, 1998.

Moussette, Marcel, 'La recherche en culture matérielle à la Place-Royale. Essai de redéfinition d'une orientation', Quebec: Ministère des Affaires culturelles du Québec, 1981.

Le site du Palais de l'intendant à Québec: genèse et structuration d'un lieu urbain, Quebec: Septentrion, 1994.

Mrozowski, Stephen A., 'Interdisciplinary perspectives on the production of urban industrial space', in Geoff Egan and R. L. Michael (eds.), *Old and New Worlds*, Oxford: Oxbow Books, 1999, pp. 136–46.

'Landscapes of inequality', in McGuire and Paynter (eds.), *The Archaeology of Inequality*, pp. 79–101.

'Managerial capitalism and the subtleties of class analysis in historical archaeology', in James A. Delle, Stephen A. Mrozowski and Robert Paynter (eds.), *Lines That Divide: Historical Archaeologies of Race, Class, and Gender*, Knoxville: University of Tennessee Press, 2000.

Mrozowski, Stephen A. and Beaudry, Mary C., 'Archaeology and the landscape of corporate ideology', in W. M. Kelso and R. Most (eds.), *Earth Patterns: Essays in Landscape Archaeology*, Charlottesville: University Press of Virginia, 1990, pp. 189–208.

Mrozowski, Stephen A., Ziesing, Grace H. and Beaudry, Mary C., *'Living on the Boott': Historical Archaeology at the Boott Mills Boardinghouses, Lowell, Massachusetts*, Amherst: University of Massachusetts Press, 1996.

Mullens, Wayne, 'Just who are the people in your neighbourhood? The archaeology of "the neighbourhood" in the Rocks and Millers Point', BA thesis, University of Sydney, 1993.

Muller, D., *Whitey*, Johannesburg: Ravan, 1977.

Mullins, Paul R., 'The contradictions of consumption: an archaeology of African American and consumer culture, 1850–1930', PhD thesis, University of Massachusetts Amherst, 1996.

Murray, Tim and Mayne, Alan, '(Re) constructing a lost community: "Little Lon", Melbourne, Australia', *Historical Archaeology* (in press).

Muthesius, S., *The English Terraced House*, New Haven and London: Yale University Press, 1982.

Myler, Elizabeth A. and Dent, Richard J. Jr, *Archaeological Survey and Evaluation of Squares 367 and 368, Washington, D.C.*, submitted to Traceries, Inc., Washington, DC, 1989.

Nasson, B., 'Oral history and the reconstruction of District Six', in Jeppie and Soudien, *The Struggle for District Six*, pp. 44–66.

National Association of Home Builders, *A New Face for America: A Program of Action Planned to Stop Slums and Rebuild Our Cities*, Washington, DC: Department of Housing Rehabilitation, 1953.

Newman, O., *Defensible Space: People and Design in the Violent City*, London: Architectural Press, 1973.

Ngcelwane, N., *Sala Kahle, District Six: An African Woman's Perspective*, Cape Town: Kwela Books 1998.

Nicholls, William L., II, *Poverty and Poverty Programs in Oakland*, Survey Research Center, University of California, Berkeley, 1966.

Niellon, Françoise, Cloutier, Céline, Fortin, Catherine and Yasui, Cathy, *Les modes de vie de la population de Place-Royale entre 1820 et 1859, Annexe 2*, Collection Patrimoines, Dossier 66, Quebec: Les Publications du Québec, 1990.

Niellon, Françoise and Moussette, Marcel, *Le site de l'Habitation de Champlain à Québec, étude de la collection archéologique (1976–1980)*, Collection Patrimoines, Dossier 57, Quebec: Les Publications du Québec, 1981.

Nord, Deborah E., *Walking the Victorian Streets: Women, Representation, and the City*, Ithaca, NY: Cornell University Press, 1995.

Oakland Citizens Committee for Urban Renewal, *Neighbourhood Profiles: West Oakland*, 1988, on file at Environmental Design Library, University of California, Berkeley.

Oakland Cultural Heritage Survey, *Historic Property Survey Report*, 4 vols., Oakland City Planning Department, 1990.

Ogle, Maureen, *All the Modern Conveniences: American Household Plumbing, 1840–1890*, Baltimore: Johns Hopkins University Press, 1996.

Olive, M. (ed.), *Central Sheffield*, Stroud: Chalford Publishing, 1994.

Olmsted, Nancy and Roger W., 'History of West Oakland', in Praetzellis (ed.), *West Oakland*, pp. 9–223.

Orser, Charles E., Jr, 'The challenge of race to American historical archaeology', *American Anthropologist* 100 (1998), 661–8.

A Historical Archaeology of the Modern World, New York: Plenum Press, 1996.

Paterson, Alexander, *Across the Bridges, or Life by the South London River-Side*, London: Edward Arnold, 1911.

Pearson, Hugh, *The Shadow of the Panther: Huey Newton and the Price of Black Power in America*, Menlo Park, CA: Addison-Wesley, 1994.

Pember Reeves, Maud, *Round About a Pound a Week*, first published 1913, London: Virago Books, 1979.

Pennybacker, Susan, *A Vision for London 1889–1914: Labour, Everyday Life and the LCC Experiment*, London: Routledge, 1995.

Peralta Improvement League, vertical file at Oakland Public Library, Oakland History Room.

Percy, J., *Metallurgy – Iron and Steel*, London: John Murray, 1864.

Peterson, M. Jeanne, *Family, Love and Work in the Lives of Victorian Gentlewomen*, Bloomington: Indiana University Press, 1989.

Picard, François, *Les traces du passé*, Sillery: Québec Science–Les Presses de l'Université du Québec, 1979, pp. 151–7.

Pidgeon, Nathaniel, *The Life, Experience and Journal of Nathaniel Pidgeon*, Sydney: Smith and Gardener, 1852.

Pollard, S., *History of Labour in Sheffield*, Liverpool: Liverpool University Press, 1959.

Poovey, Mary, *Making a Social Body: British Cultural Formation, 1830–1864*, Chicago: University of Chicago Press, 1995.

Potter, Beatrice, 'A Lady's View on the Unemployed in the East', *Pall Mall Gazette*, 18 February 1886, p. 11.

Poulin, Suzie, 'Etude architecturale de la maison Hunt', CELAT, Université Laval, 1995.

Praetzellis, Adrian (ed.), *Archaeologists as Storytellers*, special issue, *Historical Archaeology* 32:1 (1998).

Praetzellis, Adrian and Praetzellis, Mary, 'Faces and façades: Victorian ideology in early Sacramento', in Yentsch and Beaudry (eds.), *The Art and Mystery of Historical Archaeology*, pp. 75–100.

Praetzellis, Mary (ed.), *West Oakland – A Place to Start From. Research Design and Treatment Plan Cypress I-880 Replacement Project*, vol. 1, *Historical Archaeology*, Anthropological Studies Center, Sonoma State University, Rohnert Park, CA: 1994.

Praetzellis, Mary and Praetzellis, Adrian, *Junk! Archaeology of the Pioneer Junk Store, 1877–1908*, Papers in Northern California Anthropology 4, Anthropological Studies Center, Sonoma State University, Rohnert Park, CA: 1990.

Prochaska, Frank K., 'Body and soul: Bible nurses and the poor in Victorian London', *Historical Research* 143 (October 1987), 336–48.

'A mother's country: mothers' meetings and family welfare in Britain, 1850–1950', *History* 74 (October 1989), 336–48.

The Voluntary Impulse: Philanthropy in Modern Britain, London: Faber and Faber, 1988.

Women and Philanthropy in Nineteenth Century England, Oxford: Clarendon Press, 1980.

Proudfoot, Helen, Bickford, Anne, Egloff, Brian and Stocks, Robyn, *Australia's First Government House*, Sydney: Allen & Unwin and the New South Wales Department of Planning, 1991.

Provencher, Jean (Les Recherches Arkhis Inc.), *Les modes de vie de la population de Place-Royale entre 1820 et 1859: synthèse*, Collection Patrimoines, Dossier 66, Quebec: Les Publications du Québec, 1990.

Rancière, Jacques, 'The myth of the artisan: critical reflections on a category of social history', in S. L. Kaplan and C. J. Koepp (eds.), *Work in France: Representations, Meaning, Organisation and Practice*, Ithaca and London: Cornell University Press, 1986, pp. 317–34.

Ranyard, Ellen, *Nurses for the Needy*, London: James Nesbet, 1875.

Rapoport, Amos, 'Systems of activities and systems of settings', in Kent (ed.), *Domestic Architecture*, pp. 9–20.

Rappaport, Erika D., *Shopping for Pleasure: Women and the Making of London's West End*, Princeton: Princeton University Press, 1999.

Reason, Will (ed.), *University and Social Settlements*, London: Methuen, 1898.

Reckner, Paul, 'Negotiating patriotism at Five Points: clay tobacco pipes and patriotic imagery among trade unionists and nativists in a nineteenth-century New York neighbourhood', in Yamin (ed.), *Tales of Five Points*, vol. 2, pp. 105–17.

Redevelopment Agency of the City of Oakland, *GNRP Progress Report to City Council*, Oakland, 1958.

Redevelopment Area Organization, *Provisional Economic Development Program for the City of Oakland*, Oakland, 1964, on file, Environmental Design Library, University of California, Berkeley.

Reinhard, Karl, 'Parasitic disease at Five Points: parasitological analysis of sediments from the Courthouse Block', in Yamin (ed.), *Tales of Five Points*, vol. 2, pp. 391– 404.

Reinhard, Karl J., 'Sanitation and parasitism at Harper's Ferry, West Virginia', *Historical Archaeology* 28:4 (1994), 62–7.

Reeves, Maud Pember, *Round About a Pound a Week*, 1913; reprinted London, Virago Books, 1979.

Revel, Jacques, 'Microanalysis and the construction of the social', in Jacques Revel and Lynn Hunt (eds.), *Histories: French Constructions of the Past. Postwar French Thought Volume 1*, New York: The New Press, 1995, pp. 492–502.

Riis, Jacob A., *How the Other Half Lives: Studies among the Tenements of New York*, New York: Dover Publications, 1971; first published 1890.

Rive, R., *'Buckingham Palace', District Six*, Cape Town: David Philip, 1986.

Emergency, Cape Town: David Philip, 1988.

Roberts, Katherine, *Five Months in a London Hospital*, Letchworth: Garden City Press, 1911.

Pages from the Diary of a Militant Suffragette, Letchworth: Garden City Press, 1910.

Robinson, Portia, *Women of Botany Bay: A Reinterpretation of Women in Australian Society*, revised edition, Ringwood: Penguin, 1993.

Rodenhiser, Lorinda B. and Dutton, David H. 'Material culture from the Kirk Street Agent's House', in Beaudry and Mrozowski (eds.), *Interdisciplinary Investigations*, vol. 2, pp. 73–95.

Ross, Ellen, 'Good and bad mothers: lady philanthropists and London housewives before World War I', in Dorothy O. Helly and Susan M. Reverby (eds.), *Gendered Domains: Rethinking Public and Private in Women's History*, Ithaca, NY: Cornell University Press, 1992, pp. 199–216.

'Hungry children: housewives and London charity, 1870–1918', in Peter Mandler, (ed.), *The Uses of Charity: The Poor on Relief in the Nineteenth-Century Metropolis*, Philadelphia: University of Pennsylvania Press, 1990, pp. 161–96.

Love and Toil: Motherhood in Outcast London, 1870–1918, New York: Oxford University Press, 1993.

Rouleau, Serge, 'Les installations portuaires des marchands Lymburner, Monro et Bell (CeEt-536)', Quebec: Ville de Québec, Centre de Développement Economique et Urbain,1997.

'Le site de la maison Aubert-de-la-Chesnaye XVIIe–XXe siècle: perspective archéologique', in Moss, *L'archéologie de la maison Aubert-de-la-Chesnaye*, pp. 11–233.

Roy, Alain, 'Saint-Roch projeté, Saint-Roch inachevé: les schémas d'aménagement au XXe siècle', in Archithème, *Patrimoine du quartier Saint-Roch: études sectorielles,* Quebec: Ville de Québec, Service de l'Urbanisme, 1996, pp. 47–84.

'Le Vieux-Québec, 1945–1963. Construction et fonctions sociales d'un lieu de mémoire nationale', Masters thesis, Université Laval, 1995.

Rule, J., *The Experience of Labour in Eighteenth-Century Industry*, London: Croom Helm, 1981.

Ryan, Mary P., *Cradle of the Middle Class: The Family in Oneida County, New York 1790–1865*, Cambridge: Cambridge University Press, 1983.

Salwen, Bert and Yamin, Rebecca, 'The archaeology and history of six 19th century lots, Sullivan Street, Greenwich Village, New York: New York City. CEQR#83–225M', New York: New York University, 1990.

Sampson, Davenport, and Company, *The Lowell Directory, 1871*, Lowell, MA: Joshua Merrill and Son and B. C. Sargeant, 1871.

The Lowell Directory, 1881, Lowell, MA: Joshua Merrill and Son, 1881.

Sampson, Murdock, and Company, *The Lowell Directory, 1891,* Lowell, MA: Joshua Merrill and Son, 1891.

Sante, Luc, *Evidence*, New York: Farrar, Straus and Giroux, 1991.

Low Life, Lures and Snares of Old New York, New York: Farrar, Straus and Giroux, 1991.

Saunders, C., 'The creation of Ndabeni: urban segregation and African resistance in Cape Town', *Studies* 1 (1984), 165–93.

Schama, Simon, *Landscape and Memory*, London: Fontana Press, 1995.

Schoeman, Chris, *District Six: The Spirit of Kanala*, Cape Town: Human en Rousseau, 1994.

Portrait of a City (forthcoming).

Schrire, Carmel, *Digging through Darkness: Chronicles of an Archaeologist*, Charlottesville: University Press of Virginia, 1995.

Scott, Elizabeth M. (ed.), *Those of Little Note: Gender, Race, and Class in Historical Archaeology*, Tucson: University of Arizona Press, 1994.

Scott, James C., *Weapons of the Weak: Everyday Forms of Peasant Resistance*, New Haven: Yale University Press, 1985.

Scurfield, G., 'Seventeenth-century Sheffield and its environs', *Yorkshire Archaeological Journal* 58 (1986).

Seale, Bobby, *Seize the Time: The Story of the Black Panther Party and Huey P. Newton*, New York: Random House, 1970.

Seifert, Donna J., 'Within site of the Whitehouse: the archaeology of working women', *Historical Archaeology* 25:4 (1991), 82–108.

Sennet, Richard, and Cobb, Johnathan, *The Hidden Injuries of Class*, New York: Vantage Books, 1972.

Sims, George (ed.), *Living London*, 3 vols., London: Cassell, 1902.

Singleton, Theresa A., 'Facing the challenges of a public African-American archaeology', in *In the Realm of Politics: Prospects for Public Participation in African-American and Plantation Archaeology* (thematic issue), *Historical Archaeology* 31:3 (1997), 146–52.

Small, A., *Oos Wes Tuis Bes: Distrik Ses*, Kaapstad: Human en Rousseau, 1973.

Small, A. and Wissema, Jansje, *District Six*, Linden: Fontein, 1986.

Smith, Bonnie, *On Writing Women's Work*, pamphlet, European University Institute Working Papers in History, Florence, 1991.

Smith, D., 'The buttonmaking industry in Sheffield', in M. Jones (ed.), *Aspects of Sheffield 1*, Barnsley: Wharncliffe Publishing, 1997.

Smith, J., 'A report on the condition of the town of Sheffield', in the *Report of the Royal Commission on the Health of Towns*, London, 1841.

[Stanley, Maude], *Work about the Five Dials*, London: Macmillan, 1878.

Stansell, Christine, *City of Women: Sex and Class in New York 1789–1860*, Urbana: University of Illinois Press, 1987.

Staski, Edward, 'Studies of ethnicity in North American historical archaeology', *North American Archaeologist* 11 (1990), 121–45.

Steele, Dominic, 'Trench G report', in Godden Mackay, *The Cumberland/Gloucester Streets Site*, vol. 3, pp. 287–334.

Steele, Dominic, 'Artefact report – animal bone and shell collections', in Godden Mackay, *The Cumberland/Gloucester Streets Site*, vol. 4, part 2, pp. 141–23.

Stewart, Suzanne and Praetzellis, Mary (eds.), *Sights and Sounds: Essays in Celebration of West Oakland*, Rohnert Park, CA: Anthropological Studies Center, 1997.

Stokes, J., *The History of the Cholera Epidemic of 1832 in Sheffield*, Sheffield: J. W. Northend, 1921.

Storch, R. D., 'The problem of working-class leisure. Some roots of middle-class moral reform in the industrial north: 1825–50', in A.P. Donajgrodzki (ed.), *Social Control in Nineteenth Century Britain*, London: Croom Helm, 1977, pp. 138–62.

Stott, Richard B., *Workers in the Metropolis: Class, Ethicity, and Youth in Antebellum New York City*, Ithaca, NY: Cornell University Press, 1990.

Ström, K., 'Nineteenth-century working-class housing in Cape Town', MA thesis, University of Cape Town (in preparation).

Summers, Anne, *Damned Whores and God's Police*, first published 1975, Melbourne: Penguin, 1982.

'Public functions, private premises: female professional identity and the domestic-service paradigm in Britain, c. 1850–1930', in Billie Melman (ed.), *Borderlines: Genders and Identities in War and Peace, 1870–1930*, New York: Routledge, 1998, pp. 353–76.

Swanson, M. W., 'The sanitation syndrome: bubonic plague and urban native policy in the Cape Colony, 1900–1909', *Journal of African History* 16:3 (1977), 387–410.

Symonds, J. C., *Report into the Sanitary Conditions of the Working Classes in Sheffield*, Sheffield: J. W. Northend, 1841.

Tagg, John, *The Burden of Representation: Essays on Photographs and Histories*, Minneapolis: University of Minnesota Press, 1983.

Tebbutts, Melanie, *Women's Talk: A Social History of 'Gossip' in Working-Class Neighbourhoods, 1880–1960*, Aldershot, Hants: Scolar Press, 1995.

Thompson, E. P., *Customs in Common*, London: Penguin Books, 1991.

The Making of the English Working Class, New York: Vintage Books, 1963.

'The poverty of theory or an orrery of errors', in E. P. Thompson, *The Poverty of Theory and Other Essays,* New York: Monthly Review Press, 1978.

Thorp, Wendy, 'Report on the excavation at Lilyvale', draft report prepared for CRI, Sydney, 1994.

Tilley, Christopher, *A Phenomenology of Landscape*, Oxford: Berg Publishing, 1994.

Tilley, Louise A. and Scott, Joan W., *Women, Work, and Family*, New York: Holt, Rinehart, and Winston, 1978.

Tobin, Beth Fowkes, *Superintending the Poor – Charitable Ladies and Paternal Landlords in British Fiction, 1770–1860*, New Haven: Yale University Press, 1993.

Todd, Janet (ed.), *British Women Writers: A Critical Reference Guide*, New York: Continuum Books, 1989.

Tremblay, Micheline (Ethnotech Inc.), *Etude de la population de Place-Royale 1660–1760*, Collection Patrimoines, Dossier 82, Québec: Les Publications du Québec, 1993, pp. 9–55.

Trinder, Barrie, *The Making of the Industrial Landscape*, Gloucester: Alan Sutton, 1987.

Turner, Victor, *On the Edge of the Bush: Anthropology as Experience*, Tuscon: University of Arizona Press, 1985.

Turner, Victor and Bruner, Edward M. (eds.), *The Anthropology of Experience*, Urbana: University of Illinois Press, 1986.

Tweedale, G., *The Sheffield Knife Book: A History and Collector's Guide*, Sheffield: Hallamshire Press, 1996.

Ulrich, Laurel Thatcher, *A Midwife's Tale: The Life of Martha Ballard, Based on Her Diary 1785–1812*, New York: Alfred A. Knopf, 1990.

United States Bureau of the Census, *Ninth Census of the United States*, Massachusetts, Middlesex County, Lowell, Ward 2. Microfilm, Roll 627, Washington, DC: National Archives, 1870.

Tenth Census of the United States, Massachusetts, Middlesex County, Lowell, Enumeration District 453. Microfilm, Roll 544, Washington, D.C.: National Archives, 1880.

United States District Court, Northern District of California, Southern Division, *United States of America v. Certain Lands in the City of Oakland.* Civil Case #38477, filed 26 August 1959, amended pre-trial agenda for tracts 103, 104 and 105, on file at the National Archives, San Bruno.

Unwin, Mrs George and Telford, John, *Mark Guy Pearse: Preacher, Author, Artist*, London: Epworth, 1930.

Upton, Dell, 'The city as material culture', in Yentsch and Beaudry (eds.), *The Art and Mystery of Historical Archaeology*, pp. 51–74.

'Ethnicity, authenticity, and invented traditions', *Historical Archaeology* 30:2 (1996), 1–7.

Valentine, David T., *Valentine's Manual of the Municipal Government of the City of New York* (New York: David T. Valentine, 1855).

van Heyningen, E., 'Cape Town and the plague of 1901', *Studies* 4 (1984), 66–107.

'A liberal town planner in Africa: L. W. Thornton White and the planning of Cape Town, South Africa, Nairobi, Kenya and Port Louis, Mauritius 1939–1950', 20th Century Urban Planning Experience Conference, 15–18 July 1998, University of New South Wales, Sydney.

'Public health and society in Cape Town 1880–1910', PhD thesis, University of Cape Town, 1989.

Vicinus, Martha, *Independent Women: Work and Community for Single Women 1850–1920*, Chicago: University of Chicago Press, 1985.

Vogel, Morris, 'Urban play', in Brian Sutton-Smith (ed.), *Children's Play: Past, Present, and Future*, Philadelphia: The Please Touch Museum, 1985, pp. 8–9.

Walker, Charles R., *American City: A Rank and File History*, New York: Farrar and Rinehart, 1937.

Walker, Pat (ed.), *Between Labor and Capital: The Professional-Managerial Class*, Boston: South End Press, 1979.

Walkowitz, Judith, 'Going public: shopping, street harassment, and streetwalking in late Victorian London', *Representations* 62 (Spring 1998), 1–30.

'The Indian woman, the flower girl, and the Jew: photojournalism in Edwardian London', *Victorian Studies* 42:1 (1998–9), 3–46.

Wall, Diana di Zerera, *The Archaeology of Gender: Separating the Spheres in Urban America*, New York: Plenum Press, 1994.

'Sacred dinners and secular teas: constructing domesticity in mid-19th-century New York', *Historical Archaeology* 25:4 (1991), 69–81.

Ward, David, *Poverty, Ethnicity, and the American City, 1840–1925: Changing Conceptions of the Slum and Ghetto*, Cambridge: Cambridge University Press, 1989.

Ward, K., 'The road to Mamre: migration and community in countryside and city in the early twentieth century', *South African Historical Journal* 27 (1992), 198–224.

Warner, S. B. Jr., *The Urban Wilderness: A History of the American City*, New York: Harper and Row, 1972.

Waterhouse, Richard, *Private Pleasures, Public Leisure: A History of Australian Popular Culture since 1788*, Melbourne: Longman, 1995.

Webb, Sidney and Beatrice, *Methods of Social Study*, London: Longmans, 1932.

Weible, Robert (ed.), *The Continuing Revolution: A History of Lowell, Massachusetts*, Lowell, MA: The Lowell Historical Society, 1991.

White, Hayden, 'The historical text as literary artefact', in Hazard Adams and Leroy Searle (eds.), *Critical Theory since 1965*, Tallahassee: University Press of Florida, 1986, pp. 395–407.

'The value of narrativity in the representation of reality', in W. J. T. Mitchell (ed.), *On Narrative*, Chicago: University of Chicago Press, 1981, pp. 1–23.

Wilentz, Sean, *Chants Democratic: New York and the Rise of the American Working Class, 1788–1850*, New York: Oxford University Press, 1984.

Williams, Brackette F., 'Of straightening combs, sodium hydroxide, and potassium hydroxide in archaeological and cultural-anthropological analysis of ethnogenesis', *American Antiquity* 57 (1992), 608–12.

Williams, Raymond, *The Country and the City*, New York: Oxford University Press, 1973.

Wilson, Graham, 'Trench a report', in Godden Mackay, *The Cumberland/Gloucester Streets Site*, vol. 3, pp. 21–88.

'Artefact Report – Ceramics' in Godden Mackay, *The Cumberland/Gloucester Streets Site*, vol. 4, part 2, pp. 207–368.

Wilson, Lindy, *Last Supper in Horstley Street*, Johannesburg: Film Resource Unit, 1989.

Wood, Edith Elmer, *Slums and Blighted Areas in the United States*, Federal Emergency Administration of Public Works, Housing Division Bulletin 1, 1935.

Woolf, Virginia, *The Years*, first published 1937, New York: Harcourt Brace Jovanovich, 1965.

Worden, Nigel, van Heyningen, Elizabeth and Bickford-Smith, Vivian, *Cape Town: The Making of a City*, Cape Town: David Philip, 1998.

Wright, E. O., 'Class analysis, history and emancipation', *New Left Review* 202 (1993), 15–35.

Wurst, LuAnn, 'Internalizing Class in Historical Archaeology', *Historical Archaeology* 33:1 (1999), 7–21.

Wurst, LuAnn, and Fitts, Robert K., 'Introduction: why confront class?', *Historical Archaeology* 33:1 (1999), 1–6.

Wurst, LuAnn, and Fitts, Robert K. (eds.), *Confronting Class*, special issue, *Historical Archaeology* 33:1 (1999).

Yamin, Rebecca, 'Lurid tales and homely stories of New York's notorious Five Points', *Historical Archaeology* 32:1 (1998), 74–85.

'New York's mythic slum: digging Lower Manhattan's infamous Five Points', *Archaeology* 50:2 (1997), 44–53.

'People and Their Possessions', in Yamin (ed.), *Tales of Five Points*, vol. 1, pp. 90–145.

Yamin, Rebecca (ed.), *Tales of Five Points: Working-Class Life in Nineteenth-Century New York*, 6 vols., draft on file, Philadelphia: John Milner Associates, 1998 (and published New York, General Services Administration, 2000).

Yamin, Rebecca and Metheny, Karen Bescherer, *Landscape Archaeology: Reading and Interpreting the American Historical Landscape*, Knoxville: University of Tennessee Press, 1996.

Yentsch, Anne E., *A Chesapeake Family and Their Slaves: A Study in Historical Archaeology* Cambridge: Cambridge University Press, 1994.

Yentsch, Anne E. and Beaudry, Mary C. (eds.), *The Art and Mystery of Historical Archaeology: Essays in Honor of James Deetz*, Boca Raton, FL: CRC Press, 1992.

Young, Linda, 'The struggle for class: the transmission of genteel culture to early colonial Australia', PhD thesis, Flinders University of South Australia, 1997.

Zeising, Grace H., 'Analysis of personal effects from the excavations of the Boott Mills boardinghouse backlots in Lowell, Massachusetts', in Beaudry and Mrozowski (eds.), *Interdisciplinary Investigations*, vol. 3, pp. 141–68.

Index

Page numbers in *italics* denote illustrations. The letter n following a page number indicates that the reference will be found in a note.